1-2-3® for Windows
Made Easy

1-2-3® for Windows Made Easy

Mary Campbell

Osborne McGraw-Hill

Berkeley New York St. Louis San Francisco
Auckland Bogotá Hamburg London   Madrid
Mexico City Milan Montreal   New Delhi Panama City
Paris São Paulo Singapore Sydney
Tokyo Toronto

Osborne **McGraw-Hill**
2600 Tenth Street
Berkeley, California 94710
U.S.A.

For information on translations or book distributors outside of the U.S.A.,
please write to Osborne **McGraw-Hill** at the above address.

1-2-3® for Windows Made Easy

234567890 DOC 9987654321

ISBN 0-07-881731-5

Publisher

Kenna S. Wood

Acquisitions Editor

Jeffrey M. Pepper

Associate Editor

Emily Rader

Project Editor

Laura Sackerman

Copy Editor

Dusty Bernard

Proofing Coordinator

Wendy Goss

Proofreaders

Mick Arellano
Kelly Barr

Indexer

Valerie Robbins

Computer Designers

Helena Charm
Lance Ravella

Cover Design

Bay Graphics Design, Inc.
Mason Fong

Contents

Acknowledgments xv
Introduction xvii

1   Worksheet Basics **1**
Loading and Quitting 1-2-3 2
   Starting 1-2-3 2
   Quitting 1-2-3 3
Worksheet Organization and the 1-2-3 Window 3
   Cells and the Cell Pointer 5
   The 1-2-3 Window 6
   The Worksheet Window 9
Moving Around the Worksheet 10
   Basic Keyboard Options 10
   Moving with the Mouse 11
Review 13
   Commands and Keys 13

2   Entering Labels and Numbers **15**
Types of Worksheet Entries 16
   Entering Labels 16
   Entering Numbers 18
Correcting Errors 22
   Fixing an Entry Before It Is Finalized 23
   Fixing a Finalized Entry 23
The Undo Feature 25
Getting Help 26
Review 28
   Commands and Keys 29

Executing the Macro 335
Documenting the Macro 337
Creating Another Macro 337
Creating a Macro to Insert Rows 338
Special Macro Topics 339
Creating a Macro Library 339
Creating Automatic Macros 340
Debugging Macros 344
Review 346
Commands and Keys 347

A **Installing 1-2-3 for Windows** **349**
Requirements for 1-2-3 for Windows 349
Installing 1-2-3 350

B **Using Windows** **355**
Starting Windows 356
Exiting Windows 356
The Windows Interface 357
The Program Manager 358
Menus in Windows 359
Opening Applications 360
Switching to a Window 360
Positioning and Sizing Windows 361
The Windows File Manager 364
Deleting Files 366
Formatting a Disk 366
The Windows Print Manager 368

Index **369**

6   Changing the Appearance of Worksheet Cells ...   **97**
Using a Range of Cells 98
Changing Label Appearances 100
    Changing Label Entry Alignment 100
    Changing Worksheet Fonts 104
    Adding Borders 110
    Adding Shading 111
Changing the Display Format 112
    Formatting Options 112
    Scope of the Formatting Change 113
Review 118
    Commands and Keys 119

7   Changing Row and Column Options **121**
Altering Column Widths 121
    Changing the Width of One or More
    Columns 122
    Changing the Width of All the Columns 124
Inserting and Deleting Rows and Columns 126
    Inserting Rows and Columns 126
    Deleting Rows and Columns 128
Hiding and Displaying Columns 129
Erasing Worksheet Data 131
Review 133
    Commands and Keys 134

8   Managing Files and Sheets **135**
File Concepts 136
    Storing Information on Disk 136
    Organizing the Disk Data 137
1-2-3 File Commands 141
    Changing the Directory 142
    Saving Files 143
    Retrieving Files 148
    Opening New Worksheet Files 151
Working with Multiple Worksheet Windows 151
    Switching Between Windows 153
    Using Multiple Worksheet Files in Formulas .. 154
    Adding Worksheets 155
    Using Panes to Help Monitor Data 158

Using Worksheet Functions with Multiple
Worksheets 163
Deleting Worksheets in a Worksheet File 163
Designing Multilevel Applications 164
Review 167
Commands and Keys 168

9   **Making 1-2-3 Do Your Work** **171**
Copying Worksheet Data 172
Copying Labels 172
Copying Formulas 175
Copying Without Using the Clipboard 187
Rearranging the Worksheet 189
Moving Worksheet Data 189
Transposing Data 191
Generating Cell Entries 194
Creating Repeating Labels 195
Generating a Series of Numbers 197
Other Worksheet Commands for Expanded Data .. 198
Recalculation 199
Using Titles with Large Worksheets 201
Searching for and Replacing Worksheet Data 203
Searching for Worksheet Data 204
Replacing Worksheet Data 205
Review 208
Commands and Keys 209

10 **Printing Your Worksheet** **211**
Printing Basics 211
The Basic Printing Process 213
Previewing Your Printed Worksheet 221
Adding Printing Options 223
Margin Settings 223
Defining Headers and Footers 224
Using Borders 227
Setting the Orientation 230
Other 1-2-3 Commands That Affect Printing 231
Adding Page Breaks 231
Hiding Columns 232
Review 233
Commands and Keys 235

11   Creating Graphs **237**
　　Basic Terms 238
　　　　Data Series 238
　　　　X Axis 239
　　　　Y Axis 239
　　　　Legends 240
　　Creating a Graph 240
　　　　Deciding on a Graph Type 245
　　　　Specifying the Data for the Graph 250
　　Displaying Named Graphs 251
　　Deleting Named Graphs 252
　　Enhancing the Display 253
　　　　Adding Titles 253
　　　　Adding Legends 256
　　　　Adding Grid Lines 258
　　Adding Graphs to the Worksheet 260
　　Changing the Range of a Graph in the Worksheet .. 261
　　Printing Graphs 262
　　Review 262
　　　　Commands and Keys 264

12   Data Management Basics **267**
　　Creating a Database 268
　　　　Choosing a Location on the Worksheet 268
　　　　Entering Field Names 269
　　　　Entering Data 270
　　　　Making Changes 272
　　Sorting the Database 273
　　　　Defining the Database Location 273
　　　　Defining the Sort Sequence 274
　　Searching the Database 279
　　　　Entering Criteria 279
　　　　Defining the Database Location 282
　　　　Telling 1-2-3 the Criteria Location 283
　　　　Finding Matching Records 284
　　　　Extracting Matching Records 285
　　　　A Few More Examples 287
　　Special Features 289
　　　　Using a Shortcut Approach 289
　　　　Naming the Database 290
　　Using the Database Statistical Functions 291
　　　　Using @DAVG 292

Using @DSUM 293
Using @DCOUNT 293
Using @DMIN 294
Review 294
Commands and Keys 295

13   Advanced Problem-solving Techniques **297**
Using Solver 298
Setting Up a Problem for Solver 298
Solving a Problem 301
Saving a Section of the Worksheet 304
Saving Values 305
Saving Formulas 307
Combining Data from Other Files with Your
Worksheet 308
Setting Up a Worksheet for Combining 309
Adding a Worksheet to the Current
Worksheet 311
Subtracting from the Current Worksheet 313
Transferring Data Between Applications 314
Pasting Links Between Applications 315
Pasting Links Between Windows Applications . . 318
Exporting Data by Using the Clipboard and
Notepad 319
Extracting to a Text File 320
Using the Clipboard to Bring Data into a
Worksheet 321
Bringing Text Files into a Worksheet
Without the Clipboard 322
Review 323
Commands and Keys 324

14   Creating 1-2-3 Macros **325**
Keyboard Alternative Macros 326
Macro Building Blocks 327
Planning the Macro's Actions Before
You Begin 327
Using 1-2-3's Transcript Window 328
Recording Special Keys 330
Recording a Macro 333
Copying the Keystrokes to the Worksheet 333
Naming the Macro 335

Executing the Macro 335
Documenting the Macro 337
Creating Another Macro 337
Creating a Macro to Insert Rows 338
Special Macro Topics 339
Creating a Macro Library 339
Creating Automatic Macros 340
Debugging Macros 344
Review 346
Commands and Keys 347

A   Installing 1-2-3 for Windows **349**
Requirements for 1-2-3 for Windows 349
Installing 1-2-3 350

B   Using Windows **355**
Starting Windows 356
Exiting Windows 356
The Windows Interface 357
The Program Manager 358
Menus in Windows 359
Opening Applications 360
Switching to a Window 360
Positioning and Sizing Windows 361
The Windows File Manager 364
Deleting Files 366
Formatting a Disk 366
The Windows Print Manager

Index **369**

Acknowledgments

This book is the result of the efforts of many people. I would like to extend my special thanks to the following individuals:

Gabrielle Lawrence, who helped with every phase of the book

Eriks Usis, who created all the screens and checked all the exercises to ensure they produced the correct results

Jeff Pepper, who managed the entire process of making this a book despite his other responsibilities as editor-in-chief

Emily Rader, who prepared all of our chapters for production

Laura Sackerman, who did a fine job as project editor

Helena Charm, Fred Lass, Lance Ravella, and the others in the production department, who did their usual wonderful job with the production of this book

All of those at Lotus who were such an immense help through the beta process for 1-2-3 for Windows, including Mary Beth Butler, Karen Precourt, Alexandra Trevelyan, Kim Twist, and Lauren Wendall

Introduction

1-2-3 for Windows is an important new release of 1-2-3 designed to run under Microsoft Windows 3.0. 1-2-3 for Windows utilizes windows presentation, information management, and presentation features. It is an advanced spreadsheet product that offers a familiar 1-2-3 Classic menu interface as well as a new Windows style menu. Both spreadsheet publishing and sophisticated presentation features are an integral part of this new software.

1-2-3 for Windows Made Easy provides an introduction to Windows essentials as well as to 1-2-3 for Windows features. You will find that this book will get you started quickly whether you are new to 1-2-3 or just to the Windows version of the product.

Why 1-2-3 for Windows Is for You

There are many spreadsheet products on the market today. These include several versions of 1-2-3, such as 1-2-3 2.3 and 1-2-3 3.1. The various 1-2-3 products have a larger installed base than any other spreadsheet program available. This means that there are more users of this spreadsheet product than any other and, because so many companies use it, you can transport the knowledge you gain in working with 1-2-3 from company to company.

1-2-3 for Windows lets you run multiple applications at one time. You can have a word processing program such as Lotus Ami Pro running in one window while running 1-2-3 for Windows in another. With 1-2-3 for Windows, it is easy to transfer information from one application to another, allowing you to combine spreadsheet results with a word processing document. You also have a number of graphical user interface elements, such as pull-down menus, cascade menus, an icon palette, windows, and dialog boxes, to work with as you build your spreadsheets.

About This Book

This book is designed to present 1-2-3's features, including the new Windows options, in an easy-to-learn format. You will use these new features as you create practical application examples. Because you are introduced to these commands in the context of application examples, you not only will see the keystrokes used to make things happen but will learn what capabilities these features offer.

The exercises within this book are presented in a step-by-step tutorial format that guarantees your success. Knowing when to use a command is not left to chance, since you are offered detailed instructions throughout the model-building process. With the building block approach presented in this book, you will find your 1-2-3 skills increasing rapidly as you move from chapter to chapter.

How This Book Is Organized

This book is divided into 14 chapters and 2 appendixes. You will find that each chapter contains about the right number of new features to cover in a single session. The first few chapters provide the basic building blocks for your first spreadsheet model. After you have mastered these topics, you will progress through the remaining topics sequentially, leading gradually to more advanced topics. Because the models in the later chapters are self-contained, you can work with them without first becoming familiar with the examples in earlier chapters.

Chapter 1 gets you started with 1-2-3 for Windows. It explains the important features of 1-2-3's display.

Chapter 2 provides techniques for entering labels and numbers on the worksheet. It introduces you to error correction and the Undo feature as well as how to access 1-2-3's help features.

Chapter 3 provides an introduction to the use of formulas in the worksheet. You will learn how formulas add power to the worksheet through what-if capabilities.

Chapter 4 provides all the information you will need to use @functions in the models that you build. You will also learn how to reference data from other worksheets.

Chapter 5 focuses on the use of menus and dialog boxes. There are many new options for accomplishing tasks quickly with the Windows version of 1-2-3, and you will learn how to utilize these features in this chapter.

Chapter 6 provides information on how to tailor the format of your entries to your specific needs. You will learn how to select currency, fixed, percent, scientific notation, date, or other cell formats on the worksheet. You will also learn about features such as boldface, underline, alignment, and fonts.

Chapter 7 teaches you how to alter the attributes of one or more columns. You will also learn how to change the width of columns to display new formats and how to hide and redisplay columns.

Chapter 8 shows you how to protect your investment in model building through the use of files that can be stored permanently on your disk. You will learn about using multiple files simultaneously as well as how to use multiple sheets within one file.

Chapter 9 covers everything you need to know about copying entries that you have already made to other locations on the worksheet. In this chapter you will learn techniques for rearranging worksheet data to change your models. You will also learn to use 1-2-3's search feature to locate cell entries quickly.

Chapter 10 provides explanations and examples of 1-2-3's print features. You will learn how to do everything from printing a draft of your worksheet to adding headers and other sophisticated options.

Chapter 11 introduces 1-2-3's graphic features, which provide tools for presenting numeric data in an understandable fashion. You will learn how to print a graph by itself or along with your other worksheet entries.

Chapter 12 covers data management features. You can use these to create a simple database. You will also find examples that show you how to sort information in the database and selectively copy information to create a quick report.

Chapter 13 introduces the powerful problem-solving capabilities of Solver. The chapter also introduces advanced file management techniques such as extracting data and combining data from several worksheets.

Chapter 14 examines the basics of 1-2-3 macros, including the 1-2-3 for Windows Transcript feature, which makes macro creation easy. You will learn how to record keystrokes for execution at a later time.

Appendix A provides detailed instructions for installing 1-2-3 for Windows, and Appendix B is a reference that covers essential Windows features.

Conventions Used in This Book

Throughout this book you will be instructed to make entries in 1-2-3 models. Each of these entries will be shown in boldface type. If you are already somewhat familiar with the technique being presented in a chapter, scan the instructions quickly and enter only the information in boldface to perform each exercise.

In each instruction that requires a menu selection, the full menu command is shown. You can choose to type the boldface letter of each menu option, you can highlight the desired option and press ENTER, or you can select the desired option with a mouse.

Worksheet Basics 1
Creating Graphs 11

Entering Labels and Numbers 2
Data Management Basics 12

Defining Your Calculations 3
Advanced Problem-solving Techniques 13

@Functions and Other Formula Options 4
Creating 1-2-3 Macros 14

Getting Familiar with Menus and Dialog Boxes 5
Installing 1-2-3 for Windows .... A

Changing the Appearance of Worksheet Cells 6
Using Windows .... B

Changing Row and Column Options 7

Managing Files and Sheets 8

Making 1-2-3 Do Your Work 9

Printing Your Worksheet 10

1

Worksheet Basics

You are about to enter the world of 1-2-3 for Windows. This journey will give you a new way of working with everyday business problems—a way that is both efficient and flexible. Traditionally, accountants and business managers have worked out business problems and evaluated financial decisions using green-bar columnar pads. 1-2-3 replaces the paper versions of these worksheets by turning your computer into a larger, electronic version of this columnar pad.

You will learn to use 1-2-3's worksheet features to handle the same types of problems previously solved on columnar pads. Applications such as budgeting, financial planning, project cost projections, break-even analysis, and cost planning are some of the applications you might consider. You will also learn to pattern calculations after real-world situations and lay out models representing the problems to be solved on the electronic worksheet. Since you will be working with Windows, you will be able to switch to other applications to access information needed for problem solving.

The electronic sheet of paper that 1-2-3 places into your computer's memory has a structure organized to help you construct these models. The electronic worksheet is arranged into rows, columns, and sheets that you can use to organize your data. This structure allows you to enter numbers, text, and computations in many locations. Making entries on 1-2-3's worksheet offers significant advantages over making them on paper. For example, on a paper worksheet, you must update calculations every time you change a number; however, because 1-2-3 remembers calculations, it recalculates the worksheet automatically when you update a number.

In this chapter, you look at beginning and ending a 1-2-3 session and at worksheet organization. It is in this chapter that you will gain the understanding you need to use 1-2-3's features effectively.

Although you probably are eager to start using 1-2-3's features right away, you may have to complete some preliminary work first. Before you begin, Windows and 1-2-3 must be installed. Appendix A, "Installing 1-2-3 for Windows," provides instructions for installing your copy of 1-2-3. If you are not familiar with Windows, you may want to read Appendix B, "Using Windows," to familiarize yourself with the Windows features you may use in 1-2-3.

Loading and Quitting 1-2-3

You cannot begin to use 1-2-3 until you have loaded Windows and 1-2-3 into the memory of your computer system. Once 1-2-3 is loaded, you can continue to use it until you leave 1-2-3.

Starting 1-2-3

Since 1-2-3 for Windows is a Windows application, the first step for starting 1-2-3 is to load Windows. When you installed 1-2-3 for Windows, the installation program created a Lotus Applications group window for you. You first select this group window from the Program Manager window so it is the active window. You can press ALT, press W, and press the number next to Lotus Applications to activate the Lotus Applications group window. Next, point to the 1-2-3 for Windows icon and double-click the left button of the mouse. (For more information on using a mouse, see "Moving with the Mouse," later in this chaper.) From the keyboard, press the arrow keys so 1-2-3 for Windows is highlighted and press ENTER. 1-2-3 displays an introductory screen and then displays a 1-2-3 window.

Quitting 1-2-3

When you have finished all of your 1-2-3 tasks for the day, you will want to leave 1-2-3. To end your 1-2-3 session from the keyboard, press ALT or F10 (Menu) and then press F X to select **F**ile and **E**xit. With a mouse, point to **F**ile in the second line of the 1-2-3 window and click the left mouse button, and point to **E**xit and click the left mouse button again. A third alternative is to end your 1-2-3 session by closing the 1-2-3 window. You close a 1-2-3 window as you would close other application windows: point to the control menu box in the upper-left corner of the window and click the left mouse button, or press ALT-SPACEBAR. From the control menu that appears, press C to select **C**lose or point to **C**lose and then click the left mouse button. Another method for closing a 1-2-3 or other application window is by pressing ALT-F4.

Once you tell 1-2-3 that you want to quit, 1-2-3 displays a prompt for saving all open files. You can press Y to select **Y**es to save all open files, press N to select **N**o to remove all files without saving their contents, or press C to select **C**ancel to remain in 1-2-3. You can also select one of these options by pointing to it and clicking the left mouse button. When 1-2-3 is unloaded from memory, you are returned to the Windows interface.

Worksheet Organization and the 1-2-3 Window

When you load 1-2-3, you see only the upper-left corner of one sheet in your worksheet file. Your display should match the one shown in Figure 1-1. This initial display lets you see only a few columns and rows of the first worksheet file. The worksheet file is actually much larger than it first appears. A worksheet file has 256 columns, named A to IV, and 8192 rows, numbered from 1 to 8192. Columns use single letters first, then AA to AZ, BA to BZ, and so on.

1-2-3 lets you insert extra sheets into a worksheet file just as you might add extra sheets to a folder or notebook. Although a new worksheet file has only one sheet, sheet A, you can add as many as 255 additional sheets for a total of 256 sheets in a worksheet file. Sheets are named like columns, with single letters used first and then double-letter combinations beginning with AA and ending with IV. The first worksheet level is A, and the last is IV. You do not need to concern yourself with additional sheets just yet. You will want to explore many of 1-2-3's possibilities with one sheet before adding sheets. Figure 1-2 shows a diagram of a worksheet file, which you can compare to the small portion that is visible when you first load 1-2-3.

Figure 1-1.   *Initial 1-2-3 display*

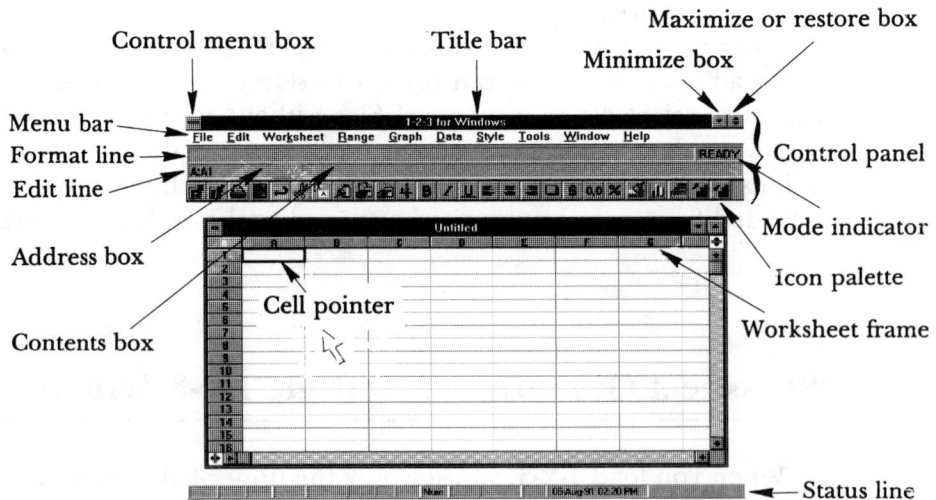

Figure 1-2.   *Structure of a 1-2-3 worksheet file*

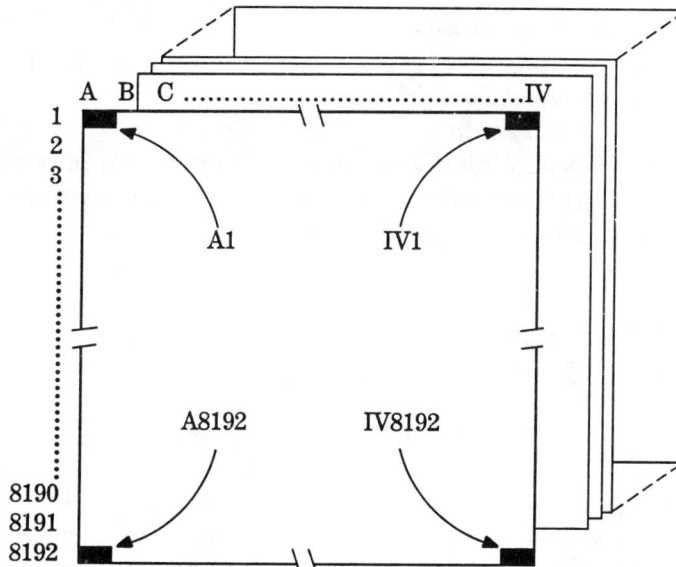

Cells and the Cell Pointer

Each location on the worksheet is referred to as a *cell*. Each cell is uniquely identified by its *worksheet level* and its *column* and *row location*. When these three pieces of information are combined, you have a *cell address*. Giving 1-2-3 a cell address is like giving someone an address, providing the city, street name, and street number to indicate the correct location. If you do not provide a worksheet level in a cell address (which is comparable to indicating which page of a notepad to use), 1-2-3 assumes you are referring to the current sheet, just as you might give someone a street name and number with the assumption that the address is in the current city.

Since you will work initially only with sheet A, when you do not specify a worksheet level, 1-2-3 automatically assumes you want to use sheet A. When you do specify a worksheet level, follow the sheet letter with a colon to indicate to 1-2-3 that it is a sheet letter. The column letter and the row

number are next. For example, you can indicate locations such as A:A1,
A:C10, D:IV8192, A:Z1025, and IJ850. 1-2-3 displays the worksheet level,
column letters, and row numbers in a *worksheet frame,* which is the top and
left border of the worksheet window in Figure 1-1.

Your worksheet has a *cell pointer,* which always marks the current
location on the worksheet with a small highlighted bar. In a new
worksheet, such as the one in Figure 1-1, the cell pointer is located in cell
A:A1. The location of the cell pointer is extremely important; it marks the
location of the *active cell,* the only cell into which you can make an entry
without first moving the cell pointer.

The 1-2-3 Window

The 1-2-3 window has several components. They are identified in
Figure 1-1.

The top four lines of the 1-2-3 window are called the control panel.
The *control panel* monitors 1-2-3's activities and tells you when 1-2-3 is
ready to proceed with new activities. In addition, the control panel
functions as a place keeper, letting you know your current location and
giving you specifics about that location. As you make entries on the
worksheet, these entries appear in the control panel.

The remaining area of the 1-2-3 window is used for the icon palette,
the status line and, mainly, the worksheet and graph windows. The icon
palette provides shortcuts for the most frequently used commands. The
status line provides information about the current 1-2-3 session. The
worksheet windows or graph windows contain the data you are using. The
rest of this chapter covers using a worksheet window. In Chapter 11,
"Creating Graphs," you learn about graph windows.

The Title Bar

The top line of the control panel is the title bar. The *title bar* contains
the control menu box, any menu description, the window name, the
minimize box, and the maximize or restore box. The control menu box
lets you control the 1-2-3 window, as described in Appendix B, "Using
Windows." The minimize box and the maximize or restore box change the
size of the 1-2-3 window, also described in Appendix B. The remaining
area of the title bar contains the window's name: 1-2-3 for Windows. When

you activate a 1-2-3 menu, the title bar displays the menu description in place of 1-2-3 for Windows. Appendix B also provides you with information about how you can use the title bar and the active window border to size and position this window.

The Menu Bar

The second line of the control panel is the menu bar. The *menu bar* displays the current menu. This menu becomes active as soon as you select one of the options with the mouse, press ALT, or press the function key labeled F10 (Menu). In later chapters, you will learn how to use the menu bar to issue 1-2-3 commands. Sometimes the menu bar uses two lines; 1-2-3 expands the menu bar to two lines when the 1-2-3 window is not wide enough to fit the menu on one line.

The Format Line

The third line of the control panel, the *format line,* displays the formatting information about the active cell. This information includes the width of the cell, whether numbers have formatting characters such as % and $ added, and any character formatting, such as boldfacing or a different character style. A sample of a cell that has formatting added and the information for the formatting displayed in the format line might look like this:

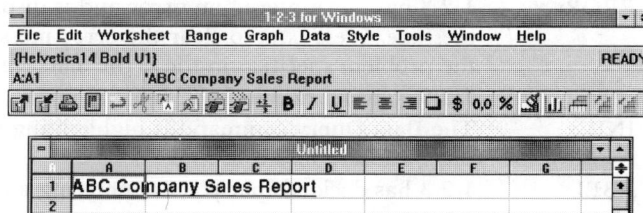

In Chapter 6, "Changing the Appearance of Worksheet Cells," you learn about several commands that you can use to add formatting to a cell.

Besides displaying the cell format information, the format line displays the *mode indicator.* When you first load 1-2-3, this indicator is READY, indicating that 1-2-3 is ready to respond to whatever you enter. The mode indicator can tell you either that 1-2-3 is busy with your previous request or that it is ready to do something new. It can also tell you to correct an error, point to a worksheet location, or select a menu choice. Once 1-2-3's mode indicator changes from READY to another mode, you must either follow along with 1-2-3 or find a way to change the indicator. Many new users become frustrated at this point, but you can avoid difficulties by watching the mode indicator and staying in sync with the current mode. Table 1-1 lists all the modes you will encounter, along with their meanings. They will also be pointed out in later chapters as new activities cause mode changes.

The Edit Line

The fourth line of the control panel is the edit line. The *edit line* displays the location of the cell pointer on the left side—the *address box*—and the contents of the cell on the right side—the *contents box*. As you make an entry, 1-2-3 also displays confirm and cancel boxes that look like a green check mark and a red X, respectively, that you can select to accept or cancel your entry.

Table 1-1.   *Mode Indicators*

Indicator	Meaning
EDIT	You are editing an entry. The entry can be in a cell or in response to a command. 1-2-3 switches to EDIT mode when you try finalizing a cell entry that contains an error
ERROR	1-2-3 has encountered an error and is displaying an error message. Press ENTER to clear the error message, and correct the problem specified in the error message
FILES	1-2-3 is listing files in its Classic menu
FIND	The **D**ata **Q**uery command is highlighting database records that you have told it to find
LABEL	1-2-3 has decided that you are entering a label
MENU	1-2-3 is waiting for you to make a selection from the menu
NAMES	1-2-3 is displaying a list of range names, external table names, @functions, graph names, or macro commands
POINT	1-2-3 is waiting for you to point to a cell or range
READY	1-2-3 is waiting for you to make a new request
VALUE	1-2-3 has decided that you are entering a value
WAIT	1-2-3 is busy processing your last command or entry. The mouse pointer will appear as an hourglass while this indicator is displayed

1

The Icon Palette

SmartIcons are symbols that represent commands you can select. The icon palette is the bar of SmartIcons you can select with a mouse to perform 1-2-3 commands. The icon palette provides shortcuts for performing the most popular 1-2-3 commands. As you use the commands for which the icon palette provides shortcuts, you will learn how to use the palette instead of entering the command. You cannot use the icon palette with the keyboard. You can display the command or feature a SmartIcon represents in the title bar by pointing to it with the mouse and clicking the right mouse button. Clicking the left mouse button selects the SmartIcon.

1-2-3 will let you select the SmartIcons to appear on the icon palette, although that feature is beyond the scope of this book. You may have different SmartIcons in your icon palette than you see in the figures and illustrations in this book. You can also put the icon palette in different positions, so the icon palette you see in the figures and illustrations may appear in a different position (many times it is moved to the bottom of the screen). To select where the icon palette appears, press ALT or F10 and then press T I for **Tools** and **SmartIcons**. Then press T, B, L, R, or F to select **T**op, **B**ottom, **L**eft, **R**ight, or **F**loating for where you want the icon palette to appear. Next, press ENTER to put the icon palette in the new position. In Chapter 5, "Getting Familiar with Menus and Dialog Boxes," you learn how you can use the mouse to make the same command selections.

The Status Line

The bottom line of the screen, the *status line,* provides a variety of information. The lower-right corner displays the date and time. The area to the left of the date and time lets you know when certain keys have been pressed. It also tells you if 1-2-3 has encountered a special situation. The four indicators designed to inform you that a certain key or key sequence has been pressed are described in Table 1-2.

There are other status indicators that monitor advanced features and have broader meanings. They will be discussed as they occur later in the book. They are Calc, Circ, CMD, File, Group, Mem, RO, SST, Step, and Zoom.

The Worksheet Window

The remaining area of your 1-2-3 window is for windows that you are using in 1-2-3. Initially, 1-2-3 puts an empty worksheet file in a worksheet

Table 1-2. *The Four Indicators on the Status Line*

Indicator	Meaning
Caps	The CAPS LOCK key has been pressed. Pressing this key causes the alphabetic keys to produce capital letters
End	The END key has been pressed. The END key moves the cell pointer to the end of entries in a given direction or to the end of a group of blank cells in a given direction. After using the END key, you must press an arrow key to indicate the direction
Num	The NUM LOCK key has been pressed and you can enter numbers from the keyboard's numeric keypad
Scroll	The SCROLL LOCK key has been pressed. When Scroll appears, the entire window shifts each time you move the cell pointer. When Scroll does not appear, the part of the worksheet that appears on the screen shifts only to show the cell that the cell pointer is moving to

window named Untitled. The worksheet window has its own title bar that includes a control menu box, a minimize box, and a maximize or restore box. These boxes in the title bar work just like the ones in the 1-2-3 window title bar within the area of the 1-2-3 window. When you save the worksheet and provide a filename, the filename will also appear on the worksheet window's title bar. You will learn how to create your models in 1-2-3 by using worksheet windows.

Moving Around the Worksheet

Now you are ready to learn about navigating 1-2-3's worksheet. This will prepare you for constructing models with entries in worksheet cells. You will look at the basic features as well as the more advanced options that let you travel long distances quickly.

Basic Keyboard Options

1-2-3's basic cell pointer movements within a sheet are accomplished with the *arrow keys*. These keys may be on the numeric keypad and in

Figure 1-3. *IBM's enhanced keyboard*

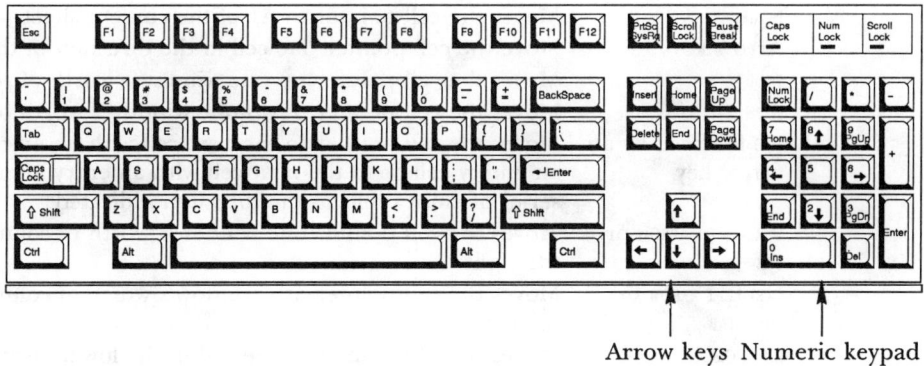

Arrow keys Numeric keypad

another location as well, depending on your computer system. Figure 1-3 shows the enhanced keyboard (standard for ATs and new computers). Even if your keyboard is slightly different, you should find it relatively easy to locate the arrow keys. The arrow keys on the numeric keypad perform two functions. When Num does not appear on the status line and you press an arrow key, the cell pointer moves in the direction indicated. When Num appears on the status line and you press one of these arrow keys, you are entering the number on the key. You can press NUM LOCK repeatedly to switch between these two functions. 1-2-3 also has other keys that move the cell pointer. The keys that you might use are listed in Table 1-3.

Moving with the Mouse

1-2-3 for Windows, like other Windows applications, is designed to be used with a mouse. Using a mouse lets you make selections by pointing to what you want and pressing a button on the mouse. Pressing the mouse button once is called *clicking* the mouse. Pressing the mouse button twice quickly is called *double-clicking* the mouse. Another term used with a mouse is *dragging,* which means that you hold down the mouse button as you move the mouse to a new position. Unless you are instructed otherwise,

Table 1-3.   *Worksheet Movement Keys*

Keys	Action
HOME	Moves the cell pointer to A1 of the current sheet
Arrow keys	Move the cell pointer one cell in the direction of the arrow
PGUP	Moves the cell pointer up one window's worth of rows
PGDN	Moves the cell pointer down one window's worth of rows
END followed by an arrow key	Moves the cell pointer to the next cell with an entry before an empty cell or to the next cell with an entry after a series of empty cells in the direction indicated
CTRL-RIGHT ARROW or TAB	Moves the cell pointer one window's worth of columns to the right
CTRL-LEFT ARROW or SHIFT-TAB	Moves the cell pointer one window's worth of columns to the left
END HOME	Moves the cell pointer to the cell in the lower corner of the area of worksheet cells containing entries
F5 (Goto)	Moves to a cell after you type its address and press ENTER

when you are told to click, double-click, or drag the mouse button, you use the left button on the mouse. You can set Windows to switch the mouse buttons, which means that when the directions refer to the left button you use the right, and vice versa.

The mouse's position on the screen is usually indicated by a pointer that looks like an arrow, but it can change to other shapes. For example, when you first load 1-2-3, the pointer looks like an hourglass; Windows and 1-2-3 are telling you to wait until 1-2-3 is loaded into memory. You will be introduced to other mouse pointers with the features that use them.

When you move in a worksheet with a mouse, usually you click the cell you want. If the cell you want is off the screen, you can change the part of the worksheet that displays in the window by using the scroll bars. The *scroll bars* are the bars on the right and at the bottom of the worksheet window. Each scroll bar has an elevator box. These *elevator boxes* represent your horizontal and vertical position in the worksheet. By clicking the scroll bar on either side of the elevator box, you can display the previous or next section of worksheet columns or rows. You can also drag the elevator box to a new position, which changes the displayed worksheet to match the elevator box's new location. If you want to shift the display one row or column at a time, click the arrows at the end of the scroll bars. As a shortcut, 1-2-3 has assigned one of the SmartIcons on the icon palette to

1

be equivalent to pressing HOME. When you click the icon that looks like a small house, the cell pointer moves to A1.

Review

In this chapter you learned how 1-2-3 organizes data and how you can move the cell pointer on the worksheet. You also learned how you can use the control panel to provide more information about your 1-2-3 session.

- To start 1-2-3 for Windows, first load Windows into your computer. Once Windows is loaded, you can start 1-2-3 for Windows by selecting 1-2-3 for Windows from the Lotus Applications group window. You can leave 1-2-3 for Windows by pressing ALT-F4, by selecting the **File Exit** command, or by selecting **C**lose from the control menu for the 1-2-3 window, which appears when you click the control menu box or press ALT-SPACEBAR.

- The cell pointer marks your place on the worksheet. Use the keys in the following section, "Commands and Keys," to move the cell pointer around, as well as using your mouse. With a mouse, click the cell you want and use the scroll bars to change the portion of the worksheet displayed in the worksheet window.

- The control panel at the top of the window provides valuable information about 1-2-3. The mode indicator indicates the type of information 1-2-3 expects from you. Other lines in the control panel display the contents, address, and format of the current cell. The status line at the bottom displays the date, time, and several indicators.

Commands and Keys

In this chapter you learned about the 1-2-3 for Windows user interface. You also learned what keys to press to move through the worksheet. Those keys and their descriptions are listed in the following table.

Keys	Action
ALT F X	**F**ile **E**xit leaves 1-2-3 and closes its application windows
ALT T I	**T**ools Smart**I**cons selects where the icon palette appears
Arrow keys	Move the cell pointer one cell in the direction of the arrow. In EDIT mode, RIGHT ARROW and LEFT ARROW move the cursor one character at a time in either direction, while UP ARROW and DOWN ARROW finalize the edit
CTRL-RIGHT ARROW or TAB	Moves the cell pointer one window's worth of columns to the right. In EDIT mode, moves the cursor to the next word
CTRL-LEFT ARROW or SHIFT-TAB	Moves the cell pointer one window's worth of columns to the left. In EDIT mode, moves the cursor to the previous word
PGUP	Moves the cell pointer one window's worth of rows up
PGDN	Moves the cell pointer one window's worth of rows down
END	Moves the cell pointer to the next cell after a series of cells with entries or empty cells in the direction of the next arrow key you press. In EDIT mode, moves the cursor to the end of the entry
END HOME	Moves the cell pointer to the cell in the last column and the last row containing entries
HOME	Moves the cell pointer to A1. In EDIT mode, moves the cursor to the beginning of the entry

2

Entering Labels and Numbers

Worksheet models represent business problems and calculations that you need to solve repeatedly. To create these models with 1-2-3, you will make entries in worksheet cells. No matter how sophisticated a model you create, it will be composed of label and value entries. Label entries describe the values on the worksheet as well as represent data that is not numeric. Value entries can consist of numeric constants and a variety of different types of formulas. Typically, you start creating a worksheet by entering labels and numbers and then move on to the more difficult task of formula creation.

In this chapter, you look at entering numbers and labels on the worksheet, correcting data-entry errors, using the Undo feature, and accessing 1-2-3's Help feature. Since this chapter covers some of the basic building blocks of worksheet-model construction, you will want to master it completely before progressing to more advanced topics.

Types of Worksheet Entries

1-2-3 has two basic types of entries for worksheet cells: labels and values. *Labels* are text characters that describe numeric data in the worksheet or store character information. Labels are not used in arithmetic calculations, even if the labels contain numbers. *Values,* on the other hand, consist of either numbers or formulas. *Formulas* result in numbers but are entered as a series of calculations to perform. 1-2-3 allows only specific entries for values. 1-2-3 determines whether you are entering a value or a label based on the first character you type. If this first character is not one of the characters that 1-2-3 considers the start of a value entry, it is a label.

Entering Labels

Entering a label is as simple as typing the characters you want to appear in the cell. If you type **Sales**, 1-2-3 treats the entry as a label because the first character in the entry is an alphabetic character. As soon as you type the **S**, 1-2-3 changes the READY mode indicator to LABEL. Since 1-2-3 always makes its determination from the first character, entering **15 Johnson St.** causes 1-2-3 to reject your entry when you attempt to finalize it; the first character is numeric and 1-2-3 attempts to treat the entire entry as a value. 1-2-3 is very stubborn once it determines the type of entry it thinks you planned for a cell. The only way you can change its mind is by editing the cell contents or pressing ESC to start over. After a little practice with entering labels, however, you will know all the tricks to put you in command of how your entries are interpreted.

Labels in 1-2-3 start with label prefixes. *Label prefixes* indicate both that an entry is a label and how the label is aligned within a cell. Most of your entries use one of three label prefixes—an apostrophe ('), a quotation mark ("), or a caret (^). The difference between these three label prefixes is how 1-2-3 aligns the contents of the cell. The ' is the default option and left aligns the label entry in the cell. This is the label prefix 1-2-3 generates for you if you do not enter one. Using " right aligns the label in the cell, and using ^ centers the label. If you choose right or center justification, first type " or ^ and then type the text that the cell will contain. If you want to enter a label that begins with a character that 1-2-3 considers to be a value, you must start your entry with one of the three label prefixes to trick 1-2-3 into treating it as a label. To start a model that contains several labels, try the following exercise:

1. Press HOME, type **Profit Report**, and, to finalize the entry, press ENTER or click the confirm box (the green check) in the edit line.

As soon as you type the **P**, the mode indicator changes from READY to LABEL. If you make a mistake, press the BACKSPACE key to remove the incorrect characters. When you finalize the entry, 1-2-3 adds an apostrophe as a label prefix since the apostrophe is the default label prefix and you did not type one.

2. Press the DOWN ARROW key or click A2, type **Prepared by Accounting**, and press the DOWN ARROW key or click another cell.

In addition to finalizing entries with ENTER or the confirm box, you can finalize entries by moving the cell pointer to another cell. The results are the same, although moving the cell pointer to finalize an entry saves you the time it takes to press a key or click another part of the screen.

3. Move the cell pointer to C4.

Whether you use the keyboard or the mouse to move to a cell makes no difference to 1-2-3. When the steps tell you to move to a cell, use the keyboard or mouse—whichever is more convenient for you. You can use any combination of keys that moves the cell pointer where you want.

4. Type **^Smith Co.**, and press ENTER or click the confirm box.

This entry is centered within the cell because you typed ^ as the label prefix.

5. Move the cell pointer to C5, type **^Division A**, and press ENTER or click the confirm box.
6. Move the cell pointer to B7, type **"Q1**, and press the RIGHT ARROW key or click C7.

This entry is right aligned within the cell because you typed " as the label prefix.

7. Type **"Q2**, and press the RIGHT ARROW key or click D7.
8. Type **"Q3**, and press the RIGHT ARROW key or click E7.
9. Type **"Q4**, and press ENTER or click the confirm box.
10. Move the cell pointer to A8, type **1990 Profit**, and press ENTER or click the confirm box.

1-2-3 changes you to EDIT mode because this entry contains an error. When you typed the **1**, 1-2-3 assumed that you were entering a value. You may have noticed that 1-2-3 changed from LABEL mode to VALUE mode. Since "Profit" is not part of a value entry, 1-2-3 did not accept the entry. To fix this entry, you need to tell 1-2-3 that you want to treat the entry as a label.

11. Press HOME to move to the beginning of the entry, type **'**, and press ENTER or click the confirm box.

1-2-3 now treats this as a label because a label prefix is the first character of the entry. Like other label prefixes that you or 1-2-3 put as the first character, the label prefix does not display in the cell on the worksheet.

12. Move the cell pointer to A9, type **'1991 Profit**, and press ENTER or click the confirm box.

This entry is automatically treated as a label since once you type the **'**, 1-2-3 changes the mode indicator from READY to LABEL. At this point, your labels look like those shown in Figure 2-1.

Entering Numbers

Numbers are one of the two types of 1-2-3 value entries. As value entries, numbers follow much more rigid rules than labels. Like labels, numbers are constant; they do not change as the result of arithmetic calculations. They do not change unless you take some direct action to change them. Numbers can contain any of the numeric digits from 0

Figure 2-1. *Worksheet with labels and numbers entered*

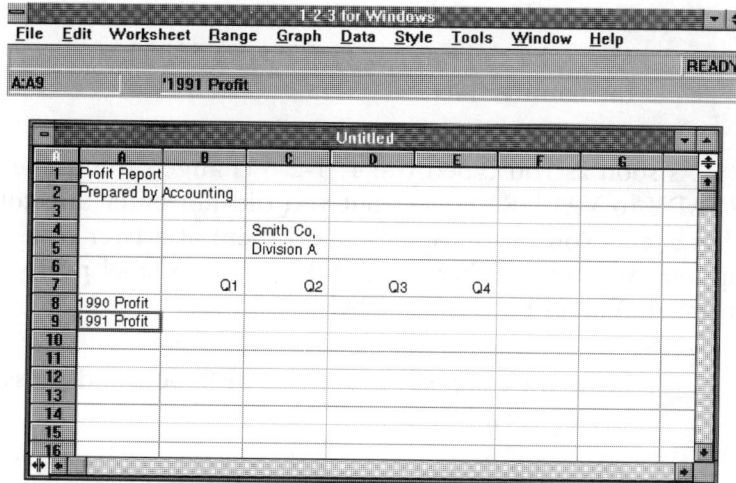

through 9. The acceptable characters for value entries are the period (.), the plus sign (+), and the minus sign (−). The . indicates a decimal point, the + indicates a positive number, and the − indicates a negative number.

Several other characters can be part of a numeric entry in special situations. A percent sign (%) can be used at the end of a numeric entry to indicate a percentage, but it is not allowed in other positions within the entry. Spaces, commas, and other formatting characters cannot be added to numeric entries. In Chapter 6, "Changing the Appearance of Worksheet Cells," you will learn how you can have 1-2-3 add these formatting characters for you. The only letter numeric entries may use is the letter E or e to represent numbers in powers of 10 (referred to as *scientific notation*). For example, 3.86E−5 is .0000386. This number can also be represented as $3.86*10^{-5}$ or 3.86 times .00001.

1-2-3 for Windows also supports the entry of special numbers that represent dates and times. These numbers are called *date and time numbers* and uniquely represent any date and time that 1-2-3 supports.

Entering Numeric Constants

The numbers you enter in a worksheet represent the constant numeric data. Once a number is entered, it changes only when you enter a new number in place of it or when you edit the existing entry as described later in this chapter. Follow these steps to add numbers to the current model:

1. Move the cell pointer to B8, type **40000**, and press ENTER or click the confirm box.

As soon as you typed the **4**, 1-2-3 changed the mode indicator from READY to VALUE. Notice that you did not enter any commas or other characters. You can have 1-2-3 add them at a later time as a formatting option. Also, notice that 1-2-3 did not add a label prefix in front of this number. Values do not use label prefixes.

2. Move the cell pointer to C8, type **80000**, and press the RIGHT ARROW key or click D8.

3. Type **20000**, and press the RIGHT ARROW key or click E8.

4. Type **−10000**, and press ENTER or click the confirm box.

Since the first character is a −, 1-2-3 treats the entry as a value and the number that you subsequently enter as a negative number.

5. Complete the entries for the 1991 profit with the following numbers:

   B9:   **−30000**
   C9:   **−20000**
   D9:   **15000**
   E9:   **45000**

Figure 2-2 shows the result of entering each number. Remember that it is easy to change any of the entries. You can type a new number or edit a cell.

Since this is the last entry you will make in the model, save a copy of the model to disk. The commands that handle saving files are covered in detail in Chapter 8, "Managing Files and Sheets." For now, all you need to know is the menu command for saving a file. You must press ALT or F10 (Menu) to activate the menu and then select **F**ile and Save **A**s by pressing

Figure 2-2. *Model created with labels and numbers*

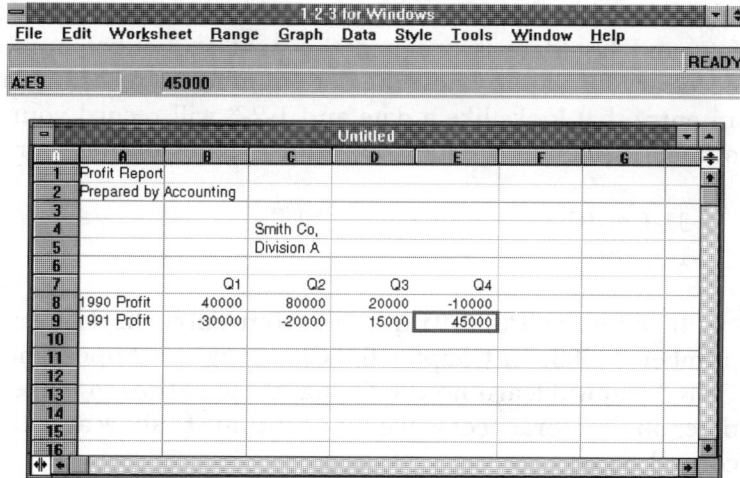

2

	A	B	C	D	E	F	G
1	Profit Report						
2	Prepared by	Accounting					
3							
4			Smith Co,				
5			Division A				
6							
7		Q1	Q2	Q3	Q4		
8	1990 Profit	40000	80000	20000	-10000		
9	1991 Profit	-30000	-20000	15000	45000		
10							
11							
12							
13							
14							
15							
16							

(Menu bar: File Edit Worksheet Range Graph Data Style Tools Window Help — READY — A:E9 45000 — title bar: 1-2-3 for Windows — worksheet title: Untitled)

the letters underlined on the screen or by clicking the selections. 1-2-3 displays a dialog box for entering information that a command uses. You will learn more about dialog boxes in Chapter 5, "Getting Familiar with Menus and Dialog Boxes."

At this point, tell 1-2-3 the filename you want to use for the worksheet by typing **PROFITS** (the filename may contain up to eight characters) and pressing ENTER or clicking the box labeled OK. To remove this data from the screen, press ALT or F10 (Menu) and then select File and Close by pressing the underlined letters or by clicking the selections. 1-2-3 closes the PROFITS worksheet window and opens a new, empty one. You can also close worksheet windows by selecting Close from that window's control menu, which appears when you select the control menu box in the window's title bar by clicking it or pressing ALT-HYPHEN.

Entering Dates and Times

Dates and times are stored as numbers in 1-2-3. Each date and time is assigned a unique number that allows you to use these entries in calculations at a later time.

1-2-3 for Windows supports date entries between January 1, 1900, and December 31, 2099. 1-2-3 assigns a date number of 1 to January 1, 1900, and a date number of 73050 to December 31, 2099. Each date between the first and last date is assigned the next sequential number. It is never necessary for you to know the date number to record a date; you can use an entry that looks like a date and 1-2-3 will record your entry as a date number. To enter a date, you can use either of these formats:

31-Dec-91
12/31/91

If you enter **12/31/91** in a cell, your entry displays exactly as the date number 33603. In Chapter 6, "Changing the Appearance of Worksheet Cells," you will learn how to format these entries to make them appear as dates on the worksheet while they continue to show as date numbers in the control panel.

You can enter a unique time for any hour, minute, and second in a day. 1-2-3 for Windows assigns a unique time number for each second in a day. This number is a decimal fraction ranging from .0 for midnight to .9999988425925926925 for 11:59:59 P.M. You can use any of these time formats for your entry:

12:59:59
12:59
12:59:59 PM
12:59 PM

You can use these dates and times in calculations. For example, you can subtract two date numbers to determine the number of elapsed days between them.

Correcting Errors

Everyone makes at least a few mistakes, and it is impossible to predict when you will make your first one, so it is best to be prepared to fix your mistakes. 1-2-3 offers several error-correction methods. The one you use depends on whether you are still entering an incorrect entry or have already finalized the entry.

Fixing an Entry Before It Is Finalized

To make a correction while making an entry in a cell, you can press the BACKSPACE key to delete the last character you entered. Suppose that you intend to enter **SALES** but that you leave out the E. To try this correction method, follow these steps:

1. Type **SALS** in A1.
2. Press the BACKSPACE key to delete the last S.
3. Type **ES**.

Using the ESC key or the cancel box (the box with a red X in the edit line) is a more dramatic way to eliminate characters. These methods eliminate all the characters you have typed in a cell, as long as you have not finalized the entry.

4. Press ESC or click the cancel box.

The entire SALES entry disappears, and 1-2-3 is ready to accept a new entry.

A third error-correction method allows you to edit an entry while you are making it. Since it functions the same whether or not the cell entry has been finalized, it is discussed in the section, "Editing a Finalized Entry."

Fixing a Finalized Entry

Once the entry is finalized, you must use other methods for correcting mistakes. The correction methods for finalized entries include retyping entries and using 1-2-3's EDIT mode.

Retyping Entries

One way to change a finalized cell entry is to retype it. Follow these steps to create and correct a finalized entry:

1. Type **SALS** and press ENTER or click the confirm box.

At this point, neither BACKSPACE nor ESC will affect the entry.

2. With the cell pointer in the same cell, type **SALES** and press ENTER or click the confirm box to make the correction.

This method gets the job done, but requires some unnecessary typing.

Editing a Finalized Entry

A better error-correction method, especially for longer entries, is to edit the entry and change only the mistakes. You must be in EDIT mode to make this type of change. To place yourself in EDIT mode, press F2 (Edit), double-click the cell containing the entry, or click the cell entry in the contents box. When the mouse is in the contents box, it appears as a thin I. This is the same EDIT mode 1-2-3 automatically places you in if you make an entry it cannot accept. Regardless of how you get there, once you are in EDIT mode, you can change the entry to make any correction you want. Your position in the entry is indicated by a vertical bar called a *cursor*. When you edit an entry, you move the cursor to where you want to add or remove characters. With a mouse, you can move the cursor by clicking the spot where you want the cursor.

Within EDIT mode, the keys that move the cell pointer around on the worksheet function differently. Now the RIGHT ARROW and LEFT ARROW keys move the cursor one character to the right or left. The HOME key also takes on a new function within EDIT mode: it moves you to the beginning of the entry. The END key moves in the opposite direction; it places the cursor at the end of the entry. You can also move a word to the right or the left with CTRL-RIGHT ARROW or CTRL-LEFT ARROW. Within the entry, you can use two different keys to eliminate characters. You can press the BACKSPACE key to delete the character to the left of the cursor, and you can press the DEL key to delete the character to the right of the cursor. Let's try an example of editing a cell by following these steps:

1. Type **SELRS** and press ENTER or click the confirm box.

2. With the cell pointer in the same cell, press F2 (Edit) or click SELRS in the contents box.

1-2-3 displays the entry in the contents box with a cursor at the end, like this:

```
┌─────────────────── 1-2-3 for Windows ─────────────────── ▼ ◆
  File  Edit  Worksheet  Range  Graph  Data  Style  Tools  Window  Help
                                                              EDIT
  A:A1        ☐ ✓ 'SELRS|
┌────────────────────── Untitled ────────────────────── ▼ ◆
        A        B       C       D       E       F       G    ◆
   1  SELRS                                                    ◆
```

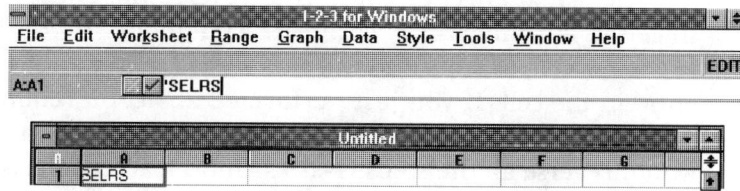

3. Press the BACKSPACE key to delete the S, and then type **Y**.

4. Press the LEFT ARROW key or click the R to position the cursor to the left of the R, and then type **A** to add the A to the left of the R.

5. Press HOME and the RIGHT ARROW twice or click the E to move the cursor to the left of the E, and then press DEL to remove the E. Type **A** so the control panel looks like this:

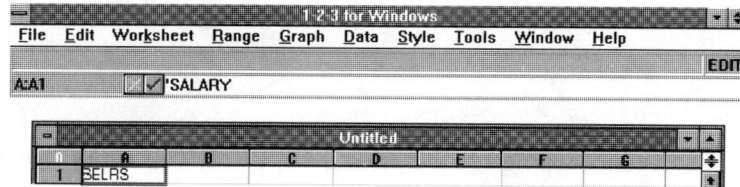

```
┌─────────────────── 1-2-3 for Windows ─────────────────── ▼ ◆
  File  Edit  Worksheet  Range  Graph  Data  Style  Tools  Window  Help
                                                              EDIT
  A:A1        ☐ ✓ 'SALARY
┌────────────────────── Untitled ────────────────────── ▼ ◆
        A        B       C       D       E       F       G    ◆
   1  SELRS                                                    ◆
```

6. Press ENTER or click the confirm box to finalize the corrected entry.

7. Press F10 (Menu) or ALT to activate the menu and press F C to select **File** and **Close** or click **File** and **Close**. Press N to select **No** or click **No** when 1-2-3 displays a prompt for saving the file. You must respond to this extra prompt because the worksheet has entries you have not saved.

The Undo Feature

1-2-3 has an Undo feature that reverses the effect of the last entry or menu command you made. The secret to using Undo effectively is to make sure that you invoke it before taking any other action since it changes only the last action performed.

The actual effect of Undo is to reverse the effect of the actions taken since the last time 1-2-3 was in READY mode. If you have just made an entry in a cell, using Undo will remove this entry and restore any previous entry in the cell. If you just performed an action requiring multiple steps and 1-2-3 did not return to READY mode between steps, using Undo would reverse all the steps. 1-2-3's Undo feature affects only changes that you make in the 1-2-3 window. Other Windows application windows are not affected by 1-2-3's Undo feature.

In Chapter 5, "Getting Familiar with Menus and Dialog Boxes," you will learn about using Undo to reverse menu commands. For now, you can use Undo to eliminate your last cell entry. All that is required is pressing ALT-BACKSPACE, pressing F10 (Menu) or ALT and pressing E U to select **Edit Undo**, or clicking the Undo icon, which looks like this,

in the icon palette. If nothing happens, Undo may be disabled. To enable the Undo feature, press ALT or F10 (Menu) and press T U or click **Tools** and **User Setup**. From the dialog box 1-2-3 presents, press ALT-E or click the box labeled **Enable Edit Undo**. Next, press ALT-U or click the box labeled **Update**. Finally, press ENTER or click OK to save the setting.

Getting Help

Navigating your way around the worksheet and entering numbers and labels in worksheet cells probably has seemed quite simple. That is because you have taken everything a step at a time. As you add more skills to your 1-2-3 toolkit, you may find that you need a quick refresher on an earlier topic. Although you can always reread the particular chapter in this book or your 1-2-3 reference manual, 1-2-3's help windows often provide just the hints you need to complete your planned task. Opening a help window is just as easy as pressing F1 (Help). 1-2-3 opens a help window that contains context-sensitive information about the task you are performing.

You can do this even if you are in the middle of a task, such as entering a label in a cell. 1-2-3 will not disrupt the in-progress task; instead, it opens a 1-2-3 help window separate from the 1-2-3 for Windows window and makes the help window the current window. Try this now: press F1 (Help) to see a help window like the one in Figure 2-3.

Another option for opening a help window is selecting **H**elp from the menu and selecting one of the topics from the Help menu. These topics include **I**ndex, **U**sing Help, **K**eyboard, **@**Functions, **M**acros, **H**ow Do I ..., **F**or Upgraders, and **A**bout 1-2-3. After you select one of the menu options, 1-2-3 opens a help window with the selected topic displayed. Regardless of how you open a help window, the information is displayed in a window separate from 1-2-3 for Windows. Because it is separate from 1-2-3, you can move and position this window like other Windows application windows. Also, when you want to close the window, you need to press ALT-F4, press ALT-SPACEBAR, or click the control menu box in the 1-2-3 for Windows title bar and select **C**lose from the control menu by typing **C** or clicking **C**lose. You can switch back to 1-2-3 just as you would switch between other Windows applications. You can always return to the help window by pressing F1 (Help) or by selecting 1-2-3 for Windows Help from the Task List window.

Figure 2-3. *Sample help window*

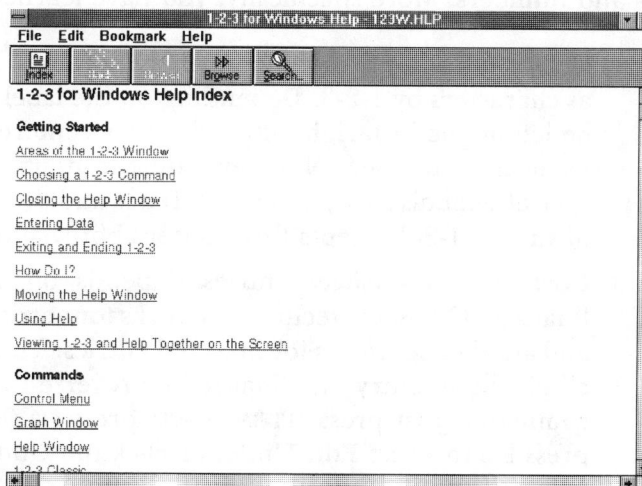

In a help window, the window displays information about 1-2-3. You can use the arrow keys, mouse, and scroll bars to change the portion of the help information displayed if it fills more than one screen. You can change the topic displayed in the window by using one of the help buttons or by selecting one of the green underlined topics. To select a help button, press the underlined letter or click it. To select an underlined topic, click it or press TAB until it is highlighted and press ENTER. You can select a glossary term, which is in lowercase letters, to have the term defined, but you must hold down the ENTER key or the left mouse button while you select it. A help window also includes a menu that includes options for printing the currently displayed information and putting the current help information into Windows' clipboard.

1-2-3 can assist you when you encounter an error message. Just select Error Messages under Reference after selecting the Index help button, the first letter of the error message, and the message. 1-2-3 displays explanations as to what might have triggered the message.

Review

In this chapter you have learned how to make simple entries such as labels and numbers. More specifically, you have learned the following:

- Cells can be empty or contain labels or values. Labels are treated as characters by 1-2-3. Depending on the label prefix, labels may be left aligned ('), right aligned ("), or centered (^). One type of value is a number. Numbers use the digits 0 through 9 and special symbols like ., +, and −. Dates and times are special types of values; 1-2-3 accepts three-letter abbreviations for the month.

- Correcting worksheet entries depends on whether they are finalized. One set of techniques works for entries you are entering and another set works for finalized entries. The Undo feature can eliminate an entry just finalized or reverse the result of a 1-2-3 command. Just press ALT-BACKSPACE; press F10 (Menu) or ALT, and press E U to select **Edit Undo**; or click the Undo icon in the icon palette.

- To save the current worksheet, press F10 (Menu) or ALT to activate the menu, press F A to select **File Save As**, type a name of not more than eight characters with no spaces, and press ENTER. To close a worksheet window and open a new empty one, press F10 (Menu) or ALT to activate the menu, and press F L to select **File Close**.

2

Commands and Keys

The keys you have learned how to use in this chapter help you make and correct entries. You have also learned commands that let you save your work and finish a worksheet window. These keys and commands are listed next.

Keys	Action
ESC	Eliminates an entry that is not finalized
F1 (Help)	Opens or switches to a 1-2-3 help window
F2 (Edit)	Places you in EDIT mode for the current cell's contents so you can change the cell's contents without retyping. In EDIT mode, many of the keys behave differently
ALT-BACKSPACE	Eliminates the last entry finalized or the effect of the last menu command. Same as the **Edit Undo** command
ALT E U	**Edit Undo** eliminates the last entry finalized or the effect of the last menu command
ALT F A	**File Save As** saves a file with a name you provide
ALT F C	**File Close** closes the worksheet file
ALT T U E	**Tools User Setup Enable Edit Undo** turns on or off the Undo feature

3

Defining Your Calculations

Calculations are an important part of many of the business tasks that you perform. Some computations, such as a 10 percent purchase discount, are easy to compute. However, not all calculations are simple. If you want to determine a yearly salary for an employee who receives a raise in the middle of the year, you need to perform a much more complex computation. Complex calculations are difficult to perform unless you write them down. Even when you write down a calculation, it is easy to make mistakes. And if conditions change even slightly, the numbers in your calculations are likely to change. You could find yourself spending a considerable amount of time redoing calculations.

1-2-3 for Windows provides many features to make your computations easier than the paper and pencil method of the past. You simply define the steps in the computational process to 1-2-3, and it performs all the calculations for you. Your instructions to 1-2-3 are called formulas. Once these formulas are entered, 1-2-3 handles all the work for you.

This chapter provides easy-to-follow instructions for entering many of the formula types that 1-2-3 supports. You learn how to use references to cells in your formula building. This powerful feature allows you to reuse applications by changing the data in cells that the formulas reference. You explore basic arithmetic formulas, as well as logical formulas and string formulas. @Functions and formulas that link to other worksheet files are covered in Chapter 4, "@Functions and Other Formula Options."

Formula Basics

Formulas, like the numbers you entered in Chapter 2, "Entering Labels and Numbers," are value entries. Unlike numbers, however, they produce results that vary, depending on the current values they reference. This variability makes formulas the backbone of worksheet features. It allows you to make *what-if projections* based on changing the entries on your worksheet. You can update the formula results without changing the formula. The only requirement is that you supply new entries for the variables referenced by the formulas, which are stored in other cells.

Entry Rules

To enter a formula in a cell, you must define for 1-2-3 the location of the variables involved and the operations you wish performed on them. 1-2-3 for Windows supports four types of formulas: arithmetic formulas, logical formulas, string formulas, and @functions. A few general rules apply to all formulas, and some special conventions must be observed for special types of formulas. The special rules are explained when each type of formula is discussed, but the general guidelines are given here.

- The first and perhaps most important rule is that the first character in a formula must be a number from 0 through 9 or an entry from the following list:

    + − (@ $ # .

- The second rule is that extraneous spaces are not allowed except in text within a string formula or a range name.

- The third and last rule pertains to the length limitation for a formula: As with other cell entries, formulas cannot exceed 512 characters.

Arithmetic Formulas

Arithmetic formulas are nothing more than instructions for certain operations: addition (+); subtraction (−); multiplication (*); division (/); and exponentiation (^), which represents raising a number to a specific power such as 3 squared or 2 cubed. These operations are the same ones that you can perform with a calculator. When you record an arithmetic formula on the worksheet, you can build it with arithmetic operators and references to the numbers contained in other worksheet cells. The results of the calculation are determined by the current values of the worksheet cells referenced. You will see the advantage of formulas more clearly when you change a referenced worksheet cell and the formula result is automatically recomputed. Anytime you wish to repeat a set of calculations on new data, you can enter the data without reentering the formulas. The sequence of required computations is stored in the cell containing the formula, and a new result is computed based on the value of the new entry.

Entering Simple Arithmetic Formulas

You can enter 1-2-3's formulas with numeric constants, as in 4*5 or 3+2. However, numeric constants within formulas are limiting; you have to change the formulas as conditions change. A better method is to store the constants in a worksheet cell. When you wish to use a value in a formula, you can use its cell address within the formula. Then, if the value changes, you need only enter a new number where it is stored; the formula will use it automatically. Using cell addresses in formulas requires an additional rule. Since cell addresses begin with nonnumeric characters, an entry's initial alphabetic character (as in A2+B3) causes it to be treated like a label entry. The entry appears in the worksheet cell just as you typed it, rather than appearing as a result of calculations. So formulas that reference other cells must start with an arithmetic character such as +.

You might use a formula in a worksheet that looks like the one in Figure 3-1 to compute the total for buying a quantity of an item. To enter the formulas, follow these steps:

1. Type the following entries in the cells specified.

A2:	**Product 1**	C1:	**"Unit Cost**
A3:	**Product 2**	C2:	**1**
A4:	**Product 3**	C3:	**3**
B1:	**"Units**	C4:	**4**
B2:	**4**	D1:	**"Cost**
B3:	**12**	E1:	**"Discount**
B4:	**8**	F1:	**"Net Cost**

2. Press the arrow keys to move the cell pointer to D4 or click the cell.

Figure 3-1.   *Simple formula entries*

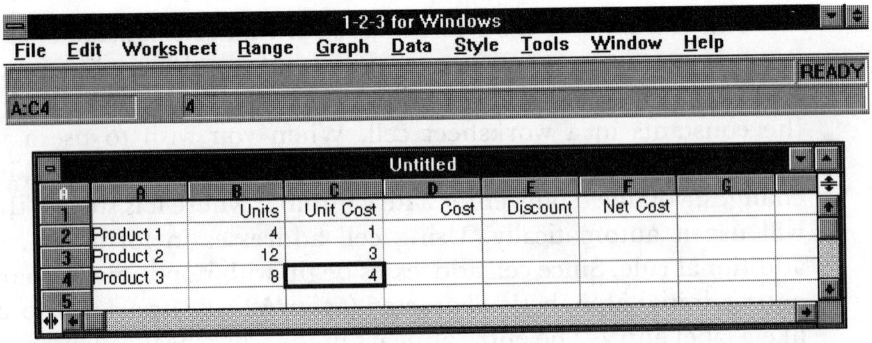

One of several arithmetic characters can begin a formula. The + is a logical choice to add to the front of the formula; it requires only one keystroke and does not affect the contents of B4, the cell containing the number of units purchased. Try it now to see the results.

3. Type **+B4∗C4**.

4. Press ENTER or click the confirm box.

When D4 is the active cell, you still see the formula in the control panel, yet you see the result in the cell. If you decide to change B4 to 10 later on, the result displayed in D4 would change to 40 as evidence that the formula was still doing its assigned task.

When you enter a formula by using cell addresses, 1-2-3 is not fussy; it will accept either upper- or lowercase characters. The formula +B4∗C4 is equivalent to +b4∗c4 or +b4∗C4 and computes the same results. Notice that 1-2-3 automatically assumes that the formula uses values from cells on the current worksheet because the cell addresses do not include sheet letters.

You can add two more formulas to compute a discount and the net amount. To compute the discount, move the cell pointer to E4, and then type **+D4∗.075** to compute a 7.5 percent discount. To compute the net amount, move the cell pointer to F4, and then type **+D4−E4** and press ENTER or click the confirm box.

Adding Notes to Formulas

1-2-3 for Windows allows you to document a formula as you enter it. Although the formula is likely to be perfectly clear to you on the day that you enter it, when you want to change the formula after a period of time has elapsed, it can be difficult to remember the logic behind your entries.

You can place the note in the same entry as the formula calculation by entering a semicolon after the formula and then the text of the note. The combined length of the entry may not exceed 1-2-3's 512-character limit. You can enter any text after the semicolon since the note is not part of the calculation and does not need to conform to 1-2-3's rules for value entries.

You can also use 1-2-3's editing features to add notes at the end of existing formula entries. Complete the following steps to add a note at the end of the formulas in the purchase discount example:

1. Move the cell pointer to D4, and then press F2 (Edit) to edit the contents of the cell.

2. Type **;Computes the total cost before discount**, and press ENTER or click the confirm box.

Your note displays in the control panel when the cell pointer is on the cell, as shown in Figure 3-2.

You can perform the same procedure for the formulas in cells E4 and F4, using "Computes a 7.5% discount" and "Computes the net amount" as the notes.

You can save this model by pressing ALT and then pressing F to select File and A to select Save **As**. Next, type **DISCOUNT** as the filename and

Figure 3-2.   *Adding a note to document a formula*

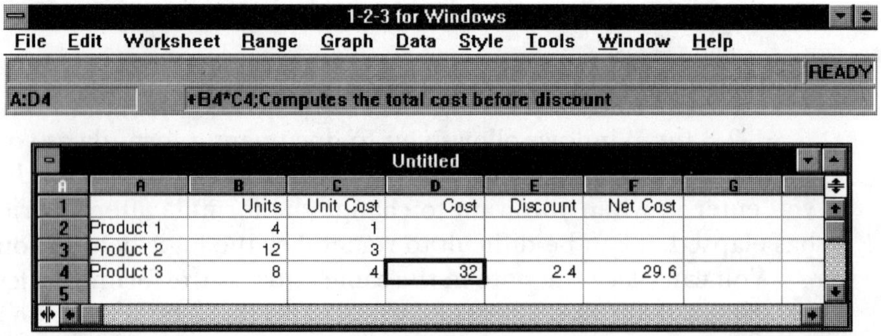

press ENTER. You can press ALT again and then press F C to select **File Close.** You can also make any of these menu selections by clicking them.

Building Formulas with the Pointing Method

1-2-3 provides a second method of formula entry that can reduce the error rate. With this method, you type only the arithmetic operators and select the cell references by pointing to the cells you wish to reference, using 1-2-3's POINT mode. You will switch to POINT mode when you point to a cell by pressing the arrow keys or by clicking the cell while you are entering a formula. 1-2-3 adds the cell address to the formula. The pointing method provides visual verification that you are selecting the correct cell and eliminates the problems of typing mistakes.

1-2-3 does not assign the same priority to each of the arithmetic operators. You can use this to your advantage in constructing the formulas. 1-2-3 evaluates formulas from left to right, but it completes all of the multiplication and division operations before coming back through the formula to perform addition and subtraction. The precedence of operators is covered in greater detail later in this chapter, along with a solution for altering the normal precedence sequence.

You can try pointing to build formulas by creating a model that computes an employee's gross pay, given an hourly rate of pay and regular and overtime hours worked. Use a multiplication process to calculate regular pay, and then use another multiplication process to calculate overtime pay before adding the results of the two multiplication operations. 1-2-3 automatically does the multiplication before the addition. Keep this model simple for now; enter just the basic information for one employee, following these steps:

1. With the cell pointer in A1, type **Employee** and press the RIGHT ARROW key.

2. Type **"Hours** and press the RIGHT ARROW key.

Notice that the " symbol is used at the beginning of the label entry. As you will recall from Chapter 2, "Entering Labels and Numbers," this causes 1-2-3 to right align the label entry in the worksheet cell so the column labels will line up with the values underneath.

3. Type **"Rate** and press the RIGHT ARROW key.

4. Type **"Overtime** and press the RIGHT ARROW key.

5. Type **"Gross Pay** and press ENTER.

6. Press HOME and the DOWN ARROW key to move the cell pointer to A2, type **J. Smith**, and press the RIGHT ARROW key.

7. Type **40** and press the RIGHT ARROW key.

8. Type **3.75** and press the RIGHT ARROW key.

9. Type **10** and press the RIGHT ARROW key. Your entries should look like this:

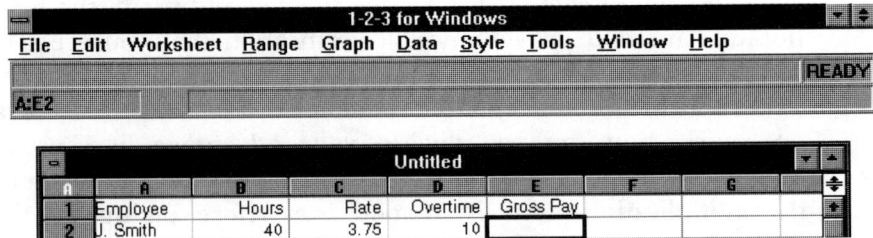

		1-2-3 for Windows						
File	Edit	Worksheet	Range	Graph	Data	Style	Tools	Window	Help

READY

A:E2

	Untitled						
	A	B	C	D	E	F	G
1	Employee	Hours	Rate	Overtime	Gross Pay		
2	J. Smith	40	3.75	10			

The next formula must calculate gross pay by multiplying regular hours by the rate of pay and then multiplying overtime hours by 1.5 times the rate of pay. The result of these two multiplication operations will be added to obtain the gross pay. This sounds complicated but can be represented succinctly in the formula that you will build with the pointing method.

10. Type **+**.

11. Use the arrow keys to point to B2 or click this cell with the mouse.

The cell address is added to the input line as B2 if you selected it with the arrow keys or as the range B2..B2 if you used the mouse.

12. Type *.

The cell pointer returns to E2, where you are entering the formula.

13. Use the arrow keys to point to C2 or click this cell.

14. Type **+**.

15. Press the arrow keys to point to D2 or click the cell D2.

16. Type ***1.5***.

17. Press the arrow keys to point to C2 or click the cell C2.

18. Press ENTER to finalize the entry.

You could add still more employees to this model, but for now, you will save it as PAY.

19. Press ALT and then press F A to select **File Save As** or click **File Save As**.

20. Type **PAY** and press ENTER to store the file as PAY.WK3 on your disk.

The .WK3 is a file extension that 1-2-3 adds to indicate the format the worksheet data is saved in.

21. Press ALT and then press F C to select **File Close** or click **File Close** to clear the worksheet and open a new one.

Logical Formulas

Logical formulas compare two or more worksheet values. They use the logical operators = for equal, < > for not equal, > for greater than, > = for greater than or equal to, < for less than, and < = for less than or equal to. You can enter logical formulas with the same methods used for arithmetic formulas but, unlike arithmetic formulas, they do not calculate numeric results. Instead, they produce a result of either a 0 or a 1, depending on whether the condition that was evaluated is true or false. If the condition is true, 1 is returned; if the condition is false, 0 is returned. For example, if D4 contains a 5, the logical formula +D4<3 returns 0, since the condition is false. This capability can evaluate a series of complex decisions or influence results in other parts of the worksheet.

If a formula contains both logical operators and arithmetic operators, the expression containing the arithmetic operators is evaluated first. For example, 1-2-3 evaluates the logical formula +D4*2>50 by first multiplying the current value in D4 by 2 and then performing the comparison.

Creating a Model to Calculate Commissions

One application of logical operators in a worksheet is the calculation of a commission bonus. In this example, sales personnel are paid a quarterly bonus, which includes a regular sales commission and a bonus paid for meeting sales quotas. The regular commission is computed as 10 percent of total sales. The bonus is calculated by product. A bonus of $1000 is paid for each product for which the sales quota is met. A salesperson could thus gain $3000 by meeting quotas for three products.

Look at the steps required to build the commission model shown in Figure 3-3. First, follow these directions to add the labels and numbers that are required:

1. Press the RIGHT ARROW key to move the cell pointer to B1 or click this cell, type **Commission Calculation**, and press ENTER.

2. Move the cell pointer to A3, type **Employee:**, and press the DOWN ARROW key.

3. Type **Sales Product 1:** and press the DOWN ARROW key.

Figure 3-3.   *Commission calculations*

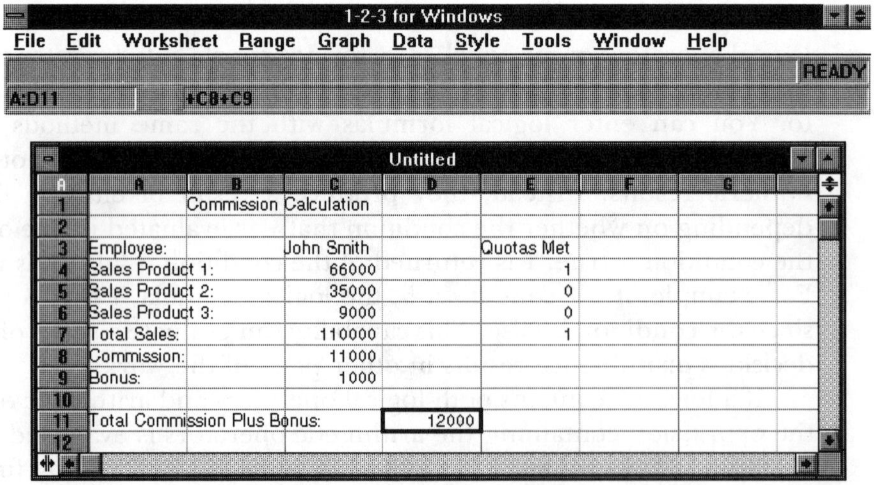

3

4. Type **Sales Product 2:** and press the DOWN ARROW key.

5. Type **Sales Product 3:** and press the DOWN ARROW key.

6. Type **Total Sales:** and press the DOWN ARROW key.

7. Type **Commission:** and press the DOWN ARROW key.

8. Type **Bonus:** and press the DOWN ARROW key twice or click A11.

9. Type **Total Commission Plus Bonus:** and press ENTER or click the confirm box.

10. Press the arrow keys to move to C3 or click this cell. Type **John Smith** and press the DOWN ARROW key to enter the name of the employee for whom you will be calculating commissions.

11. Type **66000** and press DOWN ARROW. Type **35000** and press DOWN AR-ROW. Type **9000** and press DOWN ARROW.

12. Position the cell pointer in E3 and type **Quotas Met**. Then press DOWN ARROW.

Adding Formulas to the Commission Model

The number and label entries for this model are now complete. Your model should match the one shown in Figure 3-4. At this point, you are ready to add formulas for calculating the regular and bonus commission. For computing the bonus, assume that the quota is $50,000 per product. Use the following steps to enter the logical formulas for determining whether the sales quota in each category was met:

1. With the cell pointer in E4, type **+C4>50000** and press DOWN ARROW.

This formula produces 1 if the Product 1 quota is met and 0 if it is not.

2. Type **+C5>50000** and press DOWN ARROW.

3. Type **+C6>50000** and press DOWN ARROW.

4. Total the number of quotas met by adding the result of each of the logical formulas: type **+E4+E5+E6** in E7 and press ENTER.

In Chapter 4, "@Functions and Other Formula Options," you will learn a shortcut method for summing entries, but for now you can use simple addition.

Figure 3-4.   *Numbers and labels for the commission model*

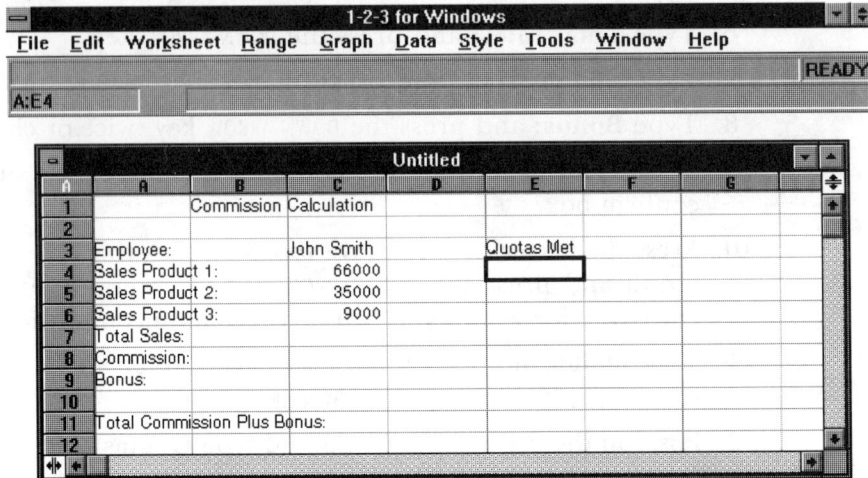

5. Total the sales of all three products in the same fashion: move the cell pointer to C7, type **+C4+C5+C6**, and press DOWN ARROW.

6. Type **+C7∗.1** and press the DOWN ARROW to enter the commission formula.

7. Type **+E7∗1000** and press ENTER or click the confirm box.

This calculates the bonus commission by multiplying the number of quotas met by 1000.

8. Position the cell pointer in D11, type **+C8+C9**, and press ENTER or click the confirm box.

Your completed model should match that shown in Figure 3-3.

The logical formulas it contains will respond to changes in the model's data. Let's try one:

1. Move the cell pointer to C6.

2. Type **73000** and press ENTER or click the confirm box.

You will find that a new commission and bonus of $19,400 are calculated immediately, as shown in Figure 3-5. Notice that the result does not display the dollar sign or the comma between hundreds and thousands. You will learn how to add these special characters in Chapter 6, "Changing the Appearance of Worksheet Cells."

note *Now that you are familiar with moving around in the worksheet, you will be given only the cell address to move the cell pointer. Remember, you can move the cell pointer by using the arrow keys and other special keys such as HOME and PGDN. You can also move to another cell by clicking it and by using the scroll bars to change the portion of the worksheet displayed in the window. It does not matter how you move the cell pointer—use whatever method you prefer.*

Figure 3-5. *Recomputing the commission*

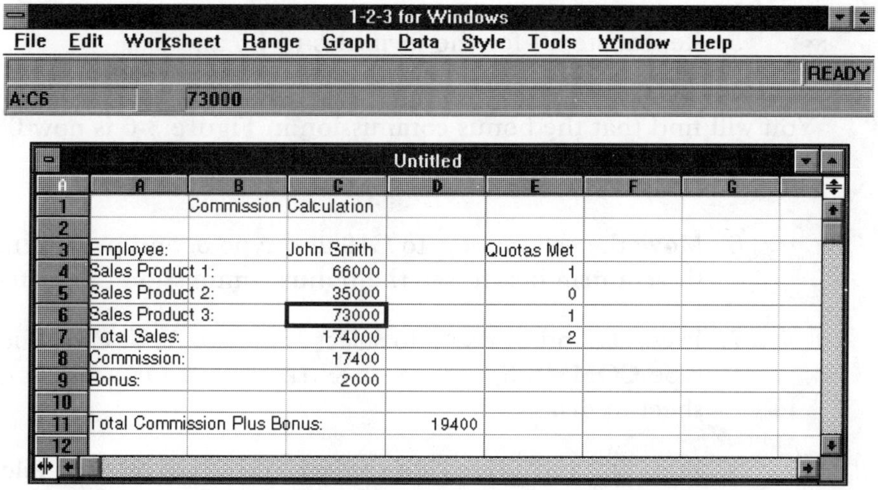

Using Compound Operators

1-2-3 also has three compound operators that you can use with logical formulas. These operators either negate an expression or join two different expressions. The negation operator #NOT# has precedence over the two compound operators #AND# and #OR#. When the compound operator #AND# joins two logical expressions, *both* expressions must be true for the compound formula to return a true value. If the two expressions are joined by #OR#, *either one* can be true for the condition to return a true value.

You can add a second condition to your commission calculation by using the compound operators. Let's say that bonus commissions require a minimum of six months of service in addition to the minimum sales level for a product. Revise the model to allow for this new condition by following these steps:

1. Move the cell pointer to A10, type **Months in Job:**, and move to C10.

2. Type **4** and press ENTER or click the confirm box.

3. Move the cell pointer to E4.

4. Press F2 (Edit), type **#AND#C10 > 6,** and then press the DOWN AR-ROW key.

5. Repeat step 4 for the formulas in E5 and E6.

You will find that the bonus commission in Figure 3-6 is now 0 since the employee has been on the job fewer than six months.

6. Move the cell pointer to C10 and type **8,** and press ENTER or click the confirm box to see the bonus commission calculated again.

7. Press ALT and press F A to select File Save **A**s or click File Save **A**s, type **COMMISS,** and press ENTER or click OK to save this work-sheet to disk.

8. Press ALT and press F C to select File **C**lose or click File **C**lose to close the open worksheet window.

Figure 3-6. *Using compound operators*

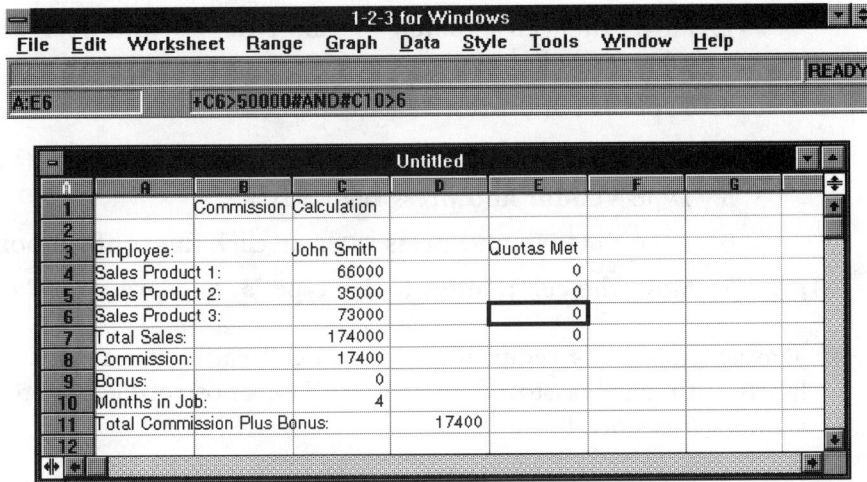

String Formulas

String formulas do not perform formula calculations as arithmetic formulas do; they let you join character strings to create headings or other data elements for the worksheet. String formulas use only one operator, the ampersand (&), which joins variables containing character strings or string constants. For example, +"John"&"Smith" results in JohnSmith, +"John"&" "&"Smith" results in John Smith, and +A1&A2&A3 results in abc if A1 contains a, A2 contains b, and A3 contains c. The quotes enclose text to distinguish it from cell addresses. As with the other types of formulas, with string formulas you can either type the complete formula or point to the cell addresses and have 1-2-3 place them in the formula for you.

Let's use a string formula to build a part number for All Parts, Incorporated. The warehouse location, bin number, product type, and vendor are all combined to create a part number. Follow these steps to enter the data for the model:

1. Move the cell pointer to B3, type **All Parts, Inc. Inventory Listing**, and press ENTER or click the confirm box.

2. Move the cell pointer to A5, type **Location**, and press the RIGHT ARROW key.

3. Type **Bin** and press RIGHT ARROW.

4. Type **Type** and press RIGHT ARROW.

5. Type **Vendor** and press RIGHT ARROW.

6. Type **Part No** and press ENTER or click the confirm box.

7. Move the cell pointer to A6, type **'5**, and press RIGHT ARROW.

The apostrophe is required because 1-2-3 cannot join entries stored as labels with entries stored as values. The apostrophe ensures that the number 5 is stored as a label.

8. Type **'12** and press RIGHT ARROW.

9. Type **AX** and press RIGHT ARROW.

10. Type **CN** and press RIGHT ARROW.

11. Type **+C6&" −"&D6&A6&B6** in E6, and press ENTER or click the confirm box.

The part number for the first item appears as shown here:

1-2-3 for Windows							▼ ▲
File **Edit** **Worksheet** **Range** **Graph** **Data** **Style** **Tools** **Window** **Help**							
							READY
A:E6	+C6&"-"&D6&A6&B6						

Untitled							▼ ▲
A	A	B	C	D	E	F	G	✧
1								▲
2								
3		All Parts, Inc.	Inventory Listing					
4								
5	Location	Bin	Type	Vendor	Part No			
6	5	12	AX	CN	AX-CN512			

For practice, you may wish to enter the data and the required string formula to build several additional part numbers. Like the other formula types, changing the values for any of the variables immediately changes the results produced by the string formula. Once you have finished with your entries, you can save the model. Press ALT and press F A to select **File**

Save **As** from the menu, or click **File** Save **As**. Next, type **PARTNO**, and press ENTER or click OK. To close the window, press ALT and then F C to select **File C**lose or click **File C**lose.

The part-number display in the last example is useful if the model contains additional information to the right that is also important to see. After using the string formula to build the part number, you can move the cell pointer to the right and view the other data without losing track of the part number.

Performing More Complex Calculations

When 1-2-3 encounters more than one operator in a formula, it does not use a left-to-right order to compute the result. Instead, it evaluates the formula based on a set precedence order for each of the operators. As you begin to build more complex formulas, you will see how important it is to understand 1-2-3's priorities in order to achieve the desired results.

When more than one operator is used in a formula, it is important to know which operation 1-2-3 performs first. Table 3-1 shows the order of precedence for each of the operators. The higher the precedence, the sooner the operation is performed. If more than one operator has the same precedence, they are evaluated from left to right.

Table 3-1. *Operation Priorities*

Precedence	Operator	Operation Performed
8	()	Parentheses to override priorities
7	^	Exponentiation
6	+ −	Positive/negative indicators
5	/ *	Division and multiplication
4	+ −	Addition and subtraction
3	= < >	Logical operators
	< <=	
	> >=	
2	#NOT#	Compound NOT indicator
1	#AND#	Compound AND, OR, and the string operator
	#OR#	
	&	

Notice that parentheses are at the top of the list in Table 3-1. This indicates that any expression enclosed within them is evaluated first. The other operators that may cause confusion are the + and − symbols shown in level 6 and level 4. The first set represents the positive or negative sign of a value. For instance, −5∗3 indicates that 5 is a negative number that is multiplied by a positive 3. However, in the expression 5−4∗2, the minus symbol represents subtraction and has a lower precedence than the multiplication operation, which is carried out first.

A short example will demonstrate this clearly. Suppose you wish to add the total number of pounds of books in a shipment by combining the 10-pound weight of the books ordered with 3 pounds of stationery items and then multiplying the total weight by the per-pound shipping rate of 25 cents. You will not get the correct result if you enter 10+3∗.25 since 1-2-3 will perform the multiplication first and then add 10 and 0.75, totaling 10.75 rather than the 3.25 you expected. To make 1-2-3 perform the calculation your way, you need to enter the formula as **(10+3)∗.25**. 1-2-3 will evaluate the expression within the parentheses first and carry out the multiplication second, resulting in the desired answer of 3.25.

Let's look at another salary model to demonstrate the importance of the precedence and of controlling precedence with parentheses. This model projects a single employee's salary based on his or her current salary, the percentage of increase, and the month of the increase. Since a lengthy formula is required, you will perform only the computation for one employee. To enter the data for the salary computation model, follow these steps:

1. Type the entries for the column headings in the worksheet cells specified:

A2:	**Name**	D1:	**"Increase**
B1:	**"1991**	D2:	**"Percent**
B2:	**"Salary**	E1:	**"1992**
C1:	**"Increase**	E2:	**"Salary**
C2:	**"Month**		

2. Type the entries for the first employee in the worksheet cells specified:

A3:   **J. Brown**
B3:   **35900**
C3:   **5**
D3:   **.06**

3. Move the cell pointer to E3 so your labels and numbers look like this:

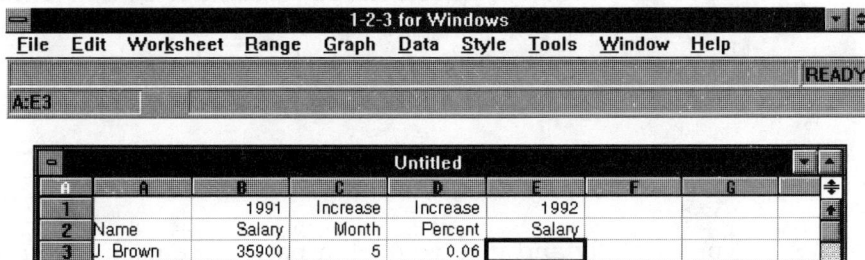

	A	B	C	D	E	F	G
1		1991	Increase	Increase	1992		
2	Name	Salary	Month	Percent	Salary		
3	J. Brown	35900	5	0.06			

The last step is the most complicated. The formula must compute the current monthly salary and multiply it by the number of months that the individual will continue to receive this salary. The result of this first computation is then added to the figure computed for the amount paid at the new salary level. The total dollars paid at the new salary level are computed by multiplying the current monthly salary by 100 percent plus the increase percentage by the number of months that the individual will receive the increased salary. Predictably, the formula is quite long, as shown in Figure 3-7. The parts of the formula are as follows:

(B3/12)	Represents the annual salary divided by 12 to compute the monthly salary
(C3−1)	The month of the increase minus 1 or the number of months the employee receives his or her current salary
(1+D3)	Indicates that the employee will receive 100% of his or her existing salary, plus an increase represented by a decimal fraction in D3
12−(C3−1)	The number of months that the employee receives the increased salary amount

4. Combining all these, enter the following formula in E3:

$$((B3/12)*(C3-1))+((B3/12)*(1+D3)*(12-(C3-1)))$$

Figure 3-7.   *Handling more complex calculations*

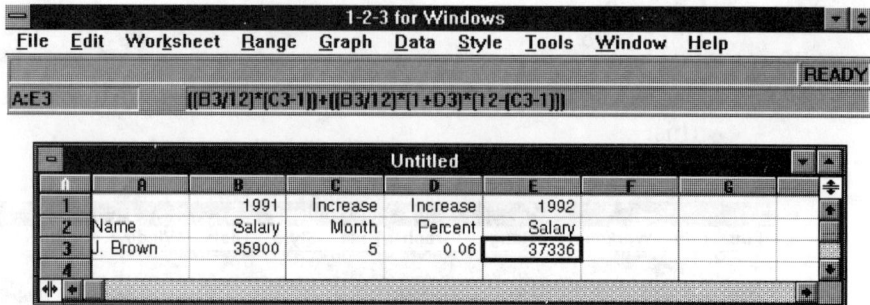

Type carefully and give yourself a pat on the back if you manage to complete the entire entry successfully on your first attempt. If you do make a few mistakes, you can always edit your entry to make the necessary corrections. If your mistakes are serious enough, 1-2-3 places you in EDIT mode without requiring you to press the F2 (Edit) key.

A few extra parentheses have been added to the formula expression to make it more readable. For example, the result would be the same if the parentheses were omitted from (B3/12), since multiplication and division have the same precedence. Using an extra pair of parentheses does not change the value of the expression as long as the parentheses do not change the order of operations. Feel free to add parentheses in this manner whenever they improve the readability of the formula without altering it. In this example, you have entered the data for only one employee, but this model could be expanded easily. In Chapter 4, "@Functions and Other Formula Options," you will use this model to add additional employees, but for now, save a copy of it. Press ALT and then press F A to select **File Save As**, or click **File Save As**. Next, type **SALARY**, and press ENTER or click OK.

Review

In this chapter you learned the basics of creating formulas, which is the backbone of 1-2-3's features. More specifically, you learned the following:

- Formulas allow you to define computations that you want 1-2-3 to perform with the contents of worksheet cells.

- Formulas must start with a value character and cannot exceed 512 characters.

- You can document a formula by adding a note at the end. Type a semicolon (;) and then type your note.

- Arithmetic formulas are the most popular type of 1-2-3 formula since they support typical business calculations such as purchase discounts, sales projections, and invoice extensions.

- You use operators to represent the type of calculation you wish to perform: addition (+), subtraction (−), multiplication (*), division (/), and exponentiation (^).

- String formulas use only one operator, the ampersand (&), to join two character strings.

- Logical formulas use the logical operators to perform a comparison: equal to (=), not equal to (< >), less than (<), less than or equal to (< =), greater than (>), or greater than or equal to (> =).

- All formula operators do not have the same order of precedence. You can use parentheses to raise the precedence of an operation. 1-2-3 evaluates entries in parentheses first. Table 3-1 lists the order of precedence for operators.

Commands and Keys

You have learned how you can activate the menu and close the worksheet window. These commands are

Keys	Action
ALT	Activates the menu
ALT F C	**File Close** closes the current worksheet window

4

@Functions and Other Formula Options

You already know quite a bit about formulas after reading Chapter 3, "Defining your Calculations," but 1-2-3 for Windows has many additional formula options. You can name worksheet cells and use the names in your formulas rather than the cell addresses. You can also reference data in other worksheet files on disk to access consistent data in all worksheets or to consolidate data from many worksheets into a summary sheet. Another more advanced option is the ability to use 1-2-3's @functions to perform computations with formulas that are already part of the package. With the techniques covered in this chapter, you will have all the skills you need to create sophisticated 1-2-3 applications. The step-by-step presentation methods make it easy to master these new skills.

Using Names in Formulas

Using cell addresses is better than using constants in formulas since a formula is updated when the contents of the cells the formula uses change without the need for editing the formula. With many entries on a worksheet, it can be difficult to remember what each cell contains. You will find that cell addresses become meaningless quickly since you are not certain of the data that a cell address represents.

You can assign a name to a range of contiguous cells. Since this range can be as small as a single cell, you can conceivably assign a unique name to each entry that you place on the worksheet. You can build new formulas by using either the cell address or the range name. Before learning how to assign names to your data, you need to learn about 1-2-3 ranges.

Range Basics

In 1-2-3, a range is a group of one or more cells that form a contiguous rectangle. You can use ranges to tell 1-2-3 to take the same action on each of the cells in the group. When used in this way, ranges can save a substantial amount of time over making a separate request to change each cell in the group. You will see more in Chapter 6, "Changing the Appearance of Worksheet Cells," about using ranges this way. For now, you will use ranges to assign names to individual worksheet cells.

Since a range can include a rectangular area of cells, you always express a range address as two separate cell addresses separated by a period. Although you need to type only one period as a separator, 1-2-3 always converts it to two, as in A1..B10 or C3..G20. The standard method of describing a range address is to first supply the upper-left cell in the range, type a period as a separator, and then supply the lower-right cell in the range, as in A1.B10 or C3.G20. When you point to a range, 1-2-3 automatically includes the sheet reference, as in A:A1..A:G2. In Chapter 8, "Managing Files and Sheets", you will learn to use multiple sheets in a worksheet file and how to create ranges that span sheets. You can assign a name to any range so that you can refer to the range by the name rather than by its cell addresses.

In Chapter 12, "Data Management Basics," and Chapter 13, "Advanced Problem-solving Techniques," you will look at applications for applying names to ranges that include more than one cell. For now, you will assign range names only to individual cells since the formulas you have used so far operate on only one cell at a time. Even though you are interested in naming one cell, you still need to refer to that cell as a range rather than using its individual cell address because 1-2-3 expects a range address for a range name. The proper way of expressing a range consisting of one cell is to use the cell address for both the beginning and the end of the range. When A1 is treated as a range, the range address is expressed as A1..A1.

Naming a Range

To name a range, you need to use a command from 1-2-3's menu. You will learn more about 1-2-3's menu in Chapter 5, "Getting Familiar with Menus and Dialog Boxes," but as you learned in Chapter 2, "Entering Labels and Numbers," you can invoke the menu by pressing ALT and select menu items by pressing the underlined letter of the option you want or by clicking the menu item you want. The complicated salary formula you entered in the SALARY worksheet in Chapter 3, "Defining Your Calculations," is a good place to try out the benefits of range names.

As you name ranges in the model, you are limited to 15 characters for the range name. Each range name must be unique. 1-2-3 does not distinguish between upper- and lowercase letters and displays all range names in uppercase when you see them in formulas.

To name the three cells used in computing the 1992 salary figure for J. Brown, follow these steps:

1. Either press ALT, press F O to select **File O**pen, type **SALARY** in the File **N**ame text box, and press ENTER; click **File O**pen, type **SALARY** in the File **N**ame text box and click OK; or make the following entries in an empty worksheet:

A2:	**Name**	E1:	**"1992**
B1:	**"1991**	E2:	**"Salary**
B2:	**"Salary**	A3:	**J. Brown**
C1:	**"Increase**	B3:	**35900**
C2:	**"Month**	C3:	**5**
D1:	**"Increase**	D3:	**.06**
D2:	**"Percent**		

2. Type the following formula in E3 if this cell does not already have an entry:

$$((B3/12)*(C3-1))+((B3/12)*(1+D3)*(12-(C3-1)))$$

Your worksheet now looks like this:

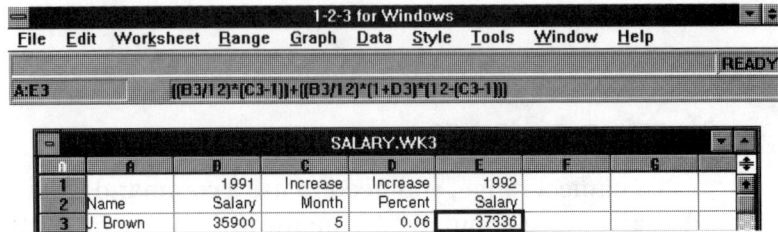

File	Edit	Worksheet	Range	Graph	Data	Style	Tools	Window	Help

```
                                   1-2-3 for Windows
 File  Edit  Worksheet  Range  Graph  Data  Style  Tools  Window  Help
                                                                        READY
 A:E3          [(B3/12)*(C3-1)]+[(B3/12)*(1+D3)*(12-(C3-1))]
```

	A	B	C	D	E	F	G
1		1991	Increase	Increase	1992		
2	Name	Salary	Month	Percent	Salary		
3	J. Brown	35900	5	0.06	37336		

3. Move the cell pointer to B3.

4. Press ALT to invoke the menu, select the **R**ange pull-down menu by pressing R, press N to select **N**ame from the **R**ange pull-down menu, and press C to select **C**reate from the **N**ame menu, or click **R**ange **N**ame **C**reate. 1-2-3 displays a dialog box that looks like this:

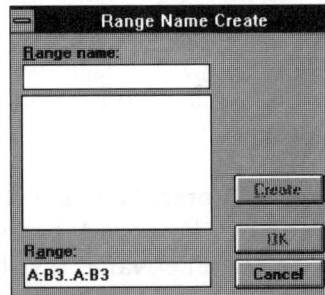

```
                    Range Name Create

  Range name:
  ┌──────────────────────────┐
  │                          │
  └──────────────────────────┘
  ┌──────────────────────────┐
  │                          │
  │                          │       ┌──────────┐
  │                          │       │  Create  │
  │                          │       └──────────┘
  │                          │       ┌──────────┐
  │                          │       │    OK    │
  Range:                     │       └──────────┘
  ┌──────────────────────────┐      ┌──────────┐
  │ A:B3..A:B3               │      │  Cancel  │
  └──────────────────────────┘      └──────────┘
```

Notice that 1-2-3 is all set to use the current cell for this command. If you forget to position the cell pointer before requesting the **R**ange **N**ame **C**reate command, you can select a new range by entering a range address in the box labeled **R**ange. You will learn how to do this in Chapter 6, "Changing the Appearance of Worksheet Cells."

5. Type **SALARY_91** and press ENTER.

A range name may contain up to 15 characters. You should avoid characters that may confuse 1-2-3 in a formula. That is why SALARY_91 uses an underscore instead of a space.

6. Move the cell pointer to C3 and then press ALT and R N C to select **R**ange **N**ame **C**reate, or click **R**ange **N**ame **C**reate. Then type **INC__MO** and press ENTER.

7. Move the cell pointer to D3 and then press ALT and R N C to select **R**ange **N**ame **C**reate or click **R**ange **N**ame **C**reate. Type **INC__%** and press ENTER.

8. Move the cell pointer to E3 to see this formula:

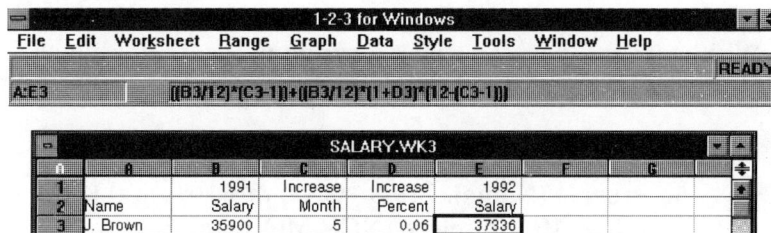

Your formula does not show the range names you have given to the cells the formula uses. This is because in the original formula, you entered cell addresses like D3 rather than range addresses like D3..D3. At this point, retyping the formula with range references would still not convert the cell addresses in the formula to range names. 1-2-3 converts a range address to a range name in an existing formula only at the time you name the range. 1-2-3 does not convert a range address to a range name in formulas you enter after naming the range. The solution is to rebuild the formula.

Using Range Names When Building Formulas

The last example showed you that range addresses in a formula do not change to range names once the ranges are named. You must assign names to a range before you reference the range name in a formula. This allows you to specify the name with the F3 (Name) key when you build a formula. Try it now by reentering the formula in E3 with these steps:

1. With your cell pointer still in E3, type ((.

2. Press F3 (Name) to display this dialog box:

Range Names

Range name:

INC_%
INC_MO
SALARY_91

OK

Cancel

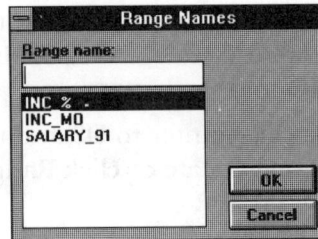

3. Press TAB once, DOWN ARROW twice, and ENTER once to select SALARY_91 from the list.

With a mouse, you can select a range name by double-clicking the range name you want.

4. Type **/12)*(**.

5. Press F3 (Name). Press TAB, DOWN ARROW, and ENTER, or double-click INC_MO to select INC_MO from the list.

6. Type **−1))+((**.

7. Press F3 (Name). Press TAB once, DOWN ARROW twice, and ENTER, or double-click SALARY_91 to select SALARY_91 from the list.

8. Type **/12)*(1+**.

9. Press F3 (Name). Press TAB and ENTER once, or double-click INC_% to select INC_% from the list.

10. Type **)*(12−(**.

11. Press F3 (Name). Press TAB, DOWN ARROW, and ENTER, or double-click INC_MO to select INC_MO from the list.

12. Type **−1)))** and press ENTER or click the confirm box to display this formula:

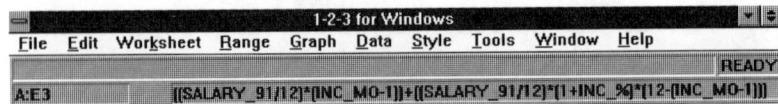

1-2-3 for Windows

File   Edit   Worksheet   Range   Graph   Data   Style   Tools   Window   Help

READY

A:E3   ([SALARY_91/12]*(INC_MO-1))+([SALARY_91/12]*(1+INC_%)*(12-(INC_MO-1)))

SALARY.WK3

A	B	C	D	E	F	G
	1991	Increase	Increase	1992		
Name	Salary	Month	Percent	Salary		
J. Brown	35900	5	0.06	37336		

Although this is still a complex formula, it is a little easier to understand since you do not need to make the mental comparison between cell address and cell contents for each entry in the formula. When you edit a formula that contains range names, the edit line continues to display the range names in the formulas (earlier releases of 1-2-3 converted them to cell addresses).

Range names are not a good solution in all models. If you expand this model to show the salary computations for a department of 100 individuals, with each individual shown on a different row, range names would be impractical—you would need to assign a unique range name to each of the entries in each of the rows. In such a situation, it is best to continue to use cell addresses in your formulas. However, a model containing a financial statement that is used to prepare ratios is a good application for the assignment of range names because similar data items would not be repeated and range names would make the formulas much more readable.

Follow these steps to build a new formula using range names.

1. With the cell pointer in E3, press ALT and then type R N C to select **R**ange **N**ame **C**reate or click **R**ange **N**ame **C**reate. Type **SALARY_92**, and press ENTER or click OK.

2. Move the cell pointer to A4, type **Salary Increase**, and press ENTER or click the confirm box.

3. Move the cell pointer to E4. Type **+** and then press F3 (Name).

4. Press TAB once, DOWN ARROW three times, and ENTER once, or double-click SALARY_92 to add SALARY_92 to the formula.

5. Type **−** and press F3 (Name).

6. Press TAB once, DOWN ARROW twice, and ENTER once, or double-click SALARY_91 to add SALARY_91 to the formula.

7. Press ENTER or click the confirm box to finalize the formula. Your display now looks like this:

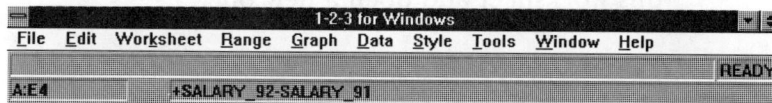

Deleting Range Names

You can delete range names that you no longer need. The command that eliminates them is **R**ange **N**ame **D**elete. When you eliminate a range name, you do not eliminate the worksheet data with the name. The formulas with references to the range names that you delete will revert to displaying the addresses of the cells, rather than the range names.

To delete the range name INC_MO from the current worksheet, follow these steps:

1. Press ALT and then R N D to select **R**ange **N**ame **D**elete, or click **R**ange **N**ame **D**elete.

2. Press TAB once, DOWN ARROW twice, and ENTER once, or double-click INC_MO to remove this range name.

When you move the highlight to E3, the formula no longer displays the deleted range name; it is replaced by the range address C3..C3. Now the formula looks like this:

```
┌──────────────────────────────── 1-2-3 for Windows ──────────────────────┐
│  File   Edit   Worksheet   Range   Graph   Data   Style   Tools   Window   Help
│                                                                    READY │
│ A:E3          [[SALARY_91/12]*[C3..C3-1]]+[[SALARY_91/12]*[1+INC_%]*[12-[C3..C3-1]]]
└──────────────────────────────────────────────────────────────────────────┘
┌──────────────────────────────── SALARY.WK3 ────────────────────────────┐
│        A         B        C         D          E        F        G        │
│  1                1991    Increase  Increase   1992                       │
│  2   Name         Salary  Month     Percent    Salary                     │
│  3   J. Brown     35900   5         0.06        37336                     │
│  4   Salary Increase                            1436                      │
└──────────────────────────────────────────────────────────────────────────┘
```

3. Press ALT and then F S to select **F**ile **S**ave or click **F**ile **S**ave to save the altered worksheet .

4. Press ALT and then F C to select **F**ile **C**lose or click **F**ile **C**lose to close this worksheet and open a new one.

Creating Linking Formulas

All of the formulas that you have entered have referenced the current worksheet. You can also create formulas in 1-2-3 for Windows that access data in other worksheet files on your disk. This allows you to access important data from other files so you can use the current worksheet to create a consolidated view of data from many other worksheets. You can use as many references to data in other worksheets as you need within a formula as long as your formula does not exceed 512 characters.

As an example, you might show the budget expenses for three different regions of the company in files named REGION1, REGION2, and REGION3. To show the total of these three regions on the current sheet, you can create a formula to link these worksheet files and obtain the correct data. This eliminates the extra work and possibility for error that would exist if you had to reenter the region data on the current worksheet.

4

The Syntax of a Link Formula

To reference data in another file, you need to tell 1-2-3 where the data is located. First, you enter the filename enclosed in double angle brackets (<< >>). If you specify only a filename in the angle brackets, as in <<REGION1>>, 1-2-3 assumes that the file is located in the default directory. If you want to use a file in another location, you must specify the entire pathname within the angle brackets. For example, if you want to use a file named WEST with a path of D:\SALES, you would use <<D:\SALES\WEST\>> in the formula. Next, you enter the cell address, range address, or range name in the other file that contains the data you want to use, as in <<REPORT>>A10 and <<D:\SALES\WEST\>>SALES. When you finalize the formula, 1-2-3 converts cell addresses to range addresses, so <<REPORT>>A10 becomes <<REPORT>>A10..A10.

A Link Example

If you want to create a consolidation sheet for the total company expenses, you can consolidate the lower level totals with link formulas, as shown here:

```
┌──────────────────────────────────────────────────────────────────┐
│ ▬                        1-2-3 for Windows                    ▼│▲ │
├──────────────────────────────────────────────────────────────────┤
│ File   Edit   Worksheet   Range   Graph   Data   Style   Tools   Window   Help │
├──────────────────────────────────────────────────────────────────┤
│                                                              READY │
├──────────────────────────────────────────────────────────────────┤
│ A:C1          │       +<<REGION1>>A:B1..A:B1+<<REGION2>>A:B1..A:B1+<<REGION3>>A:B1..A:B │
└──────────────────────────────────────────────────────────────────┘
        ┌──────────────────────────────────────────────────────────┐
        │ □                      COMPANY.WK3                   ▼│▲ │
        ├──────────────────────────────────────────────────────────┤
        │ A │    A    │   B    │   C    │   D   │   E   │   F   │ G │▲│
        ├───┼─────────┼────────┼────────┼───────┼───────┼───────┼──┤▼│
        │ 1 │Total Expenses│   │ 450000 │       │       │       │  │ │
        └──────────────────────────────────────────────────────────┘
```

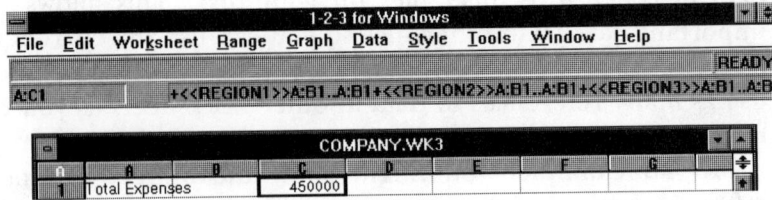

To try this, follow these steps:

1. Type **Expenses** in A1, and press the RIGHT ARROW key or click B1.

2. Type **100000** in B1 and press ENTER or click the confirm box.

3. Press ALT and then F A to select **File Save As** or click **File Save As.** Type **REGION1** as the filename and press ENTER.

4. Type **150000** in B1 and press ENTER or click the confirm box.

5. Press ALT and then F A to select **File Save As** or click **File Save As.** Type **REGION2** as the filename and press ENTER.

6. Type **200000** in B1 and press ENTER or click the confirm box.

7. Press ALT and then F A to select **File Save As** or click **File Save As.** Type **REGION3** as the filename and press ENTER.

Now you have files for the three regions. All you need now is the worksheet that totals these values.

8. Press ALT and then F C to select **File Close** or click **File Close** to close this worksheet and open a new one.

9. Type **Total Expenses** in A1 and press ENTER or click the confirm box.

10. Move to C1 and type this formula:

    **+ < <REGION1 > >B1 + < <REGION2 > >B1 +
    < <REGION3 > >B1**

11. Press ENTER or click the confirm box.

12. Press ALT and then F A to select **File Save As** or click **File Save As.** Type **COMPANY** as the filename and press ENTER.

13. Press ALT and then F C to select **File Close** or click **File Close** to close this worksheet and open a new one.

If you revise the salary number in any of the region worksheet files, the next time you retrieve the COMPANY worksheet, the result shown in C1 will include the new values in the regional worksheet files.

@Functions

Your 1-2-3 models have already shown you the importance of formulas. Formulas are actually the power behind a spreadsheet package like 1-2-3; they record your calculations and use them over and over again. However, there is a problem with formulas: it takes a long time to record them, and when you are recording a long series of calculations, it is easy to make a mistake. Also, formulas are oriented toward working with one or more individual cell addresses. Many times you want to reference a group of cells with one entry and use each value in the calculation. Fortunately, 1-2-3 has built-in functions to reduce these drawbacks. These functions are prerecorded formulas that have already been verified for accuracy. All you need to do is specify which data they should operate on each time you use them. The built-in functions also provide features that go beyond the capabilities of formulas, such as accessing the system date and calculating square roots and tangents.

To use these functions, you need to learn the syntax and the rules that provide a powerhouse of 106 prerecorded calculations that you can access easily. In the following discussion, you learn about the various function categories into which all 1-2-3 functions are grouped. You examine a variety of functions from the different categories and learn how to use them in application models.

4

Built-in Function Basics

A few general rules apply to all functions, regardless of their type, yet individual functions can differ from one another in how they expect you to convey the data with which you want them to work. You need to know the general rules and the individual exceptions, as well as which category of function is likely to handle the task you wish to address. This section provides such information. Read it before addressing the individual function categories; it is an important first step.

General Rules

Since built-in functions are formulas, they are value entries in worksheet cells. There are several rules for functions that do not apply to formulas, all of them pertaining to the syntax of recording the different components. A diagram of these components is shown in Figure 4-1. The first rule for function entry is that all functions must start with an @ symbol. After entering the @ symbol, you must include the special keyword that 1-2-3 uses to represent the function. This *keyword* is the function's name. You can enter it in either upper- or lowercase letters, but it must follow 1-2-3's spelling exactly. You can even have the package supply it for you. If you press the F3 (Name) key after typing the @ symbol, 1-2-3 displays a list of all the @ function keywords. When you highlight the word you want and press ENTER, 1-2-3 adds the function keyword and opening parenthesis to your entry.

Rules for Function Arguments

The next component within a function is its arguments. *Arguments* specify the data the function will use. Arguments are required by most functions since most functions must be defined exactly in order to be used. Arguments must be enclosed within parentheses, but if the function you are using does not require arguments you do not need to use parentheses.

When using a function that requires multiple arguments, use a comma (,) or a semicolon (;) to separate the arguments. Spaces cannot be used within a function, so they are not valid as separator characters.

Function arguments can be provided as cell addresses, range names that you assign to one or more cells, constants, or even formulas or other built-in functions. The examples you enter in this chapter may include

Figure 4-1.   *Function format*

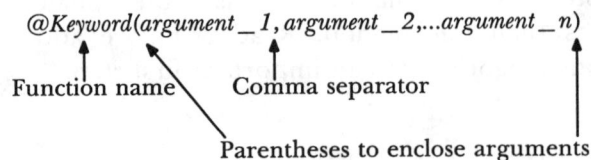

@Keyword(argument _ 1 , argument _ 2 ,...argument _ n)

Function name   Comma separator

Parentheses to enclose arguments

some constants in functions to expedite data entry. However, it is preferable to store the data needed by the function in worksheet cells and to reference these cells within the function since a change in an argument's value will not require you to edit the function. Much variety is possible; look at these examples of the @SUM function, which total the values you provide as arguments:

@SUM(9,4,8,7)
@SUM(A1;D3;Y6;Z10)
@SUM(Salaries,Rent_Exp,Equipment)
@SUM(A1..H4)
@SUM(A1,@SUM(B2..B3),<<BUDGET>>Z2)

All five are valid function entries. The last two examples reference a range of worksheet cells and use each value within the range. Ranges of cells must always form a rectangular area of contiguous worksheet cells.

Most built-in functions expect value entries for arguments. Other built-in functions require string or character data for arguments. You cannot substitute a type of data for an argument that is different from what 1-2-3 is expecting. For example, if you use 1-2-3's @UPPER function, you need to provide a label as an argument. @UPPER converts letters in a label to uppercase. If you substitute a value for the argument, @UPPER cannot convert it and returns ERR, indicating an error.

Different Types of Function Arguments

Different functions require different arguments and use them in different ways. The three basic types of functions are those that require no arguments, those that expect a list of arguments in any sequence, and those that require a specific number of arguments in a specific order.

Examples of functions that require no arguments are @NOW and @PI. @NOW supplies the current date and time number. @PI represents the special mathematical constant 3.14159265, which is used in geometric problem solving.

There are also a number of functions that expect a list of values for arguments. The entries in the list can be single cells or ranges of cells and can be provided in any order you like. All of the statistical functions fall within this category of argument types. For example, these two functions are equivalent:

@SUM(A1,B4,C5,D2..D10,F1,H2..M4)
@SUM(F1,H2..M4,A1,C5,D2..D10,B4)

In both cases, all individual values, as well as each of the values in the ranges, are totaled to produce a single sum. Functions that allow this interchangeability of argument order specify *list* as their argument. For example, since @SUM accepts this type of argument, you can expect to see @SUM(*list*) when the syntax of this function is discussed in detail.

The last type of function argument is position dependent. Functions that require arguments in a specific order cannot have their arguments reordered without erroneous results. For example, the @PMT function is designed to calculate the amount of a loan payment. The function requires three arguments: the principal, the interest, and the term of the loan. Later in this chapter, you will see the function specified like this:

@PMT(*principal,interest,term*)

When using the function, you must provide the three arguments in this exact order.

A Close Look at Each Function Category

There are seven categories of functions in 1-2-3, excluding the special database functions covered in Chapter 12, "Data Management Basics." Built-in functions are grouped into categories in which each of the functions within a category has some similarity of purpose. The various function categories form the organizational structure of the rest of this chapter. You can use the remainder of the chapter in two ways. The preferred approach is to work through the exercises in each function category to become familiar with each function's category use. There may be function categories that apply to your models, but unless you take an in-depth look at what they can do, you might not realize their potential. A second alternative, if your time is limited, is to focus on those function categories for which you have immediate use and then to come back and take a look at the other categories as you need them.

Statistical Functions

"Statistics" is a word that causes many people to be apprehensive— they recall statistics as complicated mathematical procedures from a required college math course. 1-2-3's statistical functions need not invoke this sense of alarm. They are simple to use, and they compute the most basic statistical measures, computations that you perform every day without even thinking about them as "statistical." They include computations for such operations as finding the average, summing, counting, and finding the minimum and maximum value. Table 4-1 provides a list of the statistical functions.

1-2-3's statistical functions perform their magic on lists of values. These lists are often a contiguous range of cells on the worksheet. They can also be a series of individual values or a combination of a range and individual values. Blank cells can be included within the list, but all cells in the blank range will count as zeros. When a range contains multiple blank cells, 1-2-3 ignores the cells that contain blanks.

Table 4-1. *Statistical Functions*

Function Entry	Description
@AVG(*list*)	Computes an average for the values in *list*
@COUNT(*list*)	Counts the nonblank entries in *list*
@MAX(*list*)	Locates the maximum value in *list*
@MIN(*list*)	Locates the minimum value in *list*
@STD(*list*)	Calculates the standard deviation of the values in *list*
@STDS(*list*)	Calculates the sample standard deviation of the values in *list*
@SUM(*list*)	Totals the values in *list*
@SUMPRODUCT(*list*)	Multiplies the parts of *list* and adds their results
@VAR(*list*)	Computes the variance for the values in *list*
@VARS(*list*)	Computes the sample variance for the values in *list*

Follow these steps to create a model to try out the @SUM function:

1. Place the following entries in the worksheet cells listed:

C1:	**High Profits Inc. Sales**	A12:	**Total:**
C2:	**Region 4**	C5:	**Sales**
A5:	**Salesperson**	C6:	**95800**
A6:	**Jason Rye**	C7:	**56780**
A7:	**Paul Jones**	C8:	**89675**
A8:	**Mary Hart**	C9:	**91555**
A9:	**Tom Bush**	C10:	**92300**
A10:	**Jane Hunt**		

Rather than entering a formula to total sales, you can use the @SUM function.

2. Move to C12, type **@SUM(C6.C10)**, and press ENTER or click the confirm box.

The formula you have just entered is equivalent to the formula +C6+C7+C8+C9+C10. The advantage of this formula is that it is easier to enter. Also, in Chapter 7, "Changing Row and Column Options," you will learn how to insert rows. When you insert rows in the middle of a range, 1-2-3 automatically expands the range to include the inserted rows. This means that if you add another salesperson between Jason Rye and Jane Hunt, 1-2-3 will automatically include their sales in the formula in C12.

The @COUNT function is an exception to the others in the statistical category since it often used with value and label entries. You can add this function to the worksheet.

3. Move to A11, type **Number of Salespeople**, and press ENTER or click the confirm box.

4. Move to C11, type **@COUNT(C6..C10)**, and press ENTER or click the confirm box to finish the worksheet, as shown in Figure 4-2.

5. Press ALT and then F A to select **File Save As** or click **File Save As**. Type **HIGHPROF** as the filename and press ENTER.

6. Press ALT and then F C to select **File Close**, or click **File Close** to close this worksheet and open a new one.

Figure 4-2. *Totaling values with the @SUM function and counting entries with the @COUNT function*

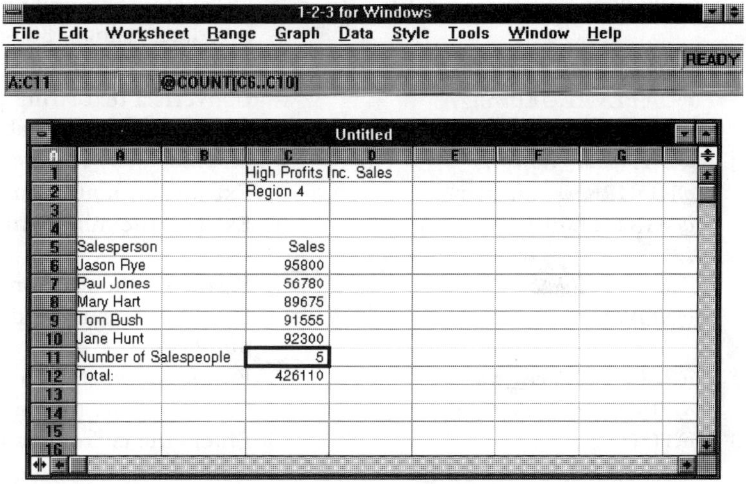

Date and Time Functions

Date information and time information are important parts of many business decisions. You need date information to know if a loan is overdue or if there is still time remaining in the discount period for an invoice. You can use time information to calculate the service time for various tasks or to log the delivery time for various carriers. In Chapter 2, "Entering Labels and Numbers," you learned how to enter a date and time number on the worksheet. The date and time functions provide an alternative approach for making these entries and allow you to work with one component of a date or time, such as the year or minute for the entry. The date and time functions are shown in Table 4-2.

You can enter **@NOW** in a worksheet cell to generate a date and time stamp. 1-2-3 accesses the system clock in your machine and places a date/time number in the cell to represent the current date and time setting of your system clock. If the date is December 31, 1991, and the time is noon, the date/time number will be 33603.5. The whole-number portion of the entry represents the date and the decimal fraction represents the time. The result of the @NOW function is updated when you open the file containing the @function and when the worksheet is recalculated, since the time is constantly changing. In Chapter 6, "Changing the Appearance

Table 4-2.   *Date and Time Functions*

Function Entry	Description
@D360(*start_date,end_date*)	Calculates the number of days between two dates using a 360-day year
@DATE(*year,month,day*)	Creates a date number
@DATEVALUE(*string*)	Converts a text string in a valid date format to a date number
@DAY(*date_number*)	Extracts a day number from a date
@HOUR(*time_number*)	Extracts an hour from a time
@MINUTE(*time_number*)	Extracts the minute number from a time
@MONTH(*date_number*)	Extracts a month from a date
@NOW	Returns the current date and time numbers
@SECOND(*time_number*)	Extracts a second from a time
@TIME(*hour,minute,second*)	Creates a time number
@TODAY	Enters the current date number
@TIMEVALUE(*string*)	Converts a text string in a valid time format to a time number
@YEAR(*date_number*)	Extracts a year from a date

of Worksheet Cells," you will learn how you can display the date and time numbers as the dates and times they represent.

To try one of these functions, type **@YEAR(@NOW)** and press ENTER or click the confirm box. The result, such as 91, indicates the year for the date number created by @NOW. Many of the date and time functions expect a time or date number as their argument.

String Functions

String functions provide a variety of character-manipulation formulas that give you flexibility in rearranging text entries. With string functions, you can work with the entire label entry for a cell or with just a part of it. The functions in this category can be real lifesavers when you have to correct data-entry errors. The same function you create for one entry could be copied down a column to correct a large portion of a worksheet. Table 4-3 provides a list of all the string functions.

Table 4-3. *String Functions*

Function Entry	Description
@CHAR(x)	Returns a Lotus Multibyte Character Set (LMBCS) character corresponding to x
@CODE(*string*)	Returns the LMBCS code of the first character in *string*
@EXACT(*string1*,*string2*)	Returns 1 if *string1* and *string2* are identical and 0 if they are not identical
@FIND(*search_string*,*string*,*start_number*)	Returns the position of *search_string* in *string*
@LEFT(*string*,*n*)	Extracts *n* number of characters from the left side of *string*
@LENGTH(*string*)	Returns the number of characters in *string*
@LOWER(*string*)	Converts *string* to lowercase
@MID(*string*,*start_number*,*n*)	Returns *n* characters from the middle of *string* beginning with the position *start_number*
@N(*range*)	Returns the entry in the first cell of *range* as a value
@PROPER(*string*)	Converts *string* to propercase (first letter of each word is capitalized and the rest is lowercased
@REPEAT(*string*,*n*)	Repeats *string* *n* times
@REPLACE(*original*,*start*,*n*,*new*)	Replaces *n* characters in *original* with *new* beginning at position *start*
@RIGHT(*string*,*n*)	Extracts *n* characters from the right side of *string*
@S(*range*)	Returns the entry from the first cell in *range* as a label
@STRING(*x*,*n*)	Converts the value *x* to a label with *n* decimal places
@TRIM(*string*)	Removes beginning, trailing, and extra spaces from *string*
@UPPER(*string*)	Converts *string* to uppercase
@VALUE(*string*)	Converts a string that looks like a value to a value

You can use the @UPPER function to correct data-entry errors involving the inconsistent use of capital letters. The syntax of the function is @UPPER(*string*) to convert an entry to uppercase. An example of the @UPPER function might look like this:

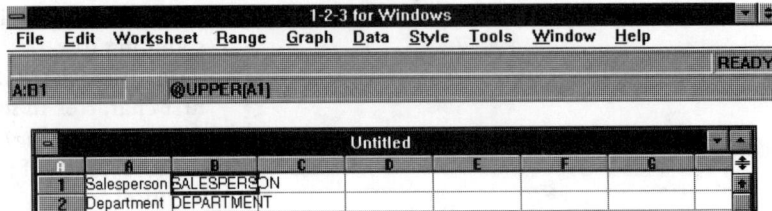

You convert the entries in A1 and A2 to uppercase by placing @UPPER(A1) and @UPPER(A2) in B1 and B2. Once you convert the entries, you can replace the original entries with the function results using the **Edit Q**uick Copy command that you will learn about in Chapter 9, "Making 1-2-3 Do Your Work."

Math Functions

1-2-3's math functions perform both simple calculations and more complex operations suited to an engineering or manufacturing application. Rather than looking at the trigonometric functions and more complex operations, you will benefit most from a general-purpose example on rounding values. You learn how to overcome rounding problems with the @INT function, which returns the whole-number portion of an entry. Table 4-4 is a complete list of math functions.

@INT requires only a single argument, the number that you want to work with. The function accepts a number, a formula, or another @function that returns a value for this entry. If you enter **@INT(@NOW)**, 1-2-3 returns the date number portion of the date/time stamp. If you enter **@INT(B3/B6)**, 1-2-3 divides the value in B3 by the value in B6 and then discards any decimal fraction in the result before returning it. For example, **@INT(10/3)** would return a 3 rather than 3.3333333.

Special Functions

1-2-3's special functions are grouped together because they do not fit neatly into any of the other function categories. Some of them trap error conditions; others count the number of rows in a range or allow you to choose a value from a list of options. Still others let you examine the contents of worksheet cells closely, thus providing information about a

Table 4-4. *Math Functions*

Function Entry	Description
@ABS(x)	Returns the absolute value of x
@ACOS(x)	Returns the arccosine of x
@ASIN(x)	Returns the arcsine of x
@ATAN(x)	Returns the arctangent of x
@ATAN2(x,y)	Returns the arctangent of y/x
@COS(x)	Returns the cosine of the angle x
@EXP(x)	Calculates the value of 2.718282 raised to the x power
@INT(x)	Returns the integer portion of x
@LN(x)	Calculates the natural log of x
@LOG(x)	Calculates the base 10 log of x
@MOD(x,y)	Returns the remainder when x is divided by y
@PI	Returns the value 3.1415926536
@RAND	Returns a random number between 0 and 1
@ROUND(x,n)	Rounds the value x to the nth place
@SIN(x)	Calculates the sine of the angle x
@SQRT(x)	Returns the square root of x
@TAN(x)	Returns the tangent of the angle x

cell's value or other attributes. For the most part, this group can be thought of as a smorgasbord of sophisticated features. Table 4-5 provides a complete list of the special functions.

One of the more interesting special @functions is the @VLOOKUP function. This function uses a table of values like the one in rows 10 through 13 of the worksheet in Figure 4-3. When you use this function, it looks in the table for either the label that exactly matches a label in the first column of the table or the highest value that is equal to or less than the value you are looking for. When it finds this label or value, it returns an entry from the same column or another column of the table, using the row from the table containing the entry it found. The format of this function is @VLOOKUP($x,range,column\_offset$). *X* is the value you are trying to find in the table. *Range* is the worksheet range that contains the table. *Column_offset* selects which column of the table the function returns the value from. The first column has an offset of 0, the second column has an

Table 4-5. *Special Functions*

Function Entry	Description
@@(*location*)	Returns the address of *location*
@CELL(*attribute,range*)	Returns specific information about the first cell in *range* as indicated by *attribute*
@CELLPOINTER(*attribute*)	Returns information about the current cell as specified by *attribute*
@CHOOSE(*x,list*)	Returns the *x* entry from *list*
@COLS(*range*)	Returns the number of columns in *range*
@COORD(*worksheet,column,row,absolute*)	Creates a cell address from the *worksheet, column,* and *row* numbers you provide
@ERR	Returns the value ERR
@HLOOKUP(*x,range,row_offset*)	Returns a value from *range* from the *row* indicated by *row_offset*
@INDEX(*range,column_offset,row_offset*)	Returns an entry from the table range as indicated by the two offsets provided
@INFO(*attribute*)	Returns information about the current 1-2-3 session
@NA	Returns the value NA
@ROWS(*range*)	Returns the number of rows in *range*
@SHEET(*range*)	Returns the number of sheets in *range*
@SOLVER(*query_string*)	Returns different types of information about the Solver utility
@VLOOKUP(*x,range,column_offset*)	Returns a value from *range* from the column indicated by *column_offset*

offset of 1, and so on. To try this function and see how it works, follow these steps:

1. Place the following entries in the worksheet cells listed here:

C1:	**High Profits Inc.**	C4:	**"Salesperson**
C2:	**Invoice Listing**	C5:	**"Number**
A5:	**"Invoice #**	D4:	**Salesperson**
B5:	**"Amount**	D5:	**Name**

A6:	**1001**	A10:	**11**
A7:	**1002**	A11:	**15**
A8:	**1003**	A12:	**16**
B6:	**15167**	A13:	**19**
B7:	**78312**	B9:	**Salesperson**
B8:	**45377**	B10:	**J. Rye**
C6:	**19**	B11:	**P. Jones**
C7:	**16**	B12:	**M. Hart**
C8:	**11**	B13:	**T. Bush**
A9:	**"Number**		

2. Enter the following formulas in the worksheet cells listed here:

D6: **@VLOOKUP(C6, A10..B13,1)**
D7: **@VLOOKUP(C7, A10..B13,1)**
D8: **@VLOOKUP(C8, A10..B13,1)**

Your worksheet now looks like the one in Figure 4-3. For each formula in column D, 1-2-3 searched the table in A10..B13 for the entry that matched the entry in column C. When 1-2-3 found a match, 1-2-3 returned the label stored in the second column of the table (column B), which has a table offset of 1.

Figure 4-3. *Using the @VLOOKUP special function in a worksheet file*

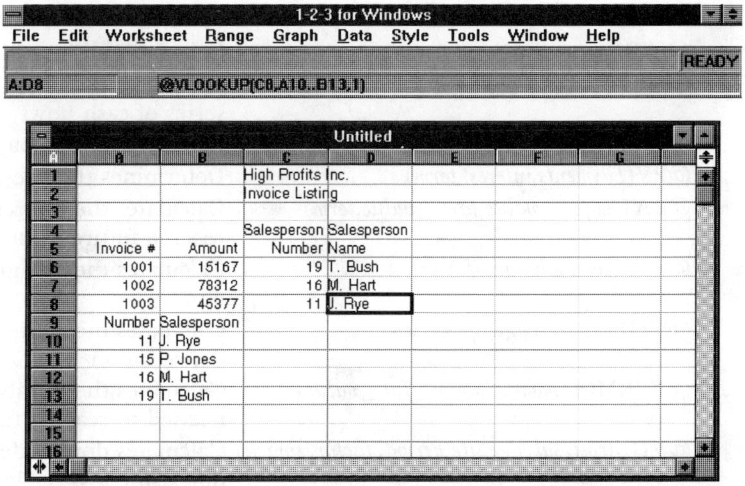

3. Press ALT and then F A to select **File Save As**, or click **File Save As**. Type **HIGH_INV** as the filename and press ENTER.

4. Press ALT and then F C to select **File Close**, or click **File Close** to close this worksheet and open a new one.

Financial Functions

1-2-3 provides an entire category of functions to use in investment calculations and other calculations concerned with the time value of money. You can use these financial functions to calculate loan payments, annuities, cash flows, and depreciation. You can quickly compare various financial alternatives since you can rely on the function to supply the correct formulas. As with the other functions, all you need to supply are arguments to tailor the calculations to your exact needs. Table 4-6 lists all of the financial functions and the arguments they use.

Table 4-6.   *Financial Functions*

Function Entry	Description
@CTERM(*int, fut_value, pres_value*)	Calculates the number of compounding periods required to attain a future value
@DDB(*cost, salvage, life, period*)	Calculates depreciation with the double-declining balance method
@FV(*payments, interest, term*)	Calculates a future value for an investment
@IRR(*guess, range*)	Calculates an internal rate of return
@NPV(*interest, range*)	Calculates the net present value of a series of cash flows
@PMT(*principal, interest, term*)	Calculates a loan payment
@PV(*payments, interest, term*)	Determines the present value
@RATE(*fut_value, pres_value, term*)	Calculates the interest rate needed to reach a future value
@SLN(*cost, salvage, life*)	Calculates the straight-line depreciation
@SYD(*cost, salvage, life, period*)	Calculates the sum-of-the-years'-digits depreciation
@TERM(*payments, interest, fut_value*)	Calculates the number of periods needed to reach a future value
@VDB(*cost, salvage, life, period, factor, switch*)	Calculates double-declining depreciation using a variable rate

When you use financial functions, it is very important that all of the arguments and the result use the same unit of time. For example, the @PMT function, which computes a loan payment, requires you to decide whether you want to calculate the payment amount on a yearly, quarterly, or monthly basis. Once you decide on some unit of time, you must apply it consistently across all arguments. If you choose to compute a monthly payment amount, the interest rate is a monthly rate. Likewise, the term is the number of months of the loan.

The following illustration shows the computation of a loan payment:

The principal in B1 is used as the first argument. The interest rate in B2 is divided by 12 to convert the yearly rate to a monthly rate. The term in B3 is multiplied by 12 to convert the number of years to a number of months. The complete function entry is

@PMT(B1,B2/12,B3*12)

Logical Functions

1-2-3's logical functions build conditional features into your models. The functions in this category return logical values (true or false) as the result of the condition tests they perform. They are a powerful addition to 1-2-3 because they allow you to alter calculations based on conditions in other locations of the worksheet. This flexibility lets you construct models patterned after real-world business conditions, where exceptions are prevalent. Table 4-7 is a complete list of the logical functions.

Logical functions let you have more than one calculation for commission payments, purchase discounts, FICA tax, or any other computation requiring multiple calculations that depend on other values in the

Table 4-7. *Logical Functions*

Function Entry	Description
@FALSE	Returns a logical 0
@IF(*condition,x,y*)	Tests *condition* and returns *x* if it is true and *y* if it is false
@ISAAF(*name*)	Tests to see if *name* is a defined add-in function; returns 1 if it is and 0 if it is not
@ISAPP(*name*)	Tests *name* to see if it is an attached add-in; returns 1 if it is and 0 if it is not
@ISERR(*x*)	Tests *x* for the value ERR and returns 0 for false and 1 for true
@ISNA(*x*)	Tests *x* for the value NA and returns 0 for false and 1 for true
@ISNUMBER(*x*)	Tests *x* to see if it is a value and returns 0 for false and 1 for true
@ISRANGE(*range*)	Tests *range* to see if it is a valid cell address, range address, or range name and returns 0 for false and 1 for true
@ISSTRING(*x*)	Tests *x* to see if it is a string and returns 0 for false and 1 for true
@TRUE	Returns the logical value 1

worksheet. The @IF function is the most popular logical function since it allows you to test a condition to determine what you want to use as the result of the @function. The function syntax is

$$@IF(condition\_test,value\_if\_true,value\_if\_false)$$

Valid entries would include

@IF(B4 > 100,.15,.08)
@IF(D4 > 500,D4*.15,D4*.08)

To create a model using the second example of the @IF function, follow these steps:

1. Place the following entries in the worksheet cells listed here:

B1:	**ABC Inc.**	F4:	**+D4−E4**
B2:	**Product Order Form**	A5:	**Printer**
A3:	**Item**	B5:	**800**
B3:	**"Cost**	C5:	**5**
C3:	**"Quantity**	D5:	**+B5*C5**
D3:	**"Subtotal**	F5:	**+D5−E5**
E3:	**"Discount**	A6:	**Cables**
F3:	**"Total**	B6:	**5.99**
A4:	**Computer**	C6:	**25**
B4:	**6780**	D6:	**+B6*C6**
C4:	**3**	F6:	**+D6−E6**
D4:	**+B4*C4**		

2. Enter the following formulas in the worksheet cells listed here:

E4:	**@IF(D4 > 15000,D4*.15,D4*.08)**
E5:	**@IF(D5 > 15000,D5*.15,D5*.08)**
E6:	**@IF(D6 > 15000,D6*.15,D6*.08)**

Now the worksheet looks like this:

The formulas in column E compute the purchase discount. The discount is 15 percent for orders over $15000 and 8 percent for orders of $15000 or less. The formula compares the order total in column D to the $15000 amount and provides a true and false alternative for the comparison. For the first item, the 15 percent discount applies, while for the other two, the 8 percent discount is used. The @IF function lets 1-2-3 make the decision based on the values stored in other cells.

Review

In this chapter, you learned more advanced 1-2-3 features that you can use with formulas. These advanced features include range names, external file links, and functions. Specifically, you learned the following:

- A range name can be assigned to any cell or range on the worksheet. To access an existing range name, use the F3 (Name) key when building the formula.

- A range name that is no longer needed can be deleted without deleting the data in the referenced cell. After the range name is deleted, the formula displays the range address rather than the range name.

- You can create formulas that reference data in other worksheet files. Use double angle brackets (<< >>) around the name of the filename or pathname in order to reference the other data, followed by the cell address, range address, or range name of the data in the other worksheet file.

- Functions are prerecorded formulas. You access them by typing an @ followed by a keyword. Most functions also have arguments that define your specific needs to 1-2-3. These arguments are enclosed in parentheses and separated by commas.

- You can press the F3 (Name) key after typing @ to list the available functions. Highlight the function you want and press ENTER or double-click it.

- There are eight categories of @functions. Statistical functions perform basic statistical calculations. Date and time functions record dates and times and work with date and time numbers. String functions manipulate character strings. Math functions access trigonometric functions and mathematical operations. Financial computations involve the time value of money or depreciation. Special functions are miscellaneous functions that do not fit into other categories. Logical functions test conditions. Data management functions perform selective computations with 1-2-3 database records, which are covered with databases in Chapter 12, "Data Management Basics."

Keys and Commands

The keys you learned to use in this chapter help you build external file links. You also learned commands that let you assign names to worksheet ranges. These keys and commands are

Keys	Action
<< >>	Encloses a filename as part of reference to data in another worksheet file
F3 (Name)	Displays a list of range names or @function names that you can add to a formula
ALT R N C	**R**ange **N**ame **C**reate assigns a name to a worksheet cell or range
ALT R N D	**R**ange **N**ame **D**elete removes the assignment of a name to a range without affecting the data in the range

4

5

Getting Familiar with Menus and Dialog Boxes

Although you can make entries on the worksheet without the use of menus, you cannot access any of 1-2-3's other features without them. Menus are your initial interface for telling 1-2-3 exactly what you want it to do for you. You can use either the keyboard or your mouse to make menu selections for you. Although the menu you see at the top of the worksheet window is not the menu used by 1-2-3 for DOS, you will soon grow to like its organization. While you are mastering its new structure, you will still be able to access the familiar menu from the past, which is called the 1-2-3 Classic menu in the Windows product. In this book, instructions for using the Classic menu to accomplish a task are highlighted by a Classic menu icon like this:

═══*classic*═══

With the new menu structure, instead of making your way through five or more levels of horizontal menu selections to define your specific needs to 1-2-3, you can now make an initial menu selection and then define your specific requirements through pull-down menus. *Pull-down menus* pull down from the main menu and allow you to see the next set of options at a glance. The pull-down menu display also indicates whether a selection will finalize a command or display a cascade menu or dialog box. *Cascade menus* display to the right of the pull-down menu and allow you to look at the entire chain of command entries. *Dialog boxes* present many items in a concise format. Dialog boxes are especially useful with a mouse since you can make changes to a number of items with a quick click of the mouse and an entry or two to fill in needed information. You will find that dialog boxes organize all your selections on one screen and provide a quick way to handle all the details.

1-2-3's Menu

1-2-3's menu is designed to make 1-2-3's commands easy to access and remember. Only one keystroke is needed to access the menu, and Lotus has chosen command names that represent their functions in building the menu. While 1-2-3 may have a wide variety of commands, do not be discouraged. You can accomplish 90 percent of your work by using only a small percentage of the total menu. The other commands are there to provide sophisticated options for 1-2-3's power users. The menu is always visible in the control panel, as shown here:

```
            1-2-3 for Windows
 File  Edit  Worksheet  Range  Graph  Data  Style  Tools  Window  Help
```

Activating the Menu

You activate 1-2-3's menu by pressing F10 (Menu) or ALT from READY mode. The menu is also activated when you click one of the options in the menu bar. If the mode indicator is not READY, 1-2-3 is not ready to accept your request for a menu option. You must take an action to return the indicator to READY before activating the menu. This action may be completing the entry you started, waiting for 1-2-3 to finish its current task, or acknowledging an error message. Once the menu is activated, the mode indicator changes to MENU. It remains MENU except for a few prompts for an entry, when it changes to EDIT, or when you are selecting the cells in the worksheet, when it changes to POINT.

The Worksheet Window Menu

Initially, the menu in the menu bar is the worksheet menu because a worksheet window is the active window. All of the worksheet commands must start from the worksheet window. Each of these menu selections will be discussed in more detail as you proceed through this book. Before you examine any one particular menu choice in further detail, take a quick look at each of the worksheet menu choices and the category of tasks it performs:

5

Menu Selection	Type of Task Handled
File	Gets and puts data on disks and prints your data
Edit	Moves and copies data between areas on a worksheet, between worksheets, and between applications, and undoes entries or commands
Worksheet	Makes changes that affect the entire worksheet file, including formatting numbers and adding and removing columns and rows
Range	Makes changes to an area within a worksheet, including formatting numbers and assigning names
Graph	Creates and names graphs created with worksheet data
Data	Sorts data, searches data for matching information, and performs other data-management features
Style	Adds word processing formatting such as fonts, lines, colors, and shading to worksheet cells
Tools	Changes global settings and provides macro, solving, and add-in features
Window	Changes the display of windows within the 1-2-3 window
Help	Opens and displays a help window on different 1-2-3 topics

Making Menu Selections

Every menu option has an underlined letter that indicates the upper- or lowercase letter you can press to select the option. For example, once the menu is active, you can select **R**ange by typing **R** or **r**. You can also make selections with the mouse by clicking the option you want.

Another way to make your selection is to use the LEFT ARROW or RIGHT ARROW key to highlight the item you want and then press ENTER. This approach is convenient when you are first learning the commands since 1-2-3 displays a description of the highlighted command in the title bar. You can continue moving between menu options until the desired option is highlighted. No action is taken until you activate a menu choice by pressing ENTER.

When you select one of the main menu options, you are shown a list of choices in a pull-down menu that looks like this:

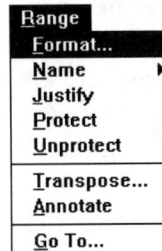

```
Range
Format...
Name          ▶
Justify
Protect
Unprotect

Transpose...
Annotate

Go To...
```

Pull-down menus let you further refine your request. When you select an option in a pull-down menu, 1-2-3 may perform a command, display another menu (called a cascade menu), or display a dialog box to prompt for more information. You can tell what will happen by looking at any characters to the right of the menu option. For example, next to **N**ame in the **R**ange pull-down menu, 1-2-3 displays a triangle. This indicates that if you select **N**ame, 1-2-3 will display a cascade menu. Next to **F**ormat, 1-2-3 displays three dots (an ellipsis). This indicates that if you select **F**ormat, 1-2-3 will display a dialog box. Options like **P**rotect do not have any characters after them, indicating that 1-2-3 will perform the **R**ange **P**rotect command as soon as you select **P**rotect.

You can try making menu selections by following these directions:

1. Press ALT or F10 (Menu) and press R or click **R**ange.

1-2-3 displays the **R**ange pull-down menu, which includes **F**ormat, **N**ame, **J**ustify, **P**rotect, **U**nprotect, **T**ranspose, **A**nnotate, and **G**o To. **N**ame has a triangle next to it indicating that if you select **N**ame, 1-2-3 will display a cascade menu. **F**ormat, **T**ranspose, and **G**o To have ellipses to indicate that if you select one of them, 1-2-3 will display a dialog box.

    2. Press N or click **N**ame to select **N**ame.

1-2-3 displays a cascade menu that contains **C**reate, **L**abel Create, **D**elete, and **P**aste Table. If you select any option except **P**aste Table, 1-2-3 will display a dialog box. If you select **P**aste Table, 1-2-3 will perform the **R**ange **N**ame **P**aste Table command.

=note= As you become more familiar with menu selections, you will be given only the names of the commands you should choose for each exercise; you will no longer be told which keys to press to make these selections. Remember, you can activate the menu with ALT or F10 (Menu). You can make menu selections by pressing the underlined letter, by pressing the arrow keys and ENTER, or by clicking the option with a mouse. It does not matter how you activate the menu or which way you choose to make menu selections—use whatever method you prefer.

Canceling a Selection

Since you are just examining the menu structure, do not make any additional selections at this time. Instead, examine the methods for backing out of menu selections to return to the previous menu and eventually to READY mode. This is useful when you accidentally make an incorrect menu selection and want to back out of it to make a new choice.

If you make a mistake in a menu selection, you can press ESC. Pressing ESC returns you to the prior level of menus. If a dialog box is displayed, pressing ESC returns you to READY mode. Try this to see how it works:

    1. Press ESC once to remove the cascade menu.

    2. Press ESC again to remove the **R**ange pull-down menu.

    3. Press ESC a third time to return to READY mode.

An easier way to return to READY mode when you are using the menu is to press CTRL-BREAK. That is, hold down the CTRL key while you press the BREAK key (which is often combined with another key such as SCROLL LOCK or

PAUSE). Regardless of the number of menu selections you have made, you are immediately returned to READY mode. With a mouse, you can switch to another pull-down menu by clicking a menu option on the menu bar. If you want to return to READY mode, click one of the worksheet cells. Once a dialog box is displayed, you can return to the worksheet without performing the command by clicking the Cancel command button.

1-2-3's Classic Menu

If you have used prior releases of 1-2-3, you may not be comfortable with the new 1-2-3 menu. To make 1-2-3 for Windows easier for you to use, 1-2-3 has included both menus. When you press /, 1-2-3 displays the 1-2-3 Classic menu:

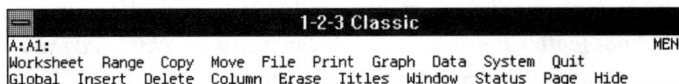

This is the same menu that 1-2-3 Release 3.1 uses. Likewise, you can press : to display the Wysiwyg menu for the add-in that Release 3.1 uses to add spreadsheet publishing capabilities to your worksheet. If you are accustomed to earlier releases, you will find all of your old commands there, as well as the new features that were added in later releases. This menu behaves just like the menu in prior releases. The two menus allow you to make the transition between the prior menu structure and the new menu structure at a pace you find comfortable.

Using Dialog Boxes

Some of 1-2-3's menu selections display dialog boxes. Dialog boxes let you provide additional information that 1-2-3 needs to perform a com-

Figure 5-1. *Tools User Setup dialog box showing dialog box components*

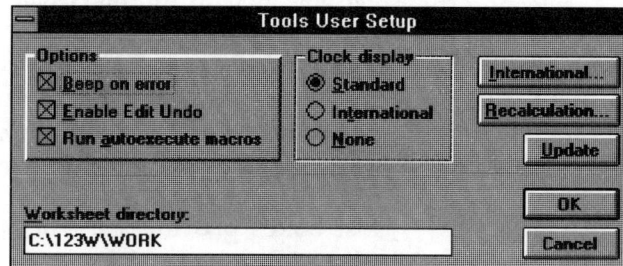

mand for you. For example, when you want to open a file, 1-2-3 needs to know the name of the file you want and where it is located. Figure 5-1 shows a dialog box.

Dialog boxes contain title bars that you can use to move the dialog box on the screen just as you can move the 1-2-3 window. Dialog boxes also have control menu boxes that let you move or close the dialog box. The dialog box is filled with the various components that allow you to make different types of entries. Dialog boxes contain the following types of components:

- **Check boxes** Check boxes add or remove features. They appear as boxes that are blank, are marked with an X, or are shaded. You can see check boxes under Options in Figure 5-1.

- **Command buttons** Command buttons perform an action, such as finalizing a command, closing a dialog box, or switching to another dialog box. All dialog boxes contain the OK command button to finalize selections and the Cancel command button to return to READY mode without performing the command.

- **Drop-down boxes** Drop-down boxes display a list that you can select from by clicking the down arrow icon or using the arrow keys to move to the icon and pressing ENTER. In Figure 5-2, you could see the list of available drives that 1-2-3 displays by selecting the down arrow icon under Drives.

- **Information boxes**   Information boxes list information without letting you make any changes. The box under File Information in Figure 5-2, which holds information for the ANSWER01.WK3 worksheet file, is an information box.

- **List boxes**   List boxes provide a list of options that you can select from. The list of files under Files in Figure 5-2 is a list box. When a list box has more options than fit in the box, the list box will include a scroll bar for changing the section of the list that appears in the list box.

- **Option buttons**   Option buttons select features from a group of exclusive choices. The option buttons that make up an exclusive set are grouped together, like the option buttons under Clock Display in Figure 5-1.

Figure 5-2.   *File Open dialog box*

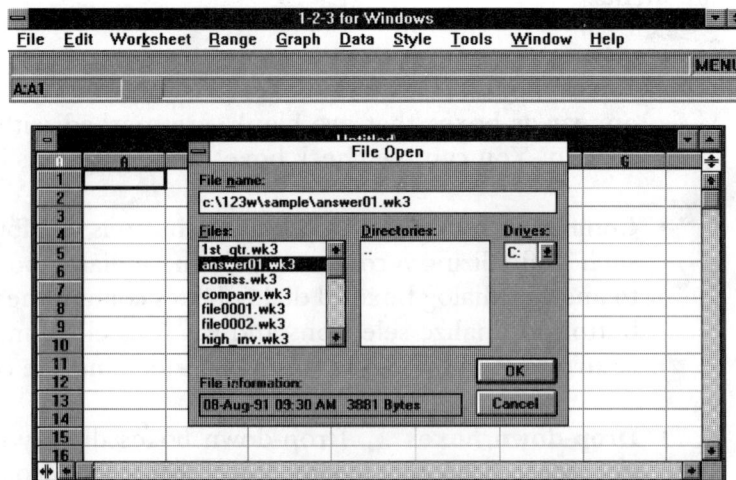

- **Text boxes**   Text boxes accept lengthy entries. The type of entry you should make is described above the text box. Text boxes are white boxes that you can fill with your entry, as in the Worksheet Directory text box in Figure 5-1.

To try using the different components of a dialog box, follow these steps:

1. Select **T**ools from the menu and **U**ser Setup to display the dialog box in Figure 5-1.

1-2-3 indicates your position on the dialog box with a dotted box around option buttons and check boxes (like the one around **B**eep on Error), by highlighting text box contents, or by outlining a command button. This dialog box has three check boxes under Options, three option buttons under Clock Display, a text box for Worksheet Directory, and five command buttons (**I**nternational, **R**ecalculation, **U**pdate, OK, and Cancel). Each dialog box option, with the exception of OK and Cancel, has an underlined letter so you can move to that option by pressing the underlined letter. If a text box or drop-down box is currently active, to select a different part of the dialog box, you need to press ALT and the underlined letter.

2. Press the SPACEBAR to remove the X before **B**eep on Error.

When a check box has an X in it, it is marked. When the check box is empty, the option is unmarked. In Chapter 6, "Changing the Appearance of Worksheet Cells," you will see that sometimes a check box is gray or shaded.

3. Press B for **B**eep on Error to select this option again.
4. Press N to move to **N**one or click the **N**one Clock Display.

When you select an option button, the previously selected option from the group is unselected. To make selections with the mouse, click the check box, option button, or command button, or the text next to it.

5. Press I or click the **I**nternational command button.

Since this command button has an ellipsis after International, 1-2-3 displays another dialog box. Most of the components in this dialog box are drop-down boxes. You can display a list of options for a drop-down box or return the drop-down box to its original size by clicking the down arrow icon. If you do not have a mouse, you cannot display the expanded list of options, but you can see them one at a time by pressing UP ARROW and DOWN ARROW.

6. If you have a mouse, select the down arrow icon to display the expanded drop-down box, as shown here:

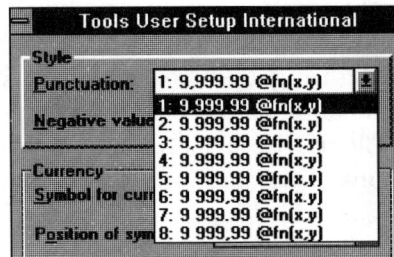

7. If you have a mouse, click the entry 5: 9 999.99 @fn(x,y). If you do not have a mouse, press DOWN ARROW four times.

Next, you will see that you can move from one dialog box option to the next by pressing TAB or SHIFT-TAB.

8. Press TAB until the Cancel command button is outlined and press ENTER, or click the Cancel command button.

When you select the Cancel command button, your changes are not retained. This provides the same result as pressing ESC. When you select a command button like OK or Cancel, 1-2-3 either returns to the previous dialog box or to READY mode.

9. Press W or click the **W**orksheet Directory text box to select this option.

The entry in a text box when that dialog box component is selected is initially highlighted. At this point, you have two options: you can entirely replace the current entry by typing a new entry or you can edit the current entry.

10. Press END or click the current setting again to tell 1-2-3 that you want to edit the current entry.

11. Press BACKSPACE until the entry is C:\ (or whatever drive your working directory is on).

12. Press ENTER to select the OK command button or click the OK command button to leave the dialog box with the changes you have made.

13. Select **T**ools and **U**ser Setup to return to the same dialog box.

14. Press S or click **S**tandard to return to the default clock display.

15. Press W or click **W**orksheet Directory, press END or click the end of the current setting, and edit the entry so it is the same directory you saw in step 11.

16. Press ENTER to select the OK command button or click the OK command button to finish the dialog box and return to READY mode.

5

Undoing Menu Commands

You have looked at 1-2-3's Undo feature for eliminating an entry from a worksheet cell, but Undo has even more power. 1-2-3 keeps track of all the activities that occur from the time that 1-2-3 is in READY mode until the next time it is in READY mode. As long as these activities involve only the current worksheet or its settings, they can be undone. External activities like printing or putting information on a disk cannot be undone. If you open a worksheet, format a range, or alter the width of a range of columns, 1-2-3 can undo these actions as long as you use Undo before performing new activities. Once you invoke another command or make a new entry, that action is the latest action and is the work that will be undone when you use Undo.

When you press ALT-BACKSPACE, select the Undo icon from the icon panel, or select **E**dit **U**ndo, the last action is undone. If you use Undo again, nothing happens because 1-2-3 remembers only the last change. 1-2-3 displays a check mark next to Undo in the **E**dit pull-down menu when

1-2-3 can undo the last action. To see how Undo can help you, first check that Undo is enabled, as described in Chapter 1, "Worksheet Basics," and then follow these steps:

1. Select **File Open**, type **ABC_SALE** in the File **N**ame text box, and select the OK command button.

2. Move the cell pointer to column A.

3. Select Worksheet **D**elete, the **C**olumn option button, and the OK command button.

4. Press ALT-BACKSPACE, select the Undo icon from the icon panel, or select **E**dit **U**ndo.

1-2-3 restores the deleted column.

5. Select **File C**lose and select **N**o when 1-2-3 asks if you want to save the file.

6. Press ALT-BACKSPACE, select the Undo icon from the icon panel, or select **E**dit **U**ndo.

1-2-3 restores the deleted worksheet window.

Review

Now you have learned how to use 1-2-3's menus. As you learn the features the different commands offer, using the new commands will be as easy as using the commands you already know. The specific skills you have learned for using menus include the following:

- Other than basic entries and function-key options, you can access all of 1-2-3's features with selections from a series of menus. You invoke the menu by pressing ALT or F10 (Menu) or by clicking an option displayed in the menu bar.

- You can select a menu option by highlighting your selection and pressing ENTER. Pressing the underlined letter of the menu selection works the same way. You can also click a menu option to select it with a mouse. You can use the ESC key to back out of a menu level.

- When 1-2-3 displays a dialog box, you can enter the additional information that 1-2-3 needs to perform the command. The type of selections you can make in a dialog box varies with the command, since different commands require different types of information. When you select the OK command button, 1-2-3 performs the command.

- You can display the 1-2-3 Classic menu, which behaves exactly as 1-2-3's Release 3.1 menu does, by pressing the / (slash) key. You can also press the : (colon) key to display the Wysiwyg menu that is available with Release 3.1.

- You can undo the effect of the last menu command by pressing ALT-BACKSPACE, selecting the Undo icon from the icon panel, or selecting **Edit Undo**.

Commands and Keys

The keys you used in this chapter let you use menus and make selections as you used the menus. You also learned how you can remove the effect of the last command with the Edit Undo command. These keys and commands are

Keys	Action
/	Displays the 1-2-3 Classic menu
:	Displays the 1-2-3 Wysiwyg menu
ALT or F10 (Menu)	Invokes the menu
CTRL-BREAK	Leaves any level of the menu and returns you to READY mode
ESC	Backs you out of the menu by one step
ALT E U	**Edit Undo** removes the effect of the last command
ALT-BACKSPACE	Undoes last menu command

6

Changing the
Appearance of
Worksheet Cells

Up to this point, you have accepted 1-2-3's choices for how to present your entries. You have used the package's *default* for the format in which the data is displayed. It is great to have this default available; it lets you build a model that produces completely accurate results without worrying about how your entries appear. But it is also great to know that 1-2-3 provides a set of powerful formatting commands that lets you change the appearance of your entries. These are commands that let you select how the characters appear and whether 1-2-3 adds numeric formatting such as currency symbols to values. Other 1-2-3 commands change the alignment of labels, either before or after you enter them. You will find that each of these 1-2-3 commands is easy to use and provides significant improvements in the appearance of your worksheet models. You will be able to use the new menu selection and dialog box skills that you learned in Chapter 5, "Getting Familiar with Menus and Dialog Boxes," to make your selections.

Using a Range of Cells

Everything you have accomplished with 1-2-3 so far has focused on individual cells. However, 1-2-3 also allows you to work with any contiguous rectangle of cells, called a *range,* to accomplish tasks. Chapter 4, "@Functions and Other Formula Options," introduced ranges when you used them in formulas that use more than one cell. Figure 6-1 shows groups of cells that are valid ranges, as well as some groups that are not. The groups on the left are invalid ranges because they do not contain contiguous cells that form rectangles. The cell groups on the right are valid ranges because each one forms a contiguous group. As long as this rule is met, the range can be as large as you wish or as small as one cell.

You can use several methods to specify cell ranges. You can type them in like a cell address or highlight them with the cell pointer. Ranges are specified by any two diagonally opposite corners separated by one or more periods. For example, the worksheet cells in rows 11 through 15 of columns E, F, G, and H can be specified as E11..H15, E15.H11, H15..E11, and H11.E15.

The most common way to specify a range is to use the upper-left cell first and the lower-right cell last, as in E11..H15. Also, since 1-2-3 supplies

Figure 6-1.   *Invalid and valid ranges*

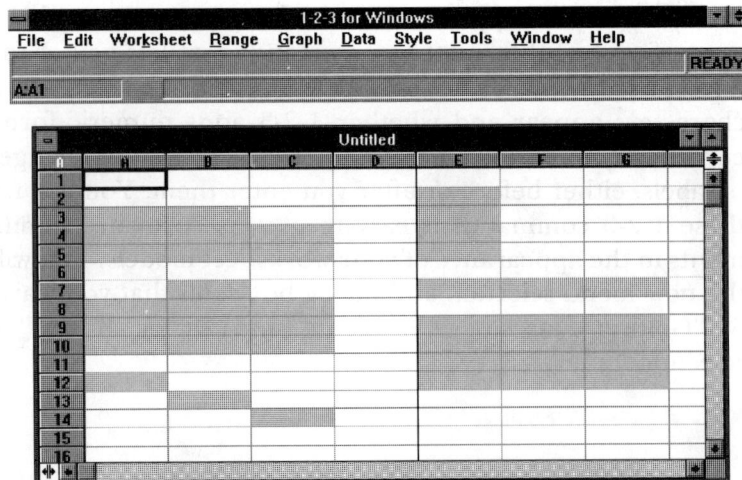

a second period, you can save yourself a keystroke by just typing **E11.H15**. If you plan to specify a range by moving the cell pointer, you can save yourself time by moving the cell pointer to one of the corners of the range to select. If you are selecting a range from within a command rather than from READY mode, positioning on a location other than a corner will require extra work since you will need to change the range to a single cell address, move the cell pointer, and respecify.

You can select a range for a command before you select the command or after you select the command. To select a range when starting from READY mode, press F4 (Abs). 1-2-3 changes from READY to POINT mode. This is the POINT mode you saw in Chapter 3, "Defining Your Calculations," when you pointed to a cell to include the cell reference in a formula.

To try selecting a range from READY mode, follow these steps:

1. Move to B3.
2. Press F4 (Abs).
3. Press the arrow keys until B3..E5 is highlighted.
4. Press ENTER to return to READY mode.

This range remains selected so you can activate the menu and select a command to use on this range. You can also select a range by holding down SHIFT as you select a range. For example, to select the range B3..E5, move to B3 and press SHIFT-DOWN ARROW twice and SHIFT-RIGHT ARROW three times. When you release the SHIFT key, 1-2-3 returns to READY mode with the range still selected.

You can also select a range with a mouse by clicking the cell to use as one corner of the range and dragging the mouse to the opposite corner of the range. As a reminder, dragging a mouse means holding down the left mouse button as you move the mouse. When you select a range with a mouse, you do not have to press F4 (Abs). To use the mouse to select the range B3..E5, click B3 and then drag the mouse to E5. You will want to preselect ranges as you learn how to use the icon palette with the mouse, as described later in this chapter under, "Adding Font Attributes."

When you select a range from READY mode, the range remains selected until you select another range or until you either press ESC or click a cell. When you select a command, 1-2-3 automatically uses the range you have selected. The range remains selected after you use the command.

6

In the section titled "Changing Label Entry Alignment," later in this chapter, you will see an example of a range that is selected after the command is invoked. You will specify the correct range through the **R**ange option in the dialog box.

Changing Label Appearances

In Chapter 2, "Entering Labels and Numbers," you learned how to enter labels. 1-2-3 has several commands that change how labels appear on the worksheet. You can change the alignment of existing cells without editing the cells individually. You can also change the appearance of the characters. This adds word processing character formatting to your 1-2-3 worksheet. You can also add borders and shading.

Changing Label Entry Alignment

You already learned one method for changing the label alignment in Chapter 1 when you entered labels by starting them with label prefixes. This method works, but if you have a large number of labels to enter, it is time consuming. It also requires you to edit the entries to replace the label prefixes if you want to change their alignment. Fortunately, 1-2-3 has several alternatives that can be real time savers. One option changes the alignment of labels that are currently on the worksheet; the other changes the default label prefix for the current worksheet so that any new labels you enter will use the new alignment setting.

Changing Previously Entered Labels

1-2-3 has two methods for altering the label alignment already recorded on the worksheet. You can use EDIT mode to alter the label prefix character, or you can use the **St**yle **A**lignment command. In Chapter 2 you learned how you can change the label alignment by using EDIT mode. The **St**yle **A**lignment command requires less work; the alignment of many cells can be changed with a single command. Not only that, but you can align cells across columns. When you select this command, you can then select from **L**eft, **R**ight, and **C**enter. The Align **O**ver Columns check box selects whether the text this command aligns spans several cells and offers an additional option, **Even,** which adds space between words. Look at the effect of altering labels by using the **S**tyle **A**lignment command with this example:

1. Type **'1991 Division Sales - Widgets** in A1.

2. Move your cell pointer to B3, type **Jan,** and move to C3.

3. Type **Feb** and move to D3.

4. Type **Mar** and move to E3.

5. Continue making these entries until you have entered **Jun** in G3 and your entries look like this:

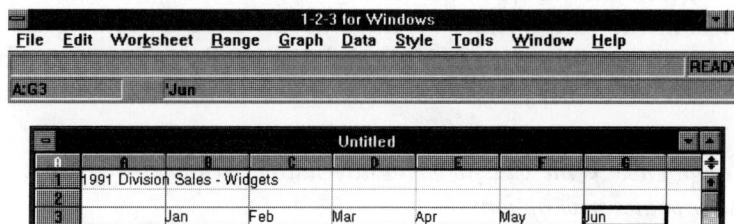

			1-2-3 for Windows				
File	**Edit**	**Worksheet**	**Range**	**Graph**	**Data**	**Style** **Tools** **Window** **Help**	**READY**

A:G3		'Jun					

			Untitled				
A	A	B	C	D	E	F	G
1	1991 Division Sales - Widgets						
2							
3		Jan	Feb	Mar	Apr	May	Jun

The labels are currently left aligned with the default setting.

6. Select **S**tyle **A**lignment, and then select the **C**enter option button.

7. Press ALT-A to select the range or use your mouse to click it. (If you wanted to accept the current range without change, you would press ENTER.)

8. Type a new range, **B3.G3,** and use the arrow keys to expand the existing range, or use the mouse to drag across the range B3..G3. If you choose to select the range with your mouse, you need to move the dialog box to allow you to select one corner of the range that you want to affect. You can use your mouse to drag the dialog box to another location.

9. Select the OK command button.

Each of the entries in row 3 is now centered in its cell. Subsequent entries in these cells will not be affected since **Style Alignment** affects only existing cell entries.

10. Move the cell pointer to A1.

11. Select **Style Alignment**, the **C**enter option button, the Align **O**ver Columns check box, the range A1..G1 in the **R**ange text box, and the OK command button.

The entry is centered in the range A1..G1 because you selected the Align **O**ver Columns check box. The entry is stored in A1 although it displays in the range A1..G1.

The **Style Alignment** command changes only the alignment of labels that are in the range at the time you use the command. If you later enter labels in the range that you have used with a **Style Alignment** command, the new label will use the default label prefix rather than the label prefix you selected with the **Style Alignment** command.

≡classic≡ */Range Label is the Classic menu alternative for Style Alignment. Style Alignment also provides new options.*

1-2-3 has three SmartIcons that you can use to change the alignment of a preselected range: Align Left, Align Center, and Align Right. These three SmartIcons look like this:

Changing Alignment Globally Before Making Entries
If you change the default label alignment, any new labels you enter will use this setting. Existing labels are not affected. This option is especially

useful when you wish to enter a series of labels with a different alignment. You can alter the default alignment without converting the data already on the worksheet, make your entries, and then change the alignment back to its original setting. To try this feature, follow these steps:

1. Select Worksheet **G**lobal Settings and the **R**ight option button under Align Labels, and select the OK command button.

2. Move the cell pointer to A4 and type **Div. A**. Then move to A5.

3. Type **Div. B** and move to A6.

4. Type **Div. C** and press ENTER or click the confirm box so your entries are right aligned, as shown here:

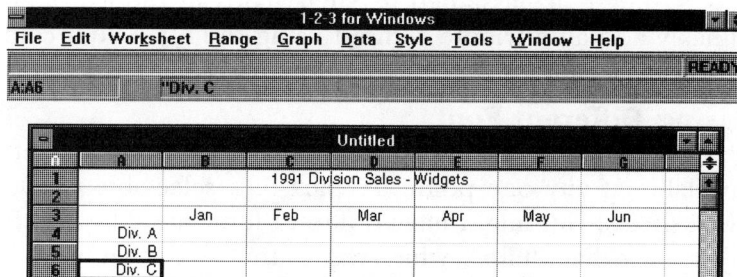

Each entry is now preceded by ", automatically generated by 1-2-3 since you have changed the default label alignment for the worksheet to right alignment.

5. Select **F**ile **C**lose and select **N**o when 1-2-3 asks if you want to save the file.

classic */Worksheet Global Label is the equivalent option in the Classic menu.*

Changing Worksheet Fonts

A font is the typeface and size of the characters 1-2-3 uses to display and print your data. So far you have seen only one font, but you can use multiple fonts to enhance your data's appearance. 1-2-3 provides several fonts, Windows provides others, and your printer can provide even more. Each worksheet can use up to eight different fonts.

The term *typeface* refers to the style of print characters. Before a typeface style is available for font replacement in 1-2-3, it must be installed for Windows. The fonts available through 1-2-3 are automatically installed when you install the product. Your printer's default fonts are installed when you select your printer during the Windows installation or setup.

The *size* of the characters is another important component of a font. Size is measured in points. A point is 1/72 of an inch. Normally, you use 10- or 12-point fonts for regular entries, 18- or 24-point fonts for headings, and 6- or 8-point fonts for fine print.

1-2-3 also lets you add font *attributes* like boldface, underlining, and italics. These are assigned to SmartIcons in the icon palette so you can quickly add an attribute without using the **Style Font** command.

Using Different Fonts

You can use as many as eight fonts in a worksheet file. The fonts available at any one point are part of a selectable *font set*. For different worksheets, you might have different font sets. The first font in any set is always the default font, which means that all entries use it unless you select a different font with the **Style Font** command. Figure 6-2 shows the default font set. Notice that the last font changes the characters into special symbols as well as changing the style.

To look at using different fonts in a worksheet, complete the entries shown in Figure 6-3. Follow these directions:

1. Move the cell pointer to C2, type **ABC Company**, and move the cell pointer to C3.

2. Type **Sales Projections** and move the cell pointer to A6.

3. Complete the following entries.

A6:	**Unit Price**	C6:	**4.75**
A7:	**Unit Sales**	C7:	**+B7*(1+C10)**
A8:	**Sales**	C8:	**+C6*C7**
A10:	**Percent Growth**	C10:	**.12**
B5:	**^1992**	D5:	**^1994**
B6:	**5**	D6:	**4.8**
B7:	**60000**	D7:	**+C7*(1+C10)**
B8:	**+B6*B7**	D8:	**+D6*D7**
C5:	**^1993**		

4. Move the cell pointer to C2 and select the range C2..C3.

5. Select **S**tyle **F**ont to change the font of the range.

The dialog box lets you select from the eight fonts that are selected for the worksheet as well as from the **B**old, **U**nderline, and **I**talics attribute check boxes.

6. Select Arial MT 14 point from the **F**onts list box and the OK command button so the entries now look like the ones in Figure 6-4.

6

Figure 6-2. *Default font set for worksheets*

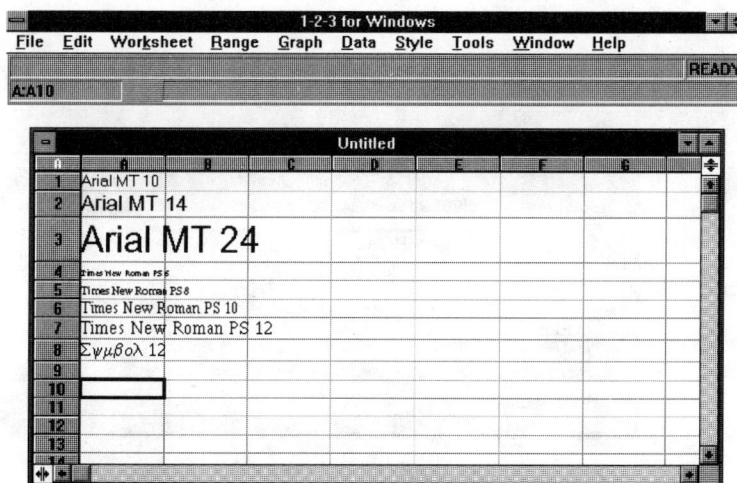

Figure 6-3. *Worksheet for demonstrating font features*

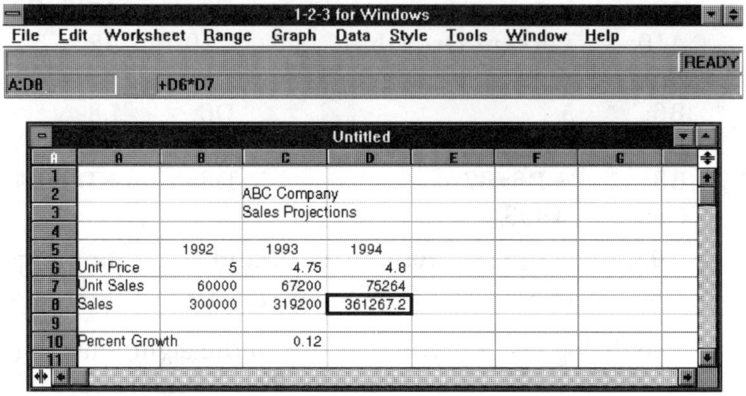

1-2-3 displays a font description in the format line since the current cell is not using the default font.

Figure 6-4. *Worksheet showing a font change*

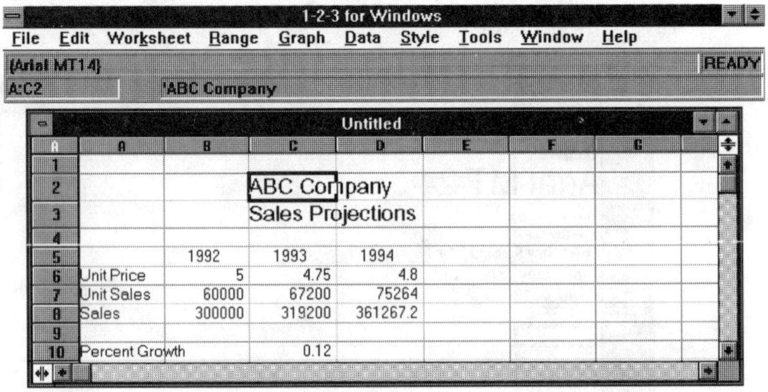

When you format part of a worksheet to use a different font, your entries may be wider or narrower than the column's width. In Chapter 7, "Changing Row and Column Options," you will learn how you can change the column's width so it will fit the wider or narrower entries. 1-2-3 automatically adjusts a row's height to match the tallest character in the row.

Changing the Font Set

Your font set is created from eight of the fonts that 1-2-3 for Windows provides. You can also replace any of these eight fonts with an installed font. Your font set may also include soft fonts and printer cartridges.

1-2-3 bases the column width on the default font, which means that a column nine characters wide that can fit the number 12345678 will adjust to fit the number regardless of the default font style and size chosen. With number entries, one less digit than the column width is shown to allow a blank space between two columns of numbers.

To replace an existing font, follow these steps:

1. Select **S**tyle **F**ont and the **R**eplace command button.

1-2-3 displays the Style Font Replace dialog box.

2. Select the font you want to replace from the **C**urrent Fonts list box.

3. Select the font style you want to use as the replacement from the **A**vailable Fonts text and list box.

For dialog box options that combine a text box with a list box, you can either type your selection in the text box or select the option from the list box below. As you type an entry in the text box, 1-2-3 highlights the option in the text box that matches your selection.

4. Select the font size for the replacement font from the **S**ize text box or list box.

5. Select the **R**eplace command button to make the font replacement.

6. Repeat steps 2 through 5 until all the fonts you want to replace are changed.

6

7. Select the OK command button twice to return to READY mode.

You can always return to the default font set by selecting the Restore command button from the Style Font Replace dialog box.

Adding Font Attributes

In addition to changing fonts, you can alter the appearance of cell entries in other ways. You can boldface, italicize, and underline text. You can underline text with single, double, or wide underlining. These font attributes are added with the **Style Font** command, but you can also add them by using icons in the icon palette. To see how you can add these attributes, follow these steps:

1. Select the range B5..D5.

2. Select **Style Font**.

Notice that the **Bold, Italics,** and **Underline** check boxes are gray, or shaded. This indicates that 1-2-3 will not change any attributes added to the currently selected range unless you mark or unmark the check box. For example, you might want to change the **B**old attribute for a range but want to leave the **Underline** and **Italics** attributes unchanged. The shaded check box will leave these settings unchanged.

3. Select the **B**old check box.

When you select a check box, 1-2-3 cycles through the three possibilities. The box will be gray or shaded to indicate that the attribute will not change, contain an X to indicate that all cells in the selected range will have the attribute, or blank to indicate that none of the cells in the selected range will have the attribute.

4. Select the OK command button.

5. Select the range B8..D8.

6. Select **St**yle **F**ont and the **U**nderline check box.

For underlining cell contents, you have the option of using single underlining, double underlining, or wide lines.

7. Click the down arrow icon and select the last option in the drop-down box or press the DOWN ARROW key twice.

8. Select the OK command button.

The font attributes are also available through the icon palette. The **B**, *I*, and U represent these three attributes. To use these SmartIcons, select the range that will use the attribute and then use the mouse to select the attribute by clicking the **B**, *I*, or U in the icon palette.

9. Move the cell pointer to C2.

10. Click the **B** SmartIcon or select **Style Font**, the **B**old check box, and the OK command button so your entries look like the ones in Figure 6-5.

The attribute applies to the entire entry even though part of it displays in other cells.

When you want to remove one of the text attributes, you must use the **Style Font** command and unmark the check box for the attribute you want to remove. You cannot use the icon palette to remove attributes.

6

Figure 6-5. *Worksheet after changing fonts and adding attributes*

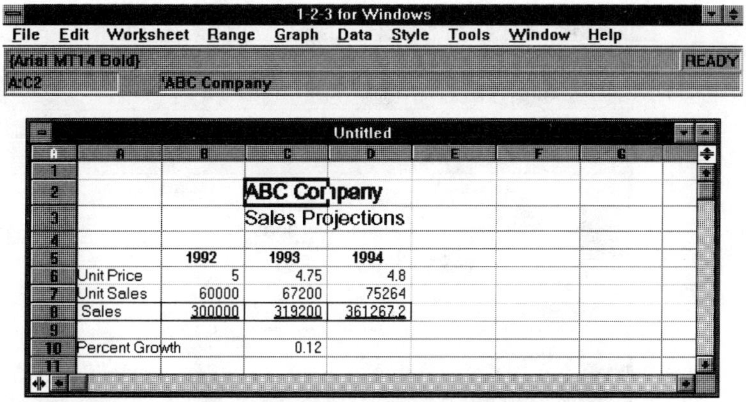

Adding Borders

You can add borders on any side of a cell or range of cells. If you use the outline feature, you can completely outline all the walls of each cell in a range. For example, you can add a border around the entries in A8..D8 by following these directions:

1. Select the range A8..D8.
2. Select **Style Border**.

The Style Border dialog box selects where the borders are added and the line style the border uses. The check boxes select the side of the range where you are adding the borders. If you select **O**utline, you will add borders around each cell in the range. As with underlining, you can also use the drop-down boxes next to the check boxes to determine if the line used as a border is a single line, a double line, or a wide line.

3. Select the All **E**dges check box and the OK command button to add a border around the selected range like that shown in Figure 6-6.

Figure 6-6.   *Outline added to worksheet range*

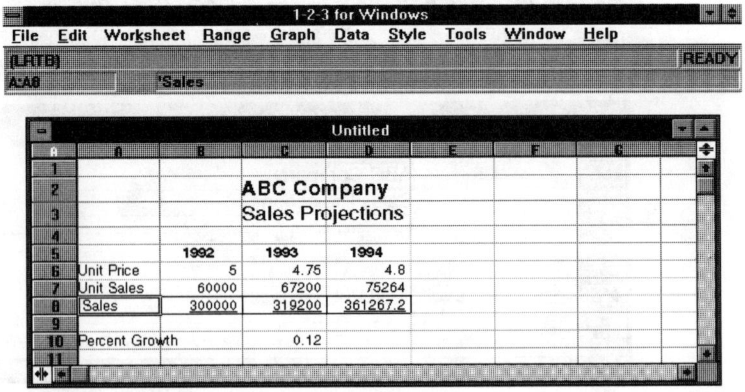

You can remove the borders by using the **Style Border** command again and unmarking the check boxes for the borders you want to remove.

Adding Shading

1-2-3 has three levels of shading that you can add to worksheet cells. The **Style Shading** command adds light, dark, and solid shading. To use light shading on numbers in the 1994 column, follow these steps:

1. Select the range D5..D8.
2. Select **Style Shading**, the **Light** option button, and the **OK** command button to add shading as shown in Figure 6-7.

Unlike other style enhancements, shading applies to the cell rather than the entry in it. This means that the entire cell is shaded even for short entries and that the cells used for displaying *long labels* (labels wider than the cell width) are shaded only if they are included in the range for the **Style Shading** command.

Figure 6-7. *Range formatted with light shading*

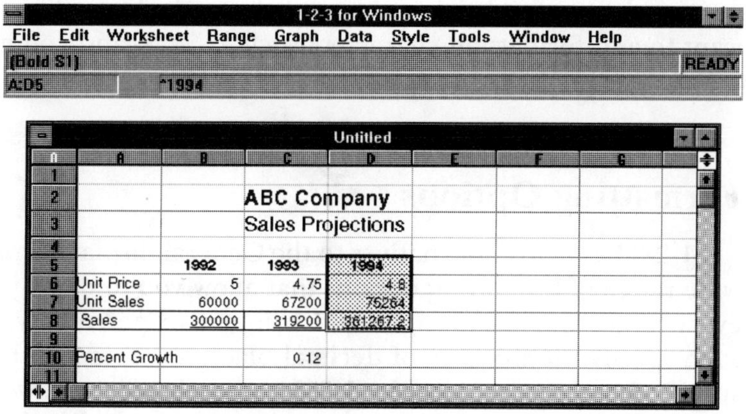

Changing the Display Format

The default format that 1-2-3 uses for all value entries is called the *General* format. This format does not provide consistent formats for all entries. The display it provides is affected by the size of the number and the number of digits after the decimal point. Some numbers display as they are entered, while others have leading zeros added or are rounded to the number of decimal digits that will fit in the cell width. Since 1-2-3 uses the number as it is stored in the cell rather than as the number appears, changing the format does not affect the results of calculations. The general format also suppresses trailing zeros after the decimal point so a column of numbers may have varying numbers of digits after the decimal point. Very large and very small numbers are displayed in scientific notation as described in Chapter 2, "Entering Labels and Numbers." If 100550000 is entered in a cell with the General format in effect, 1-2-3 uses scientific notation to display it as $1.0E+8$.

The General format handles a wide variety of formats, but it often results in a display whose results have varying numbers of decimal places. These inconsistencies make this format less than desirable for many business models. However, this inconsistency does not mean that the General format is useless; it is ideal in many situations. The General format is useful when you want to minimize the space used to display very large or very small numbers. Scientific notation ensures that these numbers will be shown in a minimum of space. It simply is not the display to use when you need to control the number of decimal places shown or when you want to add formatting characters such as %, $, and commas.

Formatting Options

1-2-3 has many alternatives to the General display format, providing a wide range of formatting options that allow you to display your data with everything from dollar signs and commas to percent symbols. You can even specify the number of decimal places for some of the formats. The specific formats supported by 1-2-3 and their effect on worksheet entries are shown in Table 6-1. The examples under Display show two decimal places selected, where appropriate.

Table 6-1. *1-2-3's Format Options*

Format	Cell Entry	Display
Fixed	5678	5678.00
	−123.45	−123.45
Scientific	5678	5.68E+03
	−123.45	−1.23E+02
Currency	5678	$5,678.00
	−123.45	($123.45)
, Comma	5678	5,678.00
	−123.45	(123.45)
General	5678	5678
	−123.45	−123.45
+/−	4	++++
	3	− − −
	0	
Percent	5	500.00%
	.1	10.00%
Text	+A2*A3	+A2*A3
Hidden	35000	
Label	+A2*A3	'+A2*A3
Date (5 formats)	31679	24-Sep-86 (1)
Time (4 formats)	.5	12:00:00 PM (6)

6

Scope of the Formatting Change

You can choose how extensive an impact you want a particular format command to have by formatting the entire worksheet or a range of cells in the worksheet. First you will examine the procedure for changing the format for a range of the worksheet.

Changing the Format for a Range of Cells

When you want to change how values in a range of worksheet cells appear, you can assign one of 1-2-3's formats to the range. Changing the format of a range affects only the appearance of the values that are part of the range.

classic */Range Format is the identical command in the Classic menu.*

You can try some of these formatting changes using the model you created earlier in the chapter. To try some of the formats you can apply to a range, follow these steps:

1. Move to B6 and select the range B6..D6.
2. Select **R**ange **F**ormat.

The **F**ormat list box lists the different formatting options you can select.

3. Select Fixed from the **F**ormat list box.

Several of the format options, such as Fixed, let you select the number of digits that are displayed after the decimal point. The default for these formats is 2, but you can enter a number between 0 and 15 in the **D**ecimal Places text box.

4. Select the OK command button so each of the values in B6..D6 appears with two digits after the decimal point.

Notice that the format line now contains (F2). The information in parentheses indicates the format assigned to the cell with a **R**ange **F**ormat command. Table 6-2 presents examples of some of the commonly used format abbreviations. For formats that allow you to specify the number of decimal places, like Fixed in this example, a numeric digit follows.

Table 6-2.   *Examples of Format Abbreviations*

Abbreviation	Format in Effect
(F6)	Fixed with six decimal places
(P2)	Percent with two decimal places
(T)	Text, to display formulas as they are entered
(G)	General
(C0)	Currency with zero decimal places
(,2)	Comma with two decimal places
(D1)	Date format 1
(D6)	Time format 1
(H)	Hidden format
(A)	Automatic format

If you have a mouse, you can use the three formatting SmartIcons in the icon palette to quickly format a selected range. The 0,0 SmartIcon formats cells with the comma format, the $ formats cells with the currency format, and the % formats cells with the percent format. All three of these formats format with zero digits after the decimal point. You can try these icons with the mouse or use their equivalent menu commands.

5. Select the range B8..D8.

6. Click the $ SmartIcon. You can also select **R**ange Format, select Currency from the **F**ormat list box, type **0** in the **D**ecimal Places text box, and select the OK command button.

7. Move the cell pointer to C10.

8. Click the % SmartIcon. You can also select **R**ange Format, select Percent from the **F**ormat list box, type **0** in the **D**ecimal Places text box, and select the OK command button.

Sometimes when you format a range, the display of the value changes to asterisks while the value still appears in the contents box. This is how 1-2-3 tells you that the column is not wide enough to display the value using the format you have selected. When this happens, you have two choices—you can either select a different format that takes less space or widen the column, as you will learn how to do in Chapter 7, "Changing Row and Column Options."

6

Making a Global Format Change

When you wish to alter the format of the entire worksheet or even most of it, a global format change is the ideal solution. A global format change alters the default format for every cell on the current worksheet, including both cells with entries and cells that are currently empty. The only cells that do not use the global format are the cells that you have formatted with **R**ange Format commands. For an empty cell, this global format is used as soon as you place a value entry in the cell. Global formatting is especially useful when most of the worksheet is formatted with the same option. You can choose a global format that meets the requirement for most of the cells and then go back and format the exceptions with a **R**ange Format command.

classic /Worksheet Global Format is the command used in earlier releases.

To alter the global format for the model, follow these steps:

1. Select Worksheet **G**lobal Settings.

2. Select the **F**ormat command button.

3. Select , Comma from the **F**ormat list box.

4. Type **0** in the **D**ecimal Places text box to specify zero decimal places, and select the OK command button twice so your final worksheet looks like the one in Figure 6-8. Since B6..D6 was formatted as a range, it will be unaffected.

5. Select File Save **A**s, type **ABC_SALE** in the File **N**ame text box, and select the OK command button to save this worksheet.

6. Select **F**ile **C**lose to close this worksheet.

Figure 6-8. *Worksheet with range and new global formats*

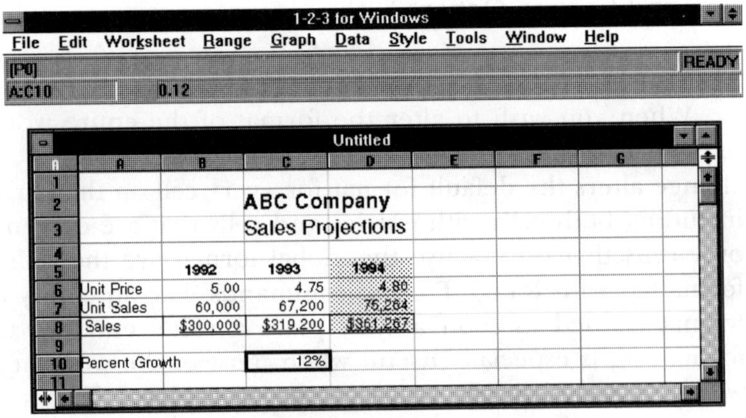

Automatically Formatting a Worksheet

1-2-3 has an *Automatic format,* which converts a number that you enter with numeric formatting characters into one of 1-2-3's numeric formats. For example, if you enter $5,432.09 in a cell with an automatic format, 1-2-3 changes the cell's format to currency with two digits after the decimal point and stores 5432.09 in the cell. When the Automatic format is selected, it remains with the cell until you enter something that 1-2-3 formats. After you make an entry that uses the automatic formatting and 1-2-3 uses one of the other acceptable formats for the cell, the cell's assigned format changes to the one it used when you made the entry. To try this formatting option, follow these steps:

1. Select **R**ange **F**ormat, select Automatic in the **F**ormat list box, select the range C1..C8 in the **R**ange text box, and select the OK command button.

2. Make the following entries so the resulting worksheet looks like the one in Figure 6-9.

6

Figure 6-9. *Automatic format for values*

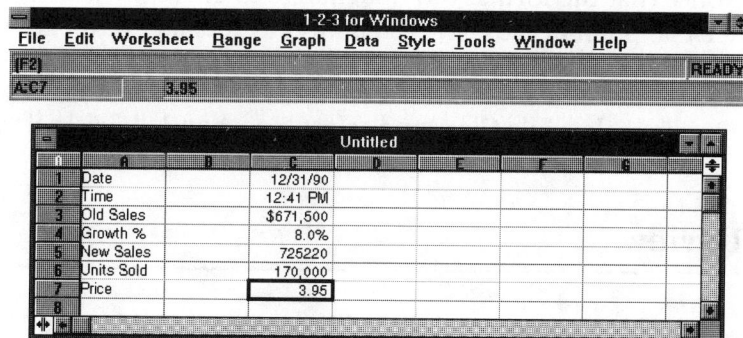

A1:	Date	C1:	12/31/90
A2:	Time	C2:	12:41 PM
A3:	Old Sales	C3:	$671,500
A4:	Growth %	C4:	8.0%
A5:	New Sales	C5:	+C3*(1+C4)
A6:	Units Sold	C6:	170,000
A7:	Price	C7:	3.95

3. Move the cell pointer to each of the entries in C1..C7 and notice how each cell is formatted.

1-2-3 converted the entries in C1 and C2 into their date and time numbers. When you move to cells in column C, you can see that the format description has changed from (A) for Automatic format to the format description that is appropriate for the entry you have made. For each of the cells, 1-2-3 used your entry to determine the format you want to use. 1-2-3 performed a **R**ange **F**ormat command on each cell in which you made an entry. Once 1-2-3 selects a format for a cell, the format does not change unless you execute another **R**ange **F**ormat command. The only cells that retained the Automatic format are C5 and C8. Cell C5 retained the Automatic format because the formula does not provide the formatting information 1-2-3 needs to assign a format to the cell. Cell C8 retained the Automatic format because it is empty.

4. Type **$60.3** in C7 and press ENTER or click the confirm box.

Notice that the format did not change to currency with one digit after the decimal point because the cell is already formatted to Fixed with two digits after the decimal point.

5. Select **F**ile **C**lose and select **N**o when 1-2-3 asks if you want to save the file.

Review

In this chapter you learned how you can add spreadsheet publishing features to your worksheets by specifying fonts and adding boldface, shading, and lines. You also learned how you can set 1-2-3 to add formatting characters to numbers to give a consistent appearance.

- Many of the 1-2-3 commands can operate on ranges, which are contiguous cells that form a rectangle. You can select the range a command uses before you select the command by pressing F4 (Abs) and selecting the range, pressing SHIFT as you select a range, or by dragging the mouse over the range you want. If you preselect a range, 1-2-3 uses the range for any commands you select while this range is still selected. You can also select a range when the command's dialog box displays. To use the icon palette with a range, you must select the range before selecting the icon.

- 1-2-3 includes several commands that change the appearance of the characters on the worksheet. These include **S**tyle **F**ont to change the font used as well as adding attributes like boldface, underlining, and italics. You can also add lines around cells with the **S**tyle **B**order command and shading with the **S**tyle **S**hading command.

- Use Worksheet **G**lobal Settings **L**abel Prefix to change the alignment for entries you are about to make. Use the **S**tyle **A**lignment command to alter the alignment of existing label entries.

- You can format numeric entries to match your needs. The **R**ange Format command formats a contiguous group of cells. The Format setting in the Worksheet Global Settings dialog box sets the default format and formats any numeric entry not formatted with a **R**ange Format command. Formats added with the **R**ange Format command are shown in the format line.

- The icon palette provides shortcuts to some of the most frequently used commands. Some of the SmartIcons you have learned about in this chapter are for the Comma format with 0 decimal places (0,0), the Currency format with 0 decimal places ($), the Percent format with 0 decimal places (%), Bold (**B**), Italics (*I*), and Underline (U). To use an icon, select the range before you select the icon.

Commands and Keys

The commands you learned in this chapter add formatting to a worksheet. You also learned how you can select the range to use before you format it. The commands and keys are

Keys	Action
ALT R F	**Range Format** applies a consistent format to mostly numeric entries
ALT S A	**Style Alignment** changes the label alignment of existing worksheet label entries
ALT S B	**Style Border** adds lines around a range or individual cells
ALT S F	**Style Font** sets the fonts and font attributes for cells
ALT S S	**Style Shading** adds light, dark, solid, and no shading to cells
ALT K G	**Worksheet Global** Settings changes the global settings of the worksheet such as the default label alignment and numeric format

7

Changing Row and Column Options

In Chapter 6, "Changing the Appearance of Worksheet Cells," you examined some of the changes you can make to the appearance of individual entries in cells. There are also several commands that allow you to make changes to one or more columns or rows at a time. 1-2-3 provides options that let you determine the width you wish to use for one or more columns. You can also hide or display columns on your worksheet, and you can insert or delete columns and rows.

Altering Column Widths

When you begin a new 1-2-3 worksheet, the default width of columns is nine characters. This is adequate for values displayed with the General format; often, however, it is not wide enough when you want to display formatted numbers or long labels. At other times, the opposite might be true. Even though you might have a column that never contains more than one character, the full width of nine characters is always reserved for the column. If you make some columns narrower, you can view more columns in the window. 1-2-3 lets you make a column wider or narrower. In fact, 1-2-3 even lets you choose whether to change the width of all the columns at once or to alter a range of columns.

Changing the Width of One or More Columns

The ability to alter the width of individual columns lets you tailor your display to meet your exact needs. This is the preferred approach when you have only a few columns to change. Any change you make for a single column will take precedence over the global column width. Follow these steps for making changes to some of the worksheet columns:

1. Select File **O**pen, type **ABC_SALE** in the File **N**ame text box, and select the OK command button.

This is the file that you created in Chapter 6, "Changing the Appearance of Worksheet Cells." If you did not complete the model entries, you can use the data in Figure 7-1 to complete the entries.

2. Select the range B8..D8.

To change the width of one or more columns, the range you select before or during the command must contain at least one cell from each column to change. Any range that contains cells from columns B, C, and D would work just as well.

3. Select Worksheet **C**olumn Width and the **S**et Width To option button.

You can type the new column width in the **S**et Width To text box to tell 1-2-3 how wide you want the selected columns.

4. Type **12** in the **S**et Width To text box.

5. Select the OK command button.

Figure 7-1. *Worksheet before widening columns*

The change is made to all of the selected columns. Since the width for these columns is different from the default for the worksheet, 1-2-3 displays the column width in brackets, as in [W12], in the format line.

6. Select **File Close** and **No** when 1-2-3 prompts for saving the files to close the worksheet window without saving your changes.

With a mouse, you can also change column widths using the worksheet border by following these directions:

1. Move the mouse to the line separating column A from column B in the worksheet border so the mouse looks like this:

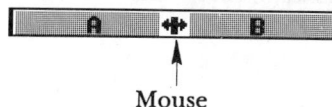

Mouse

2. Drag the mouse to the right so the temporary line 1-2-3 draws to indicate the column's new border is on top of the B, and release the mouse when the column is the desired width.

You do not see the number of characters the column is set to, but you can see where the column's boundaries will be.

3. Select **File Close** and **No** when 1-2-3 prompts for saving the files to close the worksheet window without saving your changes.

classic */Worksheet Column Set-Width and /Worksheet Column-Range are the Classic menu options used to change the width of one or more columns.*

Changing the Width of All the Columns

For certain models, all or most of the column widths need to be altered. One possibility for doing this is using the Worksheet **C**olumn Width command, but this command covers only the range you define, whereas the global option changes the entire worksheet. If you have a model like the one shown next, where most of the columns should be narrower, the Worksheet **G**lobal Settings Column **W**idth option is the method of choice:

When you change the global column width, column widths set with **W**orksheet **C**olumn Width or set by dragging the mouse on the worksheet border are not affected. The following entries alter the worksheet in Figure 7-2 so all the months can be viewed. You can record the entries yourself in a new worksheet. Follow these steps to make the global column width change.

1. Select Worksheet **G**lobal Settings, type **5** in the Column **W**idth text box, and select the OK command button.

Now all of the worksheet columns are five characters wide. The only problem with this display is that column A has also become smaller and does not display the region numbers. To fix this problem, do the following:

2. Move the cell pointer to column A.

3. Select Worksheet **C**olumn Width, select the **S**et Width To option button, type **7** in the **S**et Width To text box, and select the OK command button.

This change to an individual column width fixes the problem and produces the result shown here:

Unlike when you change the width of a range of columns, 1-2-3 does not display the global column width in the format line.

classic /Worksheet Global Col-Width *is used in the Classic menu for changing the width of all columns with one command.*

Inserting and Deleting Rows and Columns

No matter how thoroughly you plan your worksheet applications, sometimes you need to make substantial changes to a worksheet model. You might need to add an employee to a model, delete accounts that are no longer used, or add some blank space to make the worksheet more readable. 1-2-3 accommodates each of these needs by means of commands that let you insert or delete blank rows or columns in the worksheet.

Inserting Rows and Columns

You can insert blank columns and rows at any location you choose in the worksheet. When you add columns or rows to the worksheet, they are placed at the cell pointer's location. When 1-2-3 inserts rows into a worksheet, the cell addresses of the data below this location are changed. It is as though 1-2-3 pushes the data down on the worksheet to make room for the new blank rows. 1-2-3 automatically adjusts all the formulas that reference this shifted data. The same is true for data stored in cells to the right of the location at which columns are inserted.

You invoke the insert command by selecting Worksheet **I**nsert and selecting the **C**olumn or **R**ow option button. 1-2-3 does not prompt you with a straightforward question such as, "How many would you like to add?" Instead, 1-2-3 asks for the range where you want the insertion. The first column or row in this range is where the new columns or rows are inserted. The number of columns or rows in this range selects the number of columns or rows inserted. You can select this range before activating the menu or while the dialog box is on the screen. If you specify a range that includes three columns or rows, three columns or rows are inserted. If you specify a cell, only one column or row is inserted. Seeing this in action will clarify the way it works.

classic ≡ */Worksheet Insert is the Classic menu selection for inserting rows and columns in the current sheet.*

Let's add a column and a few blank rows to the ABC Company sales projections. Follow these steps to complete the changes:

1. Select File **O**pen, type **ABC_SALE** in the File **N**ame text box, and select the OK command button.

2. Move the cell pointer to C7.

Notice that the formula in C7, which projects the next year's sales, is $+B7*(1+C10)$. Be sure to look at this formula again after inserting a column and notice how 1-2-3 has adjusted it for you.

3. Move the cell pointer to any cell in column A.

4. Select Worksheet **I**nsert, the **C**olumn option button, and the OK command button to insert a single column.

5. Move the cell pointer to D7. Your worksheet should look like that shown in Figure 7-2.

Notice how 1-2-3 adjusted the worksheet: the entries that were in B7 and C10 are now in C7 and D10.

6. Select the range D8..D9. (Any range that contains cells from rows 8 and 9 would work just as well.)

Figure 7-2. *New column added for column A*

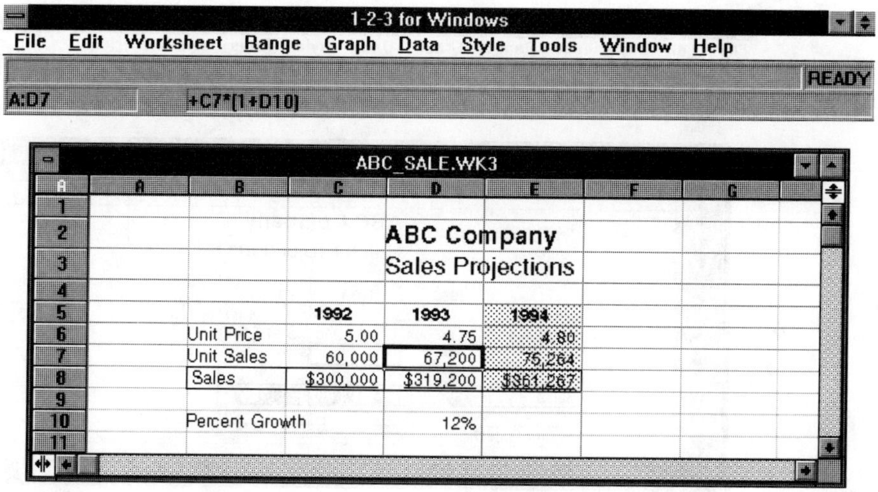

7. Select Worksheet **I**nsert, the **R**ow option button, and the OK command button to insert two rows.

1-2-3 adds two rows, as shown in Figure 7-3.

8. Select File **S**ave.

The File **S**ave command saves the worksheet without changing the name. You do not want to use the command on a worksheet you have not saved before since 1-2-3 will give it a generic name that does not describe the file's data.

Deleting Rows and Columns

You can delete rows and columns at any location in a worksheet. This allows you to eliminate blank rows and columns or rows and columns that contain entries you no longer need.

Figure 7-3.   *Two new rows added*

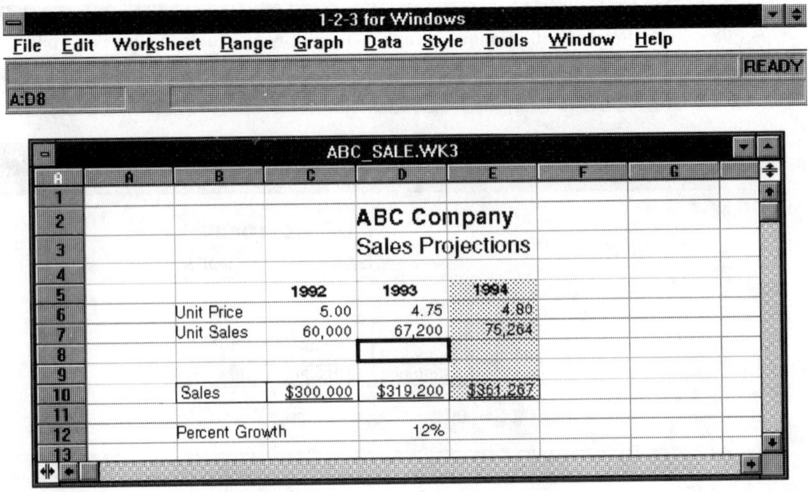

When 1-2-3 deletes rows or columns in a worksheet, the cell addresses of the data below and to the right of the deleted rows or columns are changed. It is as though 1-2-3 pushes the data up on the worksheet to replace the deleted rows or columns. 1-2-3 automatically adjusts all the formulas that reference this data. Cell references in formulas that refer to a cell in the deleted rows change to ERR. When this happens, you must edit the formula to refer to a correct range. If a formula references a range that spans the deleted rows or columns, the range the formula uses shrinks to a smaller size because of the deleted rows or columns.

Just as when you insert columns or rows, you can select a range containing the columns or rows to delete before you select the command or before you select the OK command button in the command's dialog box. You invoke the delete command by selecting Worksheet **D**elete and then selecting the **C**olumn or **R**ow option button. If you specify a range that includes three columns or rows, three columns or rows are deleted. If you specify a cell, only one column or row is deleted.

Seeing this in action will clarify the way it works. Let's remove the blank rows added in the previous section. Follow these steps to complete the changes:

1. Select the range D8..D9 (any range that contains cells from rows 8 and 9 would work just as well).

2. Select Worksheet **D**elete, the **R**ow option button, and the OK command button to delete two rows.

1-2-3 deleted the two rows you just added.

Deleting columns is just as easy. To delete a column, use the Worksheet **D**elete command and select the **C**olumn option button. This deletes the columns in the range you select before selecting the command or in the range you select before choosing the OK command button.

Hiding and Displaying Columns

1-2-3 can temporarily conceal columns from view on the display screen. The data in these columns is not altered in any way and can be displayed again at any time with the entry of another command. This feature is particularly useful if you are working with sensitive information like salary data and do not wish it to be visible, in plain view of anyone who walks by your PC.

classic ═ */Worksheet Column Hide and /Worksheet Column Display are the Classic menu options for hiding and displaying worksheet columns.*

You can hide the entries in column C by following these steps:

1. Move the cell pointer to any cell in column C.

2. Select Worksheet **Hide**, the **C**olumn option button, and the **OK** command button since the **R**ange text box shows the current cell address for the range 1-2-3 will hide.

1-2-3 hides the entries in column C, as shown in Figure 7-4.

3. Move to D7.

Figure 7-4.   *Column C hidden*

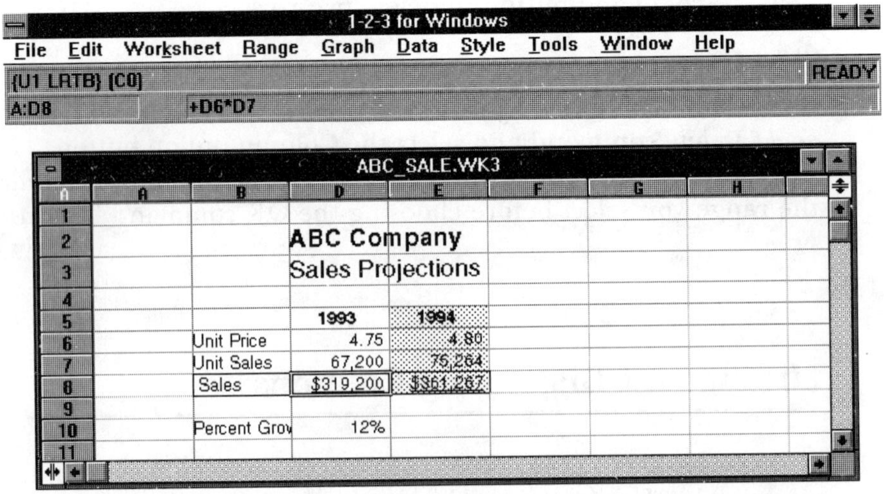

Notice that the formula still uses values in column C. When a column is hidden, it is removed only from the display and not from the worksheet.

4. Press F4 (Abs) to switch from READY to POINT mode.

When 1-2-3 is in POINT mode, hidden columns temporarily appear with an asterisk, as in C*.

To display the hidden column, follow these steps:

1. Press the LEFT ARROW key and ENTER or select a range containing at least one cell from columns B, C, and D.

2. Select Worksheet Unhide, the Column option button, and the OK command button to display the hidden column, C.

As this example shows, you can include columns in the range you select that are not hidden without affecting them.

With a mouse, you can use the worksheet border to hide and display columns. To hide columns, select the columns to hide and then drag the right border of the last column to hide to the left border of the first column to hide. To hide column C in the above example, drag the right side of the column on top of the left side. If you are hiding columns B and C, drag the right side of column C to the left side of column B. To unhide a hidden column with a mouse, drag the right column border for the column to the left of the hidden column to the right.

Erasing Worksheet Data

You have learned how to change worksheet entries and completely replace them with other data. However, you may want to eliminate entries completely; they may be mistakes or old data that is no longer required. Pressing ESC does not eliminate entries once they are finalized.

1-2-3 provides a way to delete unwanted cell entries. It does not even care what types of entries the cells contain; 1-2-3 erases labels, numbers, and formulas with equal ease. The most common way to eliminate data is to erase a range of cells, which eliminates all their contents. A second approach is more extensive and thus more dangerous since it eliminates all the entries on the entire worksheet.

To erase a range of cell entries, select the range you want to erase and select **E**dit **C**lear. This eliminates not only the cell entry but any formatting assigned with **R**ange and **S**tyle commands. You also have another choice. You can select the range to erase and press DEL. If you press DEL without selecting a range, only the current cell and its formatting are deleted.

classic   */Range Erase is the Classic command for eliminating a range of entries.*

To create and then eliminate two entries, do the following:

1. Type **Sales** in the current worksheet in A1.

2. Type **Profits** in B1.

3. Select the range A1..B1.

4. Press DEL or select **E**dit **C**lear.

You can use either of these methods, and the results are the same.

5. Select **F**ile **C**lose and select **N**o when 1-2-3 prompts if you want to save the file.

1-2-3 also offers a special version of the **E**dit **C**lear command: **E**dit **C**lear **S**pecial. The **E**dit **C**lear **S**pecial command lets you select the type of information you remove from cells. When you select **E**dit **C**lear **S**pecial, a dialog box lets you select from check boxes whether the command erases the cell's contents, the number format, the cell's text style, or the graph (introduced in Chapter 11, "Creating Graphs"). When you finish marking or unmarking the check boxes and select the OK command button, 1-2-3 erases only the cell's features that are selected and leaves intact the cell's features that are not selected. You can use this command to erase a cell's entry without erasing its numeric format or style or to remove the numeric format or its style without affecting the cell entry.

Closing the worksheet window to erase worksheet data has a much more destructive capability since it eliminates everything from the work-sheet, assuming you have not saved the worksheet. You close a worksheet window when you have saved a file and are ready to start a new task (in which case you lose no data) or if you have made a complete mess and want to start over. To close a worksheet window, you select **File C**lose, select **C**lose from the window's control menu, or press CTRL-F4. 1-2-3 displays a message about saving the files. You can select **Y**es to save the worksheet in the window and then close it, **N**o to close the window without saving the worksheet, or **C**ancel to leave the worksheet window open.

Review

In this chapter, you learned how you can rearrange your worksheet by adding and deleting columns and rows. You can also set the widths of the columns and indicate which ones to display. The procedures you learned include the following:

- You can change the column width of one or more columns. Use the Worksheet **C**olumn Width command to change the width of columns in a selected range. Use the Column **W**idth setting in the Worksheet Global Setting dialog box to set the width of all columns that you have not changed with the Worksheet **C**olumn Width command. Column widths set with the Worksheet **C**olumn Width command are displayed in the format line.

- You can insert and delete rows and columns with the Worksheet **I**nsert and Worksheet **D**elete commands. When you delete a row or column, you delete the contents of all the cells in the row or column.

- You can hide columns of data and redisplay them with the Worksheet **H**ide and Worksheet **U**nhide commands. Use this feature to hide confidential information on the screen.

- You can erase a group of cells with the **E**dit **C**lear command or by using the DEL key. To erase selected attributes from a range, select the **E**dit Clear Special command. To erase an entire worksheet, select **F**ile **C**lose, select **C**lose from the window's control menu, or press CTRL-F4.

Commands and Keys

This chapter focused on the commands you will use as you build more advanced worksheet models. You have also learned about keys that are shortcuts to commands. These keys and commands are

Keys	Action
CTRL-F4	Closes the worksheet window
DEL	Shortcut for the **Edit Clear** command
ALT E E	**Edit Clear** erases the selected range's contents and its formats
ALT E R	**Edit Clear** Special lets you select whether the selected range's contents, numeric format, style, and/or graph is deleted
ALT K C	Worksheet **Column** Width changes the width of columns in a selected range
ALT K D	Worksheet **Delete** deletes a contiguous group of worksheet rows or columns
ALT K H	Worksheet **Hide** hides columns from display without removing their contents
ALT K G	Worksheet **Global** Settings changes the global settings of the worksheet, such as the default column width
ALT K I	Worksheet **Insert** inserts blank columns and rows at the cell pointer's location
ALT K U	Worksheet **Unhide** displays columns hidden with the Worksheet **Hide** command

8

Managing Files and Sheets

New computer users frequently find the concept of files a little difficult to understand. This is partly because you cannot *see* a file the way you can see entries that you place on the worksheet. But computer files are really quite simple to work with. They are very similar to the files you use every day for storing written documents in your office. The main difference is that computer files are stored on a disk instead of in a drawer.

When you perform tasks without the computer, files and papers are the normal mediums for organizing your information. Often you need several different file folders available at once to accomplish a job. 1-2-3 lets you have several worksheet files open at once so you can access information in the different locations easily. 1-2-3 even makes it easy for you to build formulas that use entries you have stored in other worksheet files.

Just as you usually need more than one sheet of paper for each task or activity, 1-2-3 lets you have multiple sheets in one worksheet file. You can use multiple sheets in a worksheet file to help organize your information. You might store salary information on one sheet and travel expenses on another. Or perhaps you are overseeing several branch operations and want to organize the data for each branch separately. Once you have added the extra sheets, you can access information in all of the sheets as if it were on one sheet by specifying the sheet level as part of the cell's address.

In this chapter, you learn about basic file concepts and explore the basic file commands that 1-2-3 has to offer to store and retrieve your data. Next, you learn about using multiple worksheet files simultaneously in the 1-2-3 window. Finally, you learn about using more than one worksheet in each worksheet file.

File Concepts

Every day, you undoubtedly work with a number of different pieces of paper. Periodically, you probably place some of these papers into file folders in a cabinet or desk drawer to make space for new information on your desktop. Then, when you want to review these papers, you search for them in the cabinet or you ask your secretary to bring you the file folder you wish to see. Assuming that you have an organized filing system, the papers you want will arrive back on your desk.

Your computer uses very similar procedures to maintain its information. Taking a look at the similarities and differences will help you understand the important role that files can play for you.

Storing Information on Disk

When you store information in your computer, you provide the machine with an organizational challenge similar to the one faced by you or your secretary. In the computer's case, the "desktop" is *random access memory,* or *RAM,* the temporary memory of the system; and like your desktop, it has a limited amount of space. How much space is available in memory dictates how much information you can place in memory at any one time. You can use part of this space for applications such as 1-2-3; you can use another part to store the data the applications use.

Just as you use file folders to store papers, your computer uses disk files to store information. The computer's files are maintained on disk rather than in a cabinet. When you build a model in a worksheet, it is stored in the 1-2-3 window—in temporary memory. You generally will want to store a copy of this worksheet in a file on your disk before you exit 1-2-3. This makes it possible for the computer to recall the worksheet another time so you can work on it again.

When working with a computer, you need to save your worksheet; 1-2-3 does not automatically maintain a permanent record of your worksheet. As soon as you close your 1-2-3 window (whether deliberately or accidentally), the worksheet is lost from memory. In order to use this worksheet again, you must already have stored a copy of it in a file on your disk. The disk provides more permanent storage because its contents are not lost when the power is off in your computer. As long as you store the file on disk, you can retrieve a copy of the file from disk and place it in the memory of your computer system again. The screen prompt when you try to exit from 1-2-3 or close a window reminds you to save the changes to your worksheets.

When you work with data in the form of papers stored in your office files and you retrieve those papers so you can work with them again, the file is empty and no longer contains the data. But storing data in computer disk files works differently. Once you store a model on disk, it remains there until you take some special action to remove it from the disk. When you retrieve the model, you are placing a copy in memory, but the original is maintained on the disk. This feature offers a tremendous advantage over paper storage methods: if you accidentally destroy the copy in the computer's memory, you can always retrieve another copy of the model from the disk.

Organizing the Disk Data

When you create file folders for your office, you probably have a system—at least a rudimentary one—for labeling these files. One rule of your system is probably that no two folders should have exactly the same label. If they did, you would have a lot of difficulty finding the papers you need once they were filed. Perhaps your system for labeling file folders is quite organized. It may include color coding or some other scheme that makes it easy to categorize your files.

Storing files on disk also requires a system. Part of this system involves rigid rules you must follow. There is also room for some flexibility, however, so you can personalize the system to suit your needs. You need not be concerned with the specifics of how the data is stored on disk. Your only concern is the rules you need to follow when working with these files, especially the rules that center around the names you use for your files and the location of these files when they are stored.

Filenames

Before you can store a file on your disk, you must give it a name. Since the naming process follows particular, although somewhat flexible, rules, first review the rules you must follow for naming a file. Each file on a disk must have a unique name. This name consists of from one to eight characters. You can create a name by using the alphabetic characters, numeric digits, and some of the special symbols. Since it can be difficult to remember which symbols are permissible and which are not, it is best to limit your use of special symbols to the _ (underline) symbol, which is particularly useful as a separator in a filename. For example, the name SALES_91 might be used to store the sales data for 1991. Be aware that even though 1-2-3 lets you include spaces in a filename, the spaces cause confusion with some DOS commands. SALES 91 is a valid filename, but SALES_91 is a better one.

Although there is no flexibility in the rules just discussed, you can assign the eight allowable characters any way you like. It is best to develop some consistent rules for naming your data because consistency can help you determine a file's contents when you see the filename later on. If you are storing sales data for a number of years and keeping one year's worth of data in each file, you could create names such as SALES_91 and SALES_92. You could also use names such as 92_SALES or SLS1992. It really does not matter what pattern you select for your names; what is important is that once you decide on a naming pattern, you apply it consistently for each file that you create. Naming files 89_SALES, SALES_90, SLS_1991, and SALES92 is not a good strategy; the pattern is too inconsistent. It is also best not to begin a filename with a number, to ensure compatibility with other versions of 1-2-3. You can enter filenames in either uppercase or lowercase letters or in a combination of the two. Regardless of which type of entry you make, it is translated into uppercase.

You can also add filename extensions. An *extension* consists of one to three optional characters added at the end of a filename. They too can be entered in upper- or lowercase. They are separated from a filename by a period. For example, in SALES91.WK3, the filename extension is .WK3. You use extensions to categorize files or to provide an extra three characters of description. Some programs automatically add extensions for you. 1-2-3 does this. Table 8-1 shows some of the most common filename extensions that you will encounter and the types of files they are used for.

The file extension 1-2-3 assigns to a worksheet file depends on the release you are using. 1-2-3 assigns a .WK3 file extension to 1-2-3 for Windows and Release 3 worksheet files. Previous releases use .WK1 for Release 2 worksheet files and .WKS for Release 1A worksheet files. You do not need to memorize this information; 1-2-3 handles it all for you. You need to realize what these extensions are only when you want to work directly with the files stored on your disk, using your operating system. The filename extensions appear when you use operating-system commands. They could cause confusion if you were not at least aware that 1-2-3 was creating them and using them to distinguish different types of files.

Table 8-1. *Common Filename Extensions*

Extension	Type of File
.WK3	Worksheet file in Release 3 and 1-2-3 for Windows format
.WK1	Worksheet in Release 2, 2.01, and 2.2 format
.WKS	Worksheet in Release 1A format
.FM3	Formatting information about a worksheet
.FMB	Backup of worksheet formatting information
.FMT	Worksheet formatting information for Release 2.*x* files
.BAK	Backup of Release 2.2 or above worksheet
.CGM or .PIC	1-2-3 graph files
.PRN	Print files (unencoded)
.ENC	Print files (encoded)
.COM or .EXE	Executable files
.BAT	DOS batch files

8

Storing Your Data

Files can be stored on either hard or floppy disks. Hard disks, thanks to today's technology, are popular storage media for business computer systems. A floppy disk holds from 360,000 to over 1,440,000 characters, depending on whether you are using the standard double-sided, double-density disks or the new high-density disks. Today's typical hard disk installed in a computer system has a capacity of over 40,000,000 characters of information.

When new files are added to disks, their names are added to a *directory* on the disk that keeps track of every file on the disk. Although you could use a single directory to maintain a hard disk, such a directory could become so lengthy that it would be difficult to work with. This would be like having a single index to catalog a whole library of reference volumes; it would take a long time to read. It would be better if each book in the collection had its own index and if books had chapter outlines that could be referenced for contents.

To lessen the burden of the main disk index (the main directory on the disk, called the *root directory*), you can set up subdirectories for your disk. *Subdirectories* function as a second-level index to group files that are related. You can create these groupings on any basis you like, such as one for each individual that uses the system, one for each application category on the system, or one for each application program. Certain files, such as COMMAND.COM, are usually maintained in the root directory. 1-2-3 and Windows have created several subdirectories for their program files. When subdirectories are added, their names are placed in the root directory; however, the names of the files they contain are kept in the subdirectory, not in the root directory. Subdirectories are organized in a hierarchical structure, as shown in Figure 8-1. Here, the entries in the main directory include two references to subdirectories, indicated by <DIR>. These subdirectories must be created through commands in your operating system. Although 1-2-3 cannot create the directories, it uses whichever directory is current on the hard disk, and it gives you commands that let you activate another directory.

1-2-3 always assumes that you want to work with files on the *current*, or *default, directory*—the drive and subdirectory you are using. This means that if you are content to use the default directory, you do not need to specify where you want your files saved. However, if you want to use a disk

Figure 8-1. *A hierarchical directory structure*

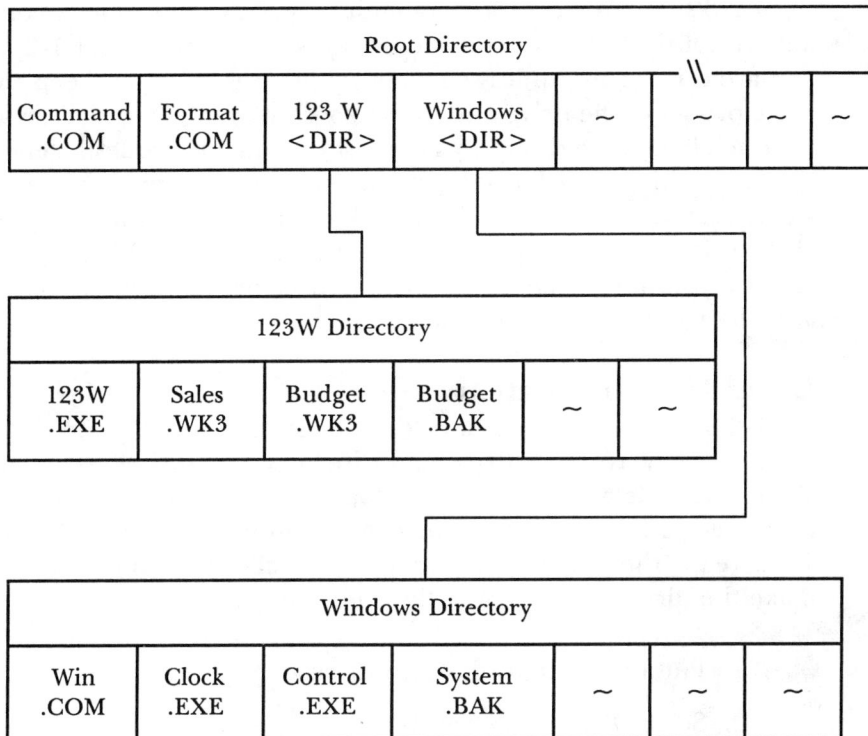

Root Directory					\\\\		
Command .COM	Format .COM	123 W \<DIR\>	Windows \<DIR\>	~	~	~	~

123W Directory					
123W .EXE	Sales .WK3	Budget .WK3	Budget .BAK	~	~

Windows Directory						
Win .COM	Clock .EXE	Control .EXE	System .BAK	~	~	~

drive or directory other than the default, you can either change the default or provide the file location along with the filename. You look at both of these possibilities in the following section on 1-2-3 commands.

1-2-3 File Commands

The commands on 1-2-3's **File** menu help you handle your file-management tasks. There are menu selections for saving your data to disk files and for retrieving copies of these files to place in memory. You have an opportunity to try these commands to save and retrieve your data in the following sections.

Changing the Directory

1-2-3's dependence on a default directory saves you a considerable amount of time. The default directory is the location that 1-2-3 assumes you are referencing unless you specify otherwise. If you keep the default directory set to the drive and directory containing your data, you will not need to change the directory for most of your file requests. Since you are working with a hard disk system, your data is probably stored in a subdirectory. To work on a hard disk for a period of time, you need to be able to change the directory you are using. Later in this chapter you will see how you can change the drive and directory for a single command and also change the default directory.

Using Another Location

1-2-3 may use solely a hard disk for storing its program files, but you can select any available drive and directory for storing your data. If you change the default drive to a floppy disk drive, you must insert a formatted disk into the drive before changing the current directory since 1-2-3 reads the current directory before allowing you to change it. To make the directory change, follow these steps:

1. Put a formatted disk into drive A.

2. Select **T**ools **U**ser Setup.

3. Type **A:** in the **W**orksheet Directory text box and then select the OK command button.

This change lasts only while the 1-2-3 window is open. If you want to permanently change the location where 1-2-3 saves and retrieves files, select the **U**pdate command button in the Tools User Setup dialog box before selecting the OK command button.

classic */File Directory and /Worksheet Global Default Directory/Update are the Classic commands for changing the default directory, depending on whether you want a change for the current session or a permanent change.*

You can store your worksheets in and retrieve them from any subdirectory on a disk. When you tell 1-2-3 which subdirectory to use, you must supply the complete path. The *path* includes the disk drive and an optional subdirectory, as in C:\123W\WORK. Each level of a subdirectory is separated from the others by a backslash (\). Follow these steps to return the previous directory setting:

1. Select **Tools User Setup.**
2. Type the directory information for where you want the files, as in **C:\123W\SAMPLE,** in the **Worksheet Directory** text box and then select the OK command button.

Saving Files

1-2-3 does not save your files automatically—it is your responsibility to save the data you enter. It is best to do this periodically; do not wait until you are ending your 1-2-3 session before you save data for the first time. A good guideline is to save every 20 to 30 minutes so you can never lose more than 20 to 30 minutes of your work, even if the power goes off unexpectedly. In previous chapters, you were briefly introduced to the **File Save** and **File Save As** commands to save your data.

Saving the First Time

When you save a file for the first time, 1-2-3 supplies a filename unless you provide a different one. The filename 1-2-3 suggests is FILE*xxxx*, where *xxxx* is replaced by the next unused sequential number (as in FILE0005). You can either accept this filename or provide one of your own. If you are saving onto floppy disks, you also need to ensure that a formatted disk is placed in the drive. In the following example, you make a few entries on the worksheet and then save the data.

classic */Worksheet Erase Yes is the Classic option used to clear the screen.*

1. Select **File Close** to erase the current worksheet and start over. You may need to select **Yes** or **No** to determine whether the current worksheet entries are saved.
2. Make the entries shown here:

3. Select **F**ile Save **A**s to display the dialog box shown in Figure 8-2.

You can use 1-2-3's suggested filename or provide a more meaningful name for the file by typing a new name.

4. Type **QTRSALES** in the File **N**ame text box and select the OK command button to save the worksheet file.

Once you select the OK command button, the disk drive light comes on momentarily while your data is being written to disk. 1-2-3 replaces the title bar entry with the file's name. At this point, you can continue to work on the model or close its window since you know that the model is saved to the disk. For now, you will make some additions to it to see how the process differs for subsequent saves.

classic */File Save is the only Classic option for saving files. Through the new menu system there are choices, depending on whether you want a quick save with the same name or want to save all the open files.*

Figure 8-2. *The File Save As dialog box*

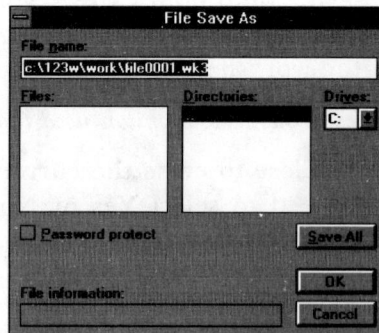

Subsequent Saves

Each time you save a model you have saved before, you can replace the copy on the disk with the information that is currently stored in memory or you can save the data to another worksheet file. If you saved the model previously, 1-2-3's default is to save the model under the same name. You can also copy the old version of the worksheet file to a backup file before saving the new version of the data. Make a few changes to the model and save the model again with these steps:

1. Move the cell pointer to A4 and type **Profit**. Type **10000** in B4, **15000** in C4, **10000** in D4 and **20000** in E4.

2. Select **File S**ave or click the File Save SmartIcon, which looks like this:

123 saves the file with the same settings you used previously.

You can save a file again using the **File Save As** command, but the steps are different.

3. Select **File Save As** and the OK command button. 1-2-3 presents this dialog box:

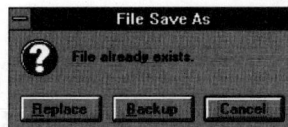

1-2-3 is asking if you wish to cancel the save request, replace the copy of the model stored on disk with the current worksheet contents, or back up the original file.

4. Select **R**eplace. 1-2-3 will save the updated model under the name you used previously.

If you want to save a model under a new name, use the **File Save As** command and enter or edit the filename in the File **N**ame text box. When you change the entry in the File **N**ame text box, you are in EDIT mode, which means you can use all of the key combinations that you use for editing cells. Then, when you select the OK command button, the file is saved under the new name. This feature is especially useful when you need to create two similar copies of a model; you can enter the data that is the same for both models and then save the model under two different names before entering the entries that are different.

Saving to Another Location

You can also use the **F**ile Save **A**s command to save a file to a directory other than the default. To do this, use the Drives drop-down box and **D**irectories list box in the File Save As dialog box to specify the location you want to use. For example, to save the file to a disk in drive A, do the following:

1. Select **F**ile Save **A**s.

2. Click the down arrow icon underneath Drives and click A:, or press TAB three times and type **A** so the drop-down box displays A:.

3. Select the OK command button to save the worksheet file in the new location.

4. Select **F**ile Save **A**s.

5. Click the down arrow icon underneath Drives and click C:, or press TAB three times and type **C** so the drop-down box displays C:.

6. Select the OK command button so the file is saved again in its original location.

7. Select **R**eplace.

Another option is to type the drive and directory information into the File **N**ame text box along with the filename.

Making a Backup Copy of the Worksheet

Sometimes when you revise a document, you keep the previous version of the document in the file cabinet along with the current version. If you revise a budget projection, for example, you may keep the previous projection for comparison purposes. You can then refer to the previous copy in case you want to revert to any of the old projections, or you can use it as a backup in case you lose the later copy.

1-2-3 offers the same feature for your worksheet files. When you select **B**ackup in response to the **C**ancel, **R**eplace or **B**ackup prompt, the worksheet file stored on disk with a .WK3 extension is renamed to a file with the same name but with a .BAK extension. Then 1-2-3 saves the current worksheet file with a .WK3 extension. Using the **B**ackup option allows you always to access the current file and its most recent previous version. As an example, make several changes to the model and save the model again with these steps:

1. Move the cell pointer to A1 and type **ABC Company**. Press ENTER or click the confirm box.

2. Select **F**ile Save **A**s and the OK command button.

1-2-3 displays the **S**ave, **B**ackup, and **R**eplace options.

3. Select **B**ackup.

1-2-3 saves the updated model under the name you used previously. The previous version of the file is saved with a .BAK extension.

4. Select **F**ile **C**lose to close this worksheet window.

For a closer look at what the Backup feature offers, imagine looking inside the QTRSALES.WK3 and QTRSALES.BAK files. Their contents are shown in Figure 8-3. On the left side, the QTRSALES.BAK file does not have "ABC Company" in A1; this file contains the worksheet as it existed after the previous save operation. On the right side, the QTRSALES.WK3 file has "ABC Company" in A1—it was created by the most recent save operation. If you ever need to use the backup version, you can retrieve it just as you would retrieve other worksheet files.

Figure 8-3.   *A Worksheet file and a backup file*

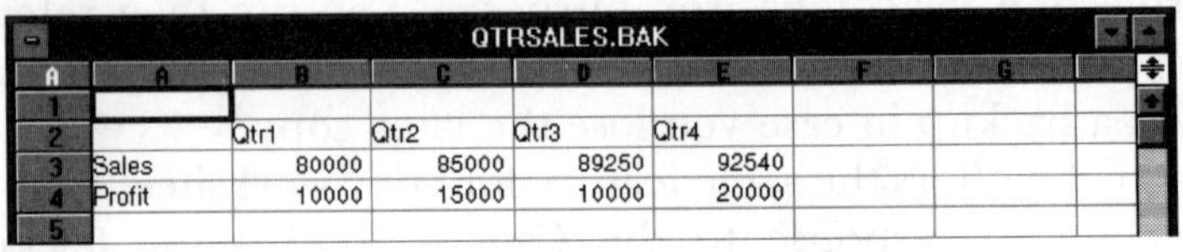

QTRSALES.BAK

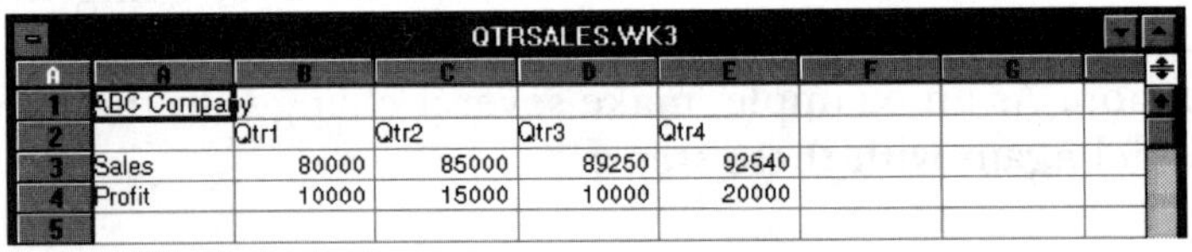

QTRSALES.WK3

Retrieving Files

Retrieving a file reads a worksheet file from disk and places it in a new worksheet window in 1-2-3's window. You can retrieve files from any location. While 1-2-3 initially lists files to retrieve in the default directory, you can always retrieve a file from another location.

Follow these steps to retrieve the QTRSALES file from the current directory:

1. Select **File Open** or click the File Open SmartIcon, which looks like this,

to display the dialog box shown in Figure 8-4.

The **Files** list box lists the worksheet files that are stored in the default directory. By changing the directory and drive, you can change which directory of files is listed. The Drives drop-down box and the **Directories** list box are identical to the ones in the File Save As dialog box that let you change the location for a command.

2. Click the down arrow icon underneath Drives and click A:, or press ALT-V and type **A** so the drop-down box displays A:.

Now the files listed in the **Files** list box are those stored in the current directory on drive A. The File **N**ame text box shows the currently selected drive and directory.

3. Click the down arrow icon underneath Drives and click C:, or type **C** so the drop-down box reads C:.

Figure 8-4. *The File Open dialog box*

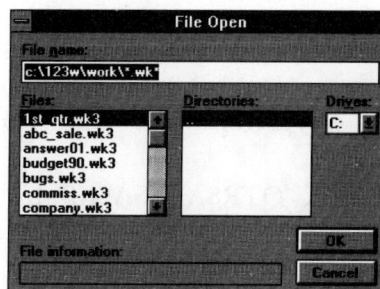

4. Click the .. in the **Directories** list box or press SHIFT-TAB and ENTER to display the parent directory of the directory currently listed. The parent directory is the directory the current subdirectory belongs to.

Now the **Directories** list box shows .. to indicate the parent directory, ADDIN, GRAPHICO, SAMPLE, SHEET1CO, and any other directories. Each of the subdirectories in the current directory is listed. You can switch to another directory by selecting the directory from the list.

5. Double-click SAMPLE in the **Directories** list box or press the DOWN ARROW key until SAMPLE is highlighted and ENTER to change to the directory containing your worksheet files. If your work-sheet files are stored in another location, substitute the directory name for SAMPLE.

The remaining part of the dialog box that you want to use is the list of files in the directory. Since 1-2-3's default directory will have more worksheet files than can fit in the list box, it has a scroll bar to shift the part of the list that appears in the **Files** list box.

6. Click the scroll bar in the **Files** list box so QTRSALES.WK3 is visible, or press SHIFT-TAB and then Q to move to the first item in the list that starts with the letter you type.

1-2-3 displays the file list in alphabetical sequence to make it easy for you to find the file you want. As you highlight a file in the **Files** list box, 1-2-3 displays the information for when the file was saved and its size in the File information box. Also, 1-2-3 displays the selected file in the File **Name** text box. Now all you have to do is tell 1-2-3 to retrieve this file.

7. Double-click QTRSALES.WK3 in the file list, click the OK command button, or press ENTER to open this worksheet file.

Most of the time when you retrieve a file, you perform only steps 1, 6, and 7 since the file you want is in the default directory. You can also just type the filename in the File **Name** text box and select the OK command button. When you retrieve a worksheet file, if the Untitled worksheet is empty, the worksheet file you select replaces the Untitled worksheet. In other cases, the worksheet file you select is added as another worksheet window.

If you need to retrieve a backup file, type **∗.BAK** in the File **N**ame text box and press ENTER so 1-2-3 lists the backup files in the **F**iles list box. For example, to retrieve the backup of QTRSALES.WK3, you would type **QTRSALES.BAK** in the File **N**ame text box or type **∗.BAK** in the text box and press ENTER so you could select QTRSALES.BAK from the **F**iles list box.

Opening New Worksheet Files

In addition to opening worksheet windows that contain existing files, you can open a worksheet window that contains an empty worksheet so you can start creating new models. The **F**ile **N**ew command creates a new worksheet file in a new worksheet window. As soon as you select the **F**ile **N**ew command, 1-2-3 opens a new window with a default filename (FILE*xxxx*). Later, you can give it a better name with the **F**ile Save **A**s command. 1-2-3 creates a placeholder on disk for the new file; if you look at the default directory, you will see the new file you are using. If you close the window without saving this new worksheet, 1-2-3 deletes the empty worksheet file placeholder.

Try the **F**ile **N**ew command now by selecting **F**ile **N**ew. Select **F**ile **N**ew again to add another worksheet window, as shown in Figure 8-5. 1-2-3 lets you continue adding new and existing worksheet files to memory until your computer runs out of memory to hold the data or until the total number of worksheets in all the open worksheet files is 256.

Working with Multiple Worksheet Windows

As you can see by the three worksheet window title bars in Figure 8-5, when you open a worksheet window, you are not putting away the one that was active before the **F**ile **O**pen or **F**ile **N**ew command. 1-2-3 lets you open as many files as you like, as long as the total number of worksheets

Figure 8-5.   *Opening a worksheet file*

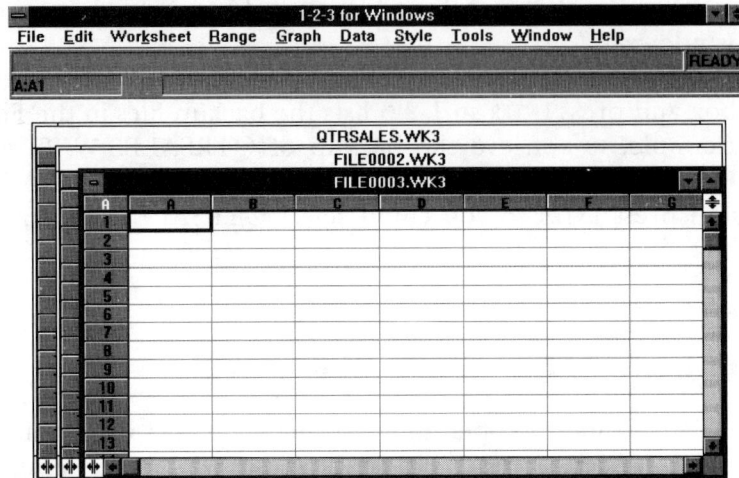

is 256 or fewer. Realistically, the true limit is likely to be the amount of memory in your machine; you may run out of memory in which to store the additional data and other Windows applications before you reach the absolute limit of 256 sheets.

Each worksheet window is separate, which means you can position and size the windows separately. The worksheet windows are document windows in this Windows application. Appendix B, "Using Windows," includes information on sizing and positioning document windows within an application window. You can use 1-2-3's **W**indow **T**ile and **W**indow **C**ascade commands to tile and cascade the worksheet windows just like you can tile and cascade the Windows application windows as described in Appendix B. These window options equally size the windows or display only the title bar of each window except the active one.

classic *1-2-3 Release 3 was the first release to include /File New and /File Open to support multiple files.*

Since 1-2-3 keeps worksheet windows open as you retrieve more, you must close the worksheet windows as you no longer need them. You do this with the **F**ile **C**lose command, which you learned about in Chapter 2,

"Entering Labels and Numbers." As you saw there, when you close the last worksheet window, 1-2-3 opens another one for you. As you open more worksheet windows, you will need to learn how to switch between them and how you can use the data from the open worksheets.

Switching Between Windows

1-2-3 lets you work with any worksheet window you want. You can switch to another window when 1-2-3 is in POINT or READY mode. With a mouse, the easiest way to switch to a worksheet window is to click the one you want. You can also switch to another window by selecting **Window** and then the number assigned to the window you want. If you want a window that is not listed (you have more than nine windows open), select **More Windows** and the window name in the list box, and select the OK command button. You can also switch between open windows on the 1-2-3 application window by pressing CTRL-F6 (Next Window). You can try some of these options by following these steps:

1. Press CTRL-F6 (Next Window) to switch to the first new worksheet window.
2. Select **File Close** to close this window without saving it.
3. Press CTRL-F6 (Next Window) to switch to the new worksheet window.
4. Select **Window 1** QTRSALES.WK3.
5. Select **Window** and 2 as the number next to the new worksheet.

You can also use the following keys to move between worksheet files:

CTRL-END HOME	Moves to the first worksheet file
CTRL-END END	Moves to the last worksheet file
CTRL-END CTRL-PGUP	Moves to the next worksheet file
CTRL-END CTRL-PGDN	Moves to the previous worksheet file

6. Press CTRL-END HOME to move to the QTRSALES.WK3 worksheet window.
7. Press CTRL-END CTRL-PGUP to move to the new worksheet window.

8

Using Multiple Worksheet Files in Formulas

The new worksheet file can use several of the values in the QTRSALES.WK3 worksheet file. You can also build this formula by using POINT mode, just as you learned how to use POINT mode to build formulas in the same worksheet in Chapter 3, "Defining Your Calculations." To create a formula that uses values from the QTRSALES.WK3 worksheet file, follow these steps:

1. Type **Total Sales** in A2 of the new worksheet file.

2. Move the cell pointer to B2 in the new worksheet file.

3. Type **@SUM(**.

4. Press CTRL-END CTRL-PGDN and move to B3 in the QTRSALES worksheet file.

The formula in the control panel looks like this:

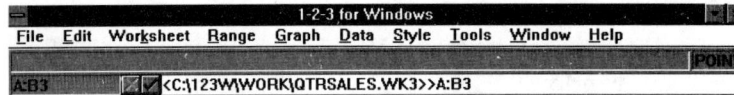

1-2-3 automatically adds the file reference for you.

5. Type **.** (a period) to change the cell address to a range address.

6. Press RIGHT ARROW three times to select the range A:B3..A:E3 in the QTRSALES worksheet file.

7. Type **)** and press ENTER or click the confirm box to finalize the formula.

The formula looks like this:

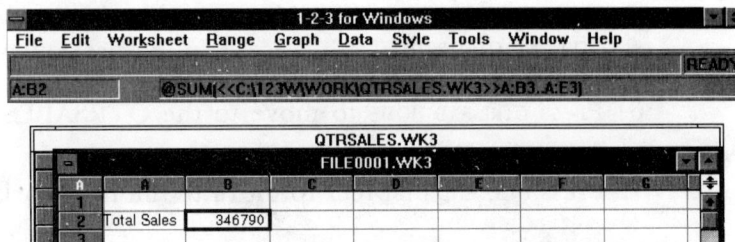

Notice that the same angle brackets you used when you built linking formulas in Chapter 4, "@Functions and Other Formula Options," are automatically added for you. Pointing is one way to include the external file links in the formulas; typing is another. For example, you could have typed

@SUM(< <C:\123W\WORK\QTRSALES.WK3> >A:B3..A:E3)

which is the formula you entered by pointing to the range in the other worksheet file.

At this point, you want to save your new file and save any changes made to the other file. To do this, follow these steps:

1. Select **File Save As**, type **TOTALSAL** in the File **Name** text box, and select the OK command button.

This saves the file with a better name than 1-2-3's default filename, but it does not save the other open worksheet window.

2. Select **File Save As** and select the **Save** All command button.

This saves every open worksheet window with the name displayed on the window's title bar just as if you selected the **File Save** command in every open window. If a window is open that does not have a filename, 1-2-3 assigns it a default filename. Now that you have learned how to open and close the worksheet windows you want, you will want to learn about adding additional worksheets to a worksheet file. This is like adding pages to a tablet to provide you with additional areas to put data.

Adding Worksheets

Adding a worksheet to a worksheet file is like adding another sheet to a notebook: you go to the sheet where you want to add the new sheets and then add one or more sheets before or after the current sheet. To try adding more sheets to a worksheet file, you will make some entries to a new worksheet file and then add worksheets. Use the following steps to create a multilevel worksheet:

1. Select Worksheet **I**nsert to display this dialog box:

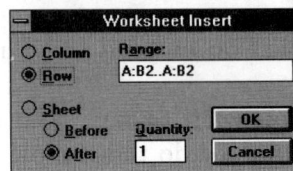

2. Select the **S**heet option button and the **B**efore option button below that.

The **Q**uantity text box is where you type the number of sheets to add. The number 1 is the default, but you can enter a higher number to add more sheets.

3. Select the OK command button to add one sheet.

The sheet indicator in the worksheet border is still an A but you do not see your worksheet entries. This is because 1-2-3 added this sheet in front of the one with entries. The new sheet is sheet A and the old sheet is sheet B. As mentioned in Chapter 1, "Worksheet Basics," 1-2-3 labels sheets with letters just like it labels columns. The first sheet is sheet A, and labeling can continue up to IV if you have 256 worksheets in one file.

4. Press CTRL-PGUP or click the Ctrl-PgUp SmartIcon, which looks like this:

As the preceding step describes, you can press CTRL-PGUP to move to the next worksheet. CTRL-PGDN moves you to the previous worksheet. Now you can see the worksheet with your entries, sheet B. The top of your worksheet looks like this:

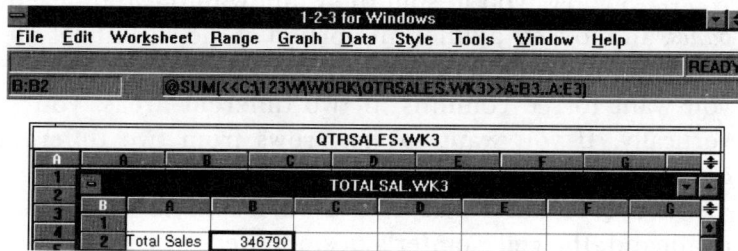

5. Press CTRL-PGDN to switch to sheet A or click the Ctrl-PgDn SmartIcon, which looks like this:

You can add other worksheets to try inserting sheets after the current one.

6. Press CTRL-PGUP or click the Ctrl-PgUp SmartIcon to switch to sheet B.

7. Select Worksheet Insert, the Sheet option button, and the After option button, type **3** in the **Q**uantity text box, and select the OK command button.

1-2-3 inserts three blank worksheets after worksheet B.

8. Press CTRL-PGUP and CTRL-PGDN to move through new worksheets labeled C, D, and E.

At this point, you can see only one worksheet at a time. You can look at two or three worksheets at a time by using 1-2-3's window features.

=classic= /Worksheet Insert Sheet was used in Release 3 to support the addition of sheets.

Using Panes to Help Monitor Data

1-2-3 allows you to split the window into two different sections, called *panes,* and to view a different portion of the worksheet file in each section. You have the option of splitting the window vertically or horizontally. If you want to see columns in two different areas, you split the window vertically. If you want to view rows from two different locations, you choose a horizontal split.

The command that creates the split is **Window Split**. With this command, the cell pointer's position determines where 1-2-3 divides the worksheet window into panes. This command is different from any other 1-2-3 command you have used: it requires you to position your cell pointer before invoking the command. You cannot select a cell or range from the dialog box. The location of the cell pointer determines the size of the two panes, and the pane size cannot be changed while the menu is active. Next, select the **Horizontal** option button if you want two horizontal panes or the **Vertical** option button if you want two vertical panes. A horizontal split is made at the cell pointer's row at the time the command is invoked. A vertical split is made at the left side of the cell pointer's column when the command is invoked.

=classic= /Worksheet Window is the Classic command used to split the screen either vertically or horizontally.

Try creating two panes in your window by following this exercise:

1. Move the cell pointer to B:D2.

2. Select the **Window Split** command, the **Vertical** option button, and the OK command button to split the window into two panes, as shown in Figure 8-6.

3. Press F6 (Window) to move the cell pointer to the right pane.

Regardless of which pane you are in, F6 (Window) always takes you to the opposite pane. With a mouse, you can click a cell in the pane where you

Figure 8-6. *Two vertical windows*

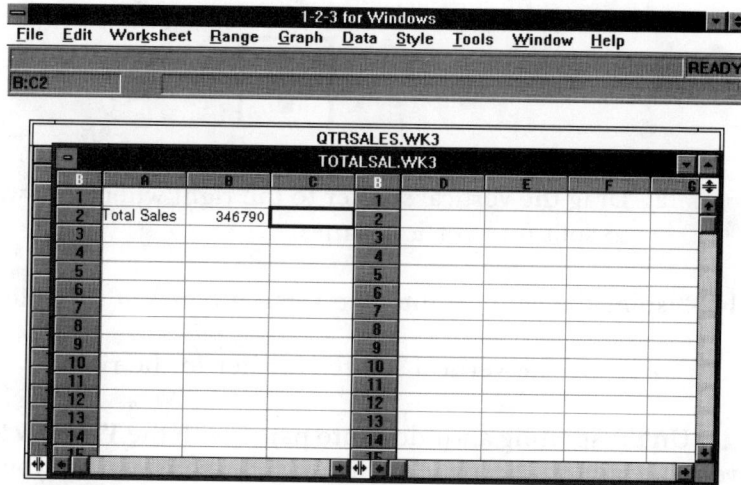

want the cell pointer. The panes have their own scroll bars so you can change the section of the worksheet that displays in the pane.

4. Move the cell pointer to I29 in the right pane.

5. Select the **W**indow **S**plit command, the **C**lear option button, and the OK command button to return to a single pane.

If you have a mouse, you can also split a window into panes by using the splitters in the window's scroll bars. Try creating two panes in the window with the splitters by following these steps:

1. Point to the vertical splitter on the scroll bar on the bottom of the worksheet window. The splitter looks like this:

8

The mouse changes to look like this:

2. Drag the vertical splitter to the right where you want the window to split into vertical panes.

1-2-3 splits the window into two vertical panes at the splitter's location.

3. Drag the vertical splitter further to the right.

Unlike splitting a window into panes with the **Window Split** command, you can adjust the pane's split with a mouse when you are using the splitters.

4. Drag the vertical splitter all the way to the left to return the display to a single pane.

Using Panes with Multiple Worksheets

Displaying your data by using panes is especially useful when you are working with multiple sheets. You can use each pane to display a separate worksheet in the worksheet file. To look at the worksheets you have added, follow these steps:

1. Move the cell pointer to A:A6 in the TOTALSAL worksheet window, which is where you want to split the worksheet window into panes.

2. Select the **Window Split** command, the **Horizontal** option button, and the OK command button to split the window into two panes.

3. Press CTRL-PGUP. Your worksheet now looks like the one in Figure 8-7.

1-2-3 moved the cell pointer to sheet B while keeping the second pane on worksheet A. You can use horizontal and vertical panes to look at two

Figure 8-7. *Using a horizontal window to view two worksheets*

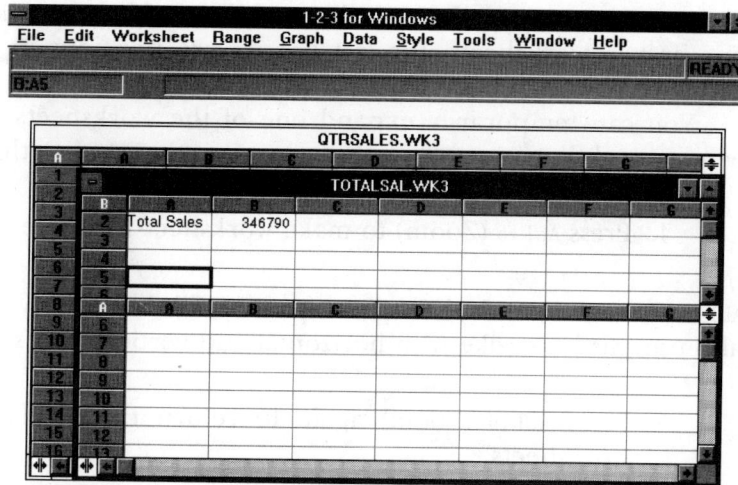

different sheets within the same worksheet file just as you used horizontal and vertical panes to look at two different areas of the same sheet.

1-2-3 has another **Window S**plit option, which displays three panes at once. To see how 1-2-3 will display your worksheet file when you use this option, follow these steps:

1. Move the cell pointer to B:A1.

2. Select the **Window S**plit command, the **C**lear option button, and the OK command button to return to a single pane.

3. Select the **Window S**plit command and then select the **P**erspective option button and the OK command button, or in the icon palette, click the Perspective SmartIcon, which looks like this:

1-2-3 changes the display to look like the worksheets in Figure 8-8. The current worksheet appears first. You can use F6 (Window), CTRL-PGUP, and CTRL-PGDN to move through the worksheets. If your worksheet has only one or two worksheets, the last one or two positions in the worksheet perspective view will appear empty.

You can temporarily expand one of the worksheets to use the full window and then contract it when you want to return to the pane display.

4. Press ALT-F6 (Zoom) to make worksheet B fill the window.

ALT-F6 (Zoom) expands the current pane to fill the entire window. You can also use this keystroke with horizontal and vertical panes.

5. Press ALT-F6 (Zoom) again to return the display to the three worksheets.

6. Select the **Window S**plit command, the **C**lear option button, and the OK command button to return to a single pane.

Figure 8-8.   *Using **Window S**plit **P**erspective to view three worksheets*

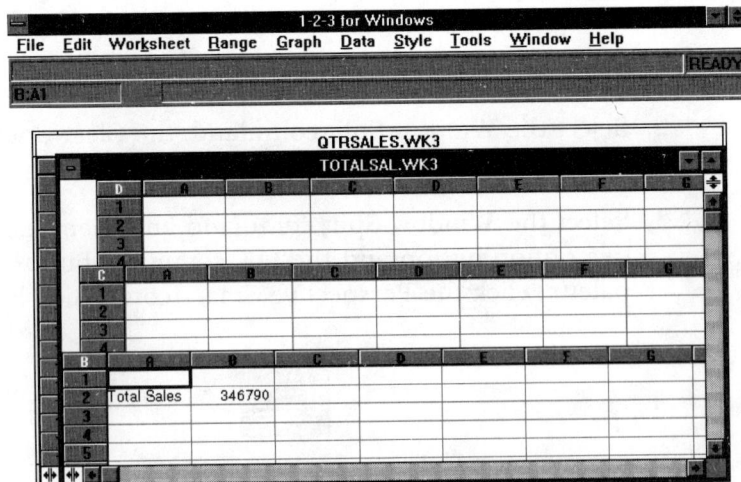

1-2-3 now displays only worksheet B, although you can go to the others by pressing CTRL-PGUP and CTRL-PGDN.

Using Worksheet Functions with Multiple Worksheets

Just as you can build formulas that reference data in other worksheets or on the same worksheet, you can also build formulas that use data on different sheets in the same worksheet file. For example, you can consolidate data by creating a formula that sums or averages data in a range that spans sheets. You can reference cells outside the current sheet by pointing to them or by typing the address, making sure that you include the worksheet letter.

To create formulas in the QTRSALES worksheet file that use multiple worksheets, follow these steps:

1. Press CTRL-HOME to move to A:A1.
2. Type **@SUM(** to start the formula you want to use.
3. Press CTRL-PGUP so the formula is now @SUM(B:A1 and you see sheet B in the worksheet window.
4. Type a period to anchor the cell reference.
5. Press the RIGHT ARROW key, the DOWN ARROW key, and CTRL-PGUP to include the range B:A2..C:B2.
6. Type), and press ENTER or click the confirm box to complete the formula, @SUM(B:A1..C:B2).

1-2-3 automatically includes the worksheet letter with the cell address when you point to cells on other sheets. Instead of pointing to cells on other sheets for cell addresses in a formula, you can type the address, but you must be sure to include the sheet letter and a colon as part of the address.

Deleting Worksheets in a Worksheet File

Just as you can insert and delete columns and rows in worksheet files, you can also insert and delete worksheets within a worksheet file. The steps for deleting a worksheet are just like those for deleting columns and rows. When you delete worksheets, you do not enter the number of sheets to delete. Instead, like deleting columns and rows, you select a worksheet range containing at least one cell in each sheet that you want to delete. Like deleting columns and rows, you can also select the range before you select the Worksheet **D**elete command or select the range in the **R**ange text box in the Worksheet Delete dialog box. You have created more worksheets than you need, so follow these steps to remove three of the worksheets:

1. Press CTRL-PGUP until the cell pointer is in worksheet C.

2. Press F4 (Abs) once, CTRL-PGUP twice, and ENTER once to select the range C:A1..E:A1.

3. Select Worksheet **D**elete, the **S**heet option button, and the OK command button.

When 1-2-3 deletes a worksheet, it reassigns letters to the remaining worksheets. If you had a worksheet F, it would become sheet C after you delete sheets C through E. You can test this by trying to move to the next worksheet.

4. Press CTRL-PGUP.

1-2-3 beeps to indicate that the worksheet file does not contain any more worksheets after B.

5. Select **F**ile Save **A**s and select the **S**ave All command button.

classic */Worksheet Delete Sheet is the corresponding command that was used in Release 3.*

Designing Multilevel Applications

1-2-3 lets you include up to 256 worksheets in one file, but you want to use multiple sheets only when they provide you with benefits. You want to plan how you lay out your data in the worksheet so you can easily access your information. While you have unlimited possibilities for arranging your worksheet, this chapter considers two different arrangements of information.

Storing the Same Type of Information

When your worksheets contain the same information for different branches, regions, or departments within the same company, use a separate worksheet for each one. Multiple sheets with similar information are useful in expense reports for different departments, where each department uses the same format and worksheet design but the department numbers and expenses differ. Figure 8-9 shows an example of multiple worksheets that contain the same type of data. Worksheet A contains the summary information for all of the departments. Worksheets B and C contain the detailed information for the accounting and advertising departments. The worksheet file also contains the same type of

Figure 8-9. *Multiple worksheets containing the same type of data*

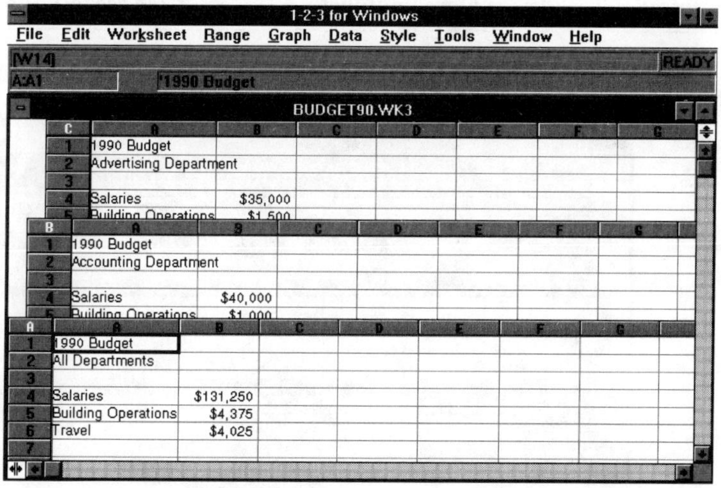

information for all of the remaining departments in the company. As numbers are entered in the worksheets for the individual departments, the formulas in the summary worksheet are immediately updated.

Storing Different Types of Information

Sometimes you have different types of information that you want to store on the same worksheet. When you create databases, as you will learn how to do in Chapter 12, "Data Management Basics," you can store the database, the entries that select database information you want to find, and the reports created with the database on different worksheets. This leaves room on each worksheet for the database and allows the reports to grow without interfering with the other information. Also, you can add and delete columns and rows in one section without affecting the other data stored in the worksheet file. Figure 8-10 shows such a database worksheet file that has the three parts on separate sheets, which minimizes the chance that a user will accidentally enter data in the wrong place.

Figure 8-10.   *An employee database using multiple worksheets*

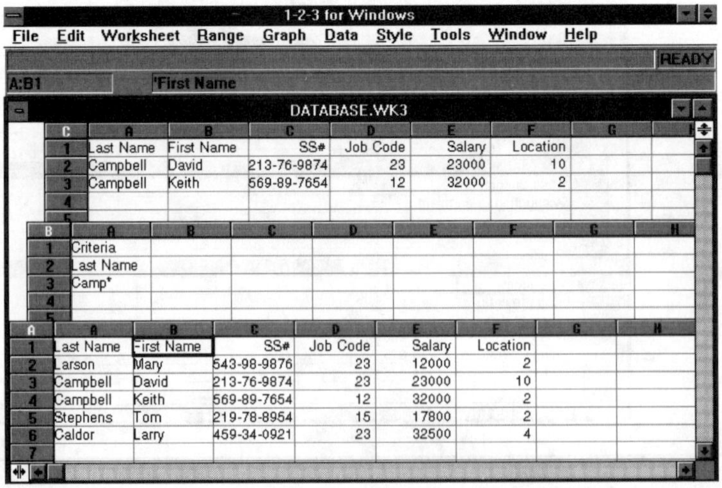

Review

Files are the basic units for storing your information. You learned some of the commands you will use to work with the files you create. The 1-2-3 features you have learned for working with files include the following:

- Files provide permanent storage for your worksheets. You can save to and retrieve worksheets from a floppy or hard disk.

- You can select where 1-2-3 looks for the files that you work with by using the **Tools Setup** command. When you use this command, you can provide a new default directory in the **Worksheet Directory** text box.

- You can save a worksheet with the **File Save As** command. When you save a file the first time, 1-2-3 displays a suggested name (FILE followed by a four-digit number). If you have saved the file before, the name currently assigned to the file displays in the File **Name** text box. You can use this filename or type a new one. You can also select a new location for where the file is saved. When you save the file again, you must choose from Cancel, Replace, and Backup.

- You can save a worksheet using the same filename and location with the **File Save** command.

- You can retrieve a worksheet with the **File Open** command. When you execute this command, you either type the filename in the FileName text box or select a file from the **Files** list box, using the Drives drop-down box and **Directories** list box to change the location of the listed files.

- A worksheet file can contain up to 256 worksheets. The total number of sheets may be limited by the other open worksheet files and your computer's memory. Sheets are added with the Worksheet Insert command and removed with the Worksheet **Delete** command.

- You can load multiple worksheet files in memory at once. You can switch between these files. 1-2-3 limits the worksheets in memory to 256, regardless of how many files make up the 256

8

worksheets. The limit may be less, depending upon the worksheet file contents and the computer's memory.

- You can use the **Window S**plit command to divide your worksheet window panes to look at two or three worksheets in a worksheet window at once. You can move in each pane to look at different sections of the same worksheet file.

- 1-2-3 lets you select ranges that span worksheets in the same file.

Commands and Keys

You learned about the commands that let you work with multiple sheets and worksheet files at once. You also learned about commands that save and retrieve your data. You were introduced to the keys you can use to switch between windows and files. These keys and commands are

Keys	Action
ALT-F6 (Zoom)	Expands the current pane to fill the entire window
CTRL-F6 (Next Window)	Switches to the next window on the 1-2-3 application window
CTRL-END HOME	Moves to the first worksheet file
CTRL-END END	Moves to the last worksheet file
CTRL-END CTRL-PGUP	Moves to the next worksheet file
CTRL-END CTRL-PGDN	Moves to the previous worksheet file
CTRL-HOME	Moves to A:A1 of the current worksheet file
CTRL-PGUP	Moves to the next worksheet in the file
CTRL-PGDN	Moves to the previous worksheet in the file
ALT F A	File Save **As** saves the file with the name and location you select
ALT F N	File **New** opens a new worksheet file in a new worksheet window
ALT F O	File **O**pen retrieves a file from disk and places it in a worksheet window
ALT F S	File **Save** saves the current worksheet using the previously defined settings

Keys	Action
ALT T U W	**Tools User Setup Worksheet Directory** sets the default directory
ALT K D S	**Worksheet Delete Sheet** removes sheets from a worksheet file
ALT K I S	**Worksheet Insert Sheet** adds sheets to a worksheet file
ALT W 1 through 9	**Window 1** through **9** makes the window with the name displayed next to the number the active window
ALT W C	**Window Cascade** sizes each open window and positions them so you can see only the title bar of each one except the active one at the top
ALT W M	**Window More Windows** lets you select which open window on the 1-2-3 window is the active one
ALT W S C	**Window Split Clear** returns the worksheet window display to a single pane
ALT W S H	**Window Split Horizontal** splits the worksheet window into two horizontal panes
ALT W S P	**Window Split Perspective** displays the worksheet file in perspective view to display three worksheets
ALT W S V	**Window Split Vertical** splits the worksheet window into two vertical panes
ALT W T	**Window Tile** resizes each open window so each window is the same size and each can be seen on 1-2-3's window

8

9

Making 1-2-3 Do Your Work

Until now, you entered every worksheet entry that you needed for your models by yourself. While that is similar to using a columnar pad for your entries, it does not take advantage of the features offered by a package like 1-2-3. This chapter introduces you to some of these features. After making only a few entries, you often can complete your model by putting 1-2-3 to work.

Copying worksheet entries has more potential than any other command to increase your productivity. In this chapter, you learn the ins and outs of copying both label and formula data. You also learn that 1-2-3 has other commands that can move worksheet data to a new location. This means that if the requirements of your application change, you can easily restructure the worksheet. You can also restructure the data stored in a column to row orientation and vice versa. Again, this is quite an improvement over the "eraser method" that manual spreadsheets require. Many of these commands use the Windows Clipboard, which is a location that all Windows applications can use to store data temporarily.

Once you have mastered rearranging your worksheet entries, you will want to learn about some of the tools that can help you monitor your expanded worksheet. You can create repeating labels and generate a series of numeric entries. You can control the recalculation of worksheet formulas. You can also freeze some of the information on your worksheet window, which helps you keep track of your location in a large worksheet. 1-2-3 can search your worksheet for an entry rather than your having to search visually for the data you want. Once 1-2-3 locates the data you want, you can have 1-2-3 replace it with another entry.

Copying Worksheet Data

Copying entries on a manual worksheet is a laborious task. To make an additional set of entries that duplicate existing ones, you must pick up your pencil and physically copy each entry that you wish to make. Naturally, duplicate entries take just as long to make as the original entries.

When you make duplicates with 1-2-3, this is not the case. For any entry that you wish to duplicate, 1-2-3 completes 95 percent of the work for you. You just tell 1-2-3 the entries you want to copy and where you want them copied to, and 1-2-3 does all the remaining work. 1-2-3 can take a column of label entries and copy it to ten new columns. It can even take a row of formulas that calculate all your sales projections for the month of January and copy it down the page to the next eleven rows, thus giving you all the calculations for February through December. The truly amazing part of this process is that 1-2-3 even adjusts the formulas as it copies them.

This chapter uses a building-block approach to cover all of the features of copying and moving worksheet data. First, you learn to duplicate a label entry. Then you look a little more closely at copying and moving entries as you examine 1-2-3's ability to adjust formulas.

Copying Labels

There are many situations in which copying labels can save you time. Perhaps you want to create a worksheet that uses account titles or months of the year in two different locations. Rather than typing the labels again, you can copy them. Not only does this save you time, it also guarantees that both sets of entries are identical. Copying labels is also useful when you have a number of similar entries to make; you can often copy your original entries and make minor editing changes in less time than it would take to type each of the entries.

Telling 1-2-3 Which Data to Copy

The copy operation is a little different from the other menu commands you have used since it is actually split into two commands. The first step is selecting the entries to copy and putting them in the Clipboard with the **E**dit **C**opy command. The second step is copying the entries from the Clipboard to the new worksheet location with the **E**dit **P**aste command. Since the **E**dit **C**opy command has no dialog box, you must select the range of entries to copy *before* you select the command.

An example will help clarify how easy it is to copy a label. Follow these steps:

1. Move the cell pointer to A1 in a new worksheet and type **Sales - Product A**. Then press ENTER or click the confirm box.

2. Select **E**dit **C**opy.

Notice that nothing appears to have happened at this point. This is because you do not see that 1-2-3 has copied this label to the Windows Clipboard. If you want to see the Clipboard's contents, you can open the Clipboard application window from the Main group window.

3. Move the cell pointer to A2, which is where you want the copy.

4. Select **E**dit **P**aste to generate these results:

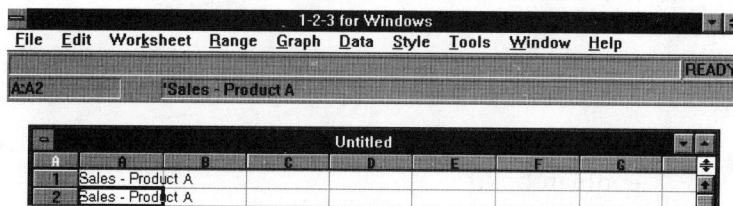

9

classic *Only one command, /Copy, is used to copy cells with the Classic menu, and the procedure is different. You must select the cells to copy, press ENTER, select where you want the copies, and press ENTER again.*

The new label is identical to the original entry, but you used far fewer keystrokes to create it. If A2 had contained an entry before you copied the label, the previous entry would have been erased.

The advantage of using the Clipboard to copy worksheet entries is that the contents remain in the Clipboard. You can make another copy of the Clipboard's contents simply by moving the cell pointer to where you want the next copy and pasting it onto the worksheet.

5. Move the cell pointer to A3, which is where you want the next copy.

6. Select **E**dit **P**aste to make another copy of the label.

Later in this chapter, you learn how to extend this productivity even further by copying to many locations with one command. You can also press some keystroke combinations that make copying entries easier. When you copy cells, you are not only copying the actual entries, you are also copying the numeric formats and text appearance settings that you learned about in Chapter 6, "Changing the Appearance of Worksheet Cells."

Modifying Copied Labels   The entry in A2 is currently identical to the original. Sometimes this situation is exactly what you need; at other times, however, a slight modification might be required. If you wanted the label "Sales - Product B" in A2 and the label "Sales - Product C" in A3, the copying the label approach is still best. Fixing the labels requires these steps:

1. Move the cell pointer to A2 and press F2 (Edit).

2. Press the BACKSPACE key, type **B**, and press ENTER or click the confirm box.

3. Move the cell pointer to A3 and press F2 (Edit).

4. Press the BACKSPACE key, type **C**, and press ENTER or click the confirm box. Your altered entries look like this:

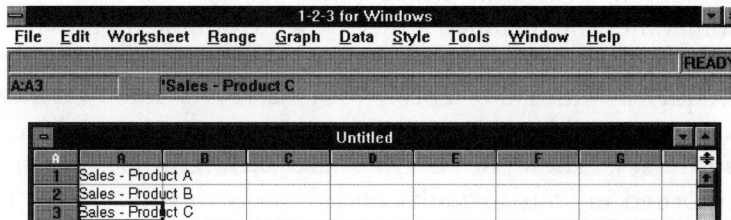

Keep this possibility in mind when you look for opportunities to copy; copying entries followed by a quick edit can still be much quicker than making new entries. Since you can use this feature with numbers as well, one potential application is to generate a list of numbers with only one digit different.

5. Select **File Close** to erase the current worksheet and start over. Select **No** so the current worksheet entries are not saved.

Copying Formulas

In one sense, copying formulas is no different from copying labels or numbers. It is accomplished with the same commands. With formulas, however, you need to control how 1-2-3 copies the cell addresses in formulas. If you have one constant interest rate and want all formulas to refer to it, you must be able to direct 1-2-3 to leave the reference to the interest rate unchanged as it copies. You need a different approach if you enter a formula for January profit that subtracts the cost of goods sold in January from the sales for January and you want to copy this formula for the other 11 months. You cannot calculate February's profit by subtracting the January cost-of-goods-sold figure from January sales—you need to subtract February's cost of goods sold from February sales. Fortunately, 1-2-3 can handle both situations. You handle these different types of calculations by using cell address types in the original formula; they are not an option during the copying process. Let's examine the different reference types to help clarify this.

9

Address Types

All the cell addresses you have entered in formulas so far have contained a column name immediately followed by a row number; sometimes you included a sheet label. Examples of these types of addresses are A1, B:E4, and IV2000. This is the cell address type that you use most frequently with 1-2-3. This type of address is called a *relative address*. There are two additional types of addresses: absolute addresses and mixed addresses. These three types are distinguished by the way they are recorded in your formulas and the way in which 1-2-3 performs a copy operation for each of them. It is important to master the differences between these types of addresses as you learn how to copy formulas; the address type you use is critical in determining how 1-2-3 copies your formulas to new worksheet locations.

Relative Addresses   Relative addresses are the only type of cell address you have used prior to this chapter. You can enter them easily in formulas by using the typing or pointing method of formula creation. When 1-2-3 records your entry, it appears to store the formula exactly as you entered it. If you move your cell pointer to any cell that holds one of the formulas you have entered, you will see the exact formula you entered in the control panel.

However, 1-2-3 remembers your instructions in a slightly different way from what it displays. If you store the formula +A1+A2 in cell A3, 1-2-3 interprets your instructions in this way: "Take the value that is located two cells above this cell and add the value that is located one cell above this cell." When your formula contains relative references, 1-2-3 remembers everything in terms of relative direction and distances from the cell that will contain the result.

When you copy this type of formula to another location, 1-2-3 adjusts the formula in the new location to reflect the same relative distances and directions. This means that 1-2-3 remembers the formula, using the same relative terms the original version of the formula uses. For example, if you copy the formula stored in A3 to B3, the formula you would see in the control panel for B3 is +B1+B2. The cell addresses are different from the original, but the formula still records the same relative directions: "Take the value that is located two cells above this cell and add the value that is located one cell above this cell." 1-2-3 automatically makes this adjustment as it copies formulas containing relative addresses.

Let's build a model that allows you to practice copying a formula that uses relative references. This model records profits for the current year and projects them for the next five years. The final result of your entries will look like the worksheet in Figure 9-1. Follow these steps to create the model:

1. Move the cell pointer to C1, type **Sales Projections 1992 - 1996**, and then press ENTER or click the confirm box.

2. Move the cell pointer to A4 and make these entries:

A4: **Sales**	D3: **^1993**
A5: **COGS**	E3: **^1994**
A6: **Profit**	F3: **^1995**
B3: **^1991**	G3: **^1996**
C3: **^1992**	

The caret (^) symbols in front of the year entries cause the numeric digits to be treated as labels and centers them within the cells.

Figure 9-1. *The completed sales projection model*

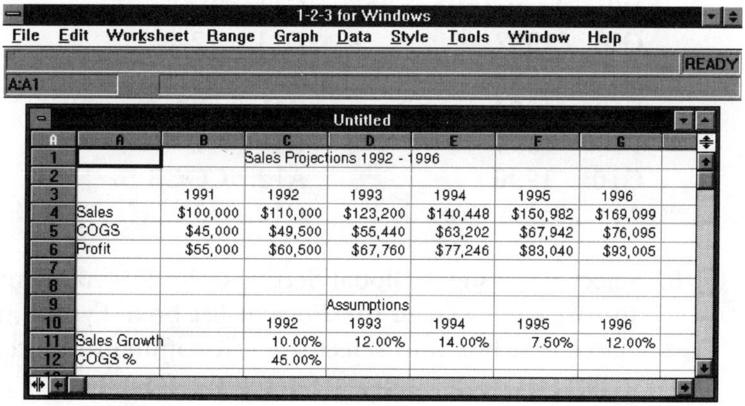

3. Move the cell pointer to B4 and make these entries for 1991:

    B4: **100000**
    B5: **45000**
    B6: **55000**

These entries are not computed, as they are assumed to be the actual numbers at the end of 1991.

It is time to think about how you want to project sales for the remaining years. You can use a constant growth rate that would apply to all years, or you can assume that sales will grow at varying percentages each year. You must also decide how to compute the cost of the goods sold each year. One method is to use a percentage of sales. Even if you select this method without evaluating other options, you must again decide whether to use one percentage rate for all years or vary the percentage by year. The profit calculation does not require you to make a decision, since it is always equal to sales minus cost of goods sold. This model assumes that sales will grow at varying rates but that cost of goods sold will be the same percentage of sales each year. You must enter these assumptions before projections can be made.

4. Complete these entries:

D9:	**Assumptions**	C11:	**.1**
C10:	**^1992**	D11:	**.12**
D10:	**^1993**	E11:	**.14**
E10:	**^1994**	F11:	**.075**
F10:	**^1995**	G11:	**.12**
G10:	**^1996**	A12:	**COGS %**
A11:	**Sales Growth**	C12:	**.45**

5. Select Worksheet **G**lobal Settings, the **F**ormat command button, and Currency from the **F**ormat list box. Type **0** in the **D**ecimal Places text box and select the OK command button twice.

This instruction sets the Global format to Currency, but you also need to use a **R**ange **F**ormat command for the percentages in the model that display as zeros.

6. Select the range C11..G12. Select **R**ange Format, and Percent from the **F**ormat list box, and the OK command button to format these percentages with two digits after the decimal point.

Your entries now look like those shown in Figure 9-2.

7. Move the cell pointer to C4, type **+B4*(1+C11)**, and press ENTER or click the confirm box.

This computes the sales projection for 1992. Rather than typing this formula for each year, a better option is to copy it.

8. Press CTRL-INS.

CTRL-INS is the shortcut for the **E**dit **C**opy command. (Edit command shortcuts appear on the right side of the **E**dit pull-down menu.) When you copy data to the Clipboard, it replaces the data that was previously in the Clipboard; the Clipboard now contains the formula that is in C4 rather than the label you copied earlier.

Figure 9-2. *The model after initial entries*

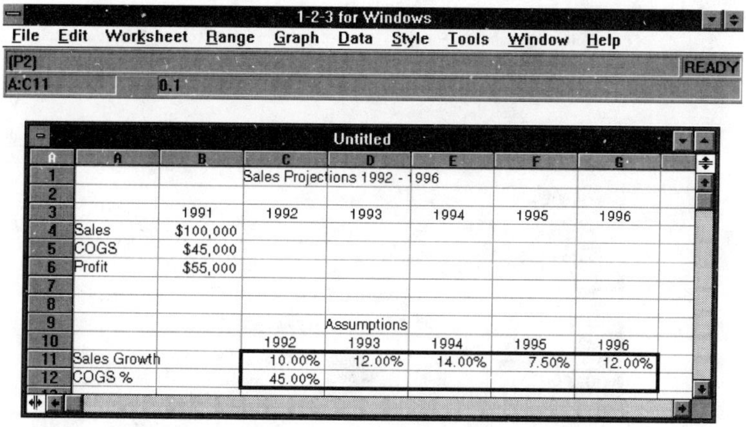

9. Move the cell pointer to D4 and press SHIFT-INS. SHIFT-INS is the shortcut for the **Edit P**aste command.

Now you can see the copied formula, which is shown in Figure 9-3.

Notice that 1-2-3 adjusted each of the cell references to take the new location of the result into account. Each reference in the formula is the same distance and direction from the result in D4 as the original references were from C4, where the original result was computed. Before completing the copy process for the other years, you will want to look at an absolute reference—a reference that is not updated by a copy operation.

Absolute Addresses   *Absolute addresses* are cell references that remain the same regardless of where the formula is copied to. The formula reference is effectively frozen in place and is not allowed to change. To create this type of reference, you must place the $ character in front of the row, column, and sheet portions of the address. $A:$A$10 or $A:$D$8 are examples of absolute cell references.

You can create an absolute reference in one of two ways: by typing or pointing. Both parallel the creation method for relative references. If you choose to build the formula by typing, you can type the dollar signs. You

Figure 9-3.   *The copied formula*

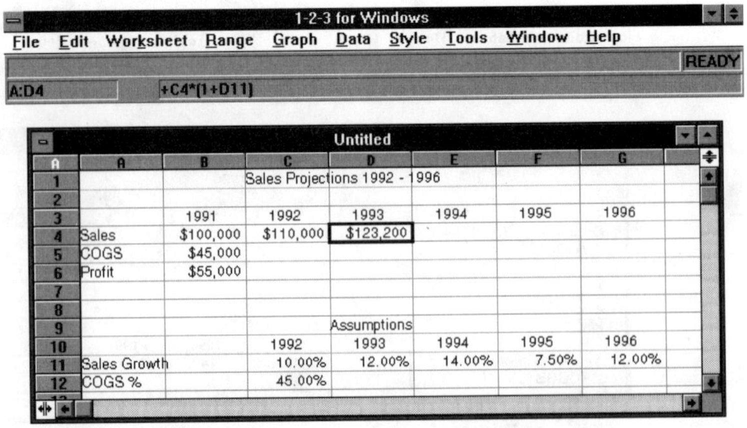

A	A	B	C	D	E	F	G
1			Sales Projections 1992 - 1996				
2							
3		1991	1992	1993	1994	1995	1996
4	Sales	$100,000	$110,000	$123,200			
5	COGS	$45,000					
6	Profit	$55,000					
7							
8							
9				Assumptions			
10			1992	1993	1994	1995	1996
11	Sales Growth		10.00%	12.00%	14.00%	7.50%	12.00%
12	COGS %		45.00%				

A:D4   +C4*(1+D11)

can also press F4 (Abs) in EDIT, VALUE or POINT mode; 1-2-3 then adds the dollar signs in front of the row, column, and sheet portions of the address. This is different than pressing F4 to switch from READY to POINT mode.

Use this approach to build the cost-of-goods-sold data. Follow these steps to enhance the sales projection model you have been working on:

1. Move the cell pointer to C5.
2. Type **+** and move the cell pointer to C4.
3. Type ***** and move the cell pointer to C12.
4. Press F4 (Abs) once to add the $ signs to the cell you are pointing to.

Your formula is now +C4*$C$12. You can also press F4 (Abs) to add the $ signs to the current cell address in the EDIT and VALUE modes. If you press F4 (Abs) on a range address, 1-2-3 changes both corners of the address.

5. Press ENTER or click the confirm box to complete the formula.
6. Press CTRL-INS to copy this formula to the Clipboard.
7. Move the cell pointer to D5 and press SHIFT-INS to copy the formula from the Clipboard to the worksheet.

You can see that the new formula also references C12 for its cost-of-goods-sold percentage, as shown in Figure 9-4.

Mixed Addresses   Mixed addresses borrow something from each of the other two types of addresses. A *mixed address* is "mixed" in that one part is fixed and the other parts are relative. This means that the row, column, or sheet portion of the address can be fixed, but not all three. When you copy a formula that uses mixed address types, the fixed portion behaves like an absolute address, and the other portion functions like a relative address and is adjusted based on the location it is copied to.

Examples of mixed addresses are A$5, $D7, and $B:A20. In A$5, the column portion of the address is adjusted as the formula is copied to different columns, but the row portion remains fixed as the formula is copied to other rows. In $D7, the exact opposite takes place: the column

9

Figure 9-4.   *The Copy operation completed for the COGS formula*

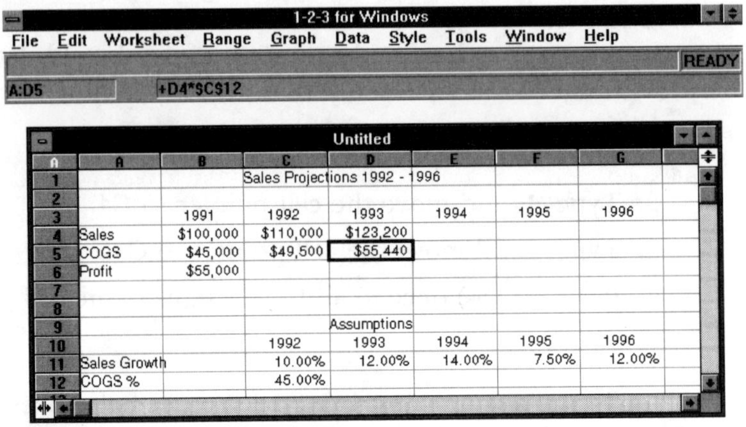

portion of the address remains fixed, regardless of where the formula containing it is copied, and the row portion is updated when the formula is copied to a different row. In $B:A20, the address always refers to sheet B, regardless of the sheet the formula containing this cell reference is copied to.

Mixed addresses are used only if you are building complex models. Still, it is important to know that they work in case you ever see a mixed address in a formula. You will want to focus your time on the relative and absolute address types as you copy formulas. Table 9-1 shows an illustration of the three types of addresses in formulas.

The Scope of Copying Entries

You have learned how to copy an entry to a new location on the worksheet by completing the preceding exercises. This is just one of the ways you can copy entries. Other options are copying the contents of one cell to many additional locations and copying many entries to many additional locations.

Copying One Entry to One New Location   You have already copied the sales and cost-of-goods-sold projections for 1992 to create the same

Table 9-1. *Different Address Reference Types*

Type of Address	Sample Formula in A3	How 1-2-3 Remembers the Sample Formula
Relative	+A1+A2	Add the value of the cell two cells above this one to the value of the cell above this one
Absolute	+$A$1+$A$2	Add A1 and A2
Mixed	+A$1+A$2	Add the value in this column from row 1 to the value in this column from row 2

projections for 1993. Now you will copy a formula that calculates the profit for 1992 and 1993. Follow these steps to add a formula for profit and then to copy the formula to one additional location:

1. Move the cell pointer to C6.
2. Type **+C4−C5** and press ENTER or click the confirm box.

Since you wish both cell addresses in this formula to be updated for the appropriate year when the formula is copied, both references are relative.

3. Press CTRL-INS or click the Edit Copy SmartIcon in the icon palette to copy this formula to the Clipboard. The Edit Copy SmartIcon looks like this:

4. Move the cell pointer to D6 and press SHIFT-INS or click the Edit Paste SmartIcon in the icon palette to copy the formula from the Clipboard to this cell. The Edit Paste SmartIcon looks like this:

9

You have been making slow but steady progress in completing the model. Now it is time to step up the pace and copy to more than one location at a time.

Copying One Entry to Many Locations   Copying entries is not restricted to the single-copy approach you have been using. By expanding the size of the target range, you can copy the entry in one cell to a range that is as large as a row or column of the worksheet. You can put this expanded version of copying entries to use in completing the sales projections for the remaining years of the model:

1. Move the cell pointer to D4.

2. Press CTRL-INS or click the Edit Copy SmartIcon in the icon palette to copy this formula to the Clipboard.

3. Select the range E4..G4 by using SHIFT, F4 (Abs) or the mouse.

4. Press SHIFT-INS or click the Edit Paste SmartIcon in the icon palette to copy the formula in the Clipboard to each cell in the selected range.

The worksheet now looks like the one in Figure 9-5.

Figure 9-5.   *Copying the sales formula to many cells*

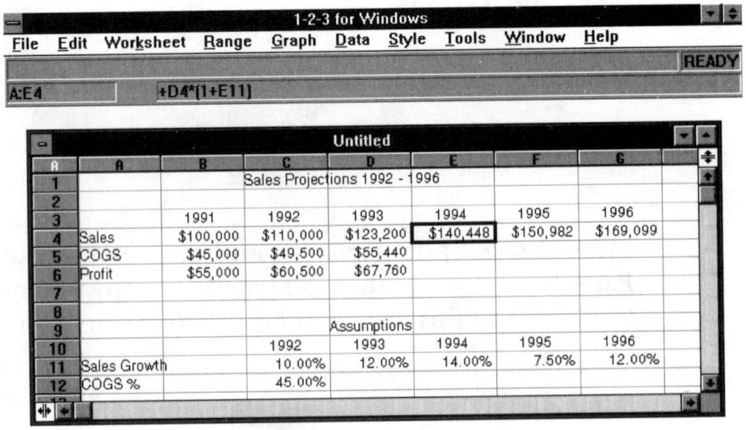

Copying Many Entries to Many New Locations You can step up the pace a little more and copy a column or a row of formulas to many columns or many rows all in one step. To accomplish this, you must select a range of cells to copy and paste. You can use this approach to complete the formulas for your model. You can copy the two formulas in D5 and D6 to columns E, F, and G. Follow these directions to complete the model:

1. Select the range D5..D6 with F4 (Abs) or the mouse.

2. Press CTRL-INS or click the Edit Copy SmartIcon to copy these two formulas to the Clipboard.

3. Select the range E5..G5.

You need to select the entire range to hold the copies because you are making more than one copy.

4. Press SHIFT-INS to copy the formulas from the Clipboard to the worksheet and to see the results shown in Figure 9-6.

Figure 9-6. *The result of the Copy operation for Cogs and Profit*

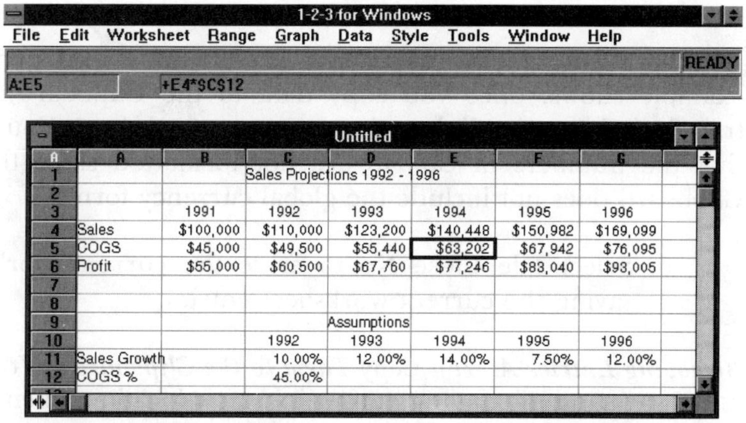

9

Copying a row of cell entries follows the same basic pattern as this example. First, you must select the row of cells to copy and copy it to the Clipboard. Next, you must select a range to tell 1-2-3 where to copy this row to and how far down the worksheet to copy it. Keep in mind that all these copy methods can be used for values and labels just as easily as for formula entries. Also, after you make these multiple copies, the data is still in the Clipboard so you can make another copy by pasting it to a worksheet range.

Copying to Other Worksheet Files   So far, the examples of copying data have used the same worksheet in the same worksheet file. You can copy your cell entries to any worksheet in any worksheet file. You do this simply by switching to the worksheet or worksheet file where you want the entries copied to after you use the **Edit Copy** command to copy the data to the Clipboard and before you use the **Edit Paste** command. You can try out this command by following these steps:

1. Select the range A1..G12 with F4 (Abs) or the mouse.
2. Press CTRL-INS or click the Edit Copy SmartIcon to copy these entries to the Clipboard.
3. Select **File New** to open a new worksheet window.
4. Move the cell pointer to B3, where you want to put the copy.
5. Press SHIFT-INS to copy the entries from the Clipboard to the worksheet.

The 1-2-3 window now looks like the one in Figure 9-7. As this example shows, once you copy data to the Clipboard, you can then transfer it from the Clipboard to any open worksheet. You will also notice that the numbers in C6..H8 are not formatted since the data in the Clipboard does not include the global currency format.

6. Select **File Close No** to erase the current worksheet without saving the current worksheet entries.

Removing Entries As You Copy Them to the Clipboard   You can use another variation of copying entries to a new location when you no longer want to retain the original. For example, you may want to remove a range from one location but copy it in three other locations. You can remove the

Figure 9-7. *Copying entries to another worksheet file*

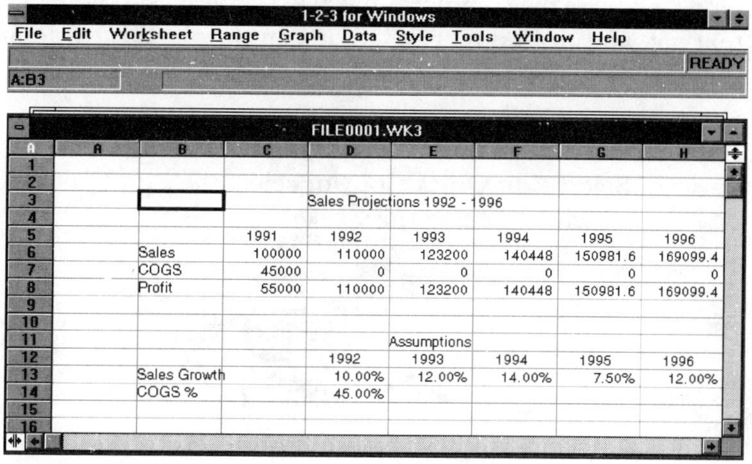

original entries as you copy the entries onto the Clipboard by using the **Edit Cut** command instead of the **Edit Copy** command. Unlike the **Edit Copy** command, once you select the **Edit Cut** command, the entries no longer appear on the worksheet. After you copy the data to the Clipboard, you can move to the location where you want the entries copied and select the **Edit Paste** command. The **Edit Cut** command also has a SmartIcon you can use in place of the command. The Edit Cut SmartIcon looks like this:

classic The Edit Cut command is equivalent to /Range Erase or /Range Move from the Classic menu, depending on whether or not you copy the data to a new location.

Copying Without Using the Clipboard

So far you have learned how to copy entries by using the Clipboard. You may sometimes want to copy without using the Clipboard. For example, you may want to copy entries without removing the current Clipboard's contents. To copy entries without the Clipboard, select **Edit Quick Copy**. This command has two text boxes to enter ranges, the **From** text box and the **To** text box. You can try out this command by following these steps:

1. Select the range A9..G12.

2. Select **Edit Quick Copy** or select the Edit Quick Copy SmartIcon, which looks like this:

The Edit Quick Copy dialog box presents two text boxes. The first is the **From** text box, which tells 1-2-3 where you want to copy from. This is like the range you select before using the **Edit Copy** command. When you preselect a range, it appears in this text box. The other text box is the **To** text box, which tells 1-2-3 where you want to copy to. This is like the range you select before using the **Edit Paste** command. You need to select only the first cell where you want each copy. If you use the Edit Quick Copy SmartIcon you only need to select the To range using the prompt in the edit line.

3. Type **A15** in the **To** text box and select the OK command button.

Figure 9-8 shows the original entries and the copy.

4. Select the range A15..G18 and press DEL or click the Edit Cut SmartIcon to remove these entries.

Copying entries with the **Edit Quick Copy** command adjusts formulas in the same way as when you copy with the Clipboard. The disadvantage of the **Edit Quick Copy** command is that if you want to make copies in several noncontiguous locations, you must use multiple **Edit Quick Copy** commands. Also, it is inconvenient to use the **Edit Quick Copy** command when you want to copy data between worksheets.

Figure 9-8. *Formulas copied without using the Clipboard*

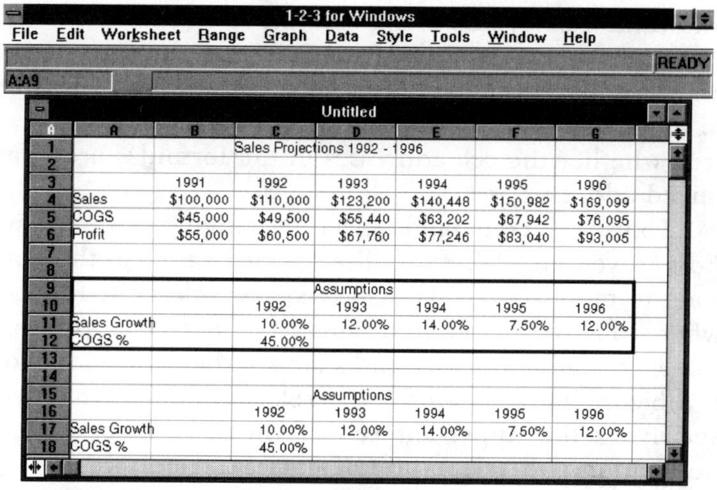

Rearranging the Worksheet

Planning is the best assurance that your completed model both looks good and meets your business needs. But even when you plan, there will be occasions when you want to rearrange the data contained in your model. 1-2-3 has commands that reorganize the worksheet for you so you do not have to reenter and erase entries the way you would with a manual version of your model. These commands include two that can move any range of data to another range that is the same size and shape. Another command allows you to take a row of data and place it in a column or to take a column of data and place it in a row.

Moving Worksheet Data

The **E**dit **M**ove Cells command moves data in one range of the worksheet to another range. This range can be a single cell, a row of cells, a column of cells, or a rectangle with multiple rows and columns. The size and shape of the relocated data are determined by the original location of the data. This means that a row of data can be moved only to another row and cannot be placed into a column of cells.

You can use the **Edit Move Cells** command to relocate labels, values, and formulas. When you move formulas, 1-2-3 adjusts the cell references in the formulas to reflect the cell's new location on the worksheet. This is true whether the cell addresses in the formulas are relative, absolute, or mixed address types.

To use this command, select the range you want to move. Next, select **Edit Move Cells.** 1-2-3 uses the selected range as the range of entries you want to move. In the **To** text box, you select the first cell of the location where to move the selected range. You need to supply only one cell; since 1-2-3 determines the size and shape of the data being moved, all you need is a beginning location for the relocated data, which you can define by specifying the upper-left cell of the new area. Once you specify the destination and select the OK command button, the move operation is complete.

You can try the **Edit Move Cells** command to relocate your assumptions on the current model by following these steps:

1. Select the range A9..G12.

2. Select **Edit Move Cells** or click the Edit Move Cells SmartIcon, which looks like this:

3. Type **B22** in the **To** text box and select the OK command button.

If you click the Edit Move Cells SmartIcon, point to B22.

4. Move the cell pointer to G26 to see where the range was moved.

classic — *Use the /Move command from the Classic menu to relocate data.*

The entire range of cells containing assumption data is relocated to B22..H26, as shown in Figure 9-9.

Figure 9-9. *Moved data*

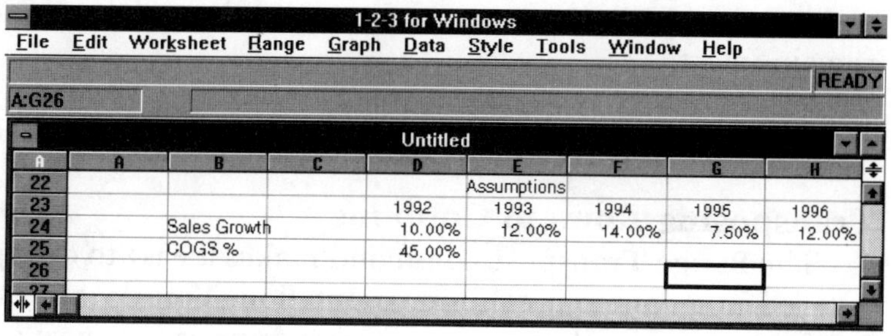

5. Select **File Save As**, type **SALESPRJ** in the File **N**ame text box, and select the OK command button to save this worksheet.

6. Select **File C**lose to erase the current worksheet and start a new one.

Transposing Data

1-2-3's Transpose feature offers another way to rearrange your worksheet data. Not only does 1-2-3's **R**ange **T**ranspose command copy data, it also alters its orientation. This command places data with a row orientation into a column. Likewise, it places data with a column orientation into a row. A third possibility is to transpose data between sheets. The power of this command will become apparent the first time you need to do major restructuring of a worksheet. In this section, you have an opportunity to try the first two types of transposition. Transposing between sheets is a more advanced topic than you will want to learn right now.

Transposition can be done with labels, numbers, and formulas. When you transpose rows or columns containing formulas, 1-2-3 copies the results of the formulas to the new locations. The resulting copy contains numbers but not formulas. This allows you to transpose formulas without concern for whether or not the new orientation will damage the resulting entries. In earlier releases, when you transposed formulas, 1-2-3 adjusted the formulas as if you were copying them to a new location rather than moving them. When you transpose worksheet data, the original entries remain intact.

≡classic≡ Use /Range Transpose from the Classic menu to change the orientation of data.

Transposing Rows to Columns

The **R**ange **T**ranspose command makes it easy to change data that was entered in a row to a column orientation. You do not even need to tell 1-2-3 whether the data you are transposing is in a row or column; 1-2-3 can figure it out from the range that you define. All you need to do is define the data to transpose and then tell 1-2-3 the upper-left cell of the area in which you wish to place the data. The following example illustrates how this command works.

    1. Make these entries in cells B2..F2:

        B2: **Sales - Balls**
        C2: **Sales - Kites**
        D2: **Sales - Rafts**
        E2: **Sales - Jacks**
        F2: **Sales - Blocks**

The entries appear as follows:

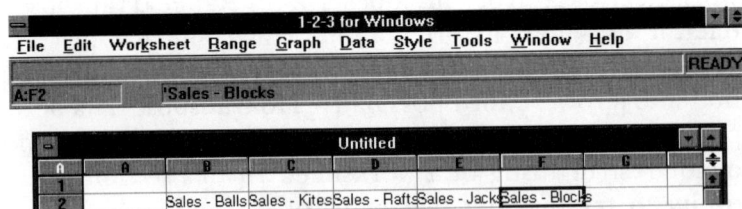

You can now try a different orientation by using the **R**ange **T**ranspose command.

    2. Select the range B2..F2 with F4 (Abs) or the mouse.

    3. Select **R**ange **T**ranspose.

1-2-3 has already put B2..F2 in the **F**rom text box as the source range. All you need to do is tell 1-2-3 where to start transposing the data.

4. Type **A4** in the **T**o text box and select the OK command button.

This places the entries in column A, but the original entries are still in row 2. Your worksheet should match the display shown in Figure 9-10.

5. Select **F**ile **C**lose **N**o to erase the current worksheet without saving the data and to start a new one.

Columns to Rows

Transposing column data to a row is just as easy as the other way around. Try this example with the months of the year:

1. Using Figure 9-11 as your guide, enter the first six months in A3..A8.

Figure 9-10. *Data in a row transposed to a column*

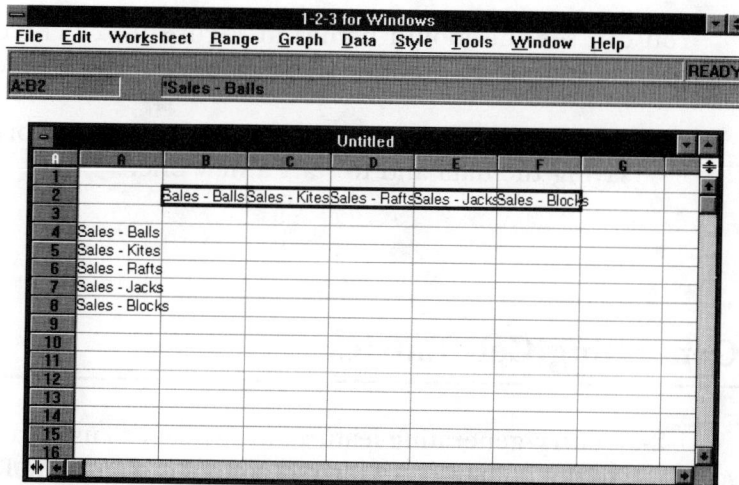

Figure 9-11. *Data entered in a column*

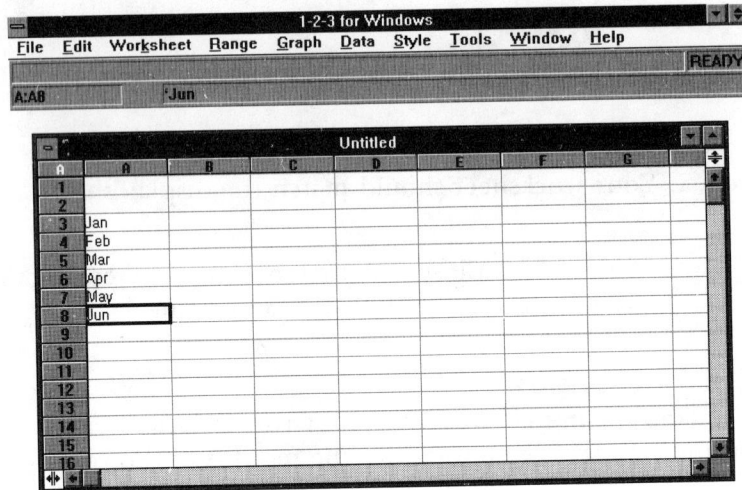

2. Select the range A3..A8 by using F4 (Abs) or the mouse.

3. Select **R**ange **T**ranspose.

4. Type **B2** in the **T**o text box and select the OK command button.

You can see the month names in Figure 9-12. The original entries remain unless you use the **E**dit **C**lear command to remove them.

5. Select **F**ile **C**lose **N**o to erase the current worksheet without saving the data and to start a new one.

Generating Cell Entries

1-2-3's entry-generating features are so easy to use that it is like having someone perform data entry for you free of charge. The Repeating Label feature provided by 1-2-3 can generate dividing lines and other quick

Figure 9-12. *Data in a column transposed to a row*

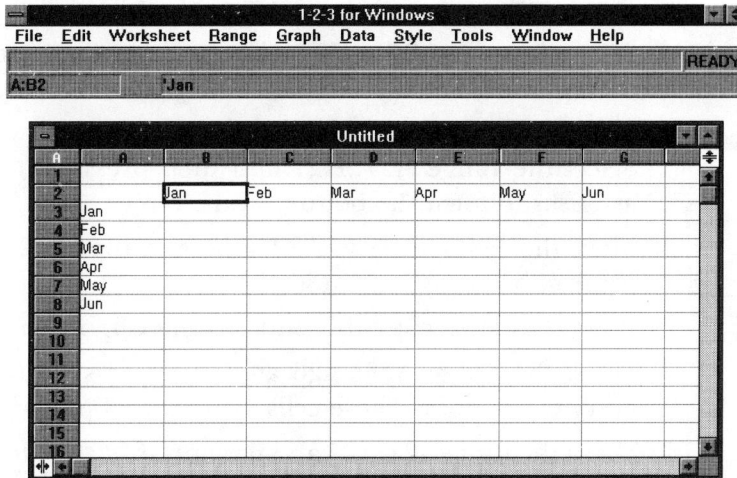

entries in worksheet cells. The other feature, a series generator, can generate a series of numbers that have the same increment between all the values in the series—for example, the series 1, 2, 3, 4 or 25, 50, 75, 100.

Creating Repeating Labels

You do not need a menu command to generate repeating labels. Instead, you accomplish the task with the special backslash (\) label prefix followed by either a single character or a series of characters. 1-2-3 duplicates your entry automatically to fill the complete display width of the cell and adjusts the entry if you change the cell width.

Follow these steps to use the repeating label prefix to draw a box of asterisks around the assumptions section of the worksheet:

1. Select **File Open**, type **SALESPRJ** in the File **N**ame text box, and select the OK command button.

2. Move the cell pointer to A21, type *****, and press ENTER or click the confirm box.

Notice that the asterisks completely fill A21.

3. Press CTRL-INS to copy this entry to the Clipboard.

4. Select the range B21..H21 with SHIFT, F4 (Abs) or the mouse and then press SHIFT-INS to copy the entry from the Clipboard to each of these cells.

5. Select the range A27..H27 and then press SHIFT-INS to copy the asterisks to form the bottom of the box.

6. Move the cell pointer to A22, type *, and press ENTER or click the confirm box.

7. Press CTRL-INS to copy this entry to the Clipboard.

8. Select the range A23..A26 and then press SHIFT-INS to copy the entry from A22 to these cells using the Clipboard.

9. Select the range I21..I27 and then press SHIFT-INS to copy the entry from A22 to I21..I27 using the Clipboard.

The final result of your entries is a line of asterisks on all four sides of the assumptions, as shown in Figure 9-13.

10. Select the **File Save** command.

11. Select **File Close** to erase the current worksheet.

Figure 9-13. *A box generated with the repeating label prefix*

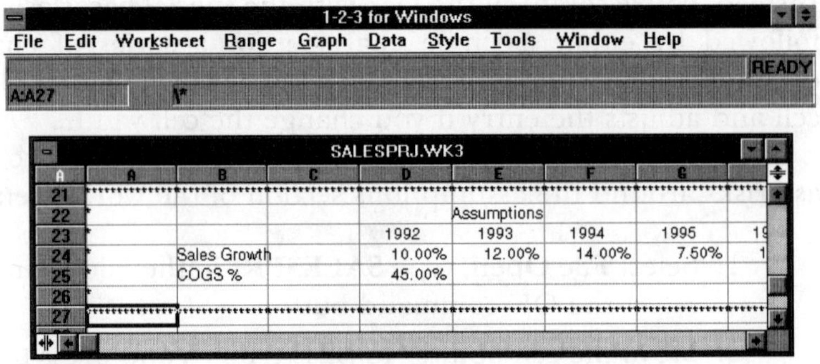

Generating a Series of Numbers

It can be tedious to enter a long list of numbers. In one special situation, you can assign this task to 1-2-3: when the list of numbers is a series with equal intervals. The interval can be either positive or negative, but it must be the same between all numbers in the series. This means that lists such as 10, 20, 30, 40; 7, 9, 11, 13, 15; 52609, 52610, 52611; and 30, 29, 28, 27 can be generated by the package. A list such as 1, 3, 7, 15 could not be generated because the intervals between the numbers in the list are not the same.

classic *The /Data Fill command is used in earlier releases to generate the series of numbers. Just as with 1-2-3 for Windows, you can provide a start value, stop value, and increment.*

Follow these instructions to try this feature by generating a list of invoice numbers:

1. Type **Inv. No.** in A3.

2. Select the range A4..A12 with F4 (Abs) or the mouse as the range you want 1-2-3 to fill with numbers.

3. Select **D**ata Fill.

4. Type **57103** in the **S**tart text box for the first number that 1-2-3 will use to fill the range.

The value in the Step text box is the value that is added to each value in the list to create the next entry. The default is one, but you can enter a different number if you want a different increment between the numbers 1-2-3 generates.

5. Type **59000** in the Stop text box so the dialog box looks like this:

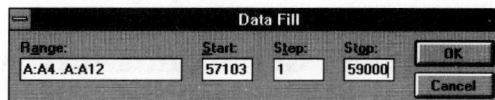

	Data Fill				
Range:		**S**tart:	St**e**p:	St**o**p:	OK
A:A4..A:A12		57103	1	59000	Cancel

9

Figure 9-14.   *Numbers generated by the Data Fill command*

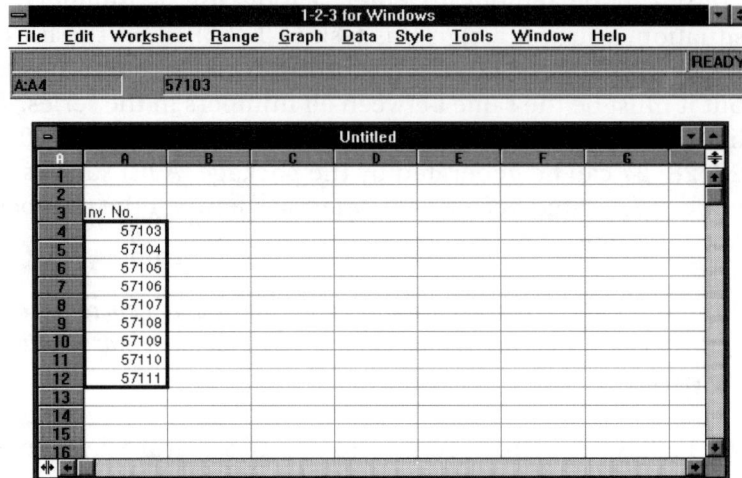

The stop value must always be as large as the last value in the list. This means that there are two factors that can end a list. 1-2-3 stops generating the fill numbers when it fills the range. The numbers can also stop sooner if the stop value is not large enough to accommodate the numbers you are generating.

> 6. Select the OK command button.

The list of numbers generated is shown in Figure 9-14. Naturally, you can make your range larger to generate a larger list of numbers. You can also choose a horizontal range of cells and create an entry for each cell in the row.

> 7. Select **File** **C**lose **N**o to erase the current worksheet without saving the data.

Other Worksheet Commands for Expanded Data

Now you have learned how to create models quickly. In this section, you find out how you can create many more models. Some of the models you create will contain data for many months or years. You will also want to learn some of the tricks that make working with these models easier, such as controlling recalculation. This is a helpful trick because, as your models grow larger, 1-2-3 takes longer to recalculate after each of your entries. 1-2-3's speed seems quite good, compared to manual alternatives, when you do what-if analyses; but if you are entering a long list of account names or invoice numbers, the constant recalculation can lower 1-2-3's performance.

You also need to use additional tools for large models since the entire model cannot be kept on the screen. You learn how you can freeze certain information on the screen and how you can have 1-2-3 find entries on the worksheet for you.

Recalculation

You access 1-2-3's recalculation options with the Tools User Setup Recalculation dialog box. This dialog box has three parts. You can select when the worksheet is recalculated, the order in which 1-2-3 recalculates formulas, and how many times 1-2-3 recalculates the worksheet. The latter two options are seldom required. If you are curious about these, check your 1-2-3 manual. The first option can be a real time-saver with any large worksheet. 1-2-3 uses *minimal recalculation,* allowing 1-2-3 to recalculate only those formulas affected by worksheet changes. 1-2-3 also uses *background recalculation,* which means that 1-2-3 performs the recalculation in between the times you are entering and editing data. Minimal and background recalculation enable you to update your worksheet formulas as quickly as possible.

=*classic*=

The /Worksheet Global Recalculation command is used in earlier releases to change recalculation options.

You can alter the timing of recalculation for the sales projection worksheet by following these steps:

1. Select **File Open,** type **SALESPRJ** in the File **N**ame text box, and select the OK command button.

9

2. Select the **T**ools **U**ser Setup command and the **R**ecalculation command button to display the Tools User Setup Recalculation dialog box.

The **A**utomatic and **M**anual option buttons let you choose whether 1-2-3 automatically updates the model after a change or you control recalculation.

3. Select the **M**anual option button once and the OK command button twice.

This selection means that 1-2-3 does not recalculate formulas after a worksheet change.

To recalculate the worksheet, you need to press the F9 (Calc) key.

4. Move your cell pointer to C4, type **120000**, and press ENTER or click the confirm box.

Notice that this change does not affect the formulas, although Calc does appear in the status line. The Calc status line indicator is a warning that the worksheet has not been recalculated since changes have been made.

5. Press F9 (Calc).

Now you will see the results of the change.

6. Change the value in C4 back to 110000 by typing **110000** and pressing ENTER or clicking the confirm box.

Again, the results are not affected.

7. Press F9 (Calc).

Your display should again show the results you started with.

8. Select the **T**ools **U**ser Setup command, the **R**ecalculation command button, and the **A**utomatic option button. Select the OK command button twice to return to READY mode.

From this point on, every worksheet entry will cause recalculation. Keep this easy-to-make change in mind; it is a great option when you have a significant amount of data to enter.

Using Titles with Large Worksheets

One of the problems with large worksheets is that you cannot see all the data on the screen at one time. This problem is magnified when you move your cell pointer to the right or down and find that the labels at the left of the rows and the top of the columns scroll off the screen. You can find yourself in a sea of numbers with no visible indication of what each of these numbers represents. The solution in 1-2-3 is to freeze some of the label information on the screen. Freezing information on the screen is another 1-2-3 feature, like splitting a window into panes (as you learned in Chapter 8, "Managing Files and Sheets"), that you may want to use with larger worksheets.

The Worksheet Titles command freezes entries on the screen. As with splitting a window into panes, the cell pointer position at the time you invoke this command is critical. If your cell pointer is in A1, you cannot create either vertical or horizontal titles—there is no information below or to the left of the cell pointer. The cell-pointer location defines what information is frozen on the screen. The command has four options: to fix titles both vertically and horizontally, to fix them vertically, to fix them horizontally, and to clear all fixed titles from the screen. This last option does not eliminate the titles themselves, but it ensures that neither vertical nor horizontal titles are frozen any longer.

If you choose to freeze vertical titles with either the **Vertical** or **Both** option button, when you invoke Worksheet Titles, any columns to the left of the cell pointer become fixed on the screen. You cannot move your cell pointer into these columns with the arrow keys or the mouse. As you move to the right of the point at which columns would normally scroll off the screen, only columns to the right of the frozen titles scroll off the screen. The columns defined as titles are always visible.

The situation is similar for horizontal titles, whether you choose **Horizontal** or **Both**. All rows above the cell pointer at the time Worksheet Titles is invoked will remain frozen on the screen, even when the cell

9

pointer moves far enough down on the worksheet to cause rows to scroll off the screen. The rows below the frozen titles can scroll off the screen, but the titles you have fixed on the screen cannot.

classic */Worksheet Titles with options for Horizontal, Vertical, Both, and Clear is the Classic menu option for creating and removing worksheet titles.*

Looking at an example of this command with the sales projection worksheet will show you how it works. If you wanted to bring the right edge of the sales projection assumptions box into view, the left edge would scroll off the screen unless you first froze the titles. Use these steps for freezing columns A through C:

1. Move the cell pointer so A21 is the cell in the upper-left corner of the worksheet window. Move the cell pointer to D25.

You could have just moved the cell pointer to D25, but this step ensures that you have only the desired rows and columns above and to the left of the cell pointer.

2. Select Worksheet **T**itles, the **V**ertical option button, and the OK command button.

3. Move the cell pointer to K25 to produce the display shown in Figure 9-15. Notice that columns A, B, and C are frozen on the screen, yet columns D, E, F, and G have scrolled off the screen.

4. Select Worksheet **T**itles, the **C**lear option button, and the OK command button.

This unfreezes the titles, and columns A through C scroll off the screen.

These title-freezing features are useful when you want to see totals at the bottom of a long column or on the right side of a long row. By freezing the titles, you can check the total and still keep the corresponding labels on the screen for readability.

Figure 9-15. *Vertical titles displaying columns A, B, and C frozen on the screen*

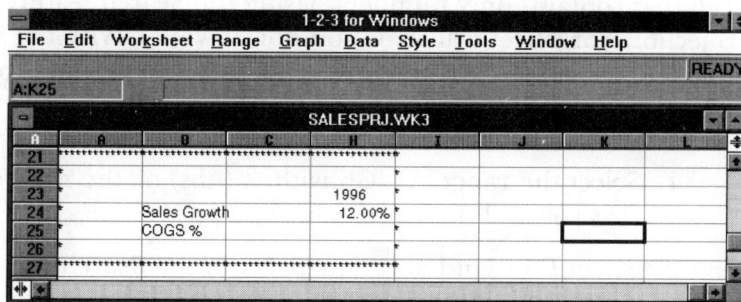

Searching for and Replacing Worksheet Data

At you create large worksheets that model your business operations, it is more difficult to find a particular entry; it is no longer practical to scan the model for a particular entry. You can have 1-2-3 scrutinize entries for you. 1-2-3 can find a string of characters in either labels or formulas. Instead of just locating the matching characters, you can also use the Replace option to change the matching characters to another set of characters. These Search and Replace features can save you time in reviewing entries, as well as the editing time required for those you want to change.

The **Edit Find** command finds and replaces worksheet data. You can find text in cell formulas and labels. Since 1-2-3 can replace text as well as find it, you can use this command to correct a misspelling and change a cell address that formulas use, as well as to find a name in a worksheet. The options for replacing text or cell addresses allow you to make changes to all the affected cells at once. If you would prefer to move a little more slowly, you can skip a matching entry, find the next matching entry to replace, or replace the current matching entry and move to the next one.

classic *The /Range Search command is the Classic menu alternative to* **Edit Find.**

Searching for Worksheet Data

1-2-3 can find text stored in formulas and labels. 1-2-3 does not search a cell that contains only numbers. Using the Search feature with the sales projection worksheet will show you how it works. With the SALESPRJ file in memory from the previous example, use these steps to find the text "Sales":

1. Select the range A1..G6 with F4 (Abs) or the mouse as the range that you will use to search.

2. Select **E**dit **F**ind and type **Sales** in the **S**earch For text box.

This step enters the characters you want to find. You can type **sales** or **SALES** for the same results.

3. Select the **L**abels option button and the Find **N**ext command button.

1-2-3 searches for the selected word since the Find option button under Action is selected. 1-2-3 finds the word "Sales" in A4 (searching a column at a time) and displays the address and entry in the edit line.

4. Select the Find **N**ext command button.

1-2-3 continues the search, column by column, finds "Sales" in C1, and shows the address and entry in the edit line.

If you select Find **N**ext, 1-2-3 will not find another Sales entry in the range selected but will beep and display a message box telling you that the range has no more matching entries.

5. Select the Cancel command button to return to READY mode.

You can also use the **E**dit **F**ind command to find text in formulas. To find which cells use the 1994 sales growth stored in F24, you can search for a cell reference to F24 in formulas within the model by using these steps:

1. Select **E**dit **F**ind and type **F24** in the **S**earch For text box.

1-2-3 has the same range from the previous **Edit Find** command in the **Range** text box. Typing **F24** replaces the word "Sales" from the previous search operation.

2. Select the **Formulas** option button and the **Find Next** command button.

Now 1-2-3 searches only formulas in the selected range for the cell reference F24. It finds F24 in E4 and displays the cell address and entry in the edit line.

3. Select the Find **Next** command button.

1-2-3 cannot find another formula that uses F24 so 1-2-3 beeps and displays this dialog box:

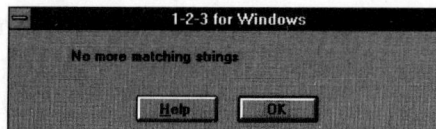

4. Select the OK command button to return to READY mode.

Replacing Worksheet Data

If you make a few mistakes when reentering labels and formulas, the **Replace** option of 1-2-3's **Edit Find** command can handle the corrections for you. The **Replace** option not only locates your text, it also changes it to whatever character string you specify. You can use the SALESPRJ worksheet and follow these steps to replace the text "Profit" with "Gross Profit":

1. Select **Edit Find** and type **Profit** in the **Search For** text box.

2. Select the **Labels** option button and the **Replace With** option button.

Now 1-2-3 will replace occurrences of the string "Profit" with the text that you enter in the text box below the **R**eplace With option button.

3. Type **Gross Profit** in the text box below the **R**eplace With option button and select the Find **N**ext command button.

1-2-3 finds Profit in A6.

4. Select the **R**eplace command button.

1-2-3 replaces "Profit" in A6 with "Gross Profit" and then searches for the next occurrence of "Profit". Since 1-2-3 cannot find another label that contains "Profit", it beeps and displays a dialog box indicating that it cannot find the search string.

5. Select the OK command button to return to READY mode.

When you use the **Edit Find** command to replace text in formulas or labels, you must be careful about what you supply as a search string. If the text that you search for is not clearly defined, you may wind up replacing text that you did not want to replace. As an example of an unintentional replacement, suppose you want to use the sales-growth rate for 1994 in 1995. One method of doing this is to replace the G24 cell reference with F24. If you use a search string of **G** and a replacement string of **F**, 1-2-3 returns unexpected results since it finds many unexpected matches. To show how this happens, follow these steps:

1. Select **E**dit **F**ind and type **G** in the **S**earch For text box.

The **B**oth option button is the default so 1-2-3 searches both labels and formulas.

2. Select the **R**eplace With option button, type **F** in the text box below, and select the Find **N**ext command button.

1-2-3 finds "G" in "COGS" in A5.

3. Select the **R**eplace All command button.

1-2-3 finds all occurrences of the letter "G" in A1..G6 and replaces them with the letter "F". When 1-2-3 cannot find another "G", it returns to READY mode. The screen looks like the one in Figure 9-16. You can see how results have changed.

4. Move the cell pointer to G6.

Since the search string is not specific enough, the **Edit Find** command replaced every "G" in the specified range, including the formula in G6 that should subtract G5 from G4. The entries in column G will highlight the error. The solution is to type **G24** as the search string and **F24** as the replacement string. Although you must type more characters, you exclude cells that you do not want to alter.

5. Select **File Close No** to erase the current worksheet without saving the data.

Figure 9-16. *The worksheet after supplying an inadequate search string*

	1-2-3 for Windows					
File	Edit	Worksheet	Range	Graph	Data	Style	Tools	Window	Help			

[W9]   READY
A:A1

SALESPRJ.WK3

	A	B	C	D	E	F	G
1		Sales Projections 1992 - 1996					
2							
3		1991	1992	1993	1994	1995	1996
4	Sales	$100,000	$110,000	$123,200	$140,448	$160,111	$179,324
5	COFS	$45,000	$49,500	$55,440	$63,202	$72,050	$72,050
6	Gross Profit	$55,000	$60,500	$67,760	$77,246	$88,061	$88,061
7							
8							
9							
10							
11							
12							
13							
14							
15							
16							

9

Review

In this chapter you learned the 1-2-3 commands and features that increase your productivity. These 1-2-3 features include the following:

- You can use the Windows Clipboard to copy data. You can use the Clipboard in 1-2-3 to copy worksheet entries from one location to another. To copy data into the Clipboard, select the range and then select the **Edit Copy** command, press CTRL-INS, or click the Edit Copy SmartIcon. To copy data from the Clipboard, select the cells where you want the Clipboard's contents to start being copied and then select the **Edit Paste** command, press SHIFT-INS, or click the Edit Paste SmartIcon. After using the **Edit Paste** command, the Clipboard's contents are still intact so you can use the **Edit Paste** command to make additional copies.

- You can make copies without using the Clipboard by using the **Edit Quick Copy** command or the Edit Quick Copy SmartIcon. For this command, you must enter the range to copy from and the range to copy to in the two text boxes in the dialog box.

- When you copy entries, you can copy one cell to one cell or one cell to many cells. You can also make one copy of an entire range of cells or make many copies of the same range. When you copy cells, 1-2-3 adjusts the formulas in the range according to whether the formulas use absolute, mixed, or relative cell addresses.

- The **Edit Move Cells** command moves cells within a worksheet. This command also has a SmartIcon in the icon palette. When you move cells, 1-2-3 adjusts the formulas so that all cell formulas reference the same cell contents as they did before cells were moved.

- The **Range Transpose** command copies a range of cells and changes the cells' orientation from row to column or column to row. If you transpose formulas, this command copies and transposes the results of the formulas rather than the formulas themselves.

- You can create a repeating label by using the backslash (\) label prefix. The characters that you enter after the backslash are repeated for the width of the cell.

- The **D**ata **F**ill command generates a series of numbers that are evenly spaced. To use this command, you must provide the worksheet range that you want to fill with numbers, the number that you want to start the series, the increment between values (positive for ascending and negative for descending), and the last value that may appear in the series.

- The Tools User Setup Recalculation dialog box determines whether 1-2-3 recalculates the worksheet whenever a worksheet entry is made or when you press the F9 (Calc) key. This command was more frequently used in earlier releases, which did not have the minimal and background recalculation that 1-2-3 for Windows features.

- The Worksheet **T**itles command locks rows and columns on the screen display so you can always see the column or row title. You can create horizontal titles (rows that always appear on the screen), vertical titles (columns that always appear on the screen), or both titles (columns and rows that always appear on the screen), and you can clear titles (unlock them on the screen).

- The **E**dit Find command can search for text in label or formula cell entries. The Replace option allows you to replace the text the command finds with different text.

Commands and Keys

This chapter introduced you to the 1-2-3 commands that duplicate and move entries as well as other commands that make working with large worksheets easier. You learned to use keys that affect labels and formulas. These commands and keys are

Keys	Action
	As a label prefix character, repeats the string that follows until the column width is filled

9

Keys	Action
F4 (Abs)	In EDIT, POINT, or VALUE mode, converts an address to an absolute, mixed, or relative address
F9 (Calc)	Updates the calculations in the worksheet
ALT D F	**D**ata **F**ill generates a series of numbers a specific interval apart
ALT E C	**E**dit **C**opy copies the selected range to the Clipboard
ALT E U	**E**dit C**u**t copies the selected range to the Clipboard and removes the original from the worksheet
ALT E F	**E**dit **F**ind finds, or finds and replaces, text in formulas and label cell entries
ALT E M	**E**dit **M**ove Cells moves a range to another location
ALT E P	**E**dit **P**aste copies the Clipboard's contents to the worksheet
ALT E Q	**E**dit **Q**uick Copy copies cell entries to another location without the Clipboard
ALT R T	**R**ange **T**ranspose copies one or more cells to a new location and changes the column and row orientation
ALT T U R	**T**ools **U**ser Setup **R**ecalculation sets when and how 1-2-3 recalculates the worksheet
ALT K T	Worksheet **T**itles sets the rows and columns that are frozen on the worksheet window

10

Printing Your Worksheet

In this chapter you have an opportunity to explore 1-2-3's printing features. You can use them to create a quick copy of your worksheet with only a few instructions. When you are ready for a final copy, you can change the page setup to create a professional-looking report.

You first learn to use the basic printing features. Then you learn more complex printing options, each skill building on those before it, until you have a set of printing features that you can use for all of your print needs. You learn about previewing your worksheet so you can see how it will appear when you print it. You also have the opportunity to explore options for printing formulas and to use worksheet commands to further customize your print output.

Printing Basics

1-2-3's basic printing features are designed to give you quick access to a printed copy. This quick access is made possible by default values that

1-2-3 has set for options such as margins. Later in this chapter, you learn to override these default settings, but for now you might as well appreciate their presence; they make it easy for you to print your files.

When you print, 1-2-3 assumes you want to print to the active printer you selected when Windows was installed. As long as this printer is attached to your system and online when you tell 1-2-3 to begin printing, your print output is sent to this device. Normally, the top or front of the printer has a series of small lights to indicate that the printer is ready to accept data. If the printer that you are using is next to your desk, verify that the printer is turned on and is online before you start to print. It is also a good idea to understand the defaults that will apply to your output before you learn about the instruction that actually starts the printing.

The **File Print** menu command is the command you use to print your data. The dialog box this command displays looks like this:

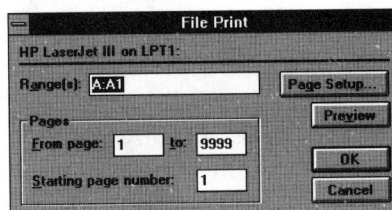

1-2-3 remembers the print settings from the last time you printed the worksheet. To have 1-2-3 remember what you want to print or any changes that you make to the print layout, first complete the definition of your print specifications, and then save the worksheet file. This saves the print settings with the worksheet for the next time you want to print the data.

classic   *From the Classic menu, type :P for the Wysiwyg Print menu. If you use the /Print Printer menu to print, your printout will not exactly match the worksheet in the window. Wysiwyg is a 1-2-3 add-in that provides spreadsheet publishing capabilities. Its features are incorporated into 1-2-3 for Windows' menu, but you can access its traditional menu by typing a colon.*

The Default Settings

One of the things that simplifies printing the first time you use a worksheet is the default settings of the page layout. These defaults affect how 1-2-3 prints the worksheet and the amount of white space, or the margin, on all four sides of a printed page. 1-2-3 fits a number of lines on the page based on the row heights in the worksheet range you select and a number of columns across based on the column width in the selected range. The **S**tyle **F**ont command you learned about in Chapter 6, "Changing the Appearance of Worksheet Cells," sets the size of the characters used in the worksheet, which in turn sets the row heights and column widths.

The page layout defined by 1-2-3 has several areas affecting the amount of data that prints on a page. A sample page layout is shown in Figure 10-1. Not all of the page contains printed data. Some of the area is reserved for top and bottom margins. In addition to the top and bottom margins, 1-2-3 reserves room at the top and bottom for a header and footer in case you use them. Similarly, on a standard 8 1/2- by 11-inch sheet of paper, the default settings reserve areas for the left and right margins. 1-2-3 initially sets the margins to one-half inch on each side (.55 of an inch on the bottom). You can use other margins, but initially, try the Print operation without modifying any of these defaults.

The Basic Printing Process

The first part of printing is telling 1-2-3 how much of the worksheet you wish to print. You can preselect a range or supply it in the File Print dialog box's **R**ange text box. If the worksheet was printed previously, when you select the **F**ile **P**rint command, the range address used from that time is still defined.

The size of the range you define affects how 1-2-3 prints your data. If your defined range contains more data than will fit on one page, 1-2-3 breaks the data into pages. If the width of the range selected exceeds the number of characters that will print across one page, 1-2-3 prints as many columns across the first page as possible. The remaining columns are printed on subsequent pages. If the number of rows in the selected range exceeds the number of rows that can print on one page, 1-2-3 generates a

10

Figure 10-1. *The layout of a printed page (default page setup)*

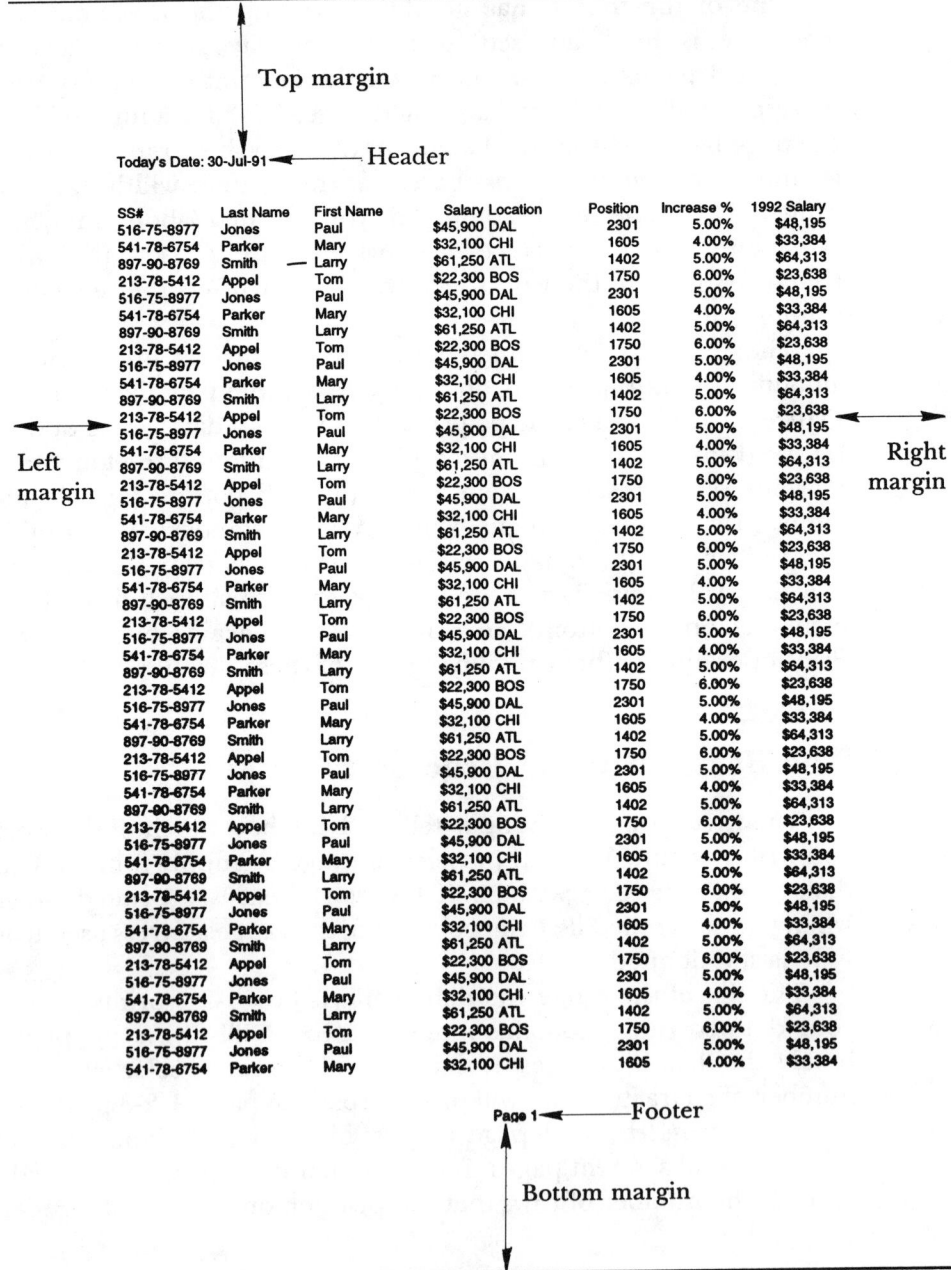

Top margin

Today's Date: 30-Jul-91 ◄———— Header

SS#	Last Name	First Name	Salary	Location	Position	Increase %	1992 Salary
516-75-8977	Jones	Paul	$45,900	DAL	2301	5.00%	$48,195
541-78-6754	Parker	Mary	$32,100	CHI	1605	4.00%	$33,384
897-90-8769	Smith	— Larry	$61,250	ATL	1402	5.00%	$64,313
213-78-5412	Appel	Tom	$22,300	BOS	1750	6.00%	$23,638
516-75-8977	Jones	Paul	$45,900	DAL	2301	5.00%	$48,195
541-78-6754	Parker	Mary	$32,100	CHI	1605	4.00%	$33,384
897-90-8769	Smith	Larry	$61,250	ATL	1402	5.00%	$64,313
213-78-5412	Appel	Tom	$22,300	BOS	1750	6.00%	$23,638
516-75-8977	Jones	Paul	$45,900	DAL	2301	5.00%	$48,195
541-78-6754	Parker	Mary	$32,100	CHI	1605	4.00%	$33,384
897-90-8769	Smith	Larry	$61,250	ATL	1402	5.00%	$64,313
213-78-5412	Appel	Tom	$22,300	BOS	1750	6.00%	$23,638
516-75-8977	Jones	Paul	$45,900	DAL	2301	5.00%	$48,195
541-78-6754	Parker	Mary	$32,100	CHI	1605	4.00%	$33,384
897-90-8769	Smith	Larry	$61,250	ATL	1402	5.00%	$64,313
213-78-5412	Appel	Tom	$22,300	BOS	1750	6.00%	$23,638
516-75-8977	Jones	Paul	$45,900	DAL	2301	5.00%	$48,195
541-78-6754	Parker	Mary	$32,100	CHI	1605	4.00%	$33,384
897-90-8769	Smith	Larry	$61,250	ATL	1402	5.00%	$64,313
213-78-5412	Appel	Tom	$22,300	BOS	1750	6.00%	$23,638
516-75-8977	Jones	Paul	$45,900	DAL	2301	5.00%	$48,195
541-78-6754	Parker	Mary	$32,100	CHI	1605	4.00%	$33,384
897-90-8769	Smith	Larry	$61,250	ATL	1402	5.00%	$64,313
213-78-5412	Appel	Tom	$22,300	BOS	1750	6.00%	$23,638
516-75-8977	Jones	Paul	$45,900	DAL	2301	5.00%	$48,195
541-78-6754	Parker	Mary	$32,100	CHI	1605	4.00%	$33,384
897-90-8769	Smith	Larry	$61,250	ATL	1402	5.00%	$64,313
213-78-5412	Appel	Tom	$22,300	BOS	1750	6.00%	$23,638
516-75-8977	Jones	Paul	$45,900	DAL	2301	5.00%	$48,195
541-78-6754	Parker	Mary	$32,100	CHI	1605	4.00%	$33,384
897-90-8769	Smith	Larry	$61,250	ATL	1402	5.00%	$64,313
213-78-5412	Appel	Tom	$22,300	BOS	1750	6.00%	$23,638
516-75-8977	Jones	Paul	$45,900	DAL	2301	5.00%	$48,195
541-78-6754	Parker	Mary	$32,100	CHI	1605	4.00%	$33,384
897-90-8769	Smith	Larry	$61,250	ATL	1402	5.00%	$64,313
213-78-5412	Appel	Tom	$22,300	BOS	1750	6.00%	$23,638
516-75-8977	Jones	Paul	$45,900	DAL	2301	5.00%	$48,195
541-78-6754	Parker	Mary	$32,100	CHI	1605	4.00%	$33,384
897-90-8769	Smith	Larry	$61,250	ATL	1402	5.00%	$64,313
213-78-5412	Appel	Tom	$22,300	BOS	1750	6.00%	$23,638
516-75-8977	Jones	Paul	$45,900	DAL	2301	5.00%	$48,195
541-78-6754	Parker	Mary	$32,100	CHI	1605	4.00%	$33,384

Left margin ◄———►   ◄———► Right margin

Page 1 ◄———— Footer

Bottom margin

page break when the data prints. Once you select a range to print, 1-2-3 displays dashed lines indicating the boundary of each page. The format line includes information about the page the cell pointer is on.

You can try several printing options with the following exercise. You will copy entries more than once to build a large file quickly so you can try out the extensive printing features covered in this chapter. Follow these steps to create the model and print it.

1. Enter the following labels across row 1:

A1: **SS#**	F1: **"Phone**
B1: **Last Name**	G1: **"Position**
C1: **First Name**	H1: **"Increase %**
D1: **"Salary**	I1: **"1992 Salary**
E1: **Location**	

2. Select the range A1..I1, and click the Underline SmartIcon or select the **Style Font** command, the **Underline** check box, and the OK command button.

When you print, 1-2-3 prints the worksheet with all of the cell formats you have added to the worksheet, including fonts and styles such as boldfacing and underlining. This means that before you print your data, you need to make any changes you want in the worksheet's appearance.

3. Make these entries in the cells shown:

A2: **'516-75-8977**	A4: **'897-90-8769**
B2: **Jones**	B4: **Smith**
C2: **Paul**	C4: **Jean**
D2: **45900**	D4: **61250**
E2: **DAL**	E4: **ATL**
F2: **980**	F4: **342**
G2: **2301**	G4: **1402**
H2: **.05**	H4: **.05**
I2: **+D2*(1+H2)**	A5: **'213-78-5412**
A3: **'541-78-6754**	B5: **Appel**
B3: **Parker**	C5: **Tom**
C3: **Mary**	D5: **22300**
D3: **32100**	E5: **BOS**

10

E3: CHI   F5: **219**
F3: **541**   G5: **1750**
G3: **1605**   H5: **.06**
H3: **.04**

4. Move the cell pointer to I2 and press CTRL-INS. Select the range I3..I5 and press SHIFT-INS.

This completes the first four records. You need more rows of data to get the full effect of 1-2-3's printing features, but typing the entries would take too long. Instead, copy these entries until you have a sufficient number to print more than one page. You will, of course, have many duplicates.

5. Select the range A2..I5 and press CTRL-INS. Move the cell pointer to A6 and press SHIFT-INS.

6. Move the cell pointer to A10 and press SHIFT-INS.

7. Repeat step 6 after moving to cells A14, A18, A22, A26, A30, A34, A38, A42, A46, A50, A54, A58, and A62.

Another option is to increase the size of the range each time you repeat step 6 since this reduces the number of copy operations that you need to perform.

8. Select the range D2..D65. Select the **R**ange **F**ormat command, select Currency in the **F**ormat list box, type **0** in the **D**ecimal Places text box, and select the OK command button.

9. Select the range H2..H65. Select the **R**ange **F**ormat command, select Percent in the **F**ormat list box, and select the OK command button.

10. Select the range I2..I65. Select the **R**ange **F**ormat command, select Currency in the **F**ormat list box, type **0** in the **D**ecimal Places text box, and select the OK command button.

The upper portion of your entries should match Figures 10-2 and 10-3.

11. Select the range A1..I65.

Figure 10-2. *The left side of the entries*

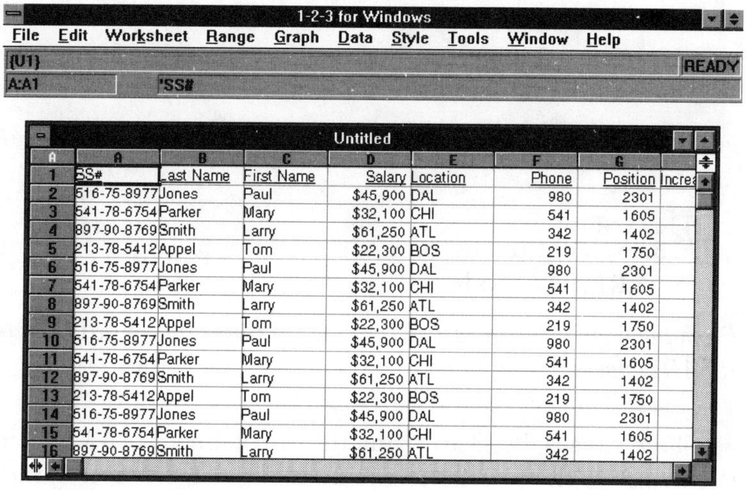

Figure 10-3. *The right side of the entries*

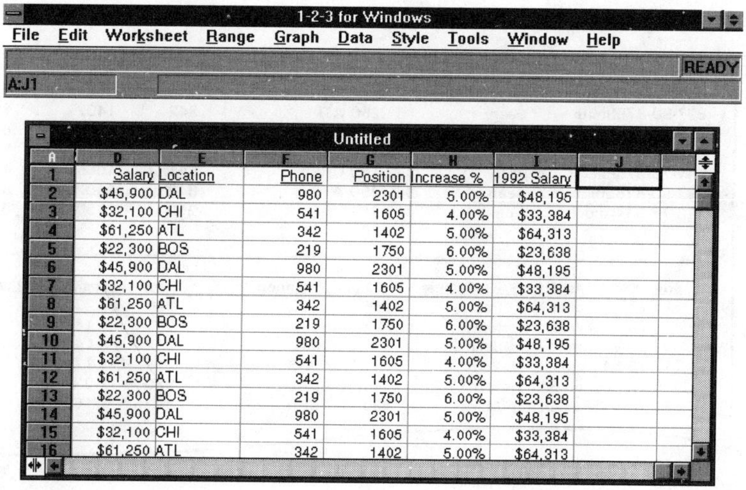

10

After moving to A1 and pressing F4 (Abs), you can use the END-HOME approach to include all of the cells.

12. Select **File Print**, and you see that 1-2-3 already has the preselected range in the **Range** text box.

classic *From the Classic menu, select the range to print with the :Print Range Set command.*

13. Select the OK command button to begin printing and return to READY mode.

classic *From the Classic menu, use the :Print Go command to start printing and return to READY mode.*

This causes 1-2-3 to print the worksheet. 1-2-3 automatically adjusts the paper in the printer to the next page. 1-2-3 uses Windows to print, so as soon as 1-2-3 sends all the information Windows needs to print the worksheet, you can return to working with 1-2-3. The printed output is shown in Figure 10-4.

Figure 10-4.   *The output from the print operation*

SS#	Last Name	First Name	Salary	Location	Phone	Position	Increase %	1992 Salary
897-90-876	Smith	Jean	$61,250	ATL	342	1402	5%	$64,313
213-78-541	Appel	Tom	$22,300	BOS	219	1750	6%	$23,638
516-75-897	Jones	Paul	$45,900	DAL	980	2301	5%	$48,195
541-78-675	Parker	Mary	$32,100	CHI	541	1605	4%	$33,384
897-90-876	Smith	Jean	$61,250	ATL	342	1402	5%	$64,313
213-78-541	Appel	Tom	$22,300	BOS	219	1750	6%	$23,638

SS#	Last Name	First Name	Salary	Location	Phone	Position	Increase %	1992 Salary
516-75-897	Jones	Paul	$45,900	DAL	980	2301	5%	$48,195
541-78-675	Parker	Mary	$32,100	CHI	541	1605	4%	$33,384
897-90-876	Smith	Jean	$61,250	ATL	342	1402	5%	$64,313
213-78-541	Appel	Tom	$22,300	BOS	219	1750	6%	$23,638
516-75-897	Jones	Paul	$45,900	DAL	980	2301	5%	$48,195
541-78-675	Parker	Mary	$32,100	CHI	541	1605	4%	$33,384

You can also quickly print a selected range by selecting the range and clicking the File Print SmartIcon. 1-2-3 prints the selected range without displaying the File Print dialog box. The File Print SmartIcon looks like this:

Printing Multiple Ranges

1-2-3 lets you select multiple ranges to print instead of selecting and printing each range separately. To select multiple print ranges, select each range and type a semicolon (;) or comma (,) when you want to select another range. You can mix typing range addresses, pointing to the range, and typing range names to print. When 1-2-3 prints the ranges, it starts in the order in which they were provided. To see how this feature works, follow these steps to print two sections of the worksheet:

1. Select **File Print**.
2. Type **A2.D5** in the Range text box as the first range to print.
3. Type **;** in the Range text box.
4. Type **A10.F15** in the Range text box as the second range to print.
5. Select the OK command button to begin printing and return to READY mode. Your output looks like Figure 10-5.

Figure 10-5. *Two ranges selected and printed*

516-75-8977	Jones	Paul	$45,900		
541-78-6754	Parker	Mary	$32,100		
897-90-8769	Smith	Jean	$61,250		
213-78-5412	Appel	Tom	$22,300		
516-75-8977	Jones	Paul	$45,900	DAL	980
541-78-6754	Parker	Mary	$32,100	CHI	541
897-90-8769	Smith	Jean	$61,250	ATL	342
213-78-5412	Appel	Tom	$22,300	BOS	219
516-75-8977	Jones	Paul	$45,900	DAL	980
541-78-6754	Parker	Mary	$32,100	CHI	541

10

Selecting Pages to Print

Initially, when you want to print your worksheet, you will want to print all of the pages in the range you select. If you then discover that one page out of several has an error, such as a misspelled name, you will not want to waste time and paper reprinting all of the pages in order to print the corrected page. You can easily print a single page or a group of pages by using the text boxes in the File Print dialog box. To try this, follow these steps:

1. Select the range A1..I65 with F4 (Abs) or the mouse.

2. Select File **P**rint.

3. Type **3** in the **F**rom Page text box and **3** in the **T**o text box.

4. Select the OK command button to print page 3.

5. Select File **P**rint.

6. Type **1** in the **F**rom Page text box and **9999** in the **T**o text box to return these to their default settings.

7. Select the OK command button to print one copy of each page.

Later in this chapter, you will learn how to add page numbers to your printed worksheets. 1-2-3 usually starts numbering pages with 1, but you can start from another page number by typing the page number for the first page in the **S**tarting Page Number text box.

Printing to a Different Printer

Usually you want to print to the printer that you installed as the active printer when you installed Windows. You can also print to any printer that is installed and connected to your system. If you want to print to a different printer than the default, you need to tell 1-2-3. To do this, select File Printer Setup. Next, select the printer to use from the ones listed in the **P**rinters list box. After you select the OK command button, when you print with the File **P**rint command, the command will go to the printer you selected with the File Printer Setup command. If you want to use a printer that is not listed, you must install it with Windows first.

While the File Printer Setup dialog box is displayed, you can select the **S**etup command button. This displays the Printer Setup dialog box, where you can change the printer settings that are set by Windows. The options you can change vary with different printers. When you select the OK command button, you are returned to the File Printer Setup dialog box.

Previewing Your Printed Worksheet

As you start changing your worksheet, you probably will be curious as to how the changes will appear when you print the data. You can see how the output will appear by *previewing* it, or displaying the worksheet data as it will appear when you print it. Previewing a worksheet before you print it lets you save time and resources since you can see if the printout is what you want before you actually print it. This is especially important if you are using a network printer and must wait for a print job in a long print queue.

To preview a worksheet you are printing, you can either use the **File Preview** command or select the Preview command button from the File Print dialog box. The difference between the methods is that when you finish previewing a printout with the **File Preview** command, you return to READY mode, and when you finish previewing with the **File Print** command, you return to the File Print dialog box. Try the two methods of previewing your output by following these steps:

1. Select **File Preview.**
2. Select the OK command button to display the printout on your screen, as shown in Figure 10-6.

You can also preview a range by selecting the range and then clicking the File Preview SmartIcon. 1-2-3 displays the previewed range without showing the File Program dialog box. The File Preview SmartIcon looks like this:

10

Figure 10-6.   *Previewing a worksheet before printing it*

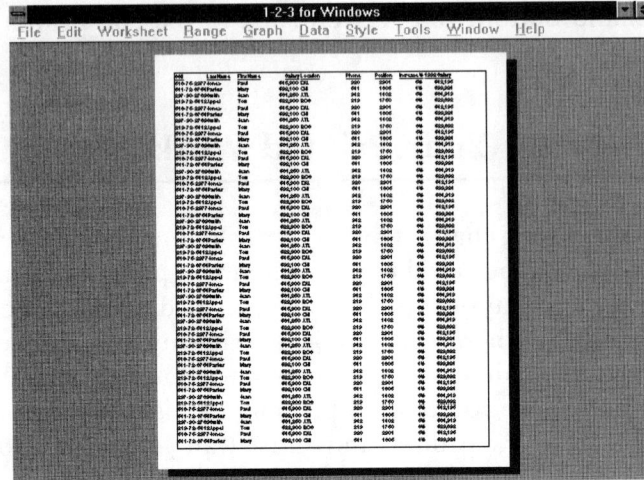

=*classic*= *From the Classic menu, select :Print Preview and then press any key to view each page and return to the :Print menu.*

The line around the edge of the paper represents the margins set for the page. You can advance through the pages by pressing any key. Pressing ESC returns you to READY mode.

3. Press any key or click the mouse until you return to READY mode.

4. Select **File Print**.

5. Select the Preview command button to display the printout on your screen, as shown in Figure 10-6.

6. Press any key until you return to the File Print dialog box.

7. Select the OK command button to begin printing and return to READY mode.

Adding Printing Options

You have already mastered the basics of printing; you do not need any other commands to get a printed copy of your data. But you may not be content with the appearance of your printout. If you want to improve it, the page setup options can assist you. The page setup is defined in the File Page Setup dialog box that appears with the **File Page** Setup command or when you select the **Page** Setup command button from the File Print or File Preview dialog box. From the File Page Setup dialog box, which appears in Figure 10-7, you can change many printing options, including margins, headers and footers, borders, and orientation. Later, if you want to return to the original page setup, you can select the **R**estore command button under Default Settings. The changes you make to the page setup are retained with the worksheet, just as 1-2-3 stores the range to print with the worksheet.

Margin Settings

The margin settings are displayed in the **T**op, **L**eft, **B**ottom, and **R**ight text boxes under Margins. The number in each text box represents the distance, for the appropriate side, from the edge of the paper to the edge

Figure 10-7. *The File Page Setup dialog box*

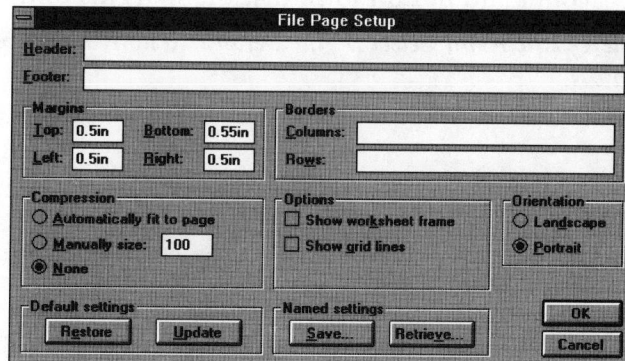

of the area where 1-2-3 can print your data. To change a margin setting, type a new number in the text box. The top and bottom margins can range from 0 to the length of the paper. The right and left margins can range from 0 to the width of the paper. Some printers require minimum margins, so if you enter 0 for the margin, 1-2-3 changes the 0 to the minimum amount. You can enter the measurement in inches, centimeters, or millimeters. By default, 1-2-3 expects your entry to be in inches, but 1-2-3 recognizes your entry as centimeters or millimeters if you type **cm** or **mm** after the number you enter for the margin.

Try the following exercise with the employee data to see how margins can affect the output:

1. Select **File Print** and select the **Page Setup** command button.

2. Type **1** in the **Left** text box under Margins.

classic — *From the Classic menu, select :Print Layout Margins, select the side to add the margin to, type the margin amount, and press* ENTER.

3. Type **1** in the **Right** text box under Margins and select the OK command button to return to the File Print dialog box.

4. Select the OK command button in the File Print dialog box.

You should find that one fewer column prints across the first page because you have reserved more space for the right and left margins.

5. Select **File Page Setup**, the **Restore** command button, and the OK command button to return the margins to the default.

classic — *From the Classic menu, select :Print Default Restore to restore the print settings to the defaults.*

Defining Headers and Footers

Headers and *footers* are lines that can appear at the top and bottom of every page of print output. Information placed in the header (at the top of a page) can include the date or time, an identifying report number, a report title, the preparer's name, or a page number. The most frequent entry in a footer (at the bottom of the page) is the page number.

Headers and footers can be up to 512 characters each and always use the first font in the Fonts list box in the Style Font dialog box. However, do not make headers and footers any longer than the number of characters that will fit on one line, or 1-2-3 will truncate the extra characters. For example, if the default font style, page width, and left and right margins fit only 100 characters on a line, do not enter a header longer than 100 characters. You create a header or footer by typing the text to appear at the top and bottom of every page in the **Header** or **Footer** text box. When either or both of these text boxes contain entries, 1-2-3 prints the header and/or footer with two blank lines separating the header and footer from the rest of the printed information. You can remove a header or footer by deleting the entry in the text box.

Using Special Symbols

You can use two special symbols anywhere in a header or footer to add special information. The @ symbol makes 1-2-3 substitute the current system date at its location when the header or footer line is printed. The # symbol makes 1-2-3 insert the current page number at its location in the header or footer. Normally, 1-2-3 starts numbering pages with page 1, by entering the first page number in the **Starting Page Number** text box in the File Print or File Preview dialog box.

These special symbols can be used alone or in combination with text characters. If you wanted the words "Page Number" to appear in front of the actual page number, you would type **Page Number #** in the **Header** text box. Likewise, if you wanted to label the date, you could type **Today's Date: @**.

The Three Sections

1-2-3 allows you to define entries for the left, middle, and right sections of a header or footer. In other words, each header or footer has the potential to be divided into three sections. The sections are separated by a vertical bar (|).

When you type a header in the **Header** text box, whatever you type will appear left aligned in the header line. When you are finished entering information for the left section, type a vertical bar (|) to indicate that you would like to begin entering the text to center. When you have completed the text to center, type another vertical bar (|) to indicate the beginning of the entry to right align. You can omit any section by entering the vertical

10

bar to end the section without entering anything in it. For example, the header ‖**Report Number: 3405** does not place anything in the left and middle sections of the header. It right aligns "Report Number: 3405" in the header line. You can also enter everything on the left side by not using any vertical bar characters in your header.

Try this exercise to see how adding a header can affect your output:

1. Select **File Print**, select the **Page Setup** command button, type **Report No: 2350‖Page #** in the **H**eader text box, and select the OK command button.

classic   *From the Classic menu, select :Print Layout Titles Header, type the header, and press ENTER.*

2. Select the OK command button twice to return to the File Print dialog box and print the worksheet.

Figure 10-8 shows the header at the top of the first two printed pages.

Figure 10-8.   *A header at the top of two pages*

Report No: 2350						Page 1
SS#	Last Name	First Name	Salary	Location	Phone	Position
516-75-8977	Jones	Paul	$45,900	DAL	980	2301
541-78-6754	Parker	Mary	$32,100	CHI	541	1605
897-90-8769	Smith	Jean	$61,250	ATL	342	1402
213-78-5412	Appel	Tom	$22,300	BOS	219	1750

Report No: 2350					Page 2
213-78-5412	Appel	Tom	$22,300	BOS	219	1750
516-75-8977	Jones	Paul	$45,900	DAL	980	2301
541-78-6754	Parker	Mary	$32,100	CHI	541	1605
897-90-8769	Smith	Jean	$61,250	ATL	342	1402

Using a Cell's Contents

In addition to entering the header or footer in the text boxes, you can enter the text for the header or footer in the worksheet and then tell 1-2-3 to use the cell's contents as the header or footer. This allows you to easily switch between multiple headers and footers. To use a cell's contents for the header or footer, type a backslash (\) and the cell address or range name that you want to use for the header or footer in the **Header** or **Footer** text box. If you enter a range name, 1-2-3 uses the cell in the upper-left corner of the range. 1-2-3 uses a cell's contents just as if you typed that cell's contents in the **Header** or **Footer** text box. This means you can include the vertical bars and the special @ and # symbols in the cell.

You may want to use this new feature to select from one of several headings when you print a report. To change a heading, all you do is type a backslash and the cell address that contains the header that you want. As an example, you can create the same header shown in Figure 10-8 by typing **Report No: 2350‖Page #** in K1. Then, from the Page Setup dialog box, type **\K1** in the **Header** or **Footer** text box. When you print the report, 1-2-3 will use **Report No: 2350‖Page #** as the header. If the **Header** or **Footer** text box contains a backslash and a cell address or range name, it cannot contain the other special header or footer characters, although the cell referenced in the header or footer can.

Using Borders

The labels you enter at the top and left side of a worksheet provide descriptive information on the first page of a printed report. When the rows in the worksheet exceed the length of one page, the rows at the top do not repeat automatically, and the second page may contain data that is meaningless without labels. Similarly, when the columns in the worksheet exceed the width of one page, the columns at the left appear only on the first page. Data further to the right appears on subsequent pages but may be meaningless without labels. When you look at worksheets that are wide and long in a worksheet window, you can freeze titles to continue displaying the identifying labels to the left and above. When you print worksheets that are wide and long, you can have *print borders,* which print the same columns and rows on each page that you would freeze with titles.

10

Print borders allow you to select rows or columns that will appear at the top or left side of every printed page. The columns or rows you select as borders should not be included in the print range. Otherwise, this data will print twice on the first page of the report: once as part of the border, and once as part of the print range.

To select the columns and rows used for the print borders, enter range addresses or names in the **C**olumns or **R**ows text box under Borders. When you want to place information at the top of the worksheet on every page, select a range that includes at least one cell in each row you want to use in the **R**ows text box. To use column information on each page, choose a range with at least one cell from every column you want to use in the **C**olumns text box.

You can put the Borders option to use for the employee file; the worksheet has more rows than will fit on one page, and the second page has no identifying labels or column heads. Follow these steps to add column and row borders:

1. Select the range D2..I65 with F4 (Abs) or the mouse.

You want to select a new range to print that does not include the columns and rows you will use for borders.

2. Select **File P**rint and the **P**age Setup command button.

3. Move to the **C**olumns text box and select the range A1..C1.

You need to select a range containing only one cell from each column you want to use; 1-2-3 automatically uses as many rows from the selected columns as it needs.

classic *Select :Print Layout Borders, then type **L** for Left to add column borders or **T** for Top to add row borders, select a range, and press ENTER.*

4. Move to the **R**ows text box and select the range A1..A1.

5. Select the OK command button twice to return to the File Print dialog box and print the data.

Figure 10-9. *The Borders option places labels on all pages*

Report No: 2350							Page 1
SS#	Last Name	First Name	Salary Location		Phone	Position	Increase %
516-75-897	Jones	Paul	$45,900	DAL	980	2301	5%
541-78-675	Parker	Mary	$32,100	CHI	541	1605	4%
897-90-876	Smith	Jean	$61,250	ATL	342	1402	5%
213-78-541	Appel	Tom	$22,300	BOS	219	1750	6%
516-75-897	Jones	Paul	$45,900	DAL	980	2301	5%

Report No: 2350							Page 2
SS#	Last Name	First Name	Salary Location		Phone	Position	Increase %
213-78-541	Appel	Tom	$22,300	BOS	219	1750	6%
516-75-897	Jones	Paul	$45,900	DAL	980	2301	5%
541-78-675	Parker	Mary	$32,100	CHI	541	1605	4%
897-90-876	Smith	Jean	$61,250	ATL	342	1402	5%
			$22,300	BOS	219	1750	6%

Report No: 2350				Page 3
SS#	Last Name	First Name	1992 Salary	
516-75-897	Jones	Paul	$48,195	
541-78-675	Parker	Mary	$33,384	
897-90-876	Smith	Jean	$64,313	
213-78-541	Appel	Tom	$23,638	
516-75-897	Jones	Paul	$48,195	

Report No: 2350				Page 4
SS#	Last Name	First Name	1992 Salary	
213-78-541	Appel	Tom	$23,638	
516-75-897	Jones	Paul	$48,195	
541-78-675	Parker	Mary	$33,384	
897-90-876	Smith	Jean	$64,313	
			$23,638	

The output contains labels at the top and left of each page, as shown in Figure 10-9. To remove these borders, you remove the range addresses in the **C**olumns or **R**ows text box.

1-2-3 has another option, which prints a different type of border. You can add a frame around the print range that displays the row and column labels. You can also print the grid lines just as you see them on the worksheet. To include a frame and grid lines in the print range, follow these steps:

10

1. Select **File** **P**rint, and the **Page** Setup command button.

2. Select the Show Worksheet Frame and the Show **G**rid Lines check boxes.

classic *From the Classic menu, select :Print Settings Frame Yes Grid Yes to add a worksheet frame and grid lines.*

3. Select the OK command button twice to return to the File Print dialog box and print the data.

4. Select **F**ile Pa**g**e Setup, unmark the Show Worksheet Frame and the Show **G**rid Lines check boxes, and select the OK command button.

Setting the Orientation

When you print a document, 1-2-3 initially prints from the top of the page to the bottom. An alternative is printing sideways. You may want to print sideways on the page so you can print a wider but shorter document. To try it, follow these steps:

1. Select the range D2..I65 for the new range to print.

2. Select **File** **P**rint, the **Page** Setup command button, and the **Land**scape option button.

classic *From the Classic menu, select :Print Configuration Orientation Landscape to rotate the printout.*

3. Select the OK command button twice to return to the File Print dialog box and print the entries sideways.

This command sequence prints the worksheet in landscape mode (if your printer has that capability). 1-2-3 automatically adjusts the range that is printed on each page to fit in the sideways area of print space on each page, so the worksheet page divisions will be different.

4. Select **F**ile Page Setup, the **P**ortrait option button, and the OK command button to return later printing to portrait mode.

Other 1-2-3 Commands That Affect Printing

1-2-3 has two commands that affect printing that are not found in the File menu. These commands are for adding page breaks and hiding columns. You learned about hiding columns in Chapter 7, "Changing Row and Column Options," but you can also use hidden columns to select which columns are printed.

Adding Page Breaks

You can add a page break at any location within a worksheet to ensure that the information following the page break starts a new page. This feature can prevent awkward breaks that can occur, for example, between the last number in a column of numbers and the total beneath it. 1-2-3 adjusts the automatic page breaks based on the size of the range and where you add manual page breaks. If you do not want automatic page breaks where 1-2-3 puts them, you must insert additional manual breaks to interrupt the automatic page-processing feature. You can add page breaks either between rows or between columns.

To insert a horizontal page break between rows, move the cell pointer to a cell in the row that you want to force to the top of a new page. Then select Worksheet **P**age Break **H**orizontal and the OK command button. To insert a vertical page break between columns, move the cell pointer to a cell in the column that you want to force to the next page and select Worksheet **P**age Break **V**ertical and the OK command button. You can also add both page breaks at once by moving the cell pointer to the cell that you want to be in the first column and first row printed on the next page and selecting Worksheet **P**age Break **B**oth and the OK command button. 1-2-3 adds dotted lines to indicate where the worksheet will be divided.

Follow these steps to insert a page break in the employee listing:

1. Move the cell pointer to F31.
2. Select Worksheet **P**age Break **B**oth and the OK command button.

From the Classic menu, select :Worksheet Page and then Column or Page to add a page break.

10

Now the pages are divided between rows 30 and 31 and between columns E and F. The format line when the cell pointer is along one of the manual page breaks displays MPage instead of Page, which is displayed for automatic page breaks.

3. Select **File P**rint and the OK command button to print this range with the new page breaks.

4. Select Worksheet **P**age Break **C**lear and the OK command button to remove these manual page breaks and return to using 1-2-3's automatic ones.

Hiding Columns

1-2-3's Worksheet **H**ide command can enhance the features of printing by letting you define a wide print range and hiding columns that you do not want printed. 1-2-3 cannot print two separate ranges side by side. However, you can effectively print separate columns of information in the same row by hiding the columns that lie between the areas you want to print.

This feature is especially advantageous when a worksheet contains confidential information. You can hide a column that contains salary information or a projected increase percentage, yet you can still create a list of employee names, locations, and phone numbers, even when the salary information is in the midst of the data columns you need. As mentioned in Chapter 7, "Changing Row and Column Options," hiding the column does not destroy the salary data—it merely removes temporarily the unwanted data from view. When you want to restore hidden data, use the Worksheet **U**nhide command. You can try this by following these steps to print a copy of the employee data without the salary or social security number columns:

1. Move the cell pointer to column A.

2. Select Worksheet **H**ide, the **C**olumn option button, and the OK command button.

3. Move the cell pointer to column D, where the salary information is stored.

Figure 10-10. *A printed worksheet with hidden columns*

Report No: 2350   Page 1

Last Name	First Name	Location	Phone	Position	Increase %	1992 Salary
Jones	Paul	DAL	980	2301	5%	$48,195
Parker	Mary	CHI	541	1605	4%	$33,384
Smith	Jean	ATL	342	1402	5%	$64,313
Appel	Tom	BOS	219	1750	6%	$23,638
Jones	Paul	DAL	980	2301	5%	$48,195

4. Select Worksheet **H**ide, the **C**olumn option button, and the OK command button.

5. Select the OK command button twice to return to the File Print dialog box and print the worksheet.

The beginning of the printed report looks like that shown in Figure 10-10.

6. Select the range E1..A1 with SHIFT, F4 (Abs) or the mouse.

When you select a range in POINT mode, 1-2-3 displays the hidden columns with an asterisk next to the column letters.

7. Select Worksheet **U**nhide, the **C**olumn option button, and the OK command button to redisplay your hidden columns.

Review

Printing your reports transfers your worksheet data from your screen to paper. 1-2-3's printing features use the worksheet features you have learned in other chapters so you can design your worksheet in the

10

worksheet window and then print it as it appears there when you want a printed copy. These 1-2-3 features include the following:

- The Print dialog boxes available with the **File Print**, **File Preview**, **File Page Setup**, and **File Printer Setup** commands provide the options that you use to print your worksheets. Only the **File Print** command starts sending information to your printer. The changes that you make with any of these commands are reflected in the settings for the other commands. Print settings are saved with the worksheet data.

- Like other commands that use a range, you can select the range to print before or after you select the **File Print** or **File Preview** command. You can print multiple ranges within one print range by separating the ranges with a comma or semicolon. 1-2-3 prints multiple worksheet ranges one at a time, immediately after each other.

- You can preview a printed worksheet with the **File Preview** command or the Preview command button in the File Print dialog box to see how 1-2-3 will print your data.

- When you have several printers installed with Windows, you can select which printer 1-2-3 uses to print by selecting the **File Printer Setup** command. Selecting a printer from the **Printers** list box selects the printer that the other printing commands will use. Selecting the **Setup** command button lets you change the setup for your printer while remaining in 1-2-3.

- 1-2-3 makes several assumptions about how it should print a worksheet. This is the default page setup. The page setup includes the margins and how the information is printed. You can change these with the **File Page Setup** command. Changes you can make include altering the margins, adding a header or footer, setting border columns and rows, setting the orientation, printing the worksheet frame, and printing grid lines indicating cell boundaries. The Restore command button in the File Page Setup dialog box returns 1-2-3's print settings to the default setting.

- A report can contain headers and footers that appear on every page. Headers and footers can contain the at sign (@) to print the current date and the number sign (#) to print the current page number. The vertical line (|) can divide the header or footer sections to left align, center, and right align header and footer text. You can enter a backslash and a cell address or range name to use the contents of the cell referenced as a header or footer.

- Print borders let you select the rows and columns that print at the top and left of every page. Borders allow lengthy reports to retain their identification labels from page to page.

- You can prevent columns from printing by hiding them with the Worksheet **H**ide command.

- The Worksheet **P**age Break command inserts a page break at a column or row in the worksheet. These manual page breaks override the automatic ones 1-2-3 adds.

Commands and Keys

In this chapter, you learned the 1-2-3 commands you will use to print. These commands and keys are

Keys	Action
ALT F G	File Page Setup sets the page setup that 1-2-3 uses when you print the worksheet. This includes margins, headers and footers, borders, orientation, and whether to print the worksheet frame and grid lines
ALT F V	File Preview displays the range or ranges on the screen as they will appear when 1-2-3 prints the data
ALT F P	File **P**rint prints the selected range or ranges
ALT F T	File Printer Setup selects the printer to use and lets you change the printer settings set by Windows
ALT K H C	Worksheet **H**ide **C**olumn hides worksheet columns and does not print them

10

Keys	Action
ALT K P	Worksheet **P**age Break inserts a page break into a worksheet
ALT K U C	Worksheet **U**nhide **C**olumn displays hidden worksheet columns

11
Creating Graphs

The worksheet provides an excellent way to *perform* all your financial projections, but it is not always the best way to *present* the results from these calculations. Important numbers that you want to highlight often get lost in a sea of other figures. How can you make sure that you and others who read your report, which contains hundreds of numbers, will focus on those conditions and trends that you think are important?

One solution is to use 1-2-3's graphics features, which let you present your data in an easy-to-interpret format. Graphs do not present all of the specific numbers; instead, they summarize your data in a way that lets you focus on general patterns and trends. When you find something in a graph that warrants more detailed analysis, you can still return to the supporting worksheet for a closer look.

You do not have to reenter your 1-2-3 data to use the graphics features; you can use the data already entered for your spreadsheet application without making any changes. Nor do you need to learn a new system to create your graphs; you access 1-2-3's graphics features through menus that are just like 1-2-3's other menus. Once you enter your worksheet data, you need to learn only a few new commands to present the data in a graph format. Any changes you make to your data will be reflected in your graph.

Creating a basic graph is really quite simple. Initially, you need only select the data you want to appear in the graph. Once you have created a graph with this data, you can proceed to change the graph type and add text. After you complete the basic graph, you can add further enhancements.

This chapter introduces you to the basics of defining a graph. You learn about some of the special options that produce a professional-looking product. You find out how to create and save multiple graphs in a single worksheet file. You also learn how to add a graph in a worksheet range and how to obtain a printed copy of your graph either separately or as part of a worksheet.

Basic Terms

Before you can begin to create your first graph, there are a few basic terms to understand. A sample graph, with the key terms and components marked, is shown in Figure 11-1. A discussion of each of the basic terms is presented here; more specialized terms are covered along with the implementation of specific features later in the chapter.

Data Series

1-2-3's graphs are designed to show from one to six sets of data values, depending on the type of graph that you select. A set of data values is referred to as a *series* and must consist of a range of contiguous cells on the worksheet. A series can represent sales of a product for a period of 6 months, the number of employees within the company each year for the last 10 years, or the number of rejects on a production line for each of the last 16 weeks. Most graphs can use up to six series. To distinguish the series, they are labeled series A through F.

Figure 11-1. *A bar graph with titles and legend*

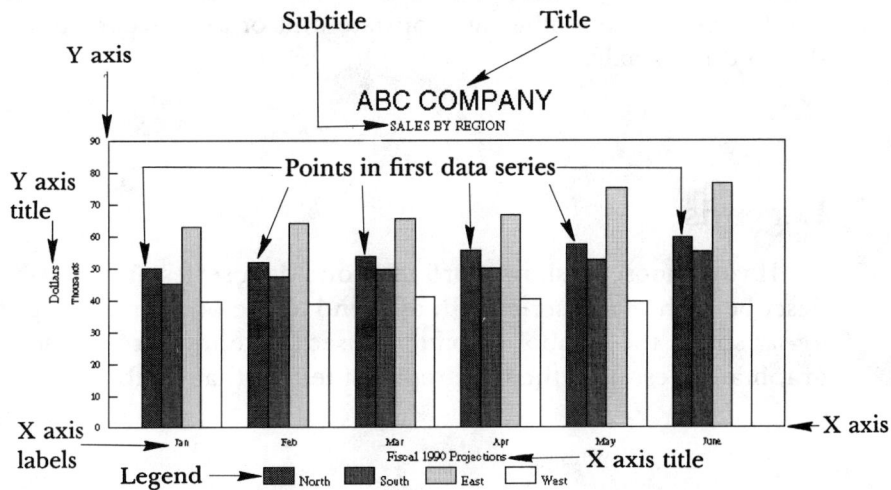

X Axis

The individual values in the series are represented as data points along the *X axis,* which is the horizontal axis at the bottom of the graph. Each point along this axis might represent a year, a month, or a quarter. It could also represent a division, a product, or a project. You can label points along the X axis to make it clear what they represent. In addition, you can place a title along the X axis to describe the general category of data it shows. For example, if each of the points on the X axis represents a month between January and December, an appropriate title for the X axis might be Fiscal 92 Projections, which describes the category to which each of these months belongs.

Y Axis

The *Y axis* is the vertical axis found on most of the graphs that 1-2-3 produces. It measures the relative size of each value within a series. Once you tell 1-2-3 which data to display on the graph, the Y axis is labeled automatically. 1-2-3 sometimes represents graph data in thousands or millions and labels the Y axis appropriately. You can also make a title for this axis; you might describe the units of measure as dollars, number of employees, or some other appropriate unit of measure for the quantities shown on this axis.

Legends

If you choose to show more than one data series on a graph, you can describe each of the series with a legend at the bottom of the graph. The *legend* shows the symbol or pattern used to represent each series in the graph and describes the data represented by that symbol or pattern.

Creating a Graph

If you have worked through the examples in this book from Chapter 1 on, you already have a number of worksheets that 1-2-3's graphics features could represent nicely. Even though you have some data for a graph, here you enter a short new worksheet designed to let you work with a small amount of data and still apply all the graphics features. Follow these steps to enter the required data for the examples in this chapter.

1. Make the following entries in the worksheet cells shown:

D1:	**ABC COMPANY**	B8:	**39550**
D2:	**SALES BY REGION**	C4:	**Feb**
A5:	**North**	C5:	**+B5*1.035**
A6:	**South**	C6:	**+B6*1.05**
A7:	**East**	C7:	**+B7*1.02**
A8:	**West**	C8:	**+B8*.98**
B4:	**Jan**	D4:	**Mar**
B5:	**50000**	E4:	**Apr**
B6:	**45000**	F4:	**May**
B7:	**62800**	G4:	**June**

11

2. Select Worksheet **G**lobal Settings, the **F**ormat command button, and Currency in the **F**ormat list box, type **0** in the **D**ecimal Places text box, and select the OK command button twice.

3. Move to D1 and then select **S**tyle **F**ont, Arial MT 14 from the **F**onts list box and the OK command button.

4. Select the range B4..G4 and then select **S**tyle **A**lignment, the **R**ight option button, and the OK command button to align the months with the numbers below them.

5. Select the range C5..C8, press CTRL-INS, select the range D5..G8, and press SHIFT-INS to copy the formulas from column C to columns D through G.

6. Move the cell pointer to the following cells and type these numbers:

   D8: **41000**
   E6: **50000**
   F7: **75000**

When you add these numbers, they replace the formulas in those cells and provide more variety in the graph than would a growth at a constant rate. Your entries should look like those in Figure 11-2.

7. Select File Save **A**s, type **MY_GRAPH** in the File **N**ame text box, and select the OK command button to save the file.

8. Select the range A5..G8 with SHIFT, F4 (Abs) or the mouse and then select **G**raph **N**ew.

1-2-3 needs to know two items to create a graph. First, 1-2-3 must know the worksheet range that contains the data you want to use in the graph. Second, 1-2-3 needs to know what you want to call the graph. 1-2-3 supplies the graph name GRAPH#, where # is the next unused number, but you can supply another name. Since each graph has its own name, 1-2-3 uses the names to distinguish among the many graphs you may have in a worksheet.

9. Type **Sales Region** in the **G**raph Name text box and select the OK command button.

Figure 11-2.   *Worksheet for using graph features*

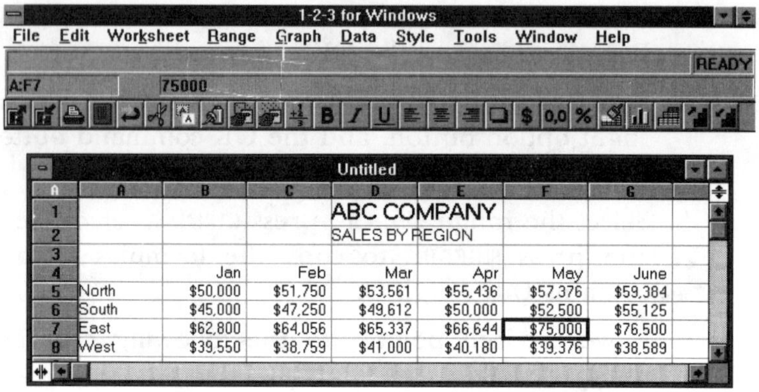

	1-2-3 for Windows	

File Edit Worksheet Range Graph Data Style Tools Window Help

READY

A:F7   75000

	A	B	C	D	E	F	G
1				ABC COMPANY			
2				SALES BY REGION			
3							
4		Jan	Feb	Mar	Apr	May	June
5	North	$50,000	$51,750	$53,561	$55,436	$57,376	$59,384
6	South	$45,000	$47,250	$49,612	$50,000	$52,500	$55,125
7	East	$62,800	$64,056	$65,337	$66,644	$75,000	$76,500
8	West	$39,550	$38,759	$41,000	$40,180	$39,376	$38,589

Another way of creating a graph is by selecting the range of data to graph and then clicking the Graph New SmartIcon. 1-2-3 creates a graph using the selected data and the default graph name. (In this case, 1-2-3 does not provide a Graph New dialog box to change the graph's data range or name.) The Graph New SmartIcon looks like this:

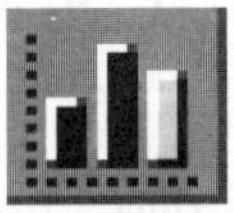

1-2-3 opens a graph window and creates a line graph with the data you have selected, as shown in Figure 11-3. The window is identified by the worksheet it uses followed by the graph name. Like worksheet windows, you can move and size the graph windows by using the same commands and mouse selections you use to move and size worksheet windows.

1-2-3 divides the range you select by columns. The X series, which appears along the X axis, uses the data in column A. The remaining six series, series A through F, use the data in columns B through G. Later in

11

Figure 11-3. *Graph created with worksheet data*

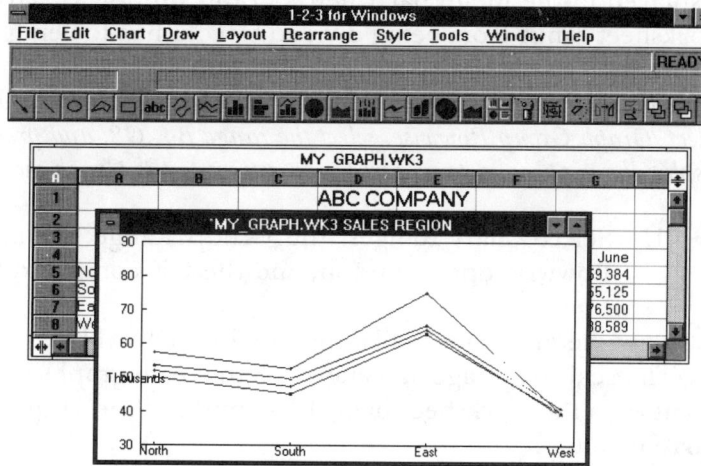

this chapter, you learn how you can change the graph type and the data the graph uses and how you can instruct 1-2-3 to divide the range you selected for the **G**raph **N**ew command by rows instead of columns.

From the Classic menu, type /GGC to select /Graph Group Columnwise, select the range A5..G8, and press ENTER. Type V to display the graph and press any key to return to the Graph menu (you need to select Quit to return to READY mode). Name this graph by selecting the /Graph Name Create command, typing SALES REGION, and pressing ENTER. You need to use this command every time you change the SALES REGION graph to ensure that the changes are saved with the graph. When you use the Classic menu to make changes to a graph, you must do so from the worksheet window that the graph uses.

10. Switch to the MY__GRAPH worksheet window by clicking it or by selecting **W**indow and the number next to MY__GRAPH.WK3.

11. Select the range B4..G8 and then select **G**raph **N**ew.

12. Type **Sales Month** in the **G**raph Name text box and select the OK command button.

This graph is not divided as you want, to show the sales by month, since 1-2-3 divided the range by columns. You can use the menu that is displayed in the menu bar when a graph window is active to change the worksheet range from being divided by columns to being divided by rows.

classic — *From the Classic menu, type /GGR from the MY_GRAPH worksheet window to select /Graph Group Rowwise, select the range B4..G8, and press ENTER. Type V to display the graph and press any key to return to the Graph menu.*

13. Select **C**hart **R**anges, the **G**roup Range command button, the **R**owwise option button, and the OK command button twice.

Now the graph looks like the one in Figure 11-4.

The real advantage of using 1-2-3 to create graphs is that as you make changes to the worksheet data, 1-2-3 updates the graphs to use the most current values.

14. Switch to the MY_GRAPH worksheet window by clicking it or by selecting **W**indow and the number next to MY_GRAPH.WK3.

15. Move to B8, type **42000**, and press ENTER or click the confirm box.

Figure 11-4. *Graph created by dividing the worksheet range by rows*

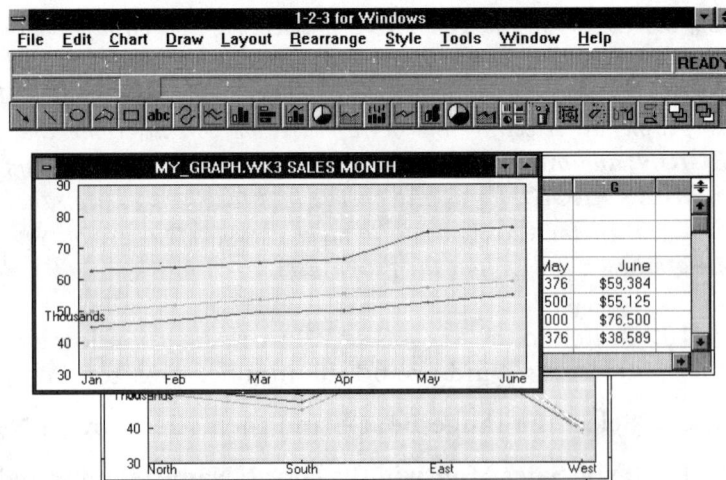

16. Switch to the SALES REGION graph window by clicking it or by selecting **Window** and the number next to MY_GRAPH.WK3 SALES REGION to see the graph with the updated values for the West region.

=*classic*= *From the Classic menu, type **/GNU** from the MY_GRAPH worksheet window to select /Graph Name Use, select SALES REGION for the graph to be the current one, and press* ENTER.

17. Switch to the SALES MONTH graph window by clicking it or by selecting **Window** and the number next to MY_GRAPH.WK3 SALES MONTH to see the graph with the updated values for the West region.

Deciding on a Graph Type

1-2-3 offers you seven different graph types: line, bar, stacked bar, XY, pie, HLCO, and mixed graphs. So far you have created only line graphs, which is the default graph type. You can change a graph to one of the other graph types by making a selection in the Chart Type dialog box. This dialog box also offers options that provide enhancements to the basic graph types.

A *line graph* shows the points in the data range you specify, plotted against the Y axis. The points may be connected with a line, shown as symbols, or both. This type of graph is an excellent choice for plotting data trends over time, such as sales or expenses. An example of a line graph is shown in Figure 11-3.

An *area graph* has points that are a distance from the X axis that represents their value. The series has a line drawn between the points, and the area from the line to the bottom is filled in with a different color or pattern. Figure 11-5 shows an area graph.

A *bar graph* looks like the one shown in Figure 11-1. It uses bars of different heights to represent the data ranges you wish to graph. Bar graphs are especially appropriate when you wish to contrast the numbers in several series.

A *pie graph* shows only one range of values. It represents each value as a percentage of the total, using a pie wedge to show the comparative size

Figure 11-5. *An area graph*

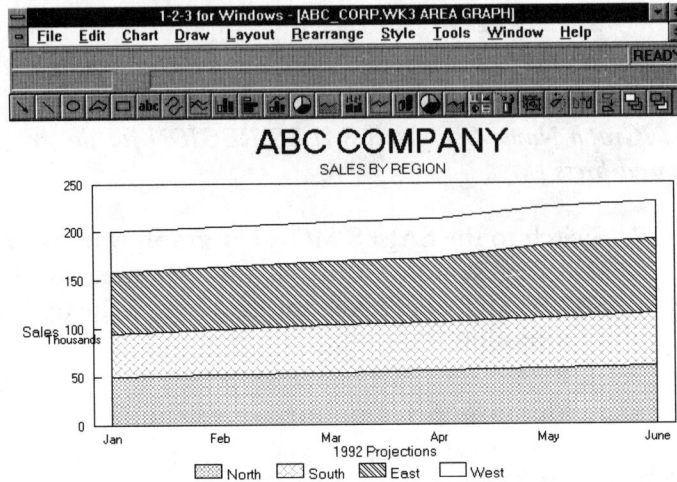

of the value. A pie graph is an effective way to show the relative size of different components of a budget or the contribution to profit from different product lines. An example of a pie chart is shown in Figure 11-6.

An *XY graph* plots the values in one series against the values from a second series. You might use this graph type to plot age against salary, time against temperature, or machine repairs against the age of the machinery. Figure 11-7 shows an example of an XY graph.

An *HLCO graph* is ideal for presenting stock and bond prices. Four different ranges are assigned to the high, low, close and open values, with the fifth range displayed as a bar graph and the sixth range as a line graph (if the fifth and sixth ranges are used). Figure 11-8 shows an example of an HLCO graph.

A *mixed graph* graphs the first three data ranges as bar graphs and the last three data ranges as line graphs. This type of graph is useful for combining different types of data. Figure 11-9 shows a mixed graph.

You can try some of the graph type options with the SALES MONTH and SALES REGION graphs by making these selections:

1. Select **Chart Type** to display the Chart Type dialog box shown in Figure 11-10.

Figure 11-6. *A pie chart*

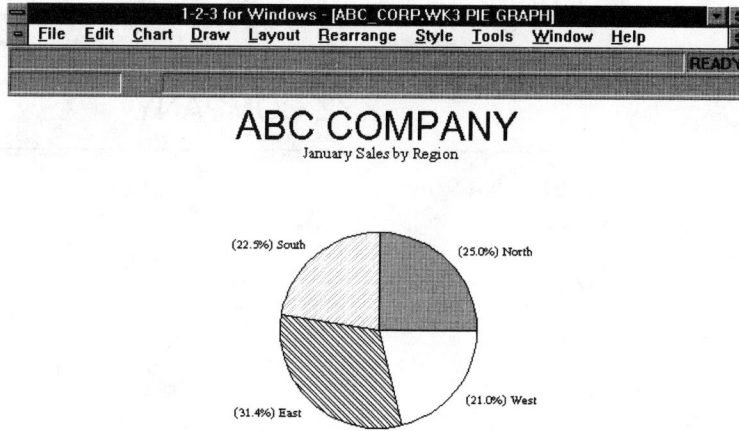

Figure 11-7. *An XY chart*

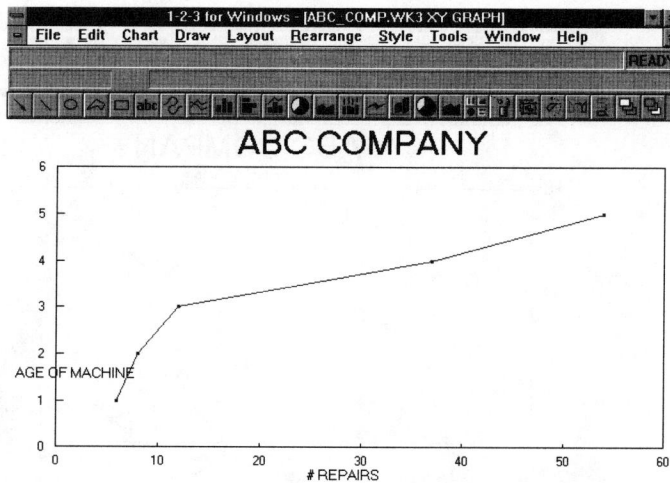

Figure 11-8. *An HLCO graph for XYZ Company's stock*

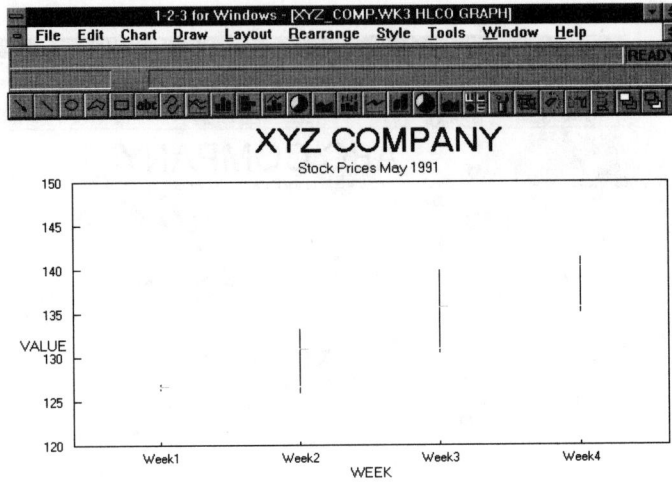

Figure 11-9. *A mixed graph*

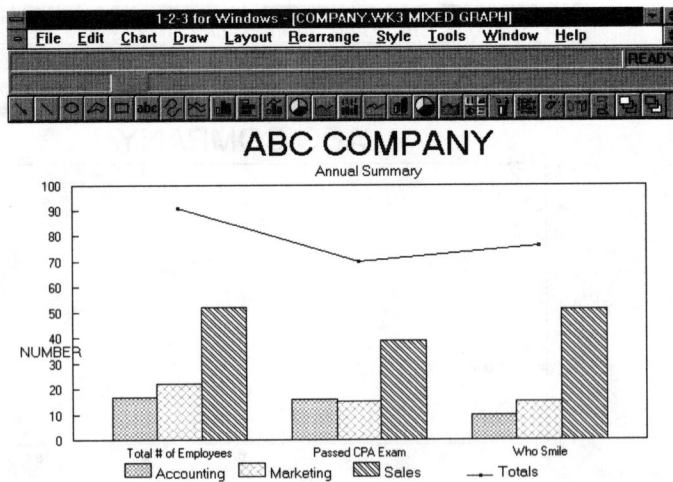

Figure 11-10.   *Chart Type dialog box*

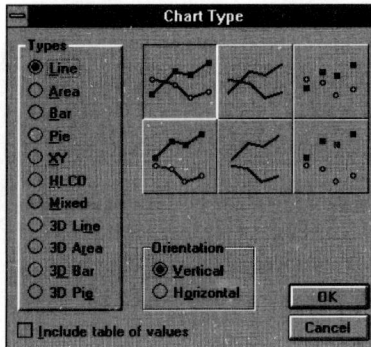

2. Select the **B**ar option button and the OK command button to create a bar graph.

You can see on the right side of the dialog box that when you select a graph type, 1-2-3 displays a gallery of icons you can select from. These icons control features such as whether 1-2-3 stacks the value for a series on top of another and whether it uses lines, symbols, or both for line graphs. You can also rotate the axes so instead of having the X axis appear on the bottom and the Y axis appear on the side, the X axis appears on the side and the Y axis appears on the bottom.

classic *From the Classic menu, change the graph type by typing /GT from READY mode to select /Graph Type, and select from Bar, Line, Pie, Stacked-Bar, XY, HLCO, and Mixed graphs.*

3. Switch to the SALES REGION graph by clicking it or by selecting **W**indow and the number next to MY_GRAPH SALES REGION.

4. Select **C**hart **T**ype, the 3D-Li**n**e option button, and the OK command button to create a three-dimensional line graph.

The 3D options are variations of Line, Bar, Area and Pie chart types.

Specifying the Data for the Graph

1-2-3 has no defaults for the data to show in a graph. If you do not tell 1-2-3 which data to display on the graph, your graph will be blank. Each graph type except the pie chart can show up to six data series or ranges. Pie charts are special; a pie chart can show only one data range, series A. So far, you have selected data to use in a graph by selecting a range that contains the X series and the A through F series. You can also assign ranges to the series the graph uses one at a time.

Follow these steps to assign data to graph ranges A through D in the current graph:

1. Switch to the MY_GRAPH worksheet window by clicking it or by selecting **Window** and the number next to the worksheet with the data you have just entered.

2. Select **Graph New**, type **East Sales** in the **Graph** Name text box, and select the OK command button.

Only the current cell is selected, so the graph is fairly empty. You want to explicitly assign the ranges the graph uses.

3. Select **Chart Ranges**.

classic *From the Classic menu, select the worksheet range for a graph series by typing /G from READY mode to select /Graph and then A through F or X for the series to assign. Next, select the range and press ENTER.*

4. Select the range B4..G4 in the **X** Data Range text box.

As soon as you press an arrow key, the dialog box shrinks to let you enter the range, and 1-2-3 displays the worksheet window in front of the graph window. This makes it easy to select a range by using the arrow keys or the mouse. You can also select a range by copying it to the Clipboard and pasting it into a text box.

5. Select the range B7..G7 in the **A** text box under Data Ranges and select the OK command button.

This assigns the data for the East region to range A of the graph; it now represents the sales for the East region in the months of January through June.

You assigned only two ranges, X and A, but you can assign up to seven ranges for the graph to use. You do not have to use all the possible ranges a graph can use. Since you did not assign ranges to series B through F, they remain unassigned. You can later remove an assigned range by deleting the range address or name in the text box for the series.

Displaying Named Graphs

While creating graphs is one way to display graph windows, you need another option for displaying named graphs that you have already created. To display an existing named graph, use the **Graph View** command. After you select the command, select the named graph you want to display from the **Graph Name** list box and select the OK command button. 1-2-3 opens a graph window that contains the named graph. You can try this by following these steps:

1. Switch to the MY_GRAPH worksheet window by clicking it or by selecting **Window** and the number next to MY_GRAPH.WK3.

2. Select **File Save** to save the current worksheet and its graphs.

When you save a worksheet that has named graphs, the graph settings are saved along with the worksheet data.

3. Select **File Close** to close the worksheet window and its graph windows.

1-2-3 closes the MY_GRAPH worksheet window as well as its three graph windows. You can close a graph window without affecting the worksheet window, but when you close the worksheet window a graph uses, the graph window automatically closes as well.

4. Select **File Open**, type **MY_GRAPH** in the File **Name** text box, and select the OK command button.

5. Select **G**raph **V**iew, select SALES REGION in the **G**raph Name list box, and select the OK command button.

This opens a graph window that contains the SALES REGIONS graph.

6. Switch to the MY_GRAPH worksheet by clicking it or by selecting **W**indow and the number next to MY_GRAPH.WK3.

7. Select **G**raph **V**iew, select SALES MONTH in the **G**raph Name list box, and select the OK command button.

8. Switch to the MY_GRAPH worksheet by clicking it or by selecting **W**indow and the number next to MY_GRAPH.WK3.

9. Select **G**raph **V**iew, select EAST SALES in the **G**raph Name list box, and select the OK command button.

Now you have all of the three named graphs you have created in separate graph windows.

Deleting Named Graphs

Each time you create a new graph, you are creating another named graph. You can continue creating new named graphs, but you will also need to remove the named graphs that you no longer want. Follow these steps to create a named graph and then delete it:

1. Switch to the MY_GRAPH worksheet by clicking it or by selecting **W**indow and the number next to MY_GRAPH.WK3.

2. Select **G**raph **N**ew, type **Extra** in the **G**raph Name text box, and select the OK command button.

This creates a graph window with only the current worksheet cell in the graph that is called EXTRA.

3. Switch to the MY_GRAPH worksheet by clicking it or by selecting **W**indow and the number next to MY_GRAPH.WK3.

4. Select **G**raph **N**ame **D**elete, select EXTRA from the **G**raph Name
   list box, and select the **D**elete command button.

=classic= *From the Classic menu, to delete a named graph, type **/GND** to select the /Graph*
Name Delete command and then select the named graph to delete and press ENTER.

5. Select the OK command button.

6. Select **W**indow.

You do not see MY _ GRAPH.WK3 EXTRA because the named graph is
deleted.

7. Press ESC twice or click the worksheet to return to READY mode.

Enhancing the Display

The current graph is not very useful — the series are distinguished by
different colors, but the only way to tell which set of bars represents which
data is by remembering the sequence in which the different regions were
assigned to the graph ranges. You also need some text to tell the reader
what the graph contains. Obviously, some additional information must be
added to the graph. In this section, you learn how to add titles to the
graph and how to add legends and grid lines.

Adding Titles

You can add titles to your graph to improve its appearance. You can
add a title along either of the axes or at the top of the graph in one or two
lines. You can add two lines to the bottom of the graph as well. You can
directly enter the text to use in the graph, or you can use an entry you
have stored in a worksheet cell. Follow these steps to enhance the SALES
REGION graph with titles in four locations:

1. Switch to the SALES REGION graph by clicking it or by selecting
   Window and the number next to MY _ GRAPH SALES REGION.

2. Select **C**hart **H**eadings to produce the Chart Headings dialog box, which contains text boxes for entering the title, subtitle, note, and second note.

classic   *From the Classic menu, to add a title, select the /Graph Options Titles First command and then enter the text for the title and press ENTER. You add subtitles by selecting Second instead of First.*

3. Type **\D1** in the **T**itle text box.

This makes the current entry in D1 the title at the top of the graph.

4. Type **Total Sales by Region** in the **S**ubtitle text box and select the OK command button.

This time, you add the text by typing it since the worksheet does not have an entry that exactly matches the desired title.

5. Select **C**hart Axis **X** and the **O**ptions command button, type **Fiscal 1992 Projections** in the Axis Title text box, and select the OK command button twice.

classic   *From the Classic menu, to add an axis title, select the /Graph Options Titles command, select X-Axis or Y-Axis, type the text for the axis title, and press ENTER.*

6. Select **C**hart Axis **Y** and the **O**ptions command button, type **Dollars** in the Axis Title text box, and select the OK command button twice.

Now your chart displays the titles, as shown in Figure 11-11.

Setting the Font for Titles

In Chapter 6, "Changing the Appearance of Worksheet Cells," you learned how you can set the font size and style for your worksheet entries. You can make the same types of changes to your graph text. Follow these

Figure 11-11. *A graph with titles*

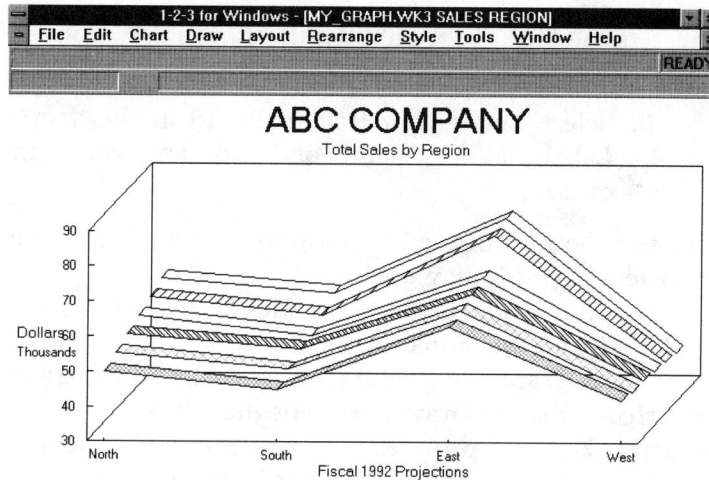

steps to add titles to the SALES MONTH graph and change the size of the titles:

1. Switch to the SALES MONTH graph by clicking it or by selecting **Window** and the number next to MY _ GRAPH SALES MONTH.

2. Select **Chart Headings**, type **\D1** in the **Title** text box, type **Sales by Month** in the **Subtitle** text box, and select the OK command button.

3. Select **Chart Axis Y** and the **Options** command button, type **Dollars** in the **Axis Title** text box, and select the OK command button twice.

4. Select **Chart Options Fonts**.

Notice that the fonts that are listed are the same ones your worksheet uses. If you want to change the fonts that are available, you must do so by replacing a font in the font set for the worksheet the graph belongs to.

classic *From the Classic menu, set the font for the chart title by selecting the /Graph Options Advanced Text First Font and selecting one of the numbers. For the subtitle, select Second instead of First, and for the name of units, select Third instead of First.*

5. Select Times New Roman PS 12 in the drop-down box under Subtitle, Axis Titles, Legend.

This sets the font of the subtitle, the X axis title, and the legend that you add in the next section.

6. Select Times New Roman PS 10 in the drop-down box under Labels, Notes, Name of Units, and select the OK command button.

This sets the font of the "Thousands" 1-2-3 adds to the Y axis as well as other text a graph may use.

Now your chart displays the titles, as shown in Figure 11-12.

An advanced graphics feature that you may want to try as you learn more about graphs is adding extra text. To add extra text, click the Text SmartIcon or select **Draw Text**, type the text and press ENTER, and then use the arrow keys and press ENTER or drag the text to the new location. Adding text this way allows you to put text in any location.

Adding Legends

Legends add clarity to any graph that presents more than one data series by identifying how each data series is represented on the graph. If

Figure 11-12. *Graph with titles after changing the font*

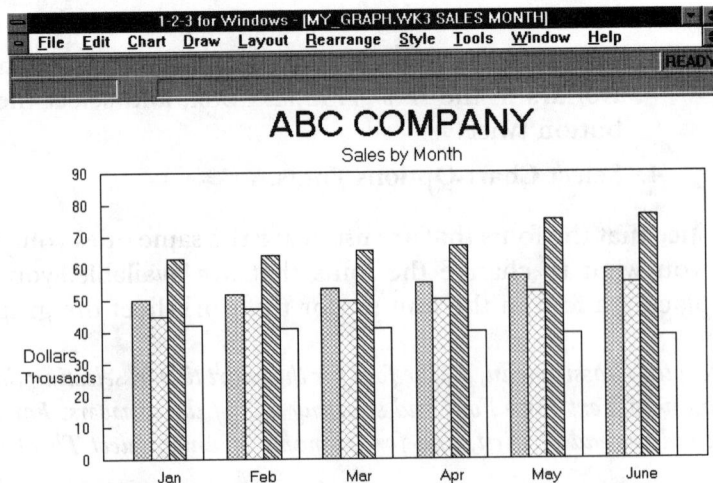

you use symbols to distinguish the different data series, the legend will consist of the series indicator and the text describing the data shown by that series. If color or hatch patterns are used, a small square of the color or pattern is placed at the bottom of the screen along with the text description of the series. You can type the legend text for each series or use entries stored in one cell or a range for the legend for one or all series. If you enter lengthy legend text, 1-2-3 automatically adjusts the legend display to use more than one line.

When you enter the text for a series, you can choose from the same six letters you used to assign worksheet ranges to the different data series for the graph. Like entering titles, you can use a cell's entry by entering a backslash and the cell address. You can even use a worksheet range for the legend text for all the series.

Follow these steps to assign the legends for the SALES MONTH graph:

1. Switch to the SALES MONTH graph by clicking it or by selecting **W**indow and the number next to MY _ GRAPH SALES MONTH.

2. Select **C**hart **L**egend and type **\A5** in the A text box under Legend Text.

The label stored in cell A5 will be used for the legend. Your other option is to type **North** in the text box. The advantage of using the label entry in the cell is that if you decide to update the entry later, the legend text is automatically updated for you.

━*classic*━ *From the Classic menu, type* **/GOLA** *from the worksheet window to select /Graph Options Legend A, type* **\A5** *as the legend this series should use, and press* ENTER.

3. Type **\A6** in the B text box, **\A7** in the C text box, and **\A8** in the D text box.

4. Select the OK command button to display the graph with the legend, as shown in Figure 11-13.

You can also assign all of the ranges at once when the text that you want to use for the series is stored in a worksheet range. Follow these steps to assign legend text for the SALES REGION graph:

1. Switch to the SALES REGION graph by clicking it or by selecting **W**indow and the number next to MY _ GRAPH SALES REGION.

2. Select **C**hart **L**egend and the **G**roup Range command button.

3. Select the range B4..G4 and the OK command button twice.

classic — *From the Classic menu, after saving the changes to the SALES REGION graph and making the SALES MONTH graph current, type **/GOLR** from the worksheet window to select /Graph Options Legend Range, select the range B4..G4, and press ENTER.*

This graph uses the first worksheet cell for the A series legend, the second worksheet cell for the B series legend, and so forth.

Adding Grid Lines

Grid lines are lines that are parallel to either the X axis or the Y axis and that originate from the markers on the axis. They help you interpret

Figure 11-13.   *Adding a legend to the bar graph*

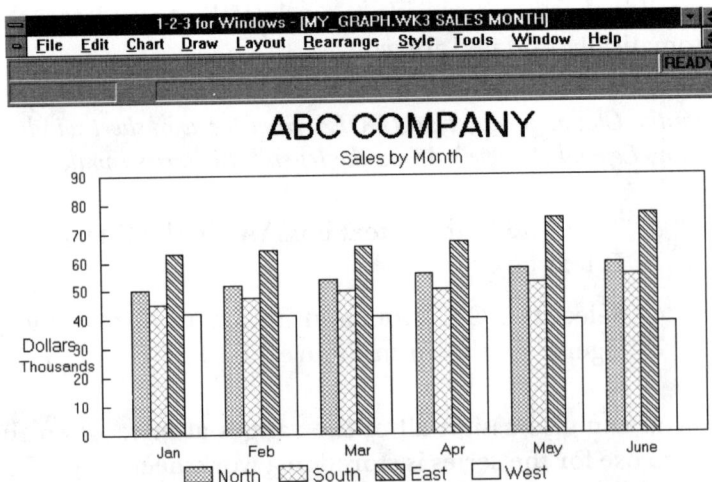

the exact value of data points by extending either up or to the right from these markers. Using grid lines in both directions at once creates a grid pattern on your graph.

To add grid lines to an axis, select **C**hart **B**orders/Grids. Next, select the check box next to the axis you want to add the grid lines to. You can add grid lines to any graph except a pie graph. Try adding grid lines to the SALES MONTH graph:

1. Click the SALES MONTH graph window or select **W**indow and MY_GRAPH.WK3 SALES MONTH.

2. Select **C**hart **B**orders/Grids, the **Y**-axis check box, and the OK command button.

The graph with the grid lines is shown in Figure 11-14.

classic *From the Classic menu, type* **/GOGH** *from the worksheet window to select /Graph Options Grid Horizontal to add horizontal grid lines.*

3. Select **C**hart **B**orders/Grids, unmark the Y-axis check box, and select the OK command button.

Figure 11-14. *Adding horizontal grid lines to the bar graph*

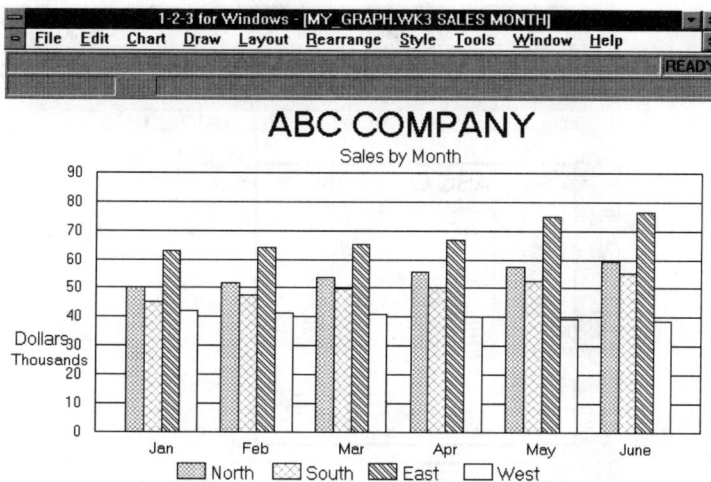

Adding Graphs to the Worksheet

You can place a graph into ranges of the worksheet. This lets you place the graph next to the data it uses. When you add a graph to a worksheet, you need to select the range the graph will fill. 1-2-3 adjusts the graph's size to fit within the range you select.

To add a couple of graphs to the current display, follow these steps:

1. Switch to the MY_GRAPH worksheet window by clicking it or by selecting **W**indow and the number next to MY_GRAPH.WK3.

2. Select the range A11..D26.

3. Select **G**raph **A**dd to Sheet.

4. Select SALES REGION from the list box under **G**raph Name and select the OK command button.

The graph now appears on your worksheet as in Figure 11-15. 1-2-3 automatically sizes each graph to fit the selected range. You can also add a graph to a worksheet by using the **E**dit **C**opy command in the graph

Figure 11-15.   *Adding a graph to the worksheet*

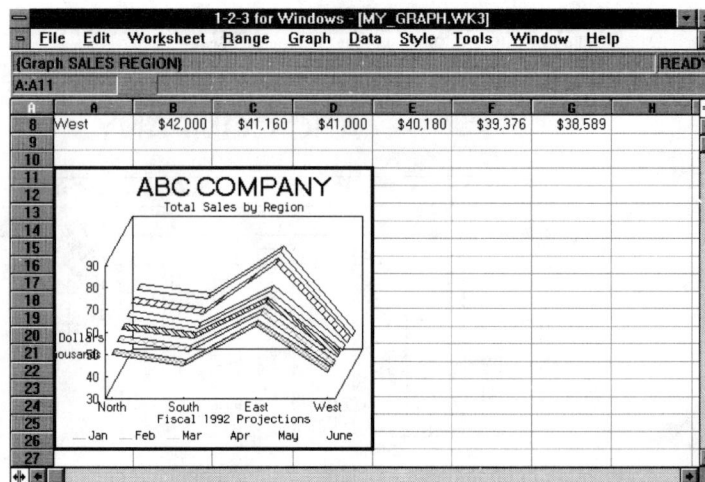

window to copy the graph to the Clipboard then paste it from the Clipboard to a selected worksheet range with the **Edit Paste** command.

classic *From the Classic menu, type :GAN to select the :Graph Add Named command, select the range A11..D26 as the range the graph should use, and press* ENTER *and type* **Q** *to return to READY mode.*

   5. Select the range A28..D50.
   6. Select **Graph Add** to Sheet.
   7. Select SALES MONTH from the list box under **Graph Name** and the OK command button to add the graph to the worksheet.

Changing the Range of a Graph in the Worksheet

When you select a range for the **Graph Add** to Sheet command, 1-2-3 fills the range with the graph. After you add a graph, you can change the range the graph uses.

To add a couple of graphs to the current display, follow these steps:

   1. Select **Graph Size**.

classic *From the Classic menu, move to a cell in the range A11..D26, type :GSR to select the :Graph Settings Range command, press* ENTER *to change the current graphic, select the range A11..F26 as the range the graphic should use, and press* ENTER *and type* **Q** *twice to return to READY mode.*

   2. Select SALES REGION from the list box under **Graph Name**.
   3. Select the range A11..F26 in the **Range** text box, and select the OK button.

The graph now changes from using A11..D26 to using A11..F26.

   4. Select **Graph Size**, SALES MONTH from the list box under **Graph Name**, the range A28..F50 in the **Range** text box, and the OK command button, to change the graph from using A11..F26 to using A28..F50.

Printing Graphs

Printing a graph on a worksheet is no different from printing a worksheet that contains text. To print a graph, you must add it to a worksheet and then include it in the range to print. 1-2-3 prints the range you select whether the range contains worksheet entries, graphs, or a combination of both. You use the same menu selections to specify the range of the worksheet that contains a graph. You can also make other menu selections to change settings if desired. When you are ready to print the worksheet range containing the graph, select the OK command button from the File Print dialog box.

To print the worksheet data and the two inserted graphs in the MY_GRAPH worksheet file, follow these steps:

1. Select the range A1..G50.

2. Select **File Preview** and the OK command button.

Since printing a graph takes longer than printing a worksheet, you should preview the graph before printing it to ensure that the graph contains the information you want to print.

3. Press any key to return to READY mode.

4. Select **File Print** and the OK command button to print the worksheet data and graphs, as shown in Figure 11-16.

5. Select **File Save** to save your worksheet.

Review

In this chapter you learned how to create graphs out of the worksheet data you already have stored in your worksheets. 1-2-3 has many graphics

Figure 11-16. *Printed graph and worksheet data*

ABC COMPANY
SALES BY REGION

	Jan	Feb	Mar	Apr	May	June
North	$50,000	$51,750	$53,561	$55,436	$57,376	$59,384
South	$45,000	$47,250	$49,612	$50,000	$52,500	$55,125
East	$62,800	$64,056	$65,337	$66,644	$75,000	$76,500
West	$42,000	$41,160	$41,000	$40,180	$39,376	$38,589

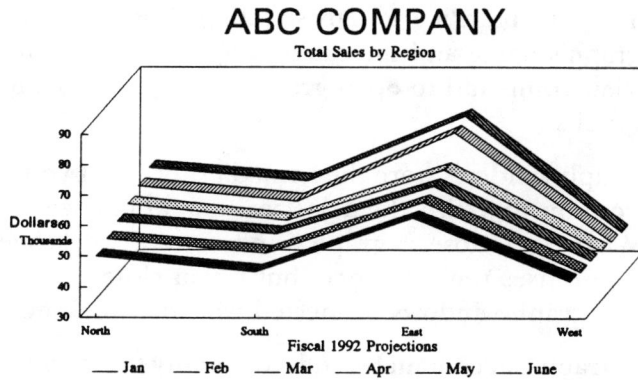

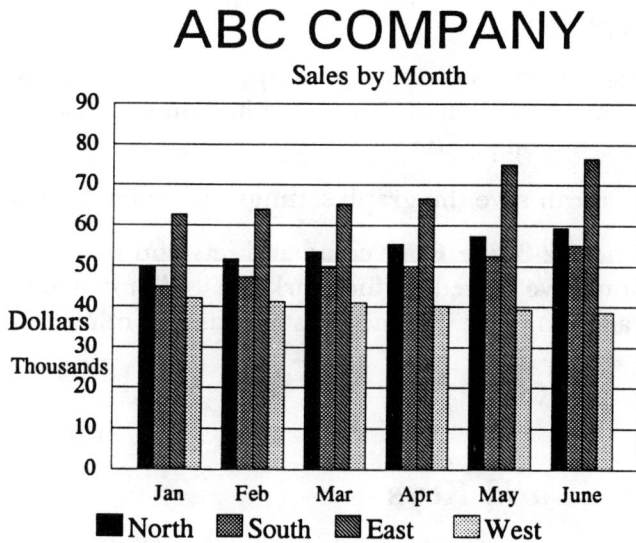

features so you do not need to learn a new package to create another way to visually present your data. These 1-2-3 features include the following:

- 1-2-3 can create seven different graph types from your worksheet data. It can create bar, line, pie, area, XY, HLCO, and mixed graphs.

- 1-2-3 can plot up to six series of data in a graph with another series along the X axis.

- You can create a graph by selecting **G**raph **N**ew and entering the graph's name and the range it will use. You can use the **G**raph **V**iew command to open graph windows that contain the named graphs.

- Graph windows store the named graphs that you create. You can position and size them just as you would worksheet windows. When you close a graph window, the worksheet window the graph uses remains open, but if you close a worksheet window, any graph windows connected with the worksheet also close.

- A graph can contain legends to identify the data ranges, grid lines for identifying data values, and titles to enhance the graph's appearance.

- Each graph is distinguished by a graph name. You can enter the graph name when you create it. You can also remove the ones you no longer use.

- You can save the graph settings by saving the worksheet.

- The 1-2-3 **File Print** command lets you print 1-2-3 graphs that you have added to the worksheet. You can select a worksheet range to print that includes graphs and other worksheet entries.

Commands and Keys

In this chapter, you learned the commands for creating and using 1-2-3 graphs. These commands and keys are

11

Keys	Action

In a worksheet window:

Keys	Action
ALT G A	**Graph Add** to Sheet displays a named graph in a worksheet range
ALT G M D	**Graph Name Delete** removes a named graph
ALT G N	**Graph New** creates a named graph starting with the data in the range you select
ALT G S	**Graph Size** selects a new range for a named graph to use to display in the worksheet
ALT G V	**Graph View** displays a named graph

In a graph window:

Keys	Action
ALT C R	**Chart Ranges** assigns worksheet data to the graph series. If you select the **Group Range** command button, you can select all the series at once and change whether the range is broken into series by rows or columns
ALT C B	**Chart Borders/Grids** adds grid lines to or removes grid lines from a graph
ALT C H	**Chart Headings** provides the title, subtitle, and notes
ALT C L	**Chart Legend** assigns legends to data ranges A through F
ALT C O F	**Chart Options Fonts** selects the fonts the graph's text uses
ALT C T	**Chart Type** selects the current graph type
ALT C X X O X	**Chart Axis X Options** Axis Title provides the title for the X axis
ALT C X Y O X	**Chart Axis Y Options** Axis Title provides the title for the Y axis

12

Data Management Basics

All the work you have done with 1-2-3 until now has been concerned with calculating some type of numeric result, which is the usual application for the 1-2-3 program. However, 1-2-3 also has features that are oriented more toward the management of information than toward calculations. These data-management features are a special group of commands that provide capabilities for the design, entry, and retrieval of information, with or without additional calculations. You can use these commands to keep track of information about your suppliers, clients, or employees.

Since this is a new area of 1-2-3 for you, the first step is to learn some new terms. A *database* is a collection of all the information you have about a set of things. These things can be customers, employees, orders, parts in your inventory, or anything else. If you created a database of employee information, you would place the information about each of your employees in it. All the information about one employee would be in one record of the database. A *record* is composed of all the pieces of information you want to record about each thing in the set, such as one employee. These individual pieces of information in the record are referred to as *fields*.

Fields you might include in each record in an employee database are name, job classification, salary, date of hire, and social security number. Every time you design a new database, you need to decide what fields will be included in each record.

A 1-2-3 database is a range of cells on the worksheet. The database can be in any area of the worksheet, but you must put the field names in the top row of the range. The records in the database, which contain data for each field, must go in the rows beneath the field names.

Creating a Database

To create a new database, you first create a list of the fields you plan to use, and then you estimate the number of records the database will contain. A database in 1-2-3 for Windows can contain up to 256 fields and 8191 records. Usually memory is more of a limitation. If you run out of memory as your database expands, you will want to either split the database into separate worksheets with the **File Extract To** command introduced in Chapter 13, "Advanced Problem-solving Techniques," or use 1-2-3's advanced database features to transfer the database to another database application file such as dBASE. (1-2-3 can use these files directly; you can continue to use the database with 1-2-3's features.)

To create an employee database, you first decide the information you want to store for each employee. For the database you create to use the database features of this chapter, this information includes the last name, first name, social security number, job code, salary, and location of the employee.

Choosing a Location on the Worksheet

You can use any area of the worksheet for a database. Normally, when your worksheet serves a dual purpose (both for calculations and as a database), you should place the database below and to the right of the calculations so it can expand easily. If nothing else is stored on the worksheet, row 1 is as good a starting location as any other. Since you can have multiple worksheets in a worksheet file, you can put the database on one sheet and the other information the worksheet file uses on separate sheets.

Entering Field Names

Whatever area you select for your database, place your field names across the top row. Always choose meaningful names; you will use them again to invoke the data-management features. Meaningful names can be self documenting, which means they can help clarify what you are doing. Each field name must be contained within a single cell. Field names that span two cells are not acceptable. Neither are spaces at the end of a field name. Spaces or special characters in the cell immediately beneath the field name can also cause a problem with some of 1-2-3's data-management features.

To enter the field names in the chosen area, simply type them in their respective cells and adjust the column widths.

1. Enter the field names for the employee database in these cells now:

A1: **Last Name**	D1: **"Job Code**
B1: **First Name**	E1: **"Salary**
C1: **"SS#**	F1: **"Location**

Pay special attention to the spelling of field names. When you use the field names in later tasks, they must match exactly if the job is to be completed properly.

2. Select the range A1..F1, and then select the Underline SmartIcon or select the **S**tyle **F**ont command, the **U**nderline check box, and the OK command button.

The entries look like this:

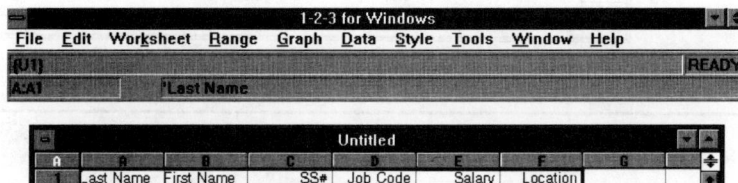

Entering Data

Now that you have entered the field names, you can begin entering the data beneath them. The first record should be entered immediately beneath the field names. Each record will occupy one row; do not skip rows as you begin to enter records.

Make sure that the data you enter in each field is the same type. If a field contains value entries, the entries in all records for this field should be value entries. If you do not have all the data for a record, you can leave the field blank, as long as you do not leave the entire row blank. Except for these simple guidelines, everything is exactly the same as entering data in the worksheet environment.

You need to complete the data entry for the database used throughout the rest of this chapter. The normal procedure for entering records in a database is to enter a complete record at once; however, since it might be easier to complete the entries in one column before moving to the next one, the directions in this chapter are written from that perspective. You can either work from the screen display shown in Figure 12-1 or follow these directions to complete the entries:

Figure 12-1.   *The employee database*

1-2-3 for Windows — EMPLOYEE.WK3

	A Last Name	B First Name	C SS#	D Job Code	E Salary	F Location	G
1	Last Name	First Name	SS#	Job Code	Salary	Location	
2	Larson	Mary	543-98-9876	23	$12,000	2	
3	Campbell	David	213-76-9874	23	$23,000	10	
4	Campbell	Keith	569-89-7654	12	$32,000	2	
5	Stephens	Tom	219-78-8954	15	$17,800	2	
6	Caldor	Larry	459-34-0921	23	$32,500	4	
7	Lightnor	Peggy	560-55-4311	14	$23,500	10	
8	McCartin	John	817-66-1212	15	$54,600	2	
9	Justof	Jack	431-78-9963	17	$41,200	4	
10	Patterson	Lyle	212-11-9090	12	$21,500	10	
11	Miller	Lisa	214-89-6756	23	$18,700	2	
12							

1. Place these entries in the Last Name field:

A2:	**Larson**	A7:	**Lightnor**
A3:	**Campbell**	A8:	**McCartin**
A4:	**Campbell**	A9:	**Justof**
A5:	**Stephens**	A10:	**Patterson**
A6:	**Caldor**	A11:	**Miller**

2. Make these entries in the First Name field:

B2:	**Mary**	B7:	**Peggy**
B3:	**David**	B8:	**John**
B4:	**Keith**	B9:	**Jack**
B5:	**Tom**	B10:	**Lyle**
B6:	**Larry**	B11:	**Lisa**

3. Select the range C2..C11, the **R**ange **F**ormat command, Label in the **F**ormat list box, and the OK command button.

This step makes labels of the social security numbers that you enter in the next step so you do not have to enter the label prefixes.

4. Make the following entries in the SS# field:

C2:	**543-98-9876**	C7:	**560-55-4311**
C3:	**213-76-9874**	C8:	**817-66-1212**
C4:	**569-89-7654**	C9:	**431-78-9963**
C5:	**219-78-8954**	C10:	**212-11-9090**
C6:	**459-34-0921**	C11:	**214-89-6756**

5. Enter the following job codes:

D2:	**23**	D7:	**14**
D3:	**23**	D8:	**15**
D4:	**12**	D9:	**17**
D5:	**15**	D10:	**12**
D6:	**23**	D11:	**23**

6. Select the range E2..E11, select the **R**ange **F**ormat command, select Currency in the **F**ormat list box, type **0** in the **D**ecimal Places text box, and select the OK command button.

7. Make the following salary entries:

E2:	**12000**	E7:	**23500**
E3:	**23000**	E8:	**54600**
E4:	**32000**	E9:	**41200**
E5:	**17800**	E10:	**21500**
E6:	**32500**	E11:	**18700**

8. Enter the following Location codes:

F2:	**2**	F7:	**10**
F3:	**10**	F8:	**2**
F4:	**2**	F9:	**4**
F5:	**2**	F10:	**10**
F6:	**4**	F11:	**2**

This completes the entries required to create a database with 10 records.

9. Select **File** Save **As**, type **EMPLOYEE** in the File **N**ame text box, and select the OK command button to save the file.

Making Changes

Making changes to entries in the database is no different from making changes in the worksheet data you use. You have two good choices: retype any entry to replace it or use the F2 (Edit) technique to make a quick correction. To feel at home with making changes, just as if you were still making worksheet entries, carry out the following steps to change the salary and social security number for Mary Larson:

1. Move the cell pointer to C2, press F2 (Edit), and move the cursor so it is to the left of the 7. Press DEL, type **4**, and press ENTER or click the confirm box to correct the social security number.

2. Move the cell pointer to E2, press F2 (Edit), and press HOME. Next, press DEL, type **2**, and press ENTER or click the confirm box.

Sorting the Database

1-2-3 provides a Sort feature that can alter the order of the records in your database to any sequence you need. If you decide that you would like an employee list in alphabetical order, 1-2-3 can do this for you. If you decide that you want the records in order by job code, salary, or location, 1-2-3 can make this change easily. You can use up to 255 fields to sort your database. You will find 1-2-3's **D**ata **S**ort command easy to work with, and you will be amazed at how rapidly 1-2-3 can rearrange your data. To sort the data, you need to fill in the Data Sort dialog box, which you can activate by selecting **D**ata **S**ort:

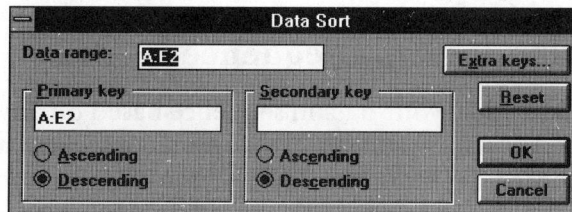

Defining the Database Location

The first step in resequencing your database is to tell 1-2-3 where the data is located. When you are sorting data, 1-2-3 is not interested in the field names, only in the data values that you expect it to sort. If you accidentally include the field names in this range, 1-2-3 sorts them just as if they were intentionally included as data values.

In defining the area to be sorted, you have the choice of defining some of the records or all of them. Always include all of the fields, even if you want to exclude some of the records. Excluded fields remain stationary and do not remain with the rest of the record to which they belong, thus jeopardizing the integrity of your file. Therefore, it is a good idea to save the file before sorting, in case you accidentally exclude some of the field names. Having Undo enabled is another safeguard, although it is effective only if you reverse the result of the sort operation before entering another command.

Follow these steps to tell 1-2-3 where the employee records are located:

1. Select the range A2..F11 as the range to sort.
2. Select **D**ata **S**ort.

As with other commands that use worksheet ranges, you can preselect a range and have 1-2-3 pick it up in the dialog box. Notice that the selected range does not include the entries in row 1. If you included the field names, 1-2-3 would put the field names in the row below Larson if you sorted by the entries in column A.

Defining the Sort Sequence

You can sort your data in sequence based on any of the database fields. If you sort by the contents of column D, the database will be in sequence by job code. If you sort by column C, the social security numbers determine the sequence. Whichever field you choose to sort on, you also have to decide whether you want the entries to be sequenced from highest to lowest (descending order) or lowest to highest (ascending order).

1-2-3 refers to the field that determines the sequence of the records after the sort as the *primary key*. 1-2-3 also allows you to establish a *secondary key* and up to 253 additional keys. The secondary key is a precaution against duplicates in the primary key. The extra keys, which are also optional, are a precaution against duplicates in the primary and secondary keys. 1-2-3 ignores the secondary key except when the primary key contains duplicate entries. It ignores the extra keys except when the primary and secondary keys contain duplicate entries. The secondary key and extra keys are used to break the tie.

Choosing a Primary Key

The way you tell 1-2-3 how you want your data sorted is by selecting keys. The first key to select is the primary key, which selects the first column of values 1-2-3 will use to sort the data. The primary key depends on the entry you make in the Primary Key text box. You can point to a cell in the column you want to use, type a cell address, or press F3 (Name) and select a range name for a cell in the column you want to use to sort. While

12

the following examples select the first entry to sort in a column, you can select any cell in the column since 1-2-3 needs to know only which column the primary key is in. You can also select whether the entries are sorted in ascending or descending order according to their primary field values by selecting the **A**scending or **D**escending option button.

Follow these steps to select a primary key and sort the database:

1. Move to the **P**rimary Key text box and either type **C2** or move the cell pointer to C2 and press ENTER (the dialog box shrinks when you press an arrow key).

This selects the social security number as the primary sort key. The default primary key sort order is descending, so you do not need to change it.

2. Select the OK command button to sort the data and change the sequence of the records to match the screen in Figure 12-2.

Like other commands, 1-2-3 does not actually perform this command until you select the OK command button.

Figure 12-2. *Records in social security number sequence*

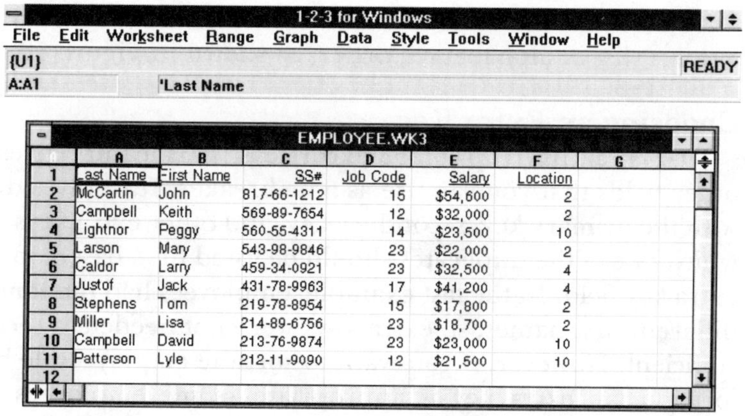

	A	B	C	D	E	F	G
1	Last Name	First Name	SS#	Job Code	Salary	Location	
2	McCartin	John	817-66-1212	15	$54,600	2	
3	Campbell	Keith	569-89-7654	12	$32,000	2	
4	Lightnor	Peggy	560-55-4311	14	$23,500	10	
5	Larson	Mary	543-98-9846	23	$22,000	2	
6	Caldor	Larry	459-34-0921	23	$32,500	4	
7	Justof	Jack	431-78-9963	17	$41,200	4	
8	Stephens	Tom	219-78-8954	15	$17,800	2	
9	Miller	Lisa	214-89-6756	23	$18,700	2	
10	Campbell	David	213-76-9874	23	$23,000	10	
11	Patterson	Lyle	212-11-9090	12	$21,500	10	
12							

Choosing a Secondary Key

The secondary key is the primary tie breaker. It resolves duplicate entries and determines which one of the duplicates should be listed first, based on the value of the secondary field. In situations like the last example, where the social security number was the controlling sequence, a secondary key is not needed. The SS# field does not contain duplicates, so there is no need for a tie breaker. However, if you want to sort the employee file by last name, a secondary key is appropriate—last names sometimes are duplicated.

The process for specifying the secondary key is the same as for the primary key, except that you make your selections under **S**econdary Key. Try this feature by sorting the employee database by name:

1. Select **D**ata **S**ort, type **A2** in the **P**rimary Key text box, and select the **A**scending option button.

This selects a cell in the Last Name field as the primary sort key.

2. Type **B2** in the **S**econdary Key text box and select the Ascending option button.

This selects a cell in the First Name field as the secondary key. This key resolves the tie when more than one employee has the same last name. In this case, the first name field determines which record is placed first.

3. Select the OK command button to resequence the data as a name list in alphabetical order, as shown in Figure 12-3.

Choosing an Extra Key

1-2-3 can have up to 253 extra keys. This feature gives you up to 253 other fields that you can use as a tie breaker. It resolves duplicate entries with the primary key, secondary key, and other extra keys and determines which one of the duplicates should be listed first, based on the value of the extra key field. In the last example, employees had the same last name but different first names, so extra keys were not needed; a secondary key was sufficient. However, if you want to sort the employee file by job code and location, an extra key is appropriate—some employees have the same information for both fields, and you can use a third field to order these duplicate entries.

Figure 12-3.   *Records in sequence by name*

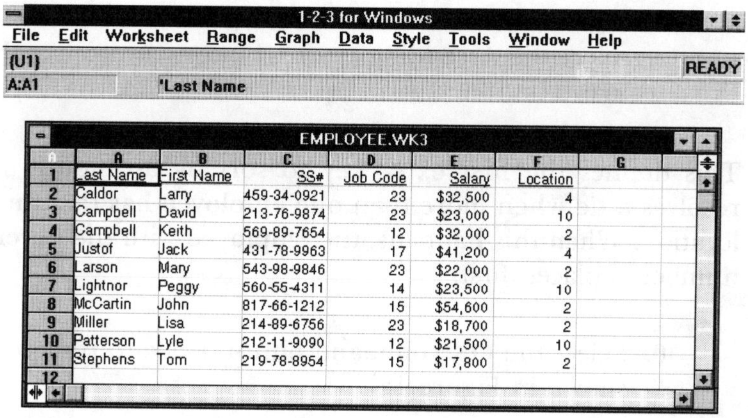

		1-2-3 for Windows						
File	Edit	Worksheet	Range	Graph	Data	Style	Tools	Window	Help

{U1}   READY

A:A1   'Last Name

EMPLOYEE.WK3

	A	B	C	D	E	F	G	
1	Last Name	First Name	SS#	Job Code	Salary	Location		
2	Caldor	Larry	459-34-0921	23	$32,500	4		
3	Campbell	David	213-76-9874	23	$23,000	10		
4	Campbell	Keith	569-89-7654	12	$32,000	2		
5	Justof	Jack	431-78-9963	17	$41,200	4		
6	Larson	Mary	543-98-9846	23	$22,000	2		
7	Lightnor	Peggy	560-55-4311	14	$23,500	10		
8	McCartin	John	817-66-1212	15	$54,600	2		
9	Miller	Lisa	214-89-6756	23	$18,700	2		
10	Patterson	Lyle	212-11-9090	12	$21,500	10		
11	Stephens	Tom	219-78-8954	15	$17,800	2		
12								

The process for specifying an extra key is different from the process for specifying the other keys. To try the extra keys feature by sorting the employee database by social security number within job code and location, follow these steps:

1. Select **Data Sort** and the **Reset** command buttons.

This cancels the current settings in the Data Sort dialog box.

2. Select the range A2..F11 in the Data Range text box for the range to sort.

3. Type **D2** in the **Primary Key** text box, select the **Ascending** option button, type **F2** in the **Secondary Key** text box, and select the Ascending option button.

This selects the Job Code field for the primary sort key and the Location field for the secondary sort key.

4. Select the **Extra Keys** command button.

1-2-3 displays a Data Sort Extra Keys dialog box to help you select the extra keys.

5. Type **1** in the **K**ey text box, type **C2** in the Key Ra**n**ge text box, select the **A**scending option button, and select the **A**ccept command button.

This defines the first extra key to sort by ascending order. This key resolves a tie when more than one employee has the same job code and location. When this happens, the employee with the lower social security number is placed first.

6. Select the OK command button twice to resequence the data as shown in Figure 12-4.

7. Press ALT-BACKSPACE to return the database to the last- and first-name sequence.

8. Select **F**ile **S**ave to save the sorted database.

Figure 12-4.   *Records in sequence by job code, location, and social security number*

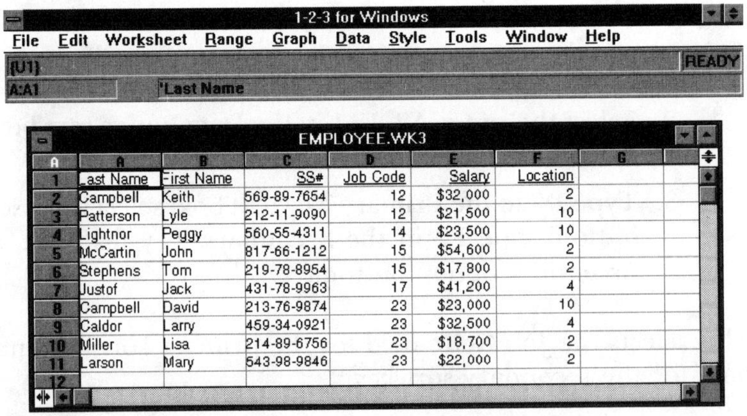

12

When you save the worksheet, 1-2-3 saves the sort settings you just entered. The next time you sort the worksheet, you will need to set only those options that are different. Be particularly careful to update the data range if you add more fields to the database; if you do not adjust the range, the new fields will remain stationary while the rest of the record is sorted to a new row.

Searching the Database

As your database increases in size, it becomes increasingly important to review selectively the information it contains. Once the employee file contains 500 records, it becomes extremely time consuming to locate all the records that have a job code of 23 by visually scanning the Job Code column.

1-2-3 gives you a way to work with information in your database selectively by means of *selective reporting* capabilities. This means you have a method of selectively presenting information that falls outside of a normal set of values you establish. This selective review feature provides an easy way to clean up the database or to create reports in response to unexpected requests.

Working with 1-2-3's selective reporting feature requires that you enter your specifications for record selection on the worksheet. These specifications are known as *criteria* and must be entered on the worksheet before you search the database.

Once the criteria are entered, you can query the database. You make all of the entries required for working with 1-2-3's selective reporting feature in the Data Query dialog box. Since selective reporting has several steps, the best approach is to look at each step and then try a few examples that combine all of the features. You begin by exploring the rules for entering your criteria on the worksheet.

Entering Criteria

You enter criteria on the worksheet to tell 1-2-3 which records you want to work with. 1-2-3 ignores records that do not match these criteria when you use the **D**ata **Q**uery command to perform a task with the database.

The first step in creating criteria is choosing a blank area on the worksheet in which to enter it. The rules for entering criteria differ, depending on whether you are working with label data or value data. However, regardless of which type of data you want to enter, the first entry represents the field containing the data you want to search. If you want to search the entries in the Job Code field, you enter **Job Code** in the blank area that you chose. You must enter the field name exactly as it is in the database, with identical spelling. You then place the criteria specification immediately beneath this field name. If you want to ensure that you have the field names spelled correctly, copy the field names from the database table.

Criteria for Value Data

You can enter two different types of criteria for matching records when you use a field that contains value entries. One option is to use *exact-entry match criteria,* which places a value that could occur in the field beneath the field name. If you want to search for all records with the number 23 in the Job Code field, all you need to do is place **23** beneath the Job Code in the criteria area.

Make the following entries to set up the exact-match criteria:

1. Select Worksheet **I**nsert, the **S**heet option button, and the OK command button to add a sheet after the sheet containing the database.

2. Move the cell pointer to B:A1 and type **Job Code**. Then move the cell pointer to B:A2 to finalize the entry.

It does not matter to 1-2-3 if the label has an alignment or style different from the copy in the database, as long as the text after the label prefix is the same.

3. Type **23** and press ENTER to create the criteria entry shown here:

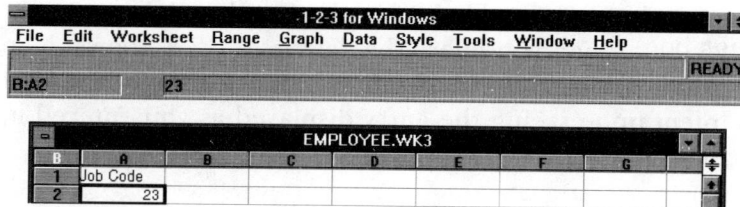

The entries you just made do not select any records; they only enable you to use the **Data Query** command to select the records you want. Before moving on to the remaining steps, look at the other types of criteria that are available. In fact, you can set up examples of several criteria on the worksheet at once.

The other type of value criteria is a *comparison formula*. This is more powerful than exact-entry criteria because it not only performs an exact match, but it also identifies records with values less than, greater than, and not equal to an established value. The logical operators that you can use to express these conditions are the same ones you were introduced to in Chapter 3, "Defining Your Calculations," to build logical formulas. You can still place the field name on the worksheet at the top of the criteria area, although 1-2-3 does not care what field name you use when you are entering formula criteria. However, it is worth entering the correct field to help document the basis of your selection.

The entry below the optional field name is the formula. The formula is designed to compare the values in a field against another value. For example, to select those records in which the salary is greater than $25,000 you could enter the formula **+SALARY > 25000**. In the formula, you can either use the field name, as in SALARY, or the cell address of the first field value, as in E2. You can also use a shortcut approach and enter **' > 25000** as long as you enter it as a label beneath the field name it uses. You can use column C for this criterion by following these directions:

1. Move the cell pointer to C1, type **Salary**, and move the cell pointer to C2 to finalize the entry.

2. Type **+SALARY > 25000** and press ENTER.

Your entry displays as ERR, but when you use it to query the database, 1-2-3 finds and displays the correct records. If you entered $+E2>25000$ instead, 1-2-3 would display the number 1 because E2 is greater than 25,000. When you query the database, 1-2-3 knows to apply this formula to every record in the database rather than just the first one. If you are intent upon seeing the entry displayed as you entered it, you can format the cell as text.

Criteria for Label Data

There are both similarities to and differences between value and label criteria. Exact-match entries work the same way as for value entries. You can place a field name in the criteria area and place the label entry you are looking for immediately beneath it. 1-2-3 is not concerned with differences in alignment, capitalization, or style between the two entries.

Wildcard characters are a special option with label entries. You can make a partial entry and use the asterisk (*) to tell 1-2-3 that you do not care which characters come at the end of the entry as long as the characters you have specified match. For example, to find all records in which the last name begins with "C," you would enter **Last Name** for the field name in the criteria area and immediately beneath it you would enter **C***. To find all the records in which the last name starts with "Camp," you would enter **Camp***. Enter a sample for this type of criterion:

1. Move the cell pointer to E1, type **Last Name**, and move the cell pointer to E2 to finalize the entry.

2. Type **Camp*** and press ENTER or click the confirm box to enter criteria in E1..E2.

The other type of wildcard character is the question mark, which represents any one character. For example, Mil??? matches Miller and Milton but does not match Million.

1-2-3 has one additional type of label criteria. This type uses string formulas. Since string formulas are an advanced topic, this chapter addresses the use of the criteria you have already entered.

Defining the Database Location

You must tell 1-2-3 where your database is stored before it can search the database for the information you need. In this case, you must include

12

the field names in the range you provide since they are an integral part of identifying the information you want to select. You can select the employee database with these steps:

1. Press CTRL-PGDN to switch to sheet A, where the database is located.

2. Select the range A:A1..A:F11.

3. Select **Data Query.**

The selected range appears in the Input Range text box. This tells 1-2-3 the location of the database to use as the input for the command buttons in the dialog box. The dialog box remains on the screen for additional selections, such as the criteria location and the type of selection you want performed.

Telling 1-2-3 the Criteria Location

1-2-3 uses criteria to select which records from the database will fill your request. You have already entered several sets of criteria on the worksheet. Now you need to choose one set that 1-2-3 can use to check each record in the database. 1-2-3 ignores records that do not meet these criteria.

To define the location of your criteria on the worksheet, enter the range in the **C**riteria Range text box. Remember that the criteria must already be stored on the worksheet before you can use this command effectively. First, use the criteria that search all of the records to find those that contain a job code of 23:

1. Press TAB or click the **C**riteria Range text box and then CTRL-PGUP to switch to sheet B.

2. Select the range B:A1..B:A2.

Now all you need to do is tell 1-2-3 what you want 1-2-3 to do with the records that match the criteria.

Finding Matching Records

The **Find** command button selects records that match the criteria you have defined. If the database has multiple records that match, the records are selected one at a time. Now, when you select the **Find** command button, 1-2-3 uses the database and criteria you have selected. Since the preliminaries have been completed, only one step is needed to select the first record:

1. Select the **Find** command button to produce the display shown in Figure 12-5.

Notice that the first record containing a job code of 23 was classified as matching the criteria and that it is currently selected. 1-2-3 begins at the top of the database, selecting the first record that matches, and lets you use the UP ARROW and DOWN ARROW keys to move to other records that match the criteria. If the number of fields exceeds the width of the screen, you can use the RIGHT ARROW and LEFT ARROW keys to view other fields within a selected record. As you select a matching record, you can edit the contents of the

Figure 12-5. *Finding the first matching record*

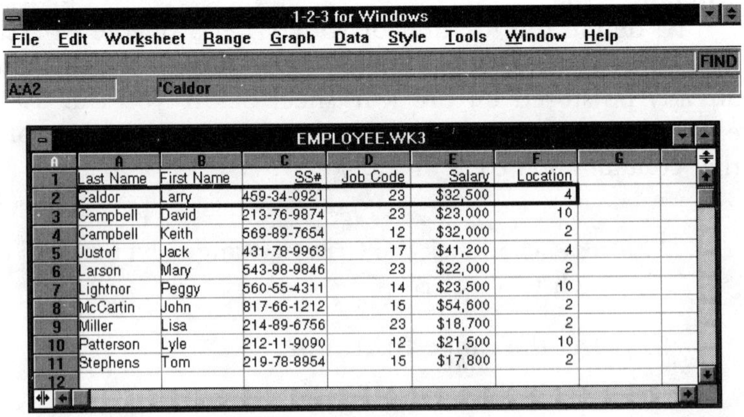

12

record just as you can from READY mode by pressing F2 (Edit) when the cell pointer is on the field you want to edit. You cannot move to records that do not match the criteria; 1-2-3 automatically skips over them.

2. Press the DOWN ARROW key to move to the next record with a job code of 23.

3. Press the UP ARROW key to move back to the previous record.

4. Press F7 (Query) to return to READY mode.

If you want to return to the Data Query dialog box after reviewing the matching records, press ESC or ENTER.

Extracting Matching Records

The Find option is useful when you need to answer a question quickly or take a quick look at someone's record. You can specify the criteria to have these records selected for you. The problem with Find is that the data does not stay on the screen. Often, when you move to the second record, the first record disappears from view (the database is probably larger than your small example). The Extract option can solve this problem; it selectively copies matching records from the database to a new area on the worksheet. As you extract this information, you can also use the fields in any sequence in the output area you are building.

To use Extract, you must complete a preliminary step from READY mode: you construct an output area in a blank area of the worksheet that will store the copied records. You can put this output area in any location that will not interfere with the database, such as below the database, to the right of it, or on a separate sheet. After choosing an area, you create the output area by placing the field names in the top row of this area. Remember, you do not need to include every field, and the fields do not need to be in the same sequence as in the database.

Try extracting matching records by following these steps:

1. Enter the field names for the output area in these cells:

B:A4: **First Name**
B:B4: **Last Name**

B:C4: **"Salary**
B:D4: **"Job Code**

This is all that is required to set up the output area as shown here:

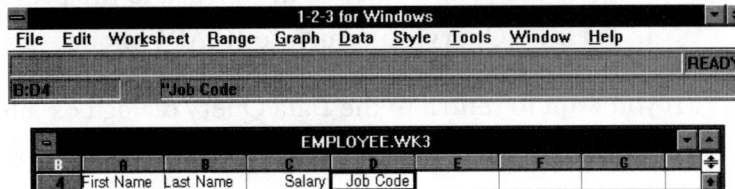

Now you are ready to extract the matching records.

2. Select **D**ata **Q**uery, and select the range B:A4..B:D4 in the **O**utput Range text box.

This tells 1-2-3 where the output area is located.

You have to tell 1-2-3 only the range containing the field names. 1-2-3 erases any data from below the field names to the bottom of the worksheet before it extracts matching records, so you do not want to put data below the field names in the output range. You can also select a range containing the field names and an appropriate number of rows beneath it. If you choose the latter approach, the output area you choose must be large enough to contain all of the selected records, or you will get an error message.

3. Select the **E**xtract command button.

4. Select the Cancel command button or press ESC.

5. Press CTRL-PGUP to view the copied records, which look like the ones in Figure 12-6.

Figure 12-6. *Extracting matching records*

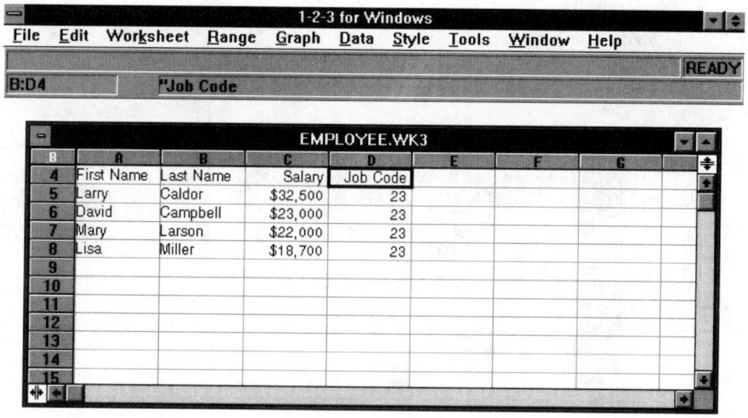

A Few More Examples

You entered more than one set of criteria as you looked at some of the ways to enter criteria in worksheet cells. You can try an extract with the two other sets of criteria, using just a few easy steps. Follow these steps to use the criteria that select records in which the salary is greater than $25,000, and then use the criteria that select records in which the last name begins with "Camp":

1. Select **Data Query** and select the range B:C1..B:C2 in the **C**riteria Range text box.

This is where you stored the criteria to select records by the Salary field. 1-2-3 continues to use the same input area and the same output area as your previous query.

2. Select the **Extract** command button to write the records to the extract area, as shown in Figure 12-7.

Figure 12-7.   *Extracting records with a salary greater than $25,000*

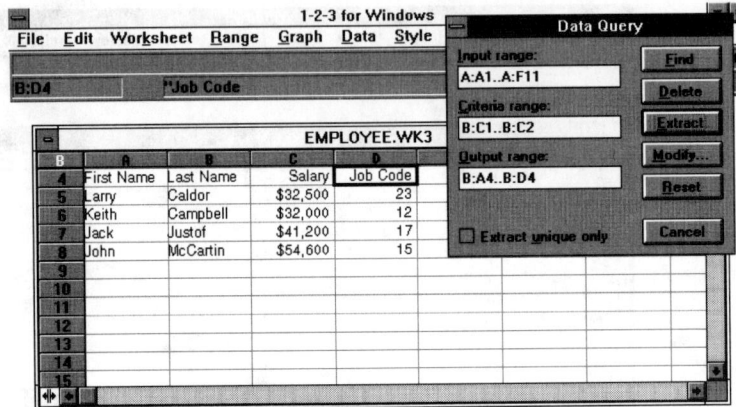

3. Select the range B:E1..B:E2 in the **C**riteria Range text box.

This uses the criteria you entered earlier to select last names that begin with "Camp."

4. Select the **E**xtract command button to produce the data shown here:

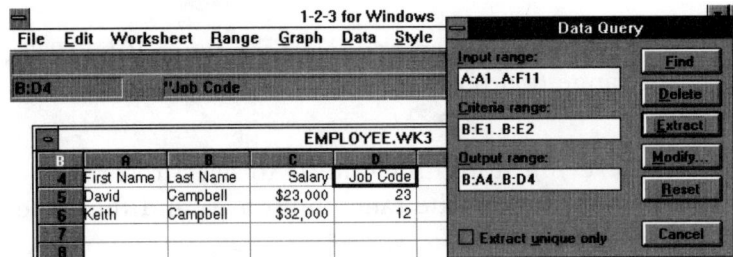

12

5. Select the Cancel command button or press ESC to return to READY mode.

Special Features

Now that you have completed the basics of data management, you may want to take a look at some of 1-2-3's data-management features. These include a shortcut approach to executing a query operation, referencing the database with a range name, and using powerful database statistical functions.

Using a Shortcut Approach

1-2-3 has a shortcut approach to reexecuting a **Data Query** command when certain conditions are met. First, the database must be in the same location and be the same size as when the last query was executed. Second, your criteria must be in the same place and with the same size and shape. The criteria can have new values or check new fields, just as long as the range you selected for the last query also applies for the query you perform with the shortcut. Third, if you are extracting records, the output area must be set up so the query performed by the shortcut can use the same output range as the previous query. Finally, you must perform the same data query operation; if you performed an extract last time, you must perform an extract this time. If all of these conditions are met, you can reexecute the last query operation by pressing F7 (Query).

Try this by carrying out the following directions to update the criteria:

1. Move the cell pointer to B:E2, type **L***, and press ENTER or click the confirm box.

2. Press F7 (Query) and then move the cell pointer to the output range to produce the display shown here:

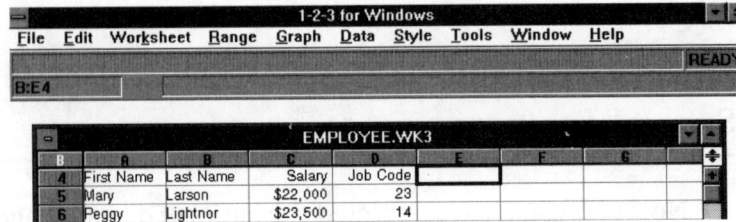

This is a handy feature if you need to perform multiple query operations. You need to use the **Data Query** command only the first time; then you can type new values in the criteria area if you wish and press F7 (Query) to have 1-2-3 use the new criteria.

Naming the Database

Using a name rather than a range address to refer to the database can provide flexibility. If you expand this named range of cells by inserting blank rows or columns in the middle, the range referenced by the name is expanded automatically. If an @function or formula rather than an address references the named database, the @function or formula automatically uses the adjusted database range.

You can assign names with the **Range Name Create** command you first used in Chapter 4, "@Functions and Other Formula Options." Try it now with the employee database:

1. Select the range A:A1..F11, select **Range Name Create**, type **EMPLOYEE** in the **R**ange Name text box, and select the OK command button.

You can now reference the range A1..F11 by the name EMPLOYEE. When you use this range name in formulas, as you will shortly, 1-2-3 automatically uses the database even if the database has changed size or location.

Using the Database Statistical Functions

The database statistical functions are @functions designed to work exclusively with databases. Like other @functions, they are prerecorded formulas that can perform calculations for you. Unlike other @functions, they operate on a database and require that you establish criteria to designate the records that are to be included in the calculations they perform. Using these @functions requires the same preliminary work as using the **D**ata **Q**uery command. Table 12-1 provides a list of the statistical functions.

All of the database statistical functions except @DQUERY have the same format for their arguments, as follows:

@DFUNCTION(*database, field in database, criteria location*)

The first argument is the location of the database. The range address or name should include the field names as well as the data. The second argument is the field name, in quotes, that you want used in the calculations. You can also select the field by providing its *offset,* which is the number of columns the field is from the left side of the database table. The offset is always one less than what you would expect with the ordinary way

Table 12-1. *Database Statistical Functions*

Function	Description
@DAVG	Averages a field for matching records
@DCOUNT	Counts the nonblank entries in a field for matching records
@DGET	Returns the value of a field for the one matching record
@DMAX	Returns the highest value of a field from the matching records
@DMIN	Returns the lowest value of a field from the matching records
@DQUERY	Returns the value of an external database function
@DSTD	Calculates the standard deviation of a field for matching records
@DSTDS	Calculates the sample standard deviation of a field for matching records
@DSUM	Totals a field for matching records
@DVAR	Computes the variance for a field for matching records
@DVARS	Computes the sample variance for a field for matching records

of counting. The first column has an offset of zero, and each column to the right has its offset incremented by one. The last argument is the range name or address specifying the location of the criteria. You define the criteria in the same way you define criteria for the **Data Query** command. Putting a few of these functions to work will clarify exactly how you use them.

Using @DAVG

The @DAVG function computes the average for a field in a selected group of database records. You can use this function to determine the average salary for employees with a job code of 23. You can use the same criteria you entered for the data query operations. Just follow these steps:

1. Move the cell pointer to B:H1, type **Average Salary for Job Code 23:**, and move the cell pointer to B:K1 to finalize your entry.

2. Type **@DAVG(EMPLOYEE,"Salary",A1.A2)** and press ENTER or click the confirm box.

Notice that the database reference uses the range name, EMPLOYEE, which includes the field names, all records, and all fields. The field name is Salary; this field contains the values you want to average. The formula uses the criteria in A1..A2 on the current sheet (sheet B) to select the records whose salary entries are averaged. The results are shown here:

Using @DSUM

The @DSUM function follows the same pattern as the @DAVG function. If you want to total the salaries for all records with a job code of 23, you can use the same criteria. Follow these steps:

1. Move the cell pointer to B:H2, type **Total Salaries for Job Code 23:**, and move the cell pointer to B:K2 to finalize your entry.

2. Type **@DSUM(EMPLOYEE,"Salary",A1.A2)** and press ENTER or click the confirm box.

The result of this calculation is 96200, which is the total of the salaries for employees with a job code of 23.

Using @DCOUNT

The @DCOUNT function selectively counts the number of nonblank entries in records that match your criteria. You can try this function to count the number of employees with a job code of 23. Follow these steps to enter the function:

1. Move the cell pointer to B:H3, type **Number of Employees in Job Code 23:**, and then move the cell pointer to B:K3 to finalize your entry.

2. Type **@DCOUNT(EMPLOYEE,"Job Code",A1.A2)** and press ENTER or click the confirm box.

The count operation is performed on the Job Code field, although you could have selected any field that contains an entry. The result is 4—the same result you would get if you manually counted records for employees with a job code of 23.

Using @DMIN

The @DMIN function searches for the minimum value in the column specified. Only records that match your criteria are eligible for this minimum comparison. You can use this function to determine the lowest salary paid to an individual in location 2 or the lowest salary paid to someone with a job code of 23. This time, you change the criteria and then enter the formula to determine the lowest salary in location 2:

1. Move to B:F1, type **Location**, move to B:F2, type **2**, and press ENTER or click the confirm box to create additional criteria to use for this function.

2. Move to B:H4, type **Minimum Salary for Location 2:**, and move the cell pointer to B:K4 to finalize your entry.

3. Type **@DMIN(EMPLOYEE,"Salary",F1.F2)** and press ENTER or click the confirm box to produce these results:

Review

In this chapter, you learned how to create, sort, and query databases in 1-2-3. The topics you covered include the following:

- You can use 1-2-3 to create and use databases. You can store a database in any location, but you want to keep other data away from it so the database can grow. The first row of the database contains the field names, with one in each cell. The rows beneath the field names contain the database records.

12

- You can resequence the records in a 1-2-3 database with the **D**ata **S**ort command. You include only the database records as the range to sort, not the field names. Primary, secondary, and extra keys control the sequence of the records.

- 1-2-3's **D**ata **Q**uery command finds records in a database that match conditions, or criteria, you create. You can select matching records with the **F**ind option or copy them to a new area on the worksheet if you set up an output area and then use **E**xtract. Only records that match your criteria are selected or copied.

- Before you query a database, you must enter the criteria a record must meet to be selected. You can use exact-match criteria for label or value data. With label data you can also use the ? and * wildcard characters to represent one or many characters. Logical formulas are another option. They describe acceptable entries for fields containing either label or value data.

- The database statistical functions are @functions that work with the records in a 1-2-3 database and the criteria you have established to select records of interest. You can obtain a total, average, minimum, maximum, and other statistical computations on a selected group of records with these functions.

Commands and Keys

The commands you learned enable you to sort and query a database. You also learned how you can repeat a query by simply pressing a function key. These commands and keys are

Keys	Action
ALT D Q	**D**ata **Q**uery finds matching records in a database and even copies them to another location
ALT D S	**D**ata **S**ort sorts a database according to the keys you select
F7 (Query)	Repeats the most recent query operation

13

Advanced
Problem-solving
Techniques

1-2-3 has several features for solving advanced problems. One of these features is Solver, which can analyze data and present the values for multiple solutions to problems. You create a model that represents the problem you want Solver to use and then develop constraints to tell Solver the limitations you place on answers.

By now you are probably an expert at the basic file-management features for opening and closing your worksheet files. These commands are the workhorses of the file commands because they play a central role in every worksheet session. A number of other file-management commands are used less commonly but provide powerful options that you will want to incorporate into your set of skills. These include dividing worksheets into multiple files and combining them. You can also share data between 1-2-3 and other applications. Together, these file commands provide ways to increase productivity by letting you reuse existing data rather than reenter it.

In this chapter, you learn to develop and solve a problem with Solver. Also, you learn to extract part of a worksheet to another worksheet file.

This feature lets you create a new worksheet that starts off with account names or end-of-period totals. You learn to combine worksheets, which lets you combine an entire file or a range of data with the file currently in memory. Finally, you explore the procedures for transferring data from 1-2-3 into other programs and transferring data from other programs into 1-2-3.

Using Solver

You use Solver for solving problems for which there may be more than one solution or for which you have many constraints. For example, when you invest money, you must decide among different alternatives. You can have Solver find different combinations of cell values that you can use in a model that meets requirements you set up. Solver is like the reverse of many what-if solutions. In many cases of using what-if analysis, you provide different values for input and 1-2-3 supplies what the answer is for each set of input values. Solver works the other way; you tell 1-2-3 what you want out of the answer and 1-2-3 finds the input values that meet the requirements you provide. You can use Solver in any model in which you want 1-2-3 to find potential what-if values.

Setting Up a Problem for Solver

Solver needs several pieces of information before you can use it to find an answer to a problem. Using Solver is like querying a database in that most of the information you will use must be entered in the worksheet before you use the command. To create a problem for 1-2-3 to solve, you must enter the model Solver will work through to calculate the answer. You must also enter logical equations that tell Solver what the limits are on the answer.

As an example of a problem that may have several solutions, suppose you have $100,000 to invest and you are thinking of investing in three stores. Each store has its gross profit, operating expenses, and initial cost, but you still have to decide which one will be the best investment. To set up a worksheet to use with Solver like the one shown in Figure 13-1, follow these steps:

1. Make the following entries:

A1:	**Store Analysis**	A6:	**Net**
B2:	**^X**	B6:	**+B3−B5−B4**
C2:	**^Y**	C6:	**+C3−C5−C4**
D2:	**^Z**	D6:	**+D3−D5−D4**
A3:	**Gross Profit**	A8:	**Investment**
B3:	**250000**	B8:	**0**
C3:	**300000**	C8:	**0**
D3:	**350000**	D8:	**0**
A4:	**Yearly Exp.**	A9:	**Percentage**
B4:	**50000**	B9:	**+B8/B5**
C4:	**75000**	C9:	**+C8/C5**
D4:	**50000**	D9:	**+D8/D5**
A5:	**Initial Exp.**	A10:	**Return**
B5:	**50000**	B10:	**+B6*B9**
C5:	**40000**	C10:	**+C6*C9**
D5:	**100000**	D10:	**+D6*D9**

The entries in columns B, C, and D represent the costs and revenues generated for the three stores, X, Y and Z, over five years. Each store has

Figure 13-1. *Worksheet setup for Solver*

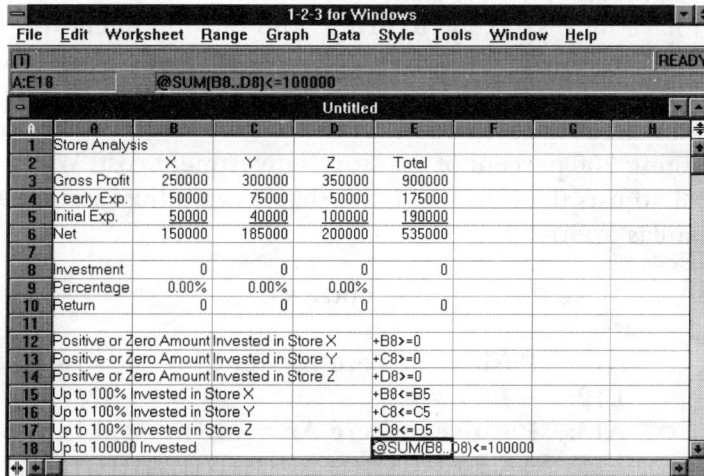

a gross profit, expenses, and an initial investment. To calculate the proceeds for each store, you have to subtract from the gross profit the yearly operating expenses and the initial cost. The amount you invest in each store determines your percentage ownership and the percentage of the net that represents your return on the store.

2. Enter ^Total in E2 and @SUM(B3..D3) in E3.

3. Press CTRL-INS or click the Edit Copy SmartIcon to copy the formula to the Clipboard.

4. Move to E4, E5, E6, E8, and E10, and at each cell press SHIFT-INS to copy the formula from the Clipboard to these cells.

5. Select the range B9..D9, and either click the Percent (%) Smart-Icon or select the **Range Format** command, Percent in the **Format** list box, and the OK command button.

6. Select the range B5..E5, and either click the Underline (U) SmartIcon or select the **Style Font** command, the **Underline** check box, and the OK command button.

The next type of entry you need to use Solver is the constraints. The constraints are logical formulas that tell Solver information, such as that E8 cannot be more than 100000. The problem you are creating to use with Solver needs several types of constraints. First, you must tell Solver that you can invest zero or more in each store. You must also tell Solver that you cannot invest more than the initial expense of each store. Finally, since you have only $100,000 to invest, you need to tell Solver that the sum of B8..D8 (the formula result in E8) must be less than or equal to 100000. If you forget one of these constraints when you solve the problem, you may get an erroneous solution, such as investing −20000 in one store or investing 200 percent of the store's investment cost. When you use Solver, 1-2-3 adjusts the cells you tell it that it can adjust so that all of the logical formulas are true.

7. Make the following entries:

A12: **Positive or Zero Amount Invested In Store X**
E12: **+B8 > =0**
A13: **Positive or Zero Amount Invested In Store Y**
E13: **+C8 > =0**

A14: **Positive or Zero Amount Invested In Store Z**
E14: **+D8 > =0**
A15: **Up to 100% invested in Store X**
E15: **+B8 < =B5**
A16: **Up to 100% invested in Store Y**
E16: **+C8 < =C5**
A17: **Up to 100% invested in Store Z**
E17: **+D8 < =D5**
A18: **Up to 100000 invested**
E18: **@SUM(B8..D8) < =100000**

13

8. Select the range E12..E18, and select the **R**ange Format command, Text in the **F**ormat list box, and the OK command button.

Displaying these logical formulas as text makes them easier to understand.
At this point, your entries look like the ones in Figure 13-1 and you are ready to use Solver to look at different investment combinations.

Solving a Problem

Once you have entered the information Solver will use to solve the problem, you are ready to use the **T**ools **S**olver command. To try this with the problem you have created, follow these steps:

1. Select **T**ools **S**olver to display this dialog box:

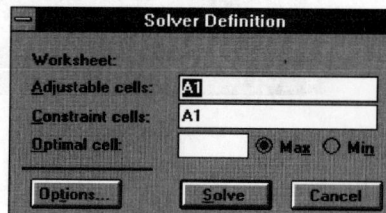

2. Select the range B8..D8 in the **A**djustable Cells text box.

The adjustable cells in a problem are the cells in which Solver is allowed to change the value in order to find answers to the problem. In the problem, the values in other worksheet cells change based on the value of these cells. In this problem, as you change the investment of each store, you are changing the percentage ownership and the return from the investment.

  3. Select the range E12..E18 in the **C**onstraint Cells text box.

These are the logical formulas you entered previously.

  4. Select the cell E10 in the **O**ptimal Cell text box and select the **Max** option button (the default).

The optimal cell is the cell containing the value that you want to be as high or low as possible. Since in this problem you want to maximize your return on the investment, you want E10, the total of the return from investment in the stores you invest in, to be as high as possible.

  5. Select the **S**olve command button.

1-2-3 solves the problem, and after a short time (larger problems may take longer), 1-2-3 displays this Solver Answer dialog box:

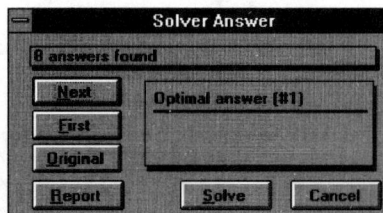

  6. Select the **F**irst command button.

1-2-3 organizes its answers according to the value of the optimal cell, so the first cell is the optimal answer. 1-2-3 replaces the adjustable cells with the values for the first answer.

  7. Select the **N**ext command button.

1-2-3 replaces the adjustable cells with the values for the second answer. You can see that the value of E10 has dropped from 355000 to 335000 since this answer is not as optimal as the first one.

   8. Select the **R**eport command button.

1-2-3 displays a Solver Report dialog box that lets you create reports about the problem Solver has solved.

   Many of the report options create a table report, which 1-2-3 puts on a new worksheet. Each report provides different information, but the most useful is the Answers report, which lists all of the answers Solver has found.

   9. Select the **A**nswer Table option button and the OK command button to generate the Answers report in a new file called ANSWER##.WK3. (## starts at 01 and continues until the next unused number.)

   The beginning of the report, when you later return to READY mode, looks like the one shown in Figure 13-2.

Figure 13-2. *Answers Table report*

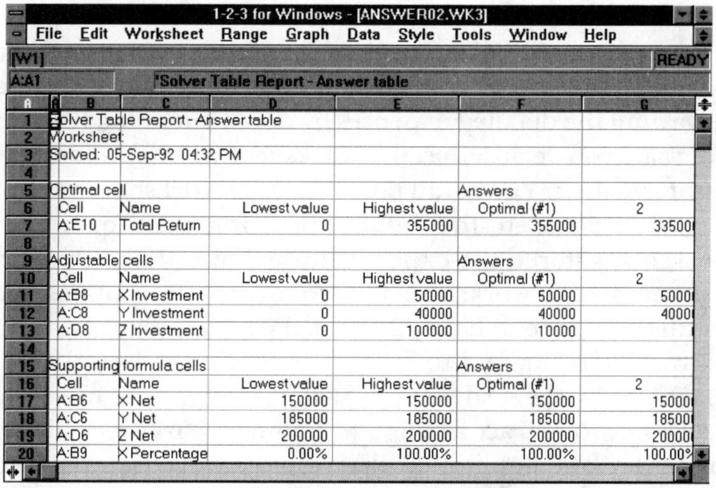

10. Select the Cancel command dialog box to return to the Solver Answer dialog box.

11. Select the **F**irst command button to return to the optimal answer.

12. Select the Cancel command button twice to return to READY mode.

13. Select **F**ile Save **A**s, type **SOLVER** in the File **N**ame text box, and select the OK command button to save the file.

14. Select **F**ile **C**lose to clear the worksheet and open a new one.

Saving a Section of the Worksheet

You can save a range on a worksheet to another worksheet file. You have complete control over the amount of data that is saved to a file. Saving part the worksheet to another file by using the **F**ile **E**xtract To command lets you split the data between the different files you want to create. You have two choices for creating the extract file: you can save just the values in the selected range, or if you prefer, you can save the formulas. You will get the chance to try both so you can become familiar with some of the potential problems encountered when you save formulas.

You may wonder why you would want to save a portion of a current worksheet to a file. You may want to do this when you are working on very large applications and are running out of memory. Suppose that you are recording the detailed expenses by department for 1992. Halfway through the year, you realize that the worksheet will not fit an entire year's worth of information. You could take this large worksheet and split it so different worksheets stored the information for each quarter or so different worksheets stored the expenses for groups of departments. You may also want to split a worksheet file when the file contains a database that is getting too large to hold all of the data. You may also want to use the **F**ile **E**xtract To command to split a multilevel worksheet into separate worksheet files by sheet so you can save them for later use with Release 2. You may want to extract a range to another worksheet file when you have a model for one application that you want to use as the basis for another model.

Saving Values

When you extract cells with the Values option, 1-2-3 saves the current values of the cells you select in a separate worksheet file. 1-2-3 extracts values, labels, and the results of formulas rather than the formulas themselves. This is a convenient way to put the result of calculations in a new worksheet without extracting the data the formula uses, as is required when you save formulas. The extracted data is placed in the new file beginning in cell A1. The data in the extracted worksheet retains the same size and shape as in the current worksheet, although each cell's addresses are determined by its offset from the beginning of the range.

You can try extracting entries to another worksheet with a small worksheet model. Although these entries are not enough data to cause a condition of insufficient memory, the concept and potential actions required are exactly the same as you would need with much larger models. Follow these steps to create this practice example:

1. Complete these entries:

A2:	**Sales:**	C4:	**5600**
A3:	**Product 1**	C5:	**7800**
A4:	**Product 2**	D2:	**"Mar**
A5:	**Product 3**	D3:	**1100**
B2:	**"Jan**	D4:	**7800**
B3:	**1200**	D5:	**9900**
B4:	**4400**	E2:	**"Qtr1**
B5:	**5400**	E3:	**@SUM(B3.D3)**
C2:	**"Feb**	E4:	**@SUM(B4.D4)**
C3:	**1500**	E5:	**@SUM(B5.D5)**

These entries produce the results shown in Figure 13-3.

2. Select the range E3..E5 as the range to extract.

3. Select **File Extract To**.

The File Extract To dialog box has many of the same options as the File Save **As** command. 1-2-3 provides a default name unless you enter another one in the File **Name** text box. In the File Extract To dialog box,

Figure 13-3.   *Data for the first quarter*

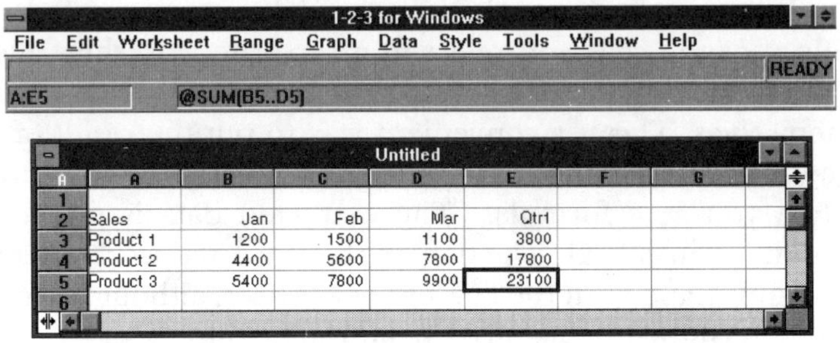

you need to indicate whether formulas in the selected range are saved as formulas or as their values and what range contains the entries you will extract. Like other commands that use ranges, 1-2-3 picks up any preselected range.

    4. Type **QTR1VALU** in the File **N**ame text box, select the Val**u**es option button, and select the OK command button.

The current values of the three cells are written to the new worksheet file, QTR1VALU.WK3.

    5. Select **File O**pen, type **QTR1VALU** in the File **N**ame text box, and select the OK command button.

The extracted worksheet looks like this:

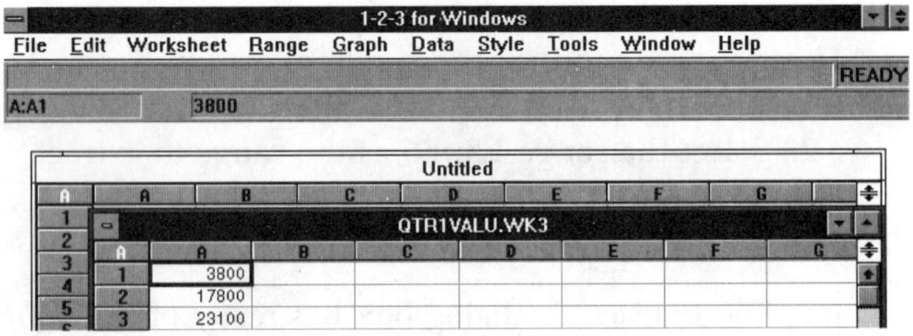

    6. Select **File C**lose to close the worksheet.

Saving Formulas

Saving formulas is just as easy as saving values, but before you use the Formulas option you must consider whether you are copying the entries the formulas use. If you save the formulas without the data they need, the formulas may return erroneous results. You extract entries by using the Formulas option when you want to retain the formulas and you are extracting the entries the formula uses. Follow these steps to complete the exercise:

1. Select the range E3..E5 as the range to extract.

2. Select File Extract To, type **QTR1FORM** in the File Name text box, select the Formulas option button, and select the OK command button.

1-2-3 extracts values, labels, and the formulas. 1-2-3 adjusts any cell references in the new worksheet just as if you had moved the selected entries to a new worksheet.

3. Select File Open, type **QTR1FORM** in the File Name text box, and select the OK command button to produce this display:

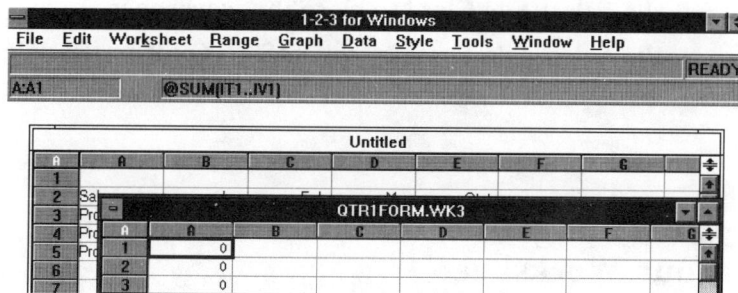

Notice that the formulas are adjusted for the new worksheet. Since you did not include the values the formulas use in the range to extract, these formulas are meaningless in the new worksheet. In this case, extracting values meets your needs better.

4. Select File Close to close the worksheet.

5. Select the range A2..E3 as the range to extract.

6. Select **File Extract To**, type **PRD1FORM** in the File **N**ame text box, select the **F**ormulas option button, and select the OK command button.

7. Select **File O**pen, type **PRD1FORM** in the File **N**ame text box, and select the OK command button.

8. Move the cell pointer to E2 to produce this display:

			1-2-3 for Windows						
File	**Edit**	**Worksheet**	**Range**	**Graph**	**Data**	**Style**	**Tools**	**Window**	**Help**

READY

A:E2   @SUM(B2..D2)

	PRD1FORM.WK3						
A	**A**	**B**	**C**	**D**	**E**	**F**	**G**
1	Sales	Jan	Feb	Mar	Qtr1		
2	Product 1	1200	1500	1100	3800		

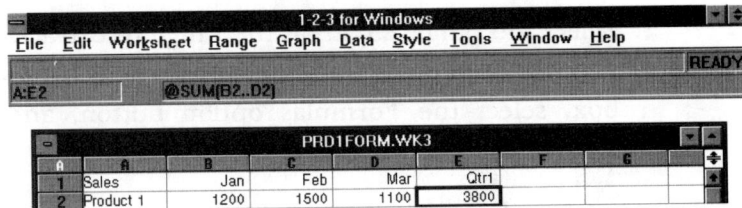

Notice that 1-2-3 adjusted the formula just like before, but since you included the values the formula uses, this formula is still useful. You extract formulas when you want to include the formulas in the new worksheet and you are including the data the formulas use in the range to extract.

9. Select **File C**lose to close the worksheet.

10. Select **File Save A**s, type **1ST_QTR** in the File **N**ame text box, and select the OK command button to save this file.

Combining Data from Other Files with Your Worksheet

1-2-3 lets you combine worksheets in three ways: you can copy the entries from one worksheet file into another, add values from one worksheet file to another, or subtract values from one worksheet file to another. You can easily copy entries by copying and pasting with the Clipboard, so you use the **File Combine From** command when you want to add or subtract values from one worksheet file to another. This section examines adding and subtracting with the **File Combine From** command to illustrate the functions they serve. You can use the **File Combine From** command to total subsidiary worksheets or to subtract a division's contribution from the total.

You have two options when combining a file with the current worksheet—to combine everything in the file or to combine a range from the file. The option you choose depends on whether the file contains other information that you do not want to combine. When you combine an entire file, everything in the file is combined with the current worksheet. For example, if you want to combine the data in Figure 13-3 with the current worksheet, 1-2-3 will use the entries stored in A2..E5. If you want to combine only the entries in E2..E5, you would combine a range because you want to use only a subset of the worksheet's entries. When you combine ranges from worksheet files, you will find that using range names makes the **File Combine From** command easier; you are more likely to remember the range name than the range address.

Setting Up a Worksheet for Combining

Before you try combining worksheet files, you will want to create a worksheet to use with the **File Combine From** command. Follow these steps to modify the 1ST_QTR worksheet file that you created earlier. You will use the modified worksheet to try adding and subtracting worksheet files.

1. Select the range E2..E5, select **R**ange **N**ame **C**reate, type **Total** in the **R**ange Name text box, and select the OK command button.

You are including the label Qtrl in this range so you can see how adding and subtracting handles labels. Both the label and formulas are now named Total. When you later add or subtract this named range with **File Combine From**, the values of the formulas are combined. (If you copy the range, the formulas are copied just as if you had copied them between worksheets.)

2. Select **File S**ave.

This saves the worksheet with the assigned range name on the disk.

3. Select **File Save As**, type **QTRTOTAL** in the File **N**ame text box, and select the OK command button.

This saves the current worksheet with a new name so you can use this newer version as the basis for creating the new model. This shortcut allows you to keep the same entries and width for column A.

4. Select the range B2..E5 and press DEL or select **E**dit Clear.

5. Make these worksheet entries to complete the model shown in Figure 13-4:

C1:   **Sales Summary by Quarter**
B2:   **"Qtr1**
C2:   **"Qtr2**
D2:   **"Qtr3**
E2:   **"Qtr4**
F2:   **"Total**
F3:   **@SUM(B3.E3)**
F4:   **@SUM(B4.E4)**
F5:   **@SUM(B5.E5)**

The **File Combine From** command provides the perfect solution for adding values from other worksheet files; using this command does not

Figure 13-4. *Worksheet before File Combine From*

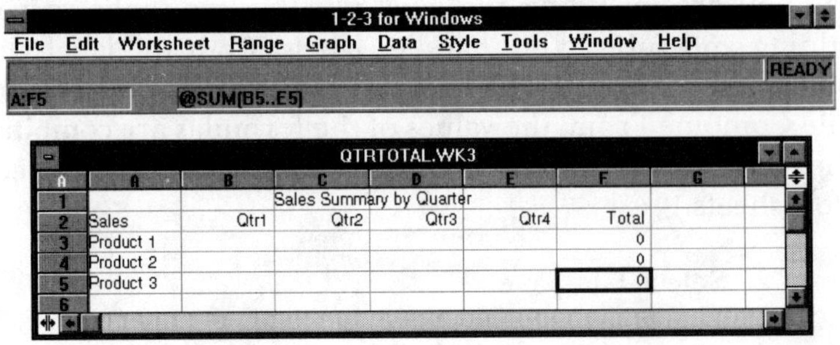

destroy the current model as you bring the quarter totals in from other files. The data that you will be bringing in must be on disk, either as range names in a completed model or as the only entries you need in the worksheet file.

Adding a Worksheet to the Current Worksheet

The **Add** option of the **File Combine From** command adds the values to the values in the current worksheet. Which values are added is determined by the cell pointer's position and the placement of the values within the file. When you add values, 1-2-3 ignores labels in the incoming worksheet, and any formulas in the current worksheet are not changed. Any formulas in the incoming worksheet are added as their values at the time you add the two files. Follow these steps to try the **Add** option:

1. Select **File Save.**

Just in case you do not combine the worksheet files the way you want, save the current worksheet before you combine the worksheets so you can retrieve the worksheet from disk and try again.

2. Move the cell pointer to B3.

The cell pointer's position for combining files is very important. The cell pointer determines the cell in the current worksheet that is combined with the first cell from the incoming worksheet (if you are combining an entire file) or the first cell in the range (if you are combining a range).

3. Select **File Combine From**, either type **1ST_QTR** in the File Name text box or select 1ST_QTR from the **Files** list box, select the **Add** option button, select the **Range** option button, and type **Total** in the text box under the **Range** option button.

4. Select the OK command button to add the range named TOTAL to the current worksheet starting at B3.

Figure 13-5 shows the range added to the worksheet. Since the Qtrl label is included in the range TOTAL, you should have positioned the cell pointer at B2. This would have caused the first value in the named range to match with B3.

5. Press ALT-BACKSPACE or select **Edit Undo** to remove the added range and return the worksheet to the way it was before you added the named range Total.

6. Move the cell pointer to B2.

7. Select **File Combine From**, either type **1ST_QTR** in the File **N**ame text box or select 1ST_QTR from the **Files** list box, select the **A**dd and the **R**ange option buttons, type **Total** in the text box under the **R**ange option button, and select the OK command button.

The added worksheet is shown in Figure 13-6. Try this again to see if it really adds.

8. Select **File Combine From**, either type **1ST_QTR** in the File **N**ame text box or select 1ST_QTR from the **Files** list box, select the **A**dd and the **R**ange option buttons, type **Total** in the text box under the **R**ange option button, and select the OK command button.

Figure 13-5.   *Misjudging the cell pointer's position for File Combine From*

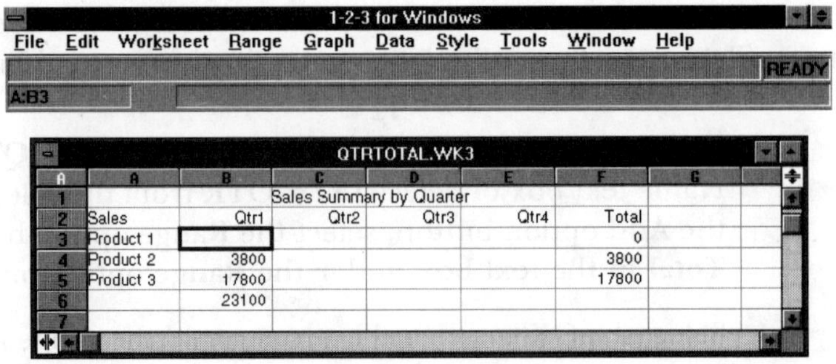

Figure 13-6. *Adding data to the worksheet with File Combine From*

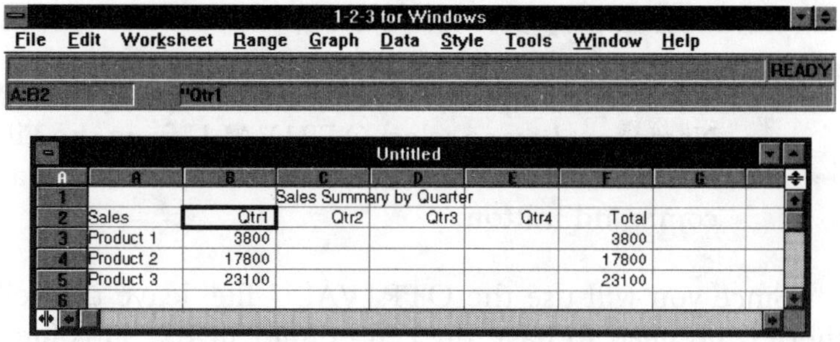

9. Move the cell pointer to B3 to see the value 7600 in B3, as shown in Figure 13-7.

You can see that each of the numbers in the current worksheet doubled as the numbers on the file were added to the current worksheet again.

Subtracting from the Current Worksheet

The Subtract option of the File Combine From command is the exact opposite of the Add option. It subtracts the values stored on disk from the current worksheet cells. This option depends on the cell-pointer location

Figure 13-7. *Adding a range to the worksheet twice*

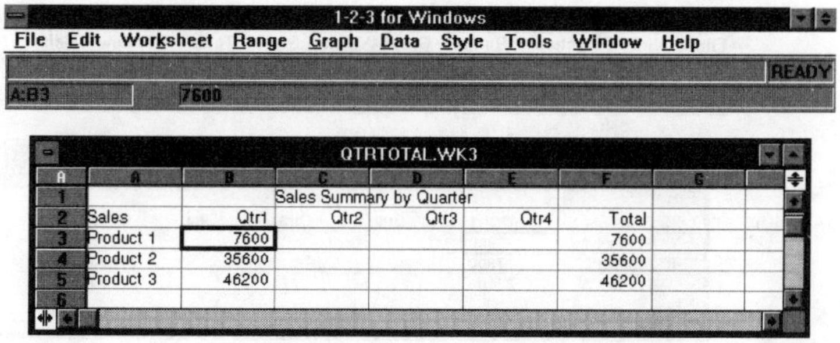

and the offset within the file that controls which numbers will be subtracted from which entries. You can try this by subtracting the values you have stored in QTR1VALU from the current worksheet:

1. Select **F**ile Com**b**ine **F**rom, either type **QTR1VALU** in the File **N**ame text box or select QTR1VALU from the **F**iles list box, select the **S**ubtract and the **E**ntire File option buttons, and select the OK command button.

Since you will use the QTR1VALU file, leave the cell pointer in B3; there is no need to have the cell pointer in B2. This file does not have a label in the first cell the way the named range did. The worksheet now looks like the one in Figure 13-8. Each of the entries returned to its original value as the subtract operation was completed.

2. Select **F**ile **S**ave.

Transferring Data Between Applications

Sharing data between applications can provide a significant savings in data-entry time. If you have account names, employee numbers, inventory items, or other lists of text data in a file for one application and need the

Figure 13-8.   *Subtracting data from the worksheet with File Combine From*

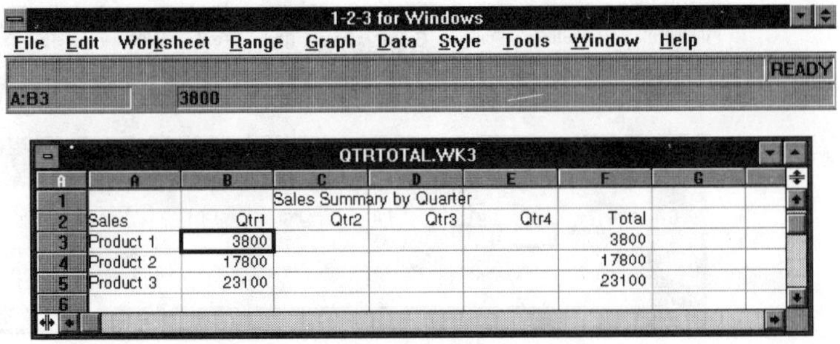

same information in another application, why retype it when you can transfer the data directly from the file? If you transfer the data, you are assured of data consistency between the two applications.

You may want to take data from another application and bring it into 1-2-3. 1-2-3 can accept data from applications that support Dynamic Data Exchange (DDE). For applications that do not support DDE, 1-2-3 can bring in data from an ASCII text file. Many programs can create text files that you can import into 1-2-3. 1-2-3 brings each line of data from a text file as a long label.

If you have worksheet data that you want to bring into another application, you need to put that worksheet information into a format the other application can use. Windows applications can often share information if you simply copy data to the Clipboard and paste it to the second application. For applications that cannot use the Clipboard, you need to put your worksheet data in a text file. You have two options for this. You can either copy the entries to the Clipboard and paste them in a Windows Notepad file that you can save as a text file, or you can extract data to a print file. Once you have the text file, you can bring it into another application. The disadvantage of transferring data to a non-Windows application is that you may lose formatting information that the data would retain if you transferred it to a Windows application.

Pasting Links Between Applications

In Chapter 9, "Making 1-2-3 Do Your Work," you learned how to copy and move data with the Clipboard. The Clipboard remembers not only the contents of the Clipboard data, but the source of the data as well. You can use the Clipboard to create links to other files. The advantage of a link over an external file link is that you can share data between 1-2-3 worksheets and other non-worksheet data formats. For example, if a report uses several numbers in a worksheet, the report can have a link to the data in the worksheet. Then, as the numbers in the worksheet change, so do the numbers in the report. You can also use entries directly from a database in a 1-2-3 worksheet without copying or entering the entries. Then, as the database changes, so do the 1-2-3 entries. Many Windows-designed applications can share information this way. The following example uses AmiPro, Lotus's Windows word processing package. If you

316 of Windows Made Easy

do not have this package, you will still want to review the example; many other Windows applications use the same steps and the same commands. Follow these steps to share data between 1-2-3 for Windows and AmiPro:

1. Make the following entries:

A1:	**Sales**	C1:	**1000000**
A2:	**Profit**	C2:	**+B3 −B5 −B4**
A3:	**Earnings Per Share**	C3:	**2.67**

2. Select the range A1..C3 and press CTRL-INS to copy these entries to the Clipboard.

3. Press CTRL-ESC to display the Task List window, and select the Program Manager.

4. Double-click the Lotus Applications icon or select **W**indow and the number next to Lotus Applications.

5. Double-click the AmiPro icon or move the highlight to AmiPro and press ENTER.

6. Select **E**dit Paste **L**ink to create a link to the current document using the source of the Clipboard's contents.

7. Press CTRL-END and type the following entries, pressing ENTER after each one.

   The past year included the following improvements:

   15 products were redesigned to reduce moveable parts and reduce assembly time.

   Distribution was expanded to include wholesale clubs.

8. Select the three sentences you have just typed by dragging the mouse over them or by moving to the beginning and holding down SHIFT as you move to cover the three lines of text.

9. Press CTRL-INS to copy these entries to the Clipboard.

10. Press ALT-ESC until you switch back to 1-2-3.

11. Move to A5 and select **E**dit Paste **L**ink to create a link to the worksheet using the source of the Clipboard's contents.

Now the data in the two applications look like the screen in Figure 13-9. (Each application window has been resized.)

12. Move to C3, type **4.87**, and press ENTER or click the confirm box.
13. Press ALT-TAB to return to AmiPro.

Notice that the document in AmiPro automatically uses the new earnings per share because this information comes from the link you created with the 1-2-3 worksheet.

14. Move to 15 and replace 15 with 23.
15. Press ALT-TAB to return to 1-2-3 for Windows.

1-2-3 automatically changes the number of products redesigned because 1-2-3 gets this information from the AmiPro document.

16. Press ALT-TAB to return to AmiPro.
17. Press ALT-F4 and select **No** to leave AmiPro without saving the document.

Figure 13-9. *1-2-3 and AmiPro files sharing data between them*

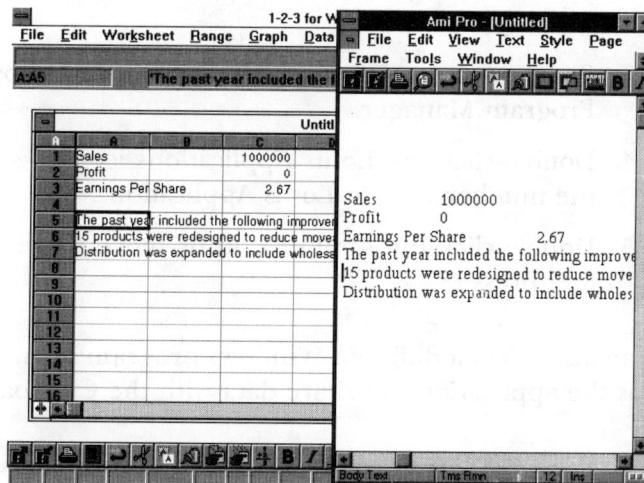

18. Select **File** **C**lose and **N**o in 1-2-3 for Windows to erase the worksheet file without saving it.

Pasting Links Between Windows Applications

If you want to export data from 1-2-3 to another Windows application, you will not always want to create a link between the two files. For example, you may want to copy a range from 1-2-3 for a year-end report in AmiPro and not want the numbers updated. You can copy information to another Windows application by using the Clipboard, just as you learned to use the Clipboard in Chapter 9, "Making 1-2-3 Do Your Work," to copy worksheet entries. Try the following steps to use the Clipboard to transfer worksheet entries to another application:

1. Make the following entries:

A1:	**Unit Price**	C1:	**4.75**
A2:	**Unit Sales**	C2:	**312000**
A3:	**Sales**	C3:	**148200**

2. Select the range A1..C3 and press CTRL-INS to copy these entries to the Clipboard.

3. Press CTRL-ESC to display the Task List window, and select the Program Manager.

4. Double-click the Lotus Applications icon or select **W**indow and the number next to Lotus Applications.

5. Double-click the AmiPro icon or move the highlight to AmiPro and press ENTER.

You can also select a different Windows program in any group window as long as the application can share data with the Clipboard.

6. Press SHIFT-INS or select **E**dit **P**aste to copy the 1-2-3 data into the current Windows application data file.

As you can see in this step, most Windows applications use the same keystroke combinations and commands to use the Clipboard. Many of them also use the same commands for procedures such as saving a file and exiting the application.

7. Press ALT-F4 and select **No** to leave AmiPro or the Windows application you are using and erase the data without saving it.

8. Press ALT-ESC until you switch back to 1-2-3.

9. Select **File** **C**lose and **No** to close the worksheet without saving the copied entries.

13

Exporting Data by Using the Clipboard and Notepad

The Notepad is an accessory Windows provides that lets you enter and store text files. You can use the Notepad with 1-2-3 to create text files from worksheet data by copying the 1-2-3 data to the Notepad, pasting the Clipboard's contents to the Notepad, and then saving the Notepad's contents as a text file. To try this, follow these steps:

1. Select **File** **O**pen, type **1ST _ QTR** in the File **N**ame text box, and select the OK command button.

2. Select the range A2..E5, and press CTRL-INS or click the Edit Copy SmartIcon to copy these cells to the Clipboard.

3. Press CTRL-ESC to display the Task List window, and select Program Manager.

4. Double-click the Accessories icon or select **W**indow and the number next to Accessories.

5. Double-click the Notepad icon or move the highlight to Notepad and press ENTER.

6. Press SHIFT-INS or select **E**dit **P**aste to copy the Clipboard's contents to the Notepad, as shown here:

```
 ─                        1-2-3 for Windows                    ▼│♦
 File  Edit  Worksheet  Range  Graph  Data  Style  Tools  Window  Help
 ┌─────────────────────────────────────────────────────────────────┐
 │  ─                    Notepad - (untitled)               ▼│▲      │
 A:A2│ File  Edit  Search  Help                                      │
 ┌────┬──────────────────────────────────────────────────────────┬─┐│
 │    │ Sales   Jan    Feb    Mar    Qtr1                         │▲││
 │ ▭  │ Product 1      1200   1500   1100   3800                  │ ││
 │ ▭  │ Product 2      4400   5600   7800   17800                 │ ││
 │    │ Product 3      5400   7800   9900   23100                 │ ││
```

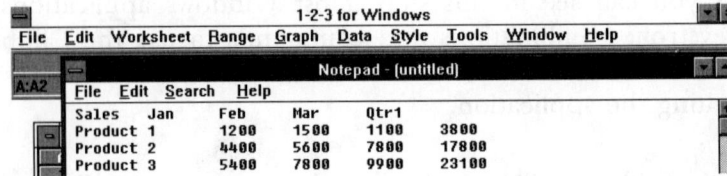

7. Select **File** Save **As**, type **C:\TEXT_QTR.DOC** in the Filename text box, and select the OK command button to save this file.

Now the worksheet entries are stored in a text file named TEXT_
QTR.DOC in the root directory of drive C.

8. Select **File New** to erase the data.

9. Press CTRL-ESC to display the Task List window, and select 1-2-3 for Windows.

Extracting to a Text File

You can also use the **File Extract To** command to create a text file to put 1-2-3 data in a format you can use with other programs, such as a word processor. The disadvantage of using the **File Extract To** command is that you must make sure the columns containing label entries are wide enough. If they are not wide enough, the long labels may be truncated. To try using the **File Extract To** command, follow these steps:

1. Select the range A2..E5 in the 1ST_QTR worksheet file, and select **File Extract To**, select the **Text** option button, type **QTR1TEXT** in the File **Name** text box, and select the OK command button.

2. Press CTRL-ESC to display the Task List window, and select Notepad.

3. Select **File Open**, type **C:\QTR1TEXT.PRN** in the Filename text box, and press ENTER to display the contents of the file in the Notepad. The display looks identical to the one you saw when you copied the data to the Notepad.

4. Select **File New** and **No** to erase the data without saving it.

Using the Clipboard to Bring Data into a Worksheet

Bringing data from a text file into the worksheet by using the Clipboard involves several steps. You can try the steps by entering text in the Notepad accessory and then copying it into 1-2-3 with the Clipboard. The steps for copying data between applications with the Clipboard are the same as you would use for data from other programs. To try this, follow these steps:

1. Type **Merchandise Inventory** in the Notepad application window, press ENTER, type **Prepaid Insurance**, press ENTER, and type **Accounts Receivable** so your text looks like this:

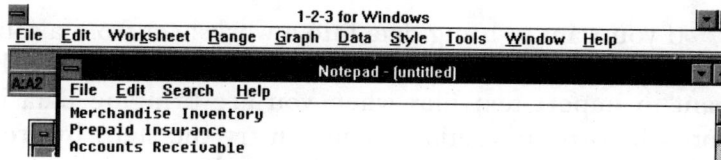

2. Select the text by either dragging the mouse to cover all of the text or selecting the **Edit Select All** command.

3. Select **Edit Copy** or press CTRL-INS to copy these entries to the Clipboard.

4. Press CTRL-ESC to display the Task List window, and select 1-2-3 for Windows.

5. Select **File New** to create a new worksheet to contain the copied data.

6. Select **Edit Paste** or press SHIFT-INS to copy the text from the Clipboard to the worksheet, as shown here:

```
┌─────────────────────────────────────────────────────────────┐
│                    1-2-3 for Windows                    ▼│⬍│
├─────────────────────────────────────────────────────────────┤
│ File  Edit  Worksheet  Range  Graph  Data  Style  Tools  Window  Help │
├───────────────────────────────────────────────────────READY──┤
│ A:A1              'Merchandise Inventory                       │
├─────────────────────────────────────────────────────────────┤
│                         1ST QTR.WK3                           │
│  ⬒                     FILE0001.WK3                    ▼│▲  │
│   │ A │     A     │    B    │  C  │  D  │  E  │  F  │  G  │⬍│
│   │ 1 │Merchandise│Inventory│     │     │     │     │     │▲│
│   │ 2 │Prepaid Insurance    │     │     │     │     │     │ │
│   │ 3 │Accounts Receivable  │     │     │     │     │     │ │
└─────────────────────────────────────────────────────────────┘
```

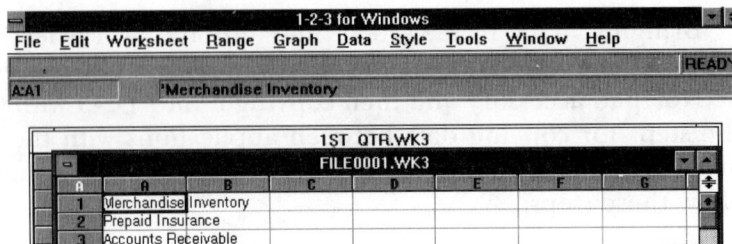

7. Select **File Close** and **No** to close the worksheet without saving the copied entries.

Bringing Text Files into a Worksheet Without the Clipboard

If you want to bring data into a worksheet from a source that cannot use the Clipboard, you can import a text file into a worksheet. You will want to import text files when you are bringing data into 1-2-3 from non-Windows applications. You can try the steps by creating a text file with the text you entered in the Notepad accessory and then importing it into 1-2-3. Once you create the text file, you use the same steps to bring text files into 1-2-3, regardless of the program you use to create the text file. To try this, follow these steps:

1. Press CTRL-ESC to display the Task List Window and select Notepad.

2. Select **File Save**, type **C:\TEXT_IN.PRN** in the Filename text box, and select the OK command button.

3. Select **File Exit** to leave the Notepad accessory.

4. Press CTRL-ESC to display the Task List window, and select 1-2-3 for Windows.

5. Select **File**, **Import From**, and **Text**.

6. Type **C:\TEXT_IN.PRN** in the File Name text box and select the OK command button so the imported text looks just like it did when you copied the entries by using the Clipboard.

7. Select **File Close** and **No** to close the worksheet without saving the imported labels.

Review

In this chapter you learned how to use Solver, save sections of a worksheet file, combine worksheet files, and transfer data between applications. The topics you covered include the following:

- The **Tools Solver** command adjusts worksheet cells that you select so the requirements that you enter by adding constraints are met. Solver also finds values for worksheet cells that result in the highest or lowest value in an optimal cell.

- You can extract a portion of a worksheet to another worksheet file with the **File Extract To** command. This command copies either values (formulas are converted to their values in the new worksheet) or formulas (formulas remain intact). You should use the Formulas option only if the cells the formulas reference are part of the range extracted to the new file. Once a file is extracted, you can open it and use it just as you do other worksheet files.

- You can combine the values of a range or an entire worksheet file into the current worksheet file with the **File Combine From** command. You must be careful where the cell pointer is when you use this command because the cells copied into the current worksheet have the same relative position in respect to the cell pointer's position as the cells have in their original file to the upper-left corner of the range or worksheet. The File Combine From options let you copy, add, and subtract entries.

- You can create links with other Windows applications that support DDE so that as the data in one application file changes, so does the linked data in the other application files. You create these links by copying the data to link to the Clipboard, transferring to the application that you want to have the link, and selecting **Edit Paste Link**.

- 1-2-3 can export data, or put it in other formats. You can use the Windows Notepad to create text files from data you copy from 1-2-3 to the Clipboard. You can also use the **File Extract To** command to create text files. In addition, you can use the

Clipboard to transfer data to other programs that can accept information from the Clipboard.

- 1-2-3 can import, or bring in, data from other another computer program if the other computer program can produce a text file. The data can be imported into the worksheet in long labels, with each line in the imported data converting into a cell's entry.

Commands and Keys

The commands you learned enable you to solve more advanced worksheet problems. You also learned how you can use the commands for transferring data to the Clipboard and then transferring the data between applications. These commands and keys are

Keys	Action
SHIFT-INS	Copies data from the Clipboard into the current Windows application (same as the **Edit Paste** command in many applications)
CTRL-INS	Copies selected data from the current Windows application to the Clipboard (same as the **Edit Copy** command in many applications)
ALT E L	**Edit Paste Link** creates a link to another application's file using the source of the data in the Clipboard.
ALT F B	**File Combine From** adds, copies, or subtracts range or worksheet data from another file to the current worksheet
ALT F E	**File Extract To** copies a portion of a range to a new worksheet file; also copies worksheet data to a text file
ALT F I T	**File Import From Text** brings data into 1-2-3 and stores the data as long labels
ALT T S	**Tools Solver** solves a problem defined on the current worksheet

14

Creating 1-2-3 Macros

Many 1-2-3 users are intimidated by macros. They have heard about the failures that others have experienced when attempting to use them. However, failure is not inevitable; in fact, if you use the step-by-step approach presented in this chapter, you have no need for concern. There is no reason why you cannot be just as successful with macros as you are with 1-2-3's **R**ange **F**ormat and **F**ile **S**ave commands.

In their simplest form, macros are nothing more than a way to automate the selections you have been making from 1-2-3's menus. Such macros are referred to as *keyboard alternative macros*. In their most complex form, macros provide an entire programming language with the special 1-2-3 command-language instructions. Attempting to use the most sophisticated form of macros without mastering the keyboard variety is a little like practicing diving before you have learned to swim — you would find yourself well over your head and doomed to failure.

This chapter focuses on keyboard alternative macros and introduces them in a logical sequence to help you avoid problems. It presents first a step-by-step approach for recording selections in the Transcript window to ensure your success. You learn how 1-2-3 for Windows records menu selections and special keyboard entries in the Transcript window for replay or later copying to worksheet cells. You also learn 1-2-3's rules for naming macros and how you can execute the macro instructions stored on the worksheet. You create several ready-to-use macros that will be your foundation for creating macros that fit your particular needs.

Keyboard Alternative Macros

Keyboard alternative macros are nothing more than a column of label entries that have a special name assigned to them. The contents of the label entries is the sequence of 1-2-3 keystrokes you want 1-2-3 to execute for you. Once the keystrokes are copied to the worksheet from the Transcript window or entered directly in a column of worksheet cells, you use the **R**ange **N**ame **C**reate command to assign a name to the top cell in the macro. You can use a backslash (\) and a single letter for the macro name or use a longer entry of up to the 15-character limit for range names. If you choose the \ and the single letter, you can execute the macro by holding down the CTRL key and pressing the letter used in the macro name, or you can press ALT-F3 (Run) and select the name from the list of macro names. If you use the longer entry option for the name, your only alternative is to press ALT-F3 (Run) and select the macro name.

When you save the worksheet on which you entered the macro, you save the macro for later use. You can use a macro on any worksheet. This means that you can create a macro on one sheet and use it on another sheet. In addition, the worksheet containing the macro and the worksheet that uses the macro can be in different worksheet files. This allows you to create a library of macros in a worksheet file that you can use with all your other worksheets.

Keyboard alternative macros provide a wealth of time-saving features. You can use them to automate printing, formatting, and any other 1-2-3 task that can be handled with menu selections. After you have learned the basics, you will want to examine the tasks you execute repeatedly. The more frequently a task is performed, the greater the potential reward of automating it with macro instructions. Some users find that data-management tasks such as sorting and extracting are the most important to automate; other users feel that printing and formatting have the highest priority because they use these commands most frequently. Although the macros in the remainder of the chapter have widespread applications, only you can decide which tasks offer you the greatest payback when automated.

Macro Building Blocks

The secret to creating macros that run correctly the first time you try them is having a structured approach that you use consistently for each macro you create. At first glance, the steps recommended here might seem unnecessarily time consuming; it might seem easier to type the macro keystrokes directly in a column of worksheet cells. However, you will find that the Transcript window approach guarantees immediate success and thereby saves time fixing errors.

The first step for successful macros is to lay out a road map of where you want to go with the macro. This is nothing more than a mental plan or a few notes jotted down about what you want the macro to accomplish. Next, you can use the Transcript window to record the macro instructions and then use the Clipboard to copy the macro on the worksheet. You will know that the macro works correctly since you will have tested it as the Transcript window was recording it. Once the instructions are stored on the worksheet, you need to name them. Documenting the workings of the macro is an often overlooked step, but it can guarantee continued trouble-free execution. Complete this step for every macro. Only then will you be ready to try your new macro. You can examine each of these steps more closely in the sections that follow.

Planning the Macro's Actions Before You Begin

You need to plan what actions a macro will take before trying the keystrokes. If you do not at least make a mental road map of what you want to accomplish, you will probably end up making many changes to the keystrokes captured in the Transcript window before you can use them. You can even jot a few notes on paper if it helps keep you on track for completing all aspects of the task. Proceeding to enter a macro without a plan is like going to the store without a list of what you need. As soon as you finish shopping, you remember what you forgot. You do not want to wait until your macro is recorded to begin thinking about what else it should do. The planning may be as simple as deciding that a macro will format a range of dates or insert a row.

Using 1-2-3's Transcript Window

You can use 1-2-3's Transcript window to capture the keystrokes for your keyboard alternative macros rather than typing the macro instructions into worksheet cells yourself. This approach offers a couple of major advantages. First, you can try out your plan for a macro and have 1-2-3 record your entries. If you make a few mistakes, you do not need to start over; you can edit the entries in the Transcript window with the same techniques you use for changing any entry. You can play back these keystrokes even before moving the entries to the worksheet. Second, when you have 1-2-3 record the keystrokes, you do not need to remember the keywords that 1-2-3 uses for the function keys and other special keys. All you do is press the proper keys, and 1-2-3 records them correctly in the macro cells.

Unlike the macro recorders for earlier versions of 1-2-3, 1-2-3 automatically records the keystrokes you make. 1-2-3 has a 512-byte buffer that constantly records your keystrokes. As you make entries in a worksheet, 1-2-3 is recording them in case you want to copy the keystrokes to a worksheet range. You do not need to tell 1-2-3 to start recording because 1-2-3 has been recording your keystrokes since you opened the 1-2-3 application window.

To use the Transcript window to record a macro, you must follow several steps. First, you clear the current contents of the Transcript window so you do not include your earlier keystrokes with the macro keystrokes you want to record. Then you perform the steps you want 1-2-3 to record. Finally, you copy the keystrokes to the worksheet. Since the buffer that stores your keystrokes is 512 bytes, you may perform these three steps repeatedly for a lengthy macro.

You can try out this procedure with a macro that correctly formats three date entries. First, place on the worksheet the date entries that 1-2-3 converts into serial date numbers:

1. Type **15-JUL-91** in A1 and move to A2.
2. Type **15-APR-92** in A2 and move to A3.
3. Type **9-MAY-91** in A3 and move to A1.

Now you are ready to explore the Record feature.

Activating the Transcript Window

Since 1-2-3 records every keystroke you make, you want to clear the entries in 1-2-3's Transcript window before you perform the steps that you want in a macro. You perform this step at the beginning of the macro-recording process; position your cell pointer where you want to begin recording the keystrokes for the macro before you clear the Transcript window. To display and activate the Transcript Window and then clear the window's contents, follow these steps:

1. Select **T**ools **M**acro **S**how Transcript.

1-2-3 displays a Transcript window containing a recording of as many as 512 characters. Your Transcript window might look something like this:

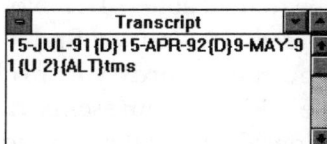

```
┌─────────────────────────┐
│ ▬  │   Transcript  │ ▼ │▲│
├─────────────────────────┤
│15-JUL-91{D}15-APR-92{D}9-MAY-9│ │
│1{U 2}{ALT}tms            │ │
│                          │ │
│                          │ │
│                          │▼│
└─────────────────────────┘
```

You can see that some of the entries are easily understandable, like 15-JUL-91 for the first date you entered. Other keystrokes, or the keystroke equivalents of actions you take with your mouse, use special representations, as described shortly.

2. Select **W**indow **T**ile to display the worksheet window and the Transcript window side by side.

This allows you to watch 1-2-3 record your entries in the Transcript window as you make them in the worksheet window. You do not need to see the Transcript window to record macros, but having it visible as you record your first macros makes creating them easier.

3. Press CTRL-F6 or click the Transcript window to make it the active window in 1-2-3.

4. Select **Edit Clear** All.

The window is now empty and ready to store your next set of keystrokes.

5. Press CTRL-F6 or click the worksheet window to make it the active window in 1-2-3.

Recording Special Keys

1-2-3 has a number of special keyboard keys, such as the function keys and cursor-movement keys, that are recorded in the Transcript window. These keys are recorded for you automatically along with menu selections and entries that you want to include in your macros. Before recording a macro, you will want to be familiar with how 1-2-3 shows the special keys. The keywords for the special keys appear even if you use a mouse to make selections because 1-2-3 converts the actions you take with the mouse into their keyboard equivalents. These keys and the macro keywords that stand for them are shown in Table 14-1. Notice that all the keywords are enclosed in curly braces: {}. You will find it easy to remember most of these words; they are the same words you probably connect with the special keys—for example, {EDIT} represents F2. The only thing you need to remember if you decide to make any editing changes to the captured keystrokes is to include the braces. Without the braces, 1-2-3 will not recognize the entry as a special key.

1-2-3 has several special keys that cannot be represented in a macro. These keys include NUM LOCK, SCROLL LOCK, CAPS LOCK, SHIFT, and PRINT SCREEN. Other key combinations for which there is no macro representation are ALT-BACKSPACE (Undo), ALT-F1 (Compose), ALT-F2 (Step), ALT-F3 (Run), INS, and CTRL-BREAK (1-2-3 instead records the number of times to press ESC to return to READY mode).

Moving the Cell Pointer

When you are creating a macro, movement of the cell pointer is represented with keywords. For example, if you move one cell to the right,

Table 14-1. *Special Keys in Macro Commands*

Special Keys	Keywords
ENTER	~
~	{~}
{	{{}
}	{}}
/ or <	/, <, or {MENU}
CTRL-*letter*	{*letter*}
ALT-*letter*	{Alt "*letter*"}

Cursor-Movement Keys

UP ARROW	{UP} or {U}
DOWN ARROW	{DOWN} or {D}
RIGHT ARROW	{RIGHT} or {R}
LEFT ARROW	{LEFT} or {L}
HOME	{HOME}
END	{END}
PGUP	{PGUP}
PGDN	{PGDN}
CTRL-RIGHT ARROW	{BIGRIGHT}
CTRL-LEFT ARROW	{BIGLEFT}
CTRL-END CTRL-PGDN	{PREVFILE}, {PF}, or {FILE}{PS}
CTRL-END CTRL-PGUP	{NEXTFILE}, {NF}, or {FILE}{NS}
CTRL-END END	{LASTFILE}, {LF}, or {FILE}{END}
CTRL-END HOME	{FIRSTFILE}, {FF}, or {FILE}{HOME}
CTRL-HOME	{FIRSTCELL} or {FC}
CTRL-PGUP	{NEXTSHEET} or {NS}
CTRL-PGDN	{PREVSHEET} or {PS}
END CTRL-HOME	{LASTCELL} or {LC}
TAB	{TAB}

Editing Keys

DEL	{DELETE} or {DEL}
INS	{INSERT} or {INS}
ESC	{ESCAPE} or {ESC}
BACKSPACE	{BACKSPACE} or {BS}

Function Keys

F1 (Help)	{HELP}
F2 (Edit)	{EDIT}
F3 (Name)	{NAME}

14

Table 14-1. *Special Keys in Macro Commands (continued)*

Special Keys	Keywords
F4 (Abs)	{ABS} or {ANCHOR}
F5 (Goto)	{GOTO}
F6 (Pane)	{WINDOW}
F7 (Query)	{QUERY}
F8 (Table)	{TABLE}
F9 (Calc)	{CALC}
F10 (Menu)	{ALT}, {MB}, or {MENUBAR}
ALT-F6 (Zoom)	{ZOOM}
ALT-F7 (App1)	{APP1}
ALT-F8 (App2)	{APP2}
ALT-F9 (App3)	{APP3}
ALT-F10 (App4)	{ADDIN} or {APP4}

1-2-3 records {R} in the Transcript window. The Transcript window uses this abbreviation to conserve its limit of 512 keystrokes. When you edit Transcript entries that you have copied to the worksheet you can use longer entries such as {RIGHT} or {right} instead of {R}. (Case is never important for the special macro keywords, although uppercase is used throughout this chapter.) You will notice that if you move the cell pointer by clicking a cell, 1-2-3 records your action as if you pressed F5 (Goto) to move to the cell.

If you move in a direction more than once, the Transcript window uses a short-cut approach. It includes a space and the number of times you move the cell pointer in the specified direction before using the closing curly brace. For example, {U 3} indicates that you moved the cell pointer up three cells.

When you are working from the keyboard, the effect of the HOME key depends on whether you are in READY or EDIT mode. This is also true in the macro environment. If you record {HOME} in a macro, its effect depends on what you are having the macro do for you. If you have placed 1-2-3 in EDIT mode, the instruction takes you to the left side of the entry in the current cell; otherwise, it places you in A1.

As you can see in Table 14-1, 1-2-3 has macro instructions for END and arrow key combinations, as in {END}{R}. You can also shift the display a window at a time with {PGUP} and {PGDN}. 1-2-3 also has macro instructions for switching between worksheets in a worksheet file and for switching between worksheet files.

The Edit Keys

In addition to F2 (Edit), which places you in EDIT mode, several other keys are used frequently for correcting cell entries. These keys are shown in Table 14-1. Most of the time when you edit a cell, 1-2-3 will record in the Transcript window the keystrokes you would have entered to make the finalized entry in the first place. For example, if you edit the label 'ABC Company to make it right aligned, 1-2-3 will record "ABC Company~ in the Transcript window rather than an entry like {EDIT}{HOME}{DEL}"~ which would represent starting EDIT mode, moving to the beginning of the label, deleting the label prefix, typing a new one, and pressing ENTER.

14

Recording a Macro

Once you have cleared the buffer, you are ready to record the macro. To record the macro, perform the steps that you want recorded in the macro, and they will automatically appear in the macro. For the current worksheet, follow these steps:

1. Select the range A1..A3 by pressing SHIFT-DOWN ARROW twice.
2. Select **R**ange **F**ormat 1 31-Dec-90 and the OK command button to select the first date format.

You will not see 1-2-3 record anything until you select the OK command button. Whether you use the mouse or the keyboard to make selections, 1-2-3 records the keyboard equivalents.

Copying the Keystrokes to the Worksheet

Once you execute the steps for the macro, you are ready to transfer the keystrokes from 1-2-3's Transcript window to a worksheet. After the keystrokes are copied to the worksheet, you can name the range, and the macro is ready to run just as if you entered the macro onto the worksheet yourself. For the date-formatting macro, follow these steps:

1. Press CTRL-F6 or click the Transcript window to make it active.

2. Select the keystrokes that you want to copy.

To select the keystrokes, move the cursor (the thin bar) to the end of the entries. With the mouse, drag the mouse pointer from this location to the beginning of the entries so all of the entries are highlighted. With the keyboard, press END and hold down the SHIFT key while you press HOME to move the cursor to the beginning of the entries so all of them are highlighted.

3. Select **E**dit **C**opy to copy the highlighted keystrokes to the Clipboard.

4. Press CTRL-F6 or click the worksheet window to make it active.

5. Move to E1 as the first cell where you want the entries copied.

6. Select **E**dit **P**aste or press SHIFT-INS to copy the keystrokes from the Clipboard to the worksheet.

The copied keystrokes look like this:

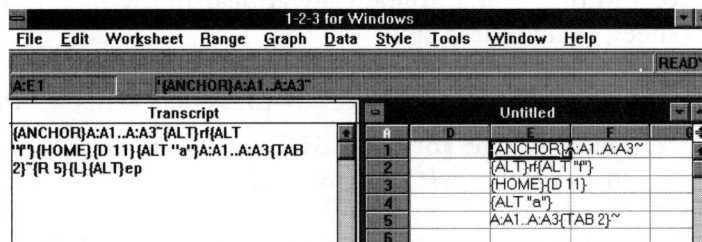

Your entries may look different since 1-2-3 may have recorded your macro slightly different. For example, 1-2-3 may record the preselected range as {ANCHOR}{D 2}– or {ANCHOR}A:A1..A:A3˜. You can edit these keystrokes so they will apply to other ranges.

7. Edit E1 so it contains {ANCHOR}{D2}˜.

8. Edit {Alt "a"} (in cell E4 in this case) so it is ˜.

9. Move to the next cell which contains A:A1..A:A3 {TAB 2}˜ and press DEL to delete this entry.

Naming the Macro

Now that you have copied all the keystrokes, you are ready to name the macro. You can use the **Range Name Create** command to apply the name to the top cell in the macro. You can also enter the name in a cell to the left of the top macro cell and then use **Range Name Label Create Right** to apply the name to the cell. You need to name only the top cell in a macro because 1-2-3 continues executing macro instructions in a column of macro commands until it reaches a nonlabel cell or an advanced macro command that tells 1-2-3 to stop executing a macro.

You must assign to the cell a name of not more than 15 characters or use a special name consisting of a backslash and a single letter. The backslash identifies your entry as a macro name, which allows you to execute the macro with the CTRL key and the letter used in the macro name. This naming convention lets you create 26 unique, quickly executable macros on one worksheet. (1-2-3 does not distinguish between upper- and lowercase letters in a macro name.)

Name the macro you have created by following these steps:

1. Move the cell pointer to D1, type **format 3 dates**, and press ENTER or click the confirm box.
2. Select Worksheet **C**olumn Width, type **11** in the text box after the **S**et Width To option box, and select the OK command button to widen the column.
3. Select **R**ange Name Label Create, the **R**ight option button, and the OK command button to use this entry to name the top cell in the macro.

The **R**ange Name Label Create **R**ight command is a different version of the **R**ange Name Create command. It assigns the labels in the range you specify to the entries in the cells immediately to the right of the cells containing the labels. This command is often used when you have several cells to name that have their names in labels in adjacent cells.

Executing the Macro

Once you have entered and named a macro, you can use it whenever you wish. Whenever you have a macro that requires the cell pointer to be positioned in a certain cell, you need to put the cell pointer there before you execute the macro. You do not need to put the cell pointer on the macro itself to execute it. After you position your cell pointer, you can execute the macro by holding down the CTRL key and, while the key is pressed, pressing the letter key used in your macro name if you used the backslash letter naming convention. If you used a longer name, you need to select **Tools Macro Run** or press ALT-F3 (Run) and select the desired macro from the list. The macro begins executing immediately.

Follow these instructions to try your new formatting macro:

1. Type three more date serial numbers, as shown here:

   B1:   **31-DEC-89**
   B2:   **8-JUN-90**
   B3:   **2-APR-90**

2. Move the cell pointer to B1 and run the macro by pressing ALT-F3 (Run). Highlight the name of the macro, as shown here:

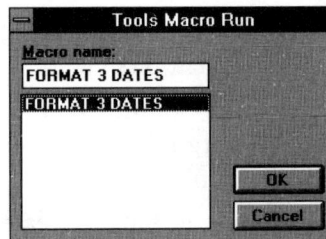

3. Select the OK command button.

1-2-3 formats the cells as dates as shown here:

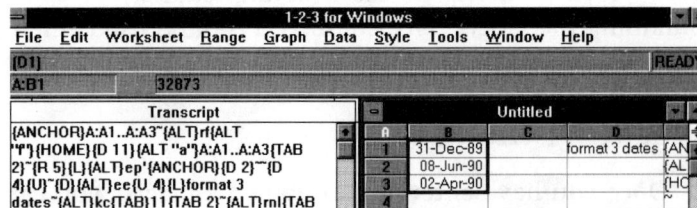

If you plan to use this macro later, you will want to document the tasks the macro executes and then save the worksheet.

Documenting the Macro

You will want to develop a few easy documentation rules for yourself so your documentation is always stored in the same place. A good strategy is to place the macro name in the cell immediately to the left of the top cell in the macro. If the macro is named \a, you would enter '\a in this cell. The apostrophe prevents 1-2-3 from interpreting the backslash as a repeating label indicator and filling your cell with the letter "a."

A good area to use for documenting the macro is the column to the right of the actual macro instructions. Entering a brief description of every command can make the purpose of the macro much clearer when you go back to examine it at a later time.

Saving a worksheet after you name it saves both the macro entries and the macro names so they will be available when you use the worksheet. Follow these steps to document the macro you have created and save it along with the other worksheet data:

1. Move to G1, type **Format 3 cells with the first date format**, and press ENTER or click the confirm box.

2. Select **File** Save **As**, type **FORMAT** in the File **N**ame text box, and select the OK command button to save the file.

3. Press CTRL-F6 or click the Transcript window to make it active.

4. Select **File** **C**lose to close the Transcript window.

5. Select **File** **C**lose to remove the current worksheet file.

Creating Another Macro

You have now created your first macro, but you have not begun to experience the variety that macros can offer. You can follow the instructions in this section to create another macro. This practice will help you improve your macro skills.

Creating a Macro to Insert Rows

You can create a macro to insert one or more blank rows in a worksheet. A macro like this is useful if you work frequently in the data-management environment and want to have some blank rows between field names. Since blank rows can cause problems for Query commands, you can have one macro to add them when you need them and another macro to remove them. Later, you can add a {GOTO} instruction to position the cell pointer right below the field names so the blanks are inserted automatically at the correct location for a database.

In this section, you create a general-purpose macro: it will insert two blank rows anywhere. You type these macro instructions rather than use the Transcript window to show you that you can type all or part of a macro when changing an existing macro or recording a new one. To create a macro to insert blank rows, follow these instructions:

1. Make the following entries that you will use for the macro:

   A1:   **Last Name**
   A2:   **Smith**

2. Place the following entries in the cells listed:

   S2:   **'\i**
   T2:   **{ANCHOR}{DOWN}~**
   V2:   **Select the current cell and the one below it**
   T3:   **{ALT}KIR~**
   V3:   **Select Worksheet Insert Rows and OK**

3. Move the cell pointer to S2 and select **R**ange **N**ame **L**abel **C**reate **R**ight and the OK command button.

4. Move the cell pointer to A2.

5. Press CTRL-I to execute the macro.

The macro will insert blank rows in the worksheet, and it looks like this:

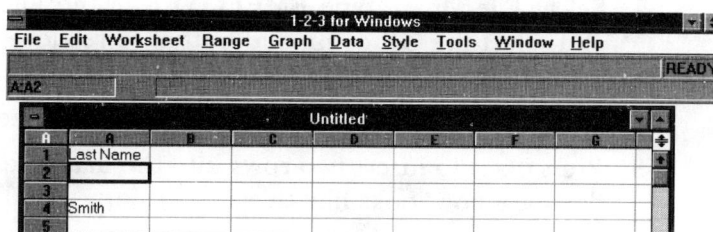

6. Select **File Save As,** type **INSERT** in the File **Name** text box, and select the OK command button to save the file.

When you have a macro that inserts and deletes rows, you must be sure that it does not insert or delete rows of the macro instructions. If you put the macro where rows are deleted or inserted, deleting the rows may also delete some of the macro instructions and the rows you insert may create a break in the macro instructions since 1-2-3 stops when it finds an empty row.

Special Macro Topics

1-2-3 has many macro options—so many, in fact, that complete books are written on the subject. This chapter cannot cover all possible options, but it can present a few of particular interest that go beyond the simpler keyboard alternatives to show you how you use macro libraries, create automatic macros, and debug macros to fix errors.

Creating a Macro Library

If you have a macro you want to use in several worksheets, you don't have to put the macro in every worksheet that uses the macro; you can create a macro library. A *macro library* is any worksheet file that contains macros that you use on other worksheets. When you execute a macro, the macro is run using the current worksheet, even if the macro is stored in another worksheet file.

You can use the INSERT worksheet file as a macro library by using the \i macro in another worksheet file. To do so, follow these steps:

1. Select **File Open**, type **EMPLOYEE** in the File **N**ame text box, and select the OK command button to retrieve the database you created in Chapter 12, "Data Management Basics."

2. Move the cell pointer to a cell in row 2 on sheet A.

3. Press CTRL-I to insert two rows into the database so the top of the database now looks like this:

4. Select **File C**lose and **N**o to remove the EMPLOYEE worksheet file without saving it.

5. Select **File C**lose to remove the INSERT worksheet file.

If you want a macro library to always be open when you use 1-2-3, name the worksheet file containing the macro library AUTO123.WK3. When you load 1-2-3, it will load a worksheet file called AUTO123.WK3 if it exists in the default directory.

Creating Automatic Macros

1-2-3 has a unique feature that lets you create an *automatic macro*. Every time a worksheet containing an automatic macro is opened, 1-2-3 immediately executes this macro as long as **Tools User Setup Run A**utoexecute Macro is checked. There are numerous applications for such macros, although they are usually used with the more advanced 1-2-3 macro features.

The only difference between an automatic macro and one that you must execute is the name that you assign to the macro. An automatic macro must have a name of \0 (zero).

For now, you can put the automatic macro to use with a model that calculates the monthly payments on a loan. The model is designed to function regardless of the principal, interest, or time. So you can easily tell what data elements have been entered for each use of the model, the old data fields will be erased and new entries will be made. Follow these directions to set up the basic model and then set up the automatic macro:

1. Move the cell pointer to B3, type **Enter desired borrowings:**, and move the cell pointer to B6.

2. Type **Enter interest rate:** and move the cell pointer to B9.

3. Type **Enter term in years:** and move the cell pointer to B12.

4. Type **✱✱ Your Payments Will Be ✱✱** and move the cell pointer to E3.

5. Select **S**tyle **B**order, the All **E**dges check box, the thick line in the drop-down box next to All Edges, and OK.

6. Press CTRL-INS to copy this cell's format to the Clipboard.

7. Move to E6, E9, and E12 and press SHIFT-INS to copy the box around the cell in E3 to these three cells.

8. Type **@PMT(E3,E6/12,E9✱12)** in E12 and press ENTER or click the confirm box.

9. Select **R**ange **F**ormat, Currency in the **F**ormat list box, and the OK command button.

You have already completed quite a bit of work, but you have yet to enter the automatic macro. Follow these instructions to create the macro:

10. Move the cell pointer to B21, type **{GOTO}E3˜{ALT}ern˜**, and move the cell pointer to B22.

This step adds the **E**dit **Cl**ear Special command and unmarks the **N**umeric format check box so only the **C**ell Contents check box is selected before the OK command button is selected. This erases the cell's contents without changing the border. You learned this command in Chapter 7, "Changing Row and Column Options."

11. Type **{D 3}{ALT}ern˜** and move the cell pointer to B23.

This moves the cell pointer from B3 to B6 before erasing the cell's entry without deleting its formatting.

12. Type **{D 3}{ALT}ern˜** and move the cell pointer to B24.

13. Type **{GOTO}E3˜** and move the cell pointer to B25.

The tilde (˜) is a very important part of the last four steps. It is easy to forget, but problems will occur if you leave it off.

14. Type **{?}˜{DOWN 3}{?}˜{DOWN 3}{?}˜** and move the cell pointer to A21.

This moves the cell pointer to where the user needs to enter information. The {?} macro instruction tells 1-2-3 to wait while you make an entry. Then, when you press ENTER or click the confirm box, 1-2-3 continues executing the macro.

15. Type **'\0** in A21, and press ENTER or click the confirm box.

16. Select **R**ange **N**ame **L**abel Create, the **R**ight option button, and the OK command button.

17. Make the following documentation entries:

D21: **Erases previous borrowing entry**
D22: **Erases previous interest rate**
D23: **Erases previous term**
D24: **Positions the cell pointer for the first entry**
D25: **Moves cell pointer for entries**

18. Make these entries to perform the first payment calculation:

E3:   **65000**
E6:   **.1025**
E9:   **30**

Your display should now match the one in Figure 14-1.

19. Select File Save **A**s, type **PAYMENT** in the File Name text box, and select the OK command button to save the file.

Figure 14-1. *Calculating a payment amount*

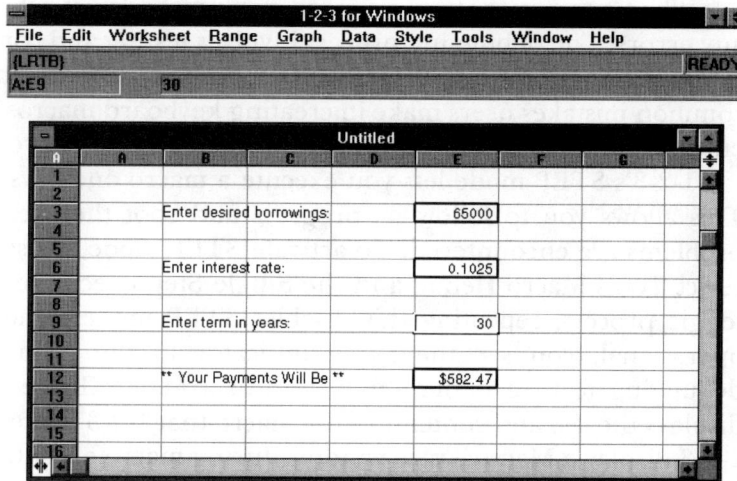

20. Select **File** **C**lose to close the worksheet file.

21. Select **File** **O**pen or click the File Open SmartIcon, type **PAY-MENT** in the File **N**ame text box, and select the OK command button to open the file.

If the macro does not begin executing immediately, select **T**ools User Setup Run **A**utoexecute Macro and the OK command button. Then close and open the worksheet again.

22. Complete entries in E3, E6, and E9 to calculate a new payment with different numbers.

23. Select **File** **C**lose and **N**o to remove the worksheet file without saving the new data.

Debugging Macros

When a macro contains an error, you must *debug* it, which means to fix any errors. The debugging process involves testing and correcting macros to ensure that you are obtaining the desired results. One of the most common mistakes users make in creating keyboard macros is forgetting to enter the tilde to represent each time the ENTER key is pressed.

1-2-3's STEP mode lets you execute a macro one keystroke at a time. This allows you to follow its progress and spot the area of difficulty if problems are encountered. To activate STEP mode, press ALT-F2 (Step) or select **T**ools **M**acro **D**ebug and the **S**ingle Step check box. Since this is a toggle process, repeating this disables STEP mode. When this mode is operational, you see the STEP indicator in the status line. Another debugging feature is the ability to add a Macro Trace window, which displays the cell and contents of the macro that 1-2-3 is executing. To have 1-2-3 display a Macro Trace window during macro execution, select **T**ools **M**acro **D**ebug and the **T**race check box.

When STEP mode is on, any macro you invoke is executed one step at a time. You must press the SPACEBAR each time you are ready for the next keystroke. You are not able to enter direct commands while the macro is executing.

To stop a malfunctioning macro, press the CTRL and BREAK keys simultaneously. This cancels the macro operation immediately and presents an error message. Select the OK command button to return to READY mode so you can make the necessary corrections to your macro.

Follow these instructions to try a macro in STEP mode:

1. Select **T**ools **M**acro **D**ebug, the **S**ingle Step and **T**race check boxes, and the OK command button.

2. Select **F**ile **O**pen, type **PAYMENT** in the **F**ile **N**ame text box, and select the OK command button.

3. Press ALT-F3 (Run), select \0 from the **M**acro Name list box, and select the OK command button.

4. Press the SPACEBAR to execute a keystroke.

Your screen now looks like the one in Figure 14-2. You can see the Macro Trace window and how 1-2-3 has highlighted the keystroke it will execute when you press the SPACEBAR.

Figure 14-2. *Running a macro in STEP mode with the Macro Trace window open*

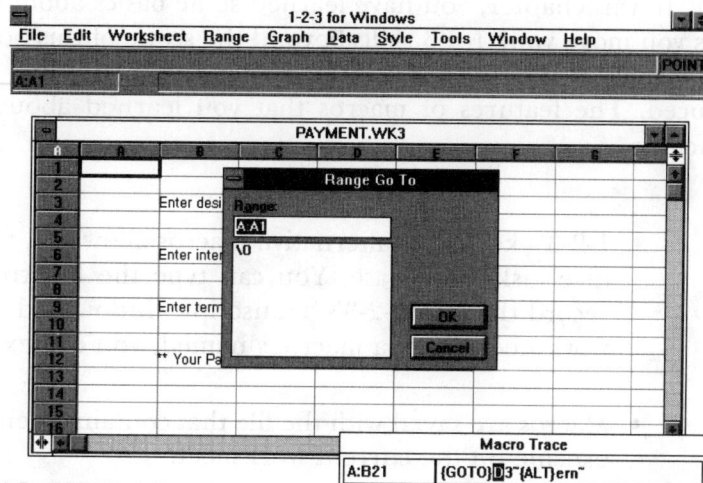

5. Continue pressing the SPACEBAR until you need to supply the amount to borrow.

6. Supply an amount to borrow, press ENTER or click the confirm box, and then continue pressing the SPACEBAR until you need to supply the interest rate.

7. Supply an interest rate, press ENTER or click the confirm box, and then continue pressing the SPACEBAR until you need to supply the number of years.

8. Supply a number of years, press ENTER or click the confirm box, and then continue pressing the SPACEBAR until the macro is done.

9. Execute step 1 again to disable STEP mode and close the Macro Trace window.

10. Select **File Close No** to close the worksheet window without saving it.

Review

In this chapter, you have learned some basics about creating macros. As you move your 1-2-3 skills beyond the scope of this book, you will find that macros provide even more features than the few that were introduced. The features of macros that you learned about in this chapter include

- 1-2-3's keyboard alternative macros allow you to perform repetitive tasks with ease. You can type the keystrokes in a cell or record them in 1-2-3's Transcript window and copy them to the worksheet. Once a macro is named, you can execute it.

- Macros are saved with the file that contains them. However, they execute on the current worksheet.

- If you edit a recorded macro and want to record function keys and special keys, you must use 1-2-3's keywords enclosed in braces: {}. To record menu selections, use the underlined character in each command name. To record entries, type them as you would without a macro.

- You enter macros in a group of contiguous cells in a column of the worksheet. If you are typing the entries, each one must be a label entry.

- You name macros the same way you name ranges. You can use either the **Range Name Create** or the **Range Name Label Create** command.

- You can use two different methods for naming macros. In both cases, only the top cell in the macro is named. Your selection determines how you can execute the macro. If you use \ and a single letter, you can press CTRL and the letter to execute the macro. If you use a regular range name, you need to use ALT-F3 (Run) or **Tools Macro Run** to execute the macro.

Commands and Keys

The keys and commands you have learned to use in this chapter provide aids to help you create and use macros. These keys and commands are

Keys	Action
CTRL-*letter*	Executes a macro named with \ and the letter
ALT-F3 (Run)	Executes a selected macro
ALT T M D	**Tools Macro Debug** starts and stops Step mode and opens and closes the Macro Trace window
ALT T M S	**Tools Macro Show** Transcript displays the Transcript window
ALT T M R	**Tools Macro Run** starts a selected macro's execution
ALT R N L R	**Range Name Label Create Right** applies names to cells immediately to the right of selected labels
ALT T U A	**Tools User Setup Run Autoexecute Macros** determines if 1-2-3 tries to execute a macro called \0 when a file is opened

14

A

Installing 1-2-3 for Windows

This appendix tells you how to install 1-2-3 for Windows. If your copy of 1-2-3 for Windows has already been installed, you do not need to read this appendix. If your copy of 1-2-3 is still covered in shrink wrap, you need to install the package. In that case, you will find this appendix a valuable reference for the steps that you must take.

Since 1-2-3 for Windows is a Windows product, you must install Windows before you install 1-2-3 for Windows. Windows includes its own installation program and directions that you must follow. If you are not familiar with Windows, read Appendix B, "Using Windows," which covers some Windows basics that you will want to use with 1-2-3 for Windows.

Requirements for 1-2-3 for Windows

1-2-3 for Windows is designed to run on a 286-, 386-, or 486-based machine such as an AT or a PS/2 from IBM or a compatible computer.

Because the compatible market is constantly changing, check with your dealer to make sure a machine you are planning to purchase runs the software you want to use. In case of doubt, have the dealer demonstrate 1-2-3 on the machine you are considering. This appendix assumes you have an IBM AT or PS/2.

1-2-3 for Windows has different minimum system requirements than its predecessors. 1-2-3 requires a minimum of 2 megabytes (2MB) of RAM. Windows and 1-2-3 can use expanded and extended memory, allowing you to take full advantage of any extra memory you have installed on your machine. If you have more than the 2MB minimum, you can run more applications and have them work more quickly. 1-2-3 must also be run from a hard disk with at least 6MB of available space to hold the 1-2-3 files. You must also have Windows 3.0 or above installed before you can use 1-2-3 for Windows.

Installing 1-2-3

Installing 1-2-3 for Windows registers your disks with your name and company, copies files to the hard disk, and sets Windows up so it is ready to run 1-2-3 for Windows. When you purchase 1-2-3, you receive several 3 1/2-inch or 5 1/4-inch disks. These disks contain all of the 1-2-3 program files. You use these disks as you follow the steps to install 1-2-3 on your computer. These instructions assume Windows is already installed on your system. If this is not the case, install Windows before you install 1-2-3.

When Windows is running, you can make many selections with either the keyboard or the mouse. With the mouse, you make selections by pointing to what you want and pressing the left mouse button. This is called clicking the mouse. The installation instructions also includes words like "dialog box," "text box," and "command button," which are the terms 1-2-3 for Windows and Windows use to describe boxes on the screen, boxes containing entries, and boxes you can select to perform commands.

Follow these steps for installation:

1. Start DOS in your system without a disk in drive A. This will make your system boot from DOS on your drive C. (You may need to respond to date and time prompts if you do not have a clock card.)

2. Start Windows by typing **WIN** and pressing ENTER. Windows displays the Program Manager window.

3. Either press ALT and type **FR** to select **F**ile and **R**un or click **F**ile and **R**un.

4. Insert the Install (Disk 1) disk into drive A and close the drive door. Type **A:INSTALL.EXE** and press ENTER or click the OK command button. (If you need to use drive B to install 1-2-3, type **B** instead of **A**.) Press ENTER or click the OK command button after viewing the opening message.

5. Install prompts you to register your name and the company's name. In the first line, enter your name. In the second line, enter your company name. If you do not have a company name to supply, reenter your name. Then press ENTER or click the OK command button to finalize the entries. The Install program prompts for a confirmation, which you supply by typing **Y** or clicking the OK command button.

6. Press ENTER or click Install 1-2-3.

7. Press ENTER or click Install with Defaults.

8. Press ENTER or click the OK command button to install 1-2-3 using the suggested drive and directory. You can change the drive or directory where 1-2-3 is installed by clicking the arrow after the drive or the directory text box and clicking or entering another selection. You can also press TAB to select the drive or directory text box and then type a new entry before you select the OK command button.

9. Install now confirms the directory that 1-2-3 will use. If the directory you chose does not exist, type **Y** or click **Y**es to have the Install program create it for you. If the directory exists and contains files, type **Y** or click **Y**es to let 1-2-3 add the 1-2-3 program files to this directory. If you type **N** or click **N**o to either prompt, you are returned to the box that let you choose the drive and directory where 1-2-3 for Windows is installed.

10. As the Install program copies the files from the disk, the program prompts for the next disk it needs. For each of the disks that the Install program requests, insert the disk in drive A (or B) and press ENTER or click the OK command button. Make sure to insert

A

the disk fully into the disk drive and close the disk drive door. Also, do not remove a disk from the disk drive until the Install program prompts for the next disk.

11. Once Install has finished copying files to your hard drive, it displays a message that it is finished. Press ENTER or click the OK command button after seeing the message, and you are ready to use 1-2-3.

12. Next, you have the option of installing the Adobe Type Manager (ATM), which makes your displayed and printed worksheets look better. Unless you have already installed a typeface manager, type **Y** or click **Y**es to install the Adobe Type Manager that 1-2-3 provides. If you type **N** or click the **N**o command button, you return to the Install Main Menu dialog box.

13. Insert the ATM Program disk in drive A (or B) and press ENTER or click the OK command button. Make sure to insert the disk fully into the disk drive and close the disk drive door.

14. Press ENTER or click the Install command button to install ATM using the suggested drive and directory. You can also change the drive and directory by clicking either text box or by pressing TAB until the text box is selected and making a new entry before you select the Install command button.

You may also see another message, about installing PCL bitmap fonts if your printer is low on memory. If your printer has more than the recommended amount of memory, press ALT-S or click the **S**kip command button. If you have less, then press ENTER or click the **I**nstall command button to install the bitmap fonts in the displayed directory.

15. Now ATM displays a message that it is finished and you must restart Windows. Press ENTER or click the OK command button and return to the Install Main Menu dialog box.

16. Type **X** or click the E**x**it Install command button to finish the Install program.

17. Close any other applications that are running by using the commands the programs use to exit, and then press ALT-F4 or click **F**ile and **E**xit to leave Windows. Next you have to press ENTER or click the OK command button from the Windows confirmation

box to indicate you want to leave Windows. At this point, you can start 1-2-3 for Windows as described in Chapter 1, "Worksheet Basics."

Once you have installed 1-2-3, you may want to use the 1-2-3 Install program again later. You use the program if you want to install other 1-2-3 programs that are not part of the defaults. You can also change other features of 1-2-3, but they are beyond the scope of this book.

A

B

Using Windows

You combine Windows with your DOS operating system to make working with programs easier. Windows features an easy-to-use interface that is more comfortable than the DOS prompt. Windows lets you run multiple applications simultaneously and share data between them. While you are in Windows, you can select which applications you are using and how the applications appear on your computer screen. If 1-2-3 for Windows is your first Windows application, read this appendix to learn about some basic Windows features you will want to use with 1-2-3 for Windows.

Windows is frequently used with a mouse. Using a mouse allows you to point to the objects on the screen you want to use. Some of the terms a mouse uses and their meanings are listed in Table B-1. Most of the time, you use the left button on the mouse. While using a mouse may be convenient for making selections, Windows has keyboard equivalents for making the same choices.

Table B-1.   *Mouse Terms*

Mouse Term	Meaning
Click	Point to the object and press the mouse button once
Double-click	Point to the object and quickly press the mouse button twice
Drag	Point to one location and hold down the mouse button as you move the mouse to another location

Starting Windows

Before you can use Windows, it must be installed. You install Windows by putting the first Windows disk into drive A. Next, type **A:**, press ENTER, type **Setup,** and press ENTER. At this point, the Windows installation program guides you with on-screen instructions. Once Windows is installed, you can start it by typing **WIN** and pressing ENTER. Once Windows is started, a display like the one in Figure B-1 appears. A Windows screen has several components, which are labeled in Figure B-1 and described in Table B-2.

With Windows, each program or application you run is put in a separate window, an *application window*. Sometimes these application windows have windows of their own, called *document windows*. Document windows are miniature versions of the application window, with a title bar, minimize button, maximize or restore button, and control menu boxes. Some applications run in full-screen mode. *Full-screen mode* means that when the application is one you are currently using, it occupies the full screen and the other application windows do not appear on the screen. When you run a non-Windows application, it runs in full-screen mode.

Exiting Windows

When you finish using Windows and its applications, you will want to exit your open applications and Windows. This is important for two reasons: it ensures that you do not lose data that you intended to save, and it enables Windows to perform any necessary housecleaning. For example,

Figure B-1. *Sample Windows screen*

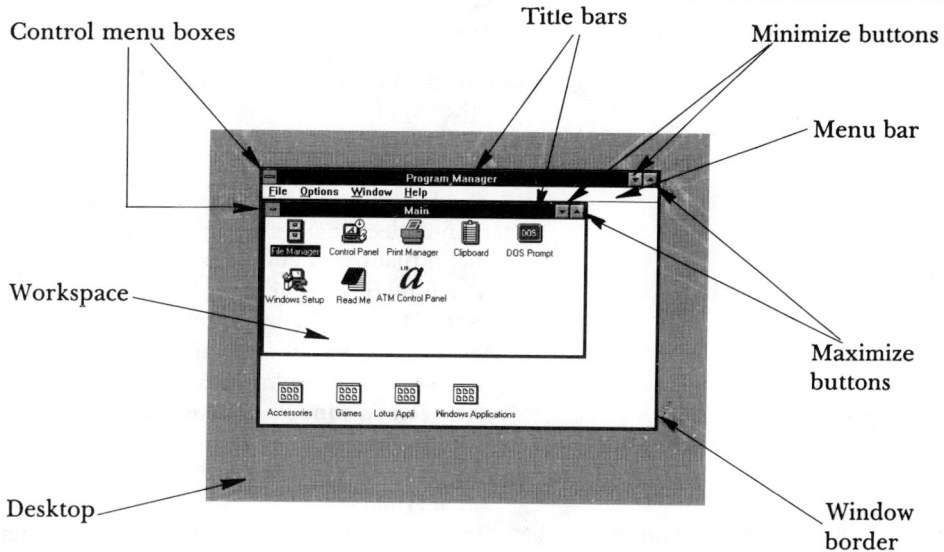

some applications create temporary files that are deleted when you exit the application.

To leave Windows, first switch to the Program Manager window by pressing CTRL-ESC, and then click Program Manager or press the DOWN ARROW until Program Manager is highlighted and press ENTER. Next, click the control menu box or press ALT-SPACEBAR to display the control menu, and select Close Windows by clicking it or pressing C. You can also press ALT-F4 from the Program Manager window. You must then select the OK command button by clicking it or pressing ENTER to confirm that you want to leave Windows. You should close and exit any applications you have running before you leave Windows.

The Windows Interface

Once you are in Windows, you can manipulate the windows you use and select which ones are open. Many of the Windows applications include

Table B-2.   *Windows Screen Components*

Component	Description
Desktop	The area of the screen that is not covered by another application
Control menu box	The box in the upper-left corner of a window that you can use for controlling the window
Menu bar	The bar in an application window that contains menu selections. Selecting one presents a pull-down menu that offers additional choices
Title bar	The top line of a window, which displays a description of the application it contains or the information a document window contains
Window border	The edge of a window, which you can use to change the size of a window with a mouse
Minimize button	The down arrow box in the upper-right corner that you can select to reduce the window to an icon (a small symbol)
Maximize button	The up arrow box in the upper-right corner that you can select to expand the window to fill the screen. (When selected, this icon changes to the Restore button with an up and down arrow.)
Workspace	The area below the menu bar (in an application window) or title bar (in a document window) area where you will work with data

menus that behave just like the menus you will learn to use in 1-2-3 for Windows. You can customize where each window appears and its size.

The Program Manager

The Program Manager is part of Windows that lets you easily decide which programs you are using. Many of the programs that you use with Windows are in the Program Manager. When you installed Windows, you probably added many of the programs installed on your machine to the Program Manager. When you install a Windows application like 1-2-3 for Windows, the installation program adds the application to the Program Manager.

The Program Manager divides the applications into group windows. These are document windows to the Program Manager application window. Many of the features you learn about using also apply to the Program Manager application window and the group windows.

Two of the group windows are Main and Accessories. Main includes programs like the Control Panel, which selects how Windows looks and operates, and the Print Manager, which controls how Windows sends information to the printer. Accessories include programs that make working with Windows easier, including the Notepad to read and write text files. You probably also have a group window called Non-Windows Applications, which includes DOS programs that were not designed for Windows. 1-2-3 for Windows is in the Lotus Applications group window. While it is beyond the scope of this appendix, you can add and delete programs from group windows, add and delete group windows, and change the properties of programs.

Menus in Windows

Most application windows have a menu in a menu bar. For example, the Program Manager window in Figure B-1 has a menu bar that contains File, Options, Window, and Help. With a mouse, you can make selections by clicking the menu item you want. For example, to select File, click File. With a keyboard, you first need to activate the menu bar by pressing ALT. Next, press the underlined letter for the menu item you want. For example, to select File from the menu, press ALT and then press F. Once you select an item from the menu bar, you usually see a pull-down menu. For example, the Program Manager's File pull-down menu looks like this:

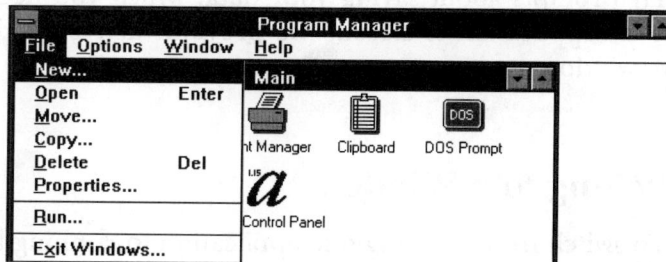

Like selecting an item on the menu bar, you can select an item in the pull-down menu by clicking the one you want or by pressing the underlined letter. After you make a selection, you may see a dialog box. In Chapter 5, "Getting Familiar with Menus and Dialog Boxes," you are introduced to dialog boxes in 1-2-3 for Windows. Dialog boxes in Windows applications behave the same way.

Opening Applications

To use an application in Windows, you must open an application window for the application from the Program Manager window. First, you must display the group window and make it active. With a mouse, double-click the window or icon. With the keyboard, press ALT to activate the menu bar, press W for **Window**, and press the number next to the group window you want to activate. With the group window active, you can double-click the application you want to run. You can also use the arrow keys to highlight the application to run and press ENTER. The application starts and an application window is added to the screen. If it is a full-screen application, the application fills the screen, so you do not see Windows in the background. If your computer's resources are limited and you have other applications running at the same time, you may not be able to start an application until you close other ones.

When you finish with an application, you want to close the application window and exit the application. For non-Windows applications, you should use the application's own commands for exiting. For Windows applications, you can press ALT-F4 when the application is the active window or select **File Exit** from the application's menu bar. You may also select **Close** from the application's control menu. Windows applications may display prompts about saving your data, which you need to respond to. Once an application is closed, the previous active window becomes the active window again.

Switching to a Window

To switch from running one application to running another one, you must select the application window or the full-screen application you want to be the active window. The *active window* is the window your keystrokes and mouse selections will affect. (If you make a selection outside of the application window with a mouse, you are selecting the other application rather than making a selection in that application.) You can press ALT-ESC to switch to the next application in the Task List. To switch to any open application, press CTRL-ESC to display the Task List, like the one shown here:

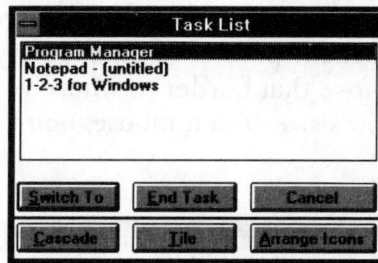

```
┌──────────────────────────────────────┐
│ ─            Task List                │
│ ┌──────────────────────────────────┐ │
│ │ Program Manager                  │ │
│ │ Notepad - (untitled)             │ │
│ │ 1-2-3 for Windows                │ │
│ │                                  │ │
│ │                                  │ │
│ │                                  │ │
│ └──────────────────────────────────┘ │
│  ┌─────────┐ ┌─────────┐ ┌─────────┐ │
│  │Switch To│ │End Task │ │ Cancel  │ │
│  └─────────┘ └─────────┘ └─────────┘ │
│  ┌─────────┐ ┌─────────┐ ┌───────────┐
│  │ Cascade │ │  Tile   │ │Arrange Icons│
│  └─────────┘ └─────────┘ └───────────┘
└──────────────────────────────────────┘
```

You can also display the Task List by double-clicking an empty desktop area (an area that is not filled with an application). You can also click an application's control menu box and select Switch To.

From the Task List, you can double-click the application you want or press the UP ARROW and DOWN ARROW keys to highlight the one you want and then press ENTER. Another option for switching to an open application is to click the application, if it is visible on the screen. In the next section, you learn how to shrink an application window into an icon. When an application window appears as an icon, you can make it active by double-clicking it.

Another special key combination is ALT-TAB. ALT-TAB switches you to the last application you were using. This means if you are using 1-2-3 for Windows and a word processor, you can press ALT-TAB to keep switching between these two applications.

Positioning and Sizing Windows

Windows lets you put your application windows anywhere on the screen and make the windows any size you want. You can make these changes with a mouse or with the control menu. The control menu appears when you click the control menu box. To display this menu for an application window, press ALT-SPACEBAR, and to display this menu for a document window, press ALT-HYPHEN. Sometimes some of the control menu selections are dimmed or grayed to indicate they cannot be selected.

B

To move a window, select **M**ove from the control menu, and then press the arrow keys to move the temporary outline of the window to a new location and press ENTER. With a mouse, drag the title bar of the window to move the temporary outline where you want the window. If you are moving a document window, you cannot move it beyond the edges of the application window.

To size a window, select **S**ize from the control menu. Next, press an arrow key to move the pointer to the border you want to change. Press the arrow keys to move that border to where you want it and press ENTER. To change a window's size with a mouse, point to the border so it looks like this:

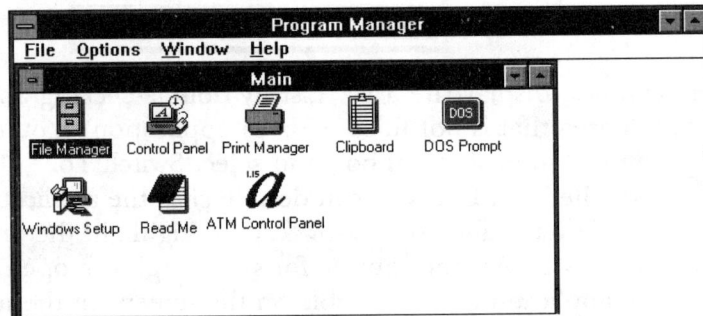

Drag the window's border to where you want it. Some document windows have size restrictions. Some other windows, like Window's Calculator, cannot change sizes. These windows have thin borders rather than the thicker borders of the windows you can resize.

Most windows have three window sizes you can select with the minimize button and the maximize or restore button, or with selections from the control menu. You can quickly enlarge a window so it fills the entire screen by clicking the maximize button or by selecting Ma**x**imize from the control menu, if the window has one. When you select a minimize button or select Mi**n**imize from the control menu, the window shrinks to an icon. An icon is a symbol that represents the application. Some applications, like 1-2-3 for Windows, even let you turn document windows into icons. While a window is an icon, you can move the icon by dragging it to a new location or selecting **M**ove from the control menu for the icon, pressing the arrow keys to move the icon, and pressing ENTER. After you minimize or maximize a window, you can return it to its previous size by selecting the restore button (the one that takes the place of the maximize button) or by selecting **R**estore from the control menu. An icon is also restored to its previous size when you double-click it.

Windows has two other quick options for positioning and sizing windows. One option is *tiling,* which divides the screen area between the non-minimized windows. Figure B-2 shows a screen that has the opened windows tiled. *Cascading,* on the other hand, makes each application window less than full size and stacks them so you can see only the title bar for each application except the top one. Figure B-3 shows a screen that has several windows cascaded. To tile or cascade windows, select the **T**ile or **C**ascade command button from the Task List by pressing CTRL-ESC and then either clicking the command button or pressing ALT-T or ALT-C. Windows does not include minimized applications in the tiling or cascading, nor does it include DOS applications, which must be run in full-screen mode. Some applications let you tile or cascade the document windows within the application window. The Program Manager and 1-2-3 for Windows are like this. For either application window, select the **W**indow pull-down menu and then select **T**ile or **C**ascade. (In some applications, you use different commands.)

B

Figure B-2.   *Windows applications tiled*

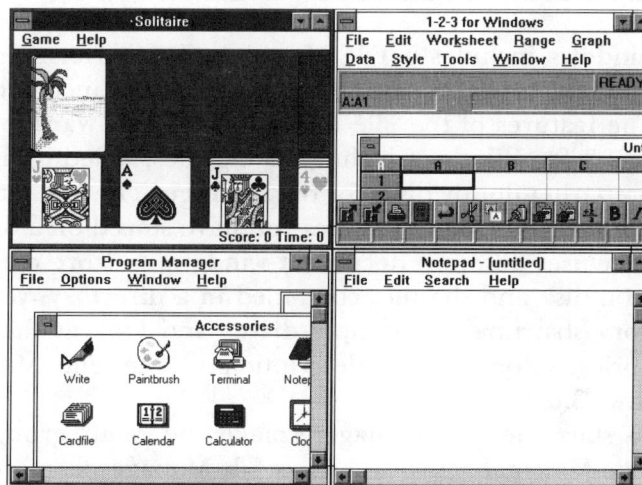

Figure B-3.   *Windows applications cascaded*

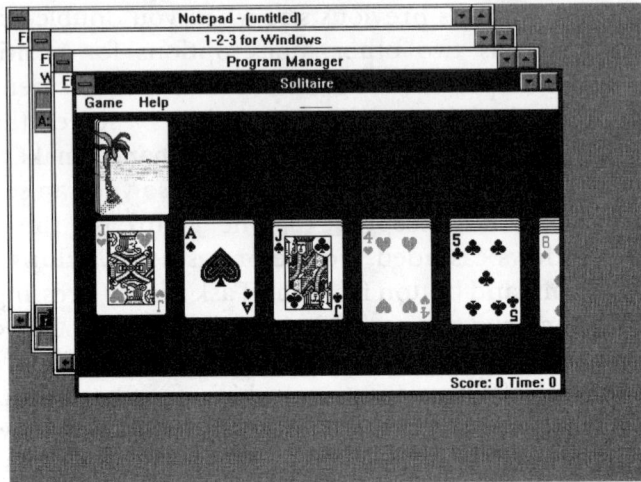

The Windows File Manager

Windows includes a File Manager that performs many of the file-management tasks that prior releases of 1-2-3 included File commands for. The features of the File Manager you may want to use as you work with 1-2-3 for Windows include listing files, deleting files, copying files, and preparing floppy disks for data storage. The File Manager provides a graphical way to look at the files you have stored on a disk. Since the File Manager uses different document windows to store diagrams of directories on a disk and the files contained in a directory, you can look at the directory structure of multiple drives and look at the files in multiple directories at once. This description of the File Manager applies to Windows 3.0.

To start the File Manager, make the Main group window in the Program Manager active and select File Manager from this group window. This displays a diagram of the directory structure of your disk, like this one:

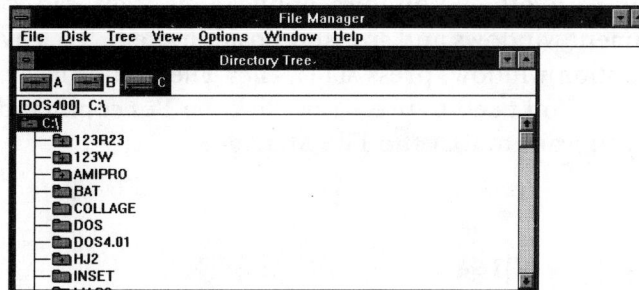

To change the disk displayed, click, at the top of the display, the drive you want or press CTRL and the letter of the drive you want, as in CTRL-A. From the directory tree, you can move between the directories you want to display. When a directory contains subdirectories, a + appears in the file next to the directory name. For example, 123W contains a SHEETICO subdirectory, so the file next to 123W has a + in it. You can add the SHEETICO directory to the display by clicking 123W or by highlighting it and typing **+**. To display the files in a directory, double-click the directory or highlight it and press ENTER. This displays another window, which contains a list of the files, like this:

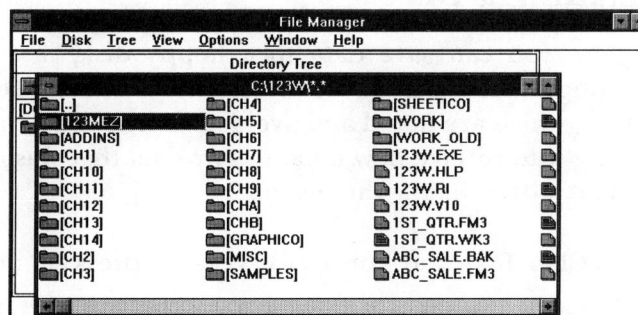

If you want to see the time and date the file was saved, its size, and its file attributes, click **V**iew and then **F**ile Details from the View pull-down menu, or press ALT and then press V F. To return to the list of just the file names, click **V**iew and then **N**ame from the View pull-down menu or press ALT and then press V N.

As with other Windows applications, you can switch between the document windows and size and position them. To leave the File Manager application window, press ALT-F4, click **File** and **Exit**, or press ALT and then press F X. You need to press Y or click the **Yes** command button to confirm that you want to exit the File Manager.

Deleting Files

To delete a file, point to the file you want to delete in the list of files in a File Manager window and then press DEL or click **File** and **Delete**. From the Delete dialog box, click the **Delete** command button or press ENTER. Next, from the File Manager dialog box that confirms that you want to delete the file, select the **Yes** command button by clicking it or by pressing Y and pressing ENTER. This removes the file from the disk. (At this point, you can recover the file only if you have a file utility like Norton that can undelete files or if you are using DOS 5, which has an UNDELETE command.) You want to delete files you no longer want since they take up space on your disk that you may later want to use for storing other data.

Formatting a Disk

Before you can save data to a floppy disk, it must be formatted. Formatting a disk sets it to receive data and checks to see if the disk has any bad spots, which are noted and avoided. When you format a disk, you are preparing it to receive new data, so any data that was on it before is lost. To format a disk, follow these steps:

1. Click **Disk** and **Format Diskette** or press ALT and then D F.

2. Select the drive to format from the Format Diskette dialog box either by pressing the UP ARROW or DOWN ARROW key until the drive you want to format is shown or by clicking the down arrow icon and the drive letter containing the disk to format.

3. Click the OK command button or press ENTER.

4. Click the **Format** command button, press F, or press ENTER to confirm that you want to format the disk.

5. Click the **High** Capacity check box or press H if you want a 3 1/2-inch disk formatted as 1.44 MB or a 5 1/4-inch disk formatted as 1.2 MB (if the disk drive is capable of it).

6. Click **Make** System Disk or press M if you want to be able to start your system with the disk in drive A.

7. Click the OK command button or press ENTER to start formatting your disk.

8. Click **Yes** or press Y to format another disk. Click **No** or press N to finish formatting.

Copying a File

You can copy a file to make a duplicate of it in another location. You may want to use this command to copy a file to a disk to make a backup copy of an important worksheet. To copy a file, follow these steps:

1. Highlight the file you want to copy.
2. Click **File Copy**, press F8, or press ALT and then F C to copy the file.
3. Type the location where you want the file copied.

You can just type the drive, as in **A:**, the drive and directory, as in **C:\123W**, or even a new filename, as in **C:\123W\MY_FILE.WK3**. If you supply the filename, make sure you use the same file extension as previously, as shown here:

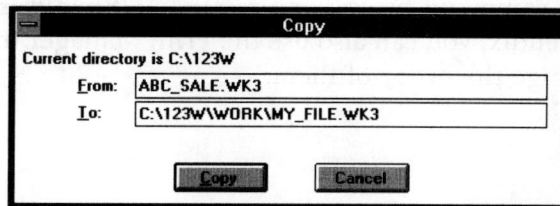

```
┌──────────────────────── Copy ────────────────────────┐
│ Current directory is C:\123W                          │
│      From:  ABC_SALE.WK3                              │
│        To:  C:\123W\WORK\MY_FILE.WK3                  │
│                                                       │
│           [  Copy  ]      [ Cancel ]                  │
└───────────────────────────────────────────────────────┘
```

4. Click the OK command button or press ENTER to copy the file.

If you are copying a 1-2-3 worksheet, make sure to copy both the file with the .WK3 extension, which contains the worksheet data, and the file with the .FM3 extension, which contains the information about how the worksheet file is formatted.

The Windows Print Manager

Windows has a Print Manager that takes information you want to send to the printer from each of the applications and sends the information to the printer, one printout at a time. This prevents your worksheet data from appearing in the middle of your word processing documents. Windows waits until it has all the information to print before it prints any data. That is why when you print, you notice a delay between when an application starts printing and when the printer starts printing.

Most of the time, you do not need to look at the Print Manager when you print in Windows. The exception is if you try to print something and your printer is not connected, is not turned on, or runs out of paper. In these instances, Windows delays sending more information to the printer until you tell it to start sending information again. To do so, after correcting the problem, make the Main group window in the Program Manager active and select Print Manager from this group window. This displays a list of the current print tasks, as shown here:

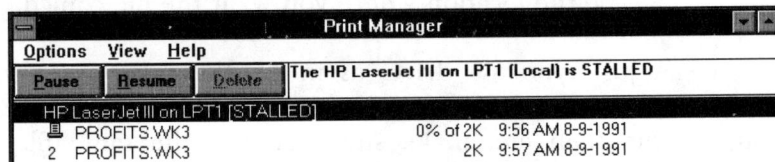

Print Manager		▼ ▲
Options View Help		
Pause Resume Delete	The HP LaserJet III on LPT1 (Local) is STALLED	

HP LaserJet III on LPT1 [STALLED]		
▤ PROFITS.WK3	0% of 2K	9:56 AM 8-9-1991
2 PROFITS.WK3	2K	9:57 AM 8-9-1991

To tell Windows to send information to the printer again, click the Resume command button or press ALT-R. While it is beyond the scope of this appendix, you can also use the Print Manager to cancel printing tasks and change the order of them.

Index

A

Absolute cell addresses, 180-181, 183
Active cell, 6
Active window, 360
Address box, 8
Address types (cell addresses), 176-183
Alignment of labels, changing, 100-103
Ami Pro, sharing files with, 316-318
Answers Table report (Solver), 303
Appearance of cells, changing, 97-120
Appearance of labels, changing, 100-111

Application windows, 356, 359-360
Applications design, 164-166
Area graphs, 245-246
Arguments (function)
    rules for, 64-65
    types of, 65-66
Arithmetic formulas, 33-39
Arrow keys, 10
AT keyboard, 11
Attributes (font), 104, 108-109
Automatic format, 117-118
Automatic macros, creating, 340-343

B

Background recalculation, 199
Backup copies of worksheets, 147-148
Bar graphs, 239, 245, 258-259
Borders, adding and using, 110-111, 227-230
Built-in functions. *See* @Functions
Buttons, 89-92

C

Calculations, 31-51
Canceling a menu selection, 87-88
Cascade menus, 84
Cascading windows, 363-364
Cell address types, 176-183
Cell addresses, 5
Cell pointer, 6, 330-333

Cell ranges, 54-55, 99-100
    changing the format for, 113-115
    erasing, 132
    invalid and valid, 98
    printing multiple, 219
    saving to a file, 304-308
Cells, 5
Chart Type dialog box, 249
Check boxes, 89, 91
Classic menu, 83, 88
Clicking the mouse, 11
Clipboard
    using to copy worksheet entries, 171-187
    using to export data, 319-320
    using to import data, 321-322
Column and row location, 5
Column widths, changing, 121-125
Columns
    deleting, 128-129
    hiding, 129-133
    inserting, 126-128
    transposing to rows, 192-195
Combining data from several worksheets, 308-314
Command buttons, 89-92
Commissions model, 40-45
Comparison formulas (database searching), 281
Compound operators, 44-45
Contents box, 8
Control panel, 6
Copying data, 172-189
Copying entries
    to another worksheet file, 186-187
    scope of, 182-187
    using the Clipboard, 171-187
    without using the Clipboard, 187-189
Copying a file, 367

Copying formulas, 175-189
Copying labels, 172-175
Correcting errors, 22-25
Criteria (database searching), 279
Current directory, 140

D

Data series, 238
Data Sort dialog box, 273
Database statistical functions, 291-294
Databases, 267-295
    choosing a worksheet location for, 268-269
    editing entries, 272
    entering data, 270-272
    entering field names, 269
    naming, 290
    searching, 279-289
    sorting, 273-279
Dates and times
    entering, 21-22
    functions for, 69-70
    numbers, 19
DDE (Dynamic Data Exchange), 315
Debugging macros, 344-345
Default directory, 140
Default format, 97
Default print settings, 213
Deleting
    files, 366
    named graphs, 252-253
    range names, 60
    rows and columns, 128-129
    worksheets, 163-164

Dialog boxes, 84, 88-93
Directories, 140-143
Disk data
    organizing, 137-141
    storage, 136-141
Disks, formatting, 366-367
Display format, changing, 112-118
Document windows, 356
Documenting formulas, 35-37
Documenting a macro, 337
Double-clicking the mouse, 11
Dragging the mouse, 11
Drop-down boxes, 89-92

E

Edit line, 8
Elevator boxes, 12
Enhanced keyboard, 11
Entering data
    arithmetic formulas, 33-35
    dates and times, 21-22
    formulas, 32-33
    labels, 16-18
    numbers, 18-22
Entries (worksheet), types of, 16-22
Entry-generating features, 194-198
Erasing worksheet data, 131-133
Error correction, 22-25
Exact-entry match criteria (database searching), 280
Executing a macro, 335-337
Exiting Windows, 356-357
Exporting data, 319-320
Extensions, filename, 138-139

F

Field names (databases), 269
Fields (databases), 267-268
File Combine From command, 308-314
File concepts, 136-141
File Manager (Windows), 364-367
File menu commands, 141-151
File Open dialog box, 90, 149
File Page Setup dialog box, 223
File Print dialog box, 212
File Save As dialog box, 144
Filename extensions, 138-139
Filenames, 138-139
Files
    adding worksheets to, 155-158
    copying, 367
    copying worksheet entries to, 186-187
    deleting, 366
    making backup copies of, 147-148
    managing, 135-151
    opening new, 151-152
    retrieving, 148-151
    saving, 143-148
    structure of, 5
Financial functions, 76-77
Font attributes, 104, 108-109
Font set, 104, 107-108
Fonts
    changing, 104-109
    selecting for graph titles, 254-256
Footers, defining, 224-227
Format line, 7-8
Formatting a disk, 366-367

Formatting options (worksheets), 97-120
    abbreviations for, 114
    automatic format, 117-118
    display format, 112-118
    global changes, 115-116
    scope of, 113-118
    table of, 113
Formula notes, 35-37
Formulas, 16, 31-51
    building with pointing, 37-39
    complex, 47-50
    copying, 175-189
    linking, 60-62
    saving to a file, 307-308
    using multiple files in, 154-155
    using range names in, 53-60
    See also @Functions
Frame (worksheet), 6
Freezing worksheet titles, 201-203
Full-screen mode (running applications), 356
Function arguments
    rules for, 64-65
    types of, 65-66
Function categories, 66-79
Function format, 64
Functions. *See* @Functions; Formulas
@Functions, 63-79
    @COUNT, 68-69
    database statistical, 291-294
    @DAVG, 292
    @DCOUNT, 293
    @DMIN, 294
    @DSUM, 293
    general rules for, 63-64

@Functions, *continued*
    @IF, 78-79
    @INT, 72
    @NOW, 65, 69
    @PI, 65
    @PMT, 66, 77
    @SUM, 68-69
    @UPPER, 71-72
    @VLOOKUP, 73-75

G

General display format, 112
Generating cell entries, 194-198
Generating a number series, 197-198
Global column width, changing, 124-125
Global format changes, 115-116
Graph grid lines, 258-259
Graph legends, 239-240, 256-258
Graph titles, 239, 253-256
Graph types, 245-249
Graphs
    adding to a worksheet, 260-261
    creating, 237-265
    deleting named, 252-253
    displaying named, 251-252
    naming, 241
    printing, 262-263
    selecting a range for, 242-245, 261
    specifying data for, 241-245, 250-251
Grid lines, adding to graphs, 258-259

H

Hardware requirements, 349-350
Headers, defining, 224-227
Help, 26-28

Help window, 27
Hiding columns, 129-131, 232-233
Hierarchical directory structure, 141
HLCO graphs, 246, 248
Horizontal windows, 161

I

IBM's enhanced keyboard, 11
Icon palette, 9
Importing data, 321-322
Information boxes, 90
Initial 1-2-3 display, 4
Inserting rows and columns, 126-128, 338-339
Installing the program, 349-353

K

Keyboard alternative macros, 325-327
Keyboard options, 10-11
Keys (special), in macro commands, 331
Keys, worksheet movement, 12
Keywords (@function), 64

L

Label entry alignment, 100-103
Label prefixes, 16
Labels, 16
    changing the appearance of, 100-111
    copying, 172-175
    creating repeating, 195-196
    database search criteria for, 282
    entering, 16-18
    wide, 111

Large worksheets, using titles with, 201-203
Legends, adding to graphs, 239-240, 256-258
Line graphs, 245
Linking formulas, 60-62
Links between applications, 315-319
List boxes, 90
Loading the program, 2-3
Logical formulas, 39-45
Logical functions, 77-79
Long labels, 111

M

Macro library, 339-340
Macros
    creating, 325-347
    creating automatic, 340-343
    debugging, 344-345
    documenting, 337
    executing, 335-337
    for inserting rows, 338-339
    naming, 335
    planning, 327-328
    recording, 333
    recording special keys, 330-333
    running in STEP mode, 344-345
    using the Transcript window, 328-330
Managing files, 135-151
Margin settings, 223-224
Math functions, 72-73
Menu bar, 7
Menus, 83-88
    in application windows, 359-360
    selecting from, 86-88
    undoing menu commands, 93-94
Minimal recalculation, 199
Mixed cell addresses, 181-183

Mixed graphs, 246, 248
Mode indicators, 7-8
Modes, 84-88
Monitoring data, 158-163
Mouse
    moving with a, 11-13
    terminology, 356
Movement keys (worksheet), table of, 12
Moving around the worksheet, 10-13
Moving worksheet data, 189-191
Multilevel applications design, 164-166
Multiple ranges, printing, 219
Multiple windows, using, 151-166
Multiple worksheets, 164-166
    using functions with, 163
    using panes with, 160-163

N

Named graphs
    deleting, 252-253
    displaying, 251-252
Named ranges, 53-60. *See also* Cell ranges
Naming a database, 290
Naming a macro, 335
Notepad, using to export data, 319-320
Number series, generating, 197-198
Numbers, entering, 18-22
Numeric constants, entering, 19-21

O

1-2-3 menu, 84-88
1-2-3 window, 3-10
Opening a new file, 151-152

Operator precedence, 44, 47-50
Option buttons, 90-91
Organization of the worksheet, 3-10
Organizing disk data, 137-141
Orientation (printing), 230

P

Page breaks, adding, 231-232
Page setup (default), 214
Pages, printing, 220
Panes (window), 158-163
Paths (directory), 143
Pie graphs, 245-247
POINT mode, 37
Pointing method, building formulas with, 37-39
Positioning windows, 361-364
Previewing before printing, 221-222
Primary key (database sorting), 274-275
Print borders, 227-230
Print Manager (Windows), 368
Print orientation, 230
Print preview, 221-222
Print settings, default, 213
Printed page layout, 214
Printers, selecting to print to, 220-221
Printing, 211-236
    graphs, 262-263
    multiple ranges, 219
    options for, 223-230
    process of, 213-219
    selected pages, 220
Program Manager (Windows), 358-359
Pull-down menus, 84, 86-87

Q

Querying a database, 279-289
Quitting 1-2-3, 3

R

RAM (random access memory), 136
Range names, deleting, 60
Ranges, cell. *See* Cell ranges
Rearranging the worksheet, 189-194
Recalculation options, 199-201
Recording a macro, 333
Records (database), 267
Relative cell addresses, 176-180, 183
Repeating labels, creating, 195-196
Replacing data, 205-207
Requirements for running the program, 349-350
Retrieving files, 148-151
Root directory, 140
Rows
    deleting, 128-129
    inserting, 126-128
    inserting with a macro, 338-339
    transposing to columns, 192-195

S

Saving
    files, 143-148
    formulas to a file, 307-308
    a range to a file, 304-308
    values to a file, 305-306

Scientific notation, 19
Scope of copying entries, 182-187
Scope of formatting changes, 113-118
Scroll bars, 12
Search criteria (databases), 279
Search strings, 206-207
Searching a database, 279-289
    entering criteria, 280-282
    extracting matching records, 285-289
    finding matching records, 284-285
    locating the criteria, 283
    locating the database, 282-283
    query shortcuts, 289-290
Searching and replacing data, 203-207
Secondary key (database sorting), 274, 276
Selective reporting (databases), 279
Series (for graphing), 238
Series of numbers, generating, 197-198
Shading, 111
Sharing data between applications, 314-322
Sizing windows, 361-364
SmartIcons, 9
Solver Answer dialog box, 302
Solver application, 298-304
Sorting a database, 273-279
Special functions, 72-76
Special keys in macro commands, table of, 331
Starting the 1-2-3 program, 2-3
Starting Windows, 356
Statistical functions, 67-69, 291-294
Status line, 9
Status line indicators, 10
STEP mode, running a macro in, 344-345
Storing information, 136-141, 164-166
String formulas, 45-47
String functions, 70-72
Subdirectories, 140

T

Text boxes, 91-92
Text files
    extracting data to, 320
    importing, 322
Tiling windows, 363
Time functions, 69-70
Times, entering, 21-22
Title bar, 6-7
Titles (graph), 239
    adding, 253-256
    freezing, 201-203
Tools Solver dialog box, 301
Tools User Setup dialog box, 89
Transcript window, 328-330
Transferring data between applications, 314-322
Transposing data, 191-195
Typeface, 104

U

Undo feature, 25-26, 93-94

V

Values, 16
    Automatic format for, 117
    saving to a file, 305-306
Vertical windows, 159

W

What-if projections, 32
Widening columns, 121-125
Wildcard characters, 282
Window panes, 158-163
Windows applications, linking, 318-319
Windows environment, 355-368
    exiting, 356-357
    File Manager, 364-367
    interface, 357-364
    and opening applications, 360
    positioning and sizing windows, 361-364
    Print Manager, 368
    Program Manager, 358-359
    sample screen, 357
    screen components, 358
    starting, 356
    switching to a window, 360-361
Windows (worksheet), 9-10, 151
    splitting, 158-163
    switching between, 153
    using multiple, 151-166
Worksheet frame, 6
Worksheet level, 5
Worksheet movement keys, table of, 12
Worksheet window menu, 85
Worksheet windows. *See* Windows (worksheet)
Worksheets
    adding to files, 155-158
    deleting, 163-164
    moving around, 10-13
    organization of, 3-10
    See also Multiple worksheets

X

X axis (graphs), 239
XY graphs, 246-247

Y

Y axis (graphs), 239-240

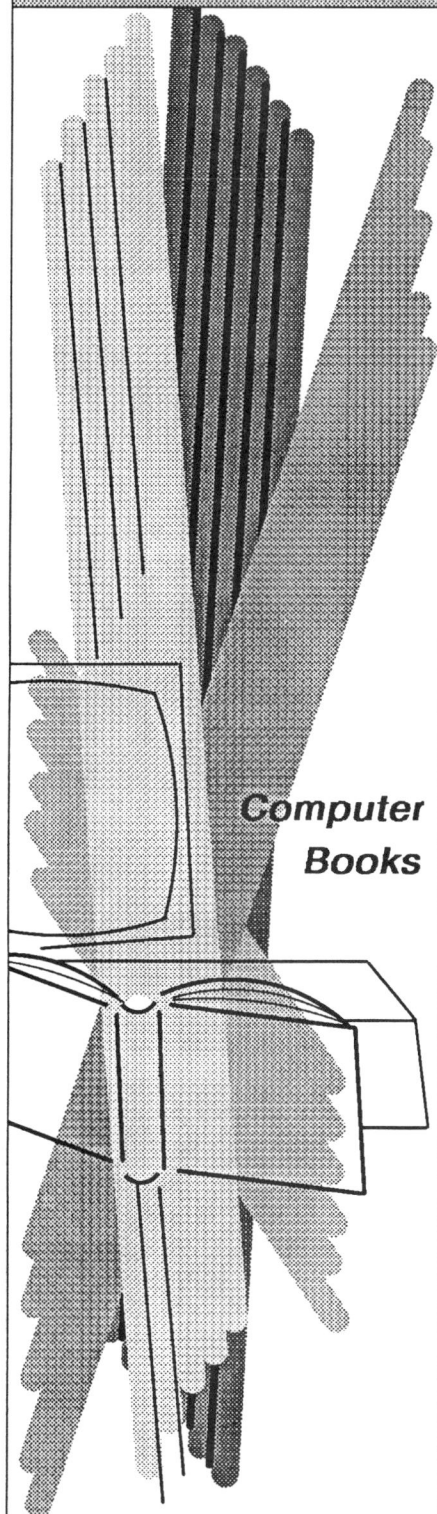

Osborne **McGraw-Hill**

Computer

Books

(800) 227-0900